THE GERMAN AIR WAR IN RUSSIA

THE GERMAN AIR WAR
IN RUSSIA

by
Richard Muller

The Nautical & Aviation Publishing Company of America
Baltimore, Maryland

Copyright © 1992 by Richard Muller. Published in 1992 by The Nautical &
Aviation Publishing Company Of America, Inc., 8 West Madison Street,
Baltimore, Maryland 21201. All rights reserved. No part of this publication may
be reprinted, stored in a retrieval system, or transmitted in any form by any
electronic or mechanical copying system without the written permission of the
publisher.

Library of Congress Catalog Card Number 92-53806

ISBN: 1-877853-13-5

Printed in the United States of America

Library of Congress Cataloging-in-Publication Data

Muller, Richard, 1961-
The German Air War in Russia by Richard Muller.

p.   cm.
Includes bibliographical references and index.
ISBN 1-877853-13-5
1. World War, 1939–1945—Aerial operations, German.
2. World War, 1939–1945—Campaigns—Soviet Union.   I. Title
D787.M82   1992
940.54'42—dc20

To my parents

CONTENTS

PREFACE

By late 1943, the German army fighting in the Soviet Union was in a strategic and operational quandary. Both Operation Barbarossa, the initial invasion of the USSR in June 1941, and the somewhat less ambitious offensive in the south the following spring failed to achieve their goals. The combat power of the Red Army remained unbroken; the territorial objectives of the German advance remained in Soviet hands. The attempt to engage and destroy the Soviet armored reserves at the battle of Kursk in July 1943 cost the Germans the bulk of their own *Panzer* force. For the staffs of the German army groups, the coming months promised only a grim battle of attrition, a campaign waged over an unwieldy, dispersed front which made conducting a defense in depth a most difficult proposition. Operational and strategic initiative had passed to the Red Army, further limiting German options. Although the German army was able to conduct a tenacious defense, the days of the great operations, of using decisive envelopment and maneuver with the potential for achieving strategic results, receded into the past.

The air force that had triumphantly spearheaded the German drive into the USSR in June 1941 likewise faced diminishing options. A major study drawn up by the Luftwaffe operations staff in November 1943 contained the following rather plaintive observation:

> Will the Luftwaffe no longer be contributing to victory in the east
> if, instead of acting as artillery and using its bomber units to drop
> bombs at the feet of the infantry, it attacks the basis of Russian
> striking power, Russian war industry?[1]

The German air force, so instrumental in the early victories of 1939–1941, found itself, like its army counterpart, at a crossroads by the time the above words were written. Its leadership had to decide whether to sacrifice the remnants of the Luftwaffe's status as an independent service and devote its dwindling resources to supporting the German army in its defensive battles or to attempt to fulfill the compelling prewar dream, shared by most air power proponents, of achieving a decisive military result in the "third dimension." Circumstances that grew beyond the control of the German air force leadership soon wrenched the decision out of its hands. Despite a remarkable ability to adapt to changing operational conditions, to recover from the most crippling losses, and to function effectively in a wide variety of roles, the German air force did not fulfill its mission as either an independent or a cooperative weapon. It failed first to bring about the swift defeat of Germany's Soviet adversary, and would finally be unable to stave off the total collapse of German arms.

Less than two and one-half years earlier, the beginning of the eastern campaign had occasioned vastly different sentiments among the Luftwaffe command. The chief of the general staff, Generaloberst Hans Jeschonnek, remarked confidently to his intelligence chief as Operation Barbarossa opened on June 22, 1941, "At last, a proper war!"[2] Jeschonnek believed that the scale and the stakes of the "drive to the east" at last represented an objective worthy of the Luftwaffe's doctrine, training, and equipment. To account for the enormous gulf between Jeschonnek's 1941 optimism and the operations staff's gloomy 1943 prognostications is the purpose of this book.

Historians have advanced many explanations for the defeat of German air power in the Second World War. In the broadest sense, one may categorize these interpretations as stressing the primacy of either "external" or "internal" factors. The external factors contributing to the Luftwaffe's collapse include Germany's economic and geopolitical situation, the unrealistic and unattainable nature of Adolf Hitler's military and foreign policy goals, and the growing imbalance between the military, population and industrial power of the Third Reich and her enemies. The nature of aerial conflict in the Second World War, with its hitherto unimagined attrition rates, helped to shatter the Nazi air arm only a few years after it had assisted the German army in subjugating the whole of Europe.[3] Victory in the air, as elsewhere, went to the "big battalions," a lesson the Luftwaffe planners absorbed too late. Even in the days of triumph, the Germans were in the process of losing the production and technological battle that was to decide the conflict.

Something of a school developed around a narrow and personalized interpretation of the external explanation following the publication of the memoirs of a number of Luftwaffe commanders. This group, which historian Edward L. Homze refers to as the "generals,"[4] placed the blame for the Luftwaffe's failure on the civilian leadership. The "generals" vented much of their anger and disillusionment on such "amateurs" and "dilettantes" as Adolf Hitler, Hermann Göring, and famed stunt flyer and WWI ace Ernst Udet, the chief of technical air armament until his suicide in November 1941. This approach shielded the professional military class from too much opprobrium. The memoirs of Adolf Galland, Werner Baumbach, H. J. Rieckhoff and Karl Koller in particular advanced the view that it was external meddling, more than any inherent defects in the Luftwaffe's own officership or operational doctrine, that doomed Germany's air weapon. In a postwar statement, Koller, the last chief of the Luftwaffe General Staff, provided an especially clear elucidation of the "generals'" viewpoint:

> But the political leadership in Germany, in its short-sightedness and in complete misjudgment of the tenacity and mentality of the Anglo-Saxons and the potential war power of the United States in the background, had believed that the war in the West had already been won in 1940 and started out on the folly of the Russian war. The calls of us outsiders and "little" General Staff officers for aircraft and more aircraft and for new types were either not heard or they were laughed off.
> We remained voices crying in vain in the wilderness . . .[5]

In many cases, these former Luftwaffe officers lent their expertise and cooperation to American and British official historians, including the compilers of the United States Strategic Bombing Survey. The result was the growth of an historical orthodoxy regarding the fundamental causes of the Luftwaffe's decline and fall that, given the destruction and dissipation of much of the primary documentation on the subject, has proved to be a most durable historical construct.

Even while the "external" interpretation, which was personality dependent and often quite engaging and dramatic, held sway, other writers tended to seek the cause for the Luftwaffe's collapse elsewhere. Popular aviation authors and historians alike have drawn attention to defects within the Nazi air arm. Some have suggested that the German air force went to war with a fundamentally unsound air power doctrine, one that emphasized direct support of and cooperation with the traditional branches of the armed services. Such an air force, so the argument runs, could not help but come up short when faced with opponents such as the United States Army Air Force or the Royal Air Force that, drawing the correct lessons from the First World War and the interwar period, emphasized strategic air operations against the enemy heartland. This rather simplistic argument, long a favorite of British and American authors, has been subjected to withering criticism in recent years.[6] The Luftwaffe leadership's optimistic view of such unproven concepts as precision bombardment and the institutional independence of the air service was strikingly similar to that of its counterparts in Britain and the United States. In fact, German solutions to the operational and doctrinal dilemmas of air power in some cases compare favorably to those reached by the Western Allies. The cause of the Luftwaffe's failure in the Second World War lies elsewhere than in a simple abandonment of strategic bombing in favor of other, less "decisive" forms of air power.

The nature of German air power doctrine, in part owing to the flexibility and the ambiguity of a number of its key principles, is perhaps more opaque than that of some of the other belligerents, and scholarly appraisal has been slow in coming. Even so, German, British, and American historians have drawn attention to important shortcomings in officer education and attitudes, especially concerning such matters as technology and logistics. German historian Horst Boog in particular identifies an attachment to "preindustrial values" within the Luftwaffe officer corps. Adherence to military ideals that predated modern warfare led to an emphasis upon operational thinking, associated with maneuvering forces in battle, rather than on the vital technical and economic aspects of twentieth century aerial conflict. Such "internal" criticisms go a long way towards explaining how it was that the Luftwaffe, when confronted with a conflict whose scope far exceeded the expectations of its leadership, proved unequal to the struggle.

It is the purpose of the present study to apply elements of both the "internal" and "external" schools of thought towards producing a new interpretation of the longest continuous offensive air campaign waged by the German Luftwaffe during the Second World War: the conflict against the Soviet Union from 1941 to 1945. An intensive study of the Luftwaffe on the eastern front reveals much about German attitudes towards the role of air power in modern warfare. Alone among the theaters in which the German armed forces fought, the four-year struggle against the "Bolshevik colossus" provided a sustained stage for the playing out and evaluation of the prewar concepts of the air force. The victorious Blitzkrieg in the west, by virtue of its brevity and dazzling success, tended to obscure any flaws in doctrine and operational practice. The Luftwaffe had, to be sure, been thwarted over the British Isles during the Battle of Britain, but German air force planners, hampered by constantly changing strategic directives and the apparent indifference or intractability of the other two services, could attribute that unhappy experience to factors beyond their control. The much-publicized campaigns of Field Marshal Erwin Rommel's Afrika Korps in the Western Desert in 1941–1942 hardly gave the Luftwaffe an opportunity to wage the type of war for which it had been designed. And the campaign in Western Europe in 1944 and 1945 took place only after the Luftwaffe had faded from the scene, the victim of losses incurred during the defense of the Reich and the sustained over-commitment in the east and in the Mediterranean. Thus, only in Russia did the German air force's offensive doctrine undergo such a protracted trial. For the Luftwaffe, the venture promised to be "a proper war" indeed. While the commitment of German air strength to the eastern theater does not quite match the preponderance of army deployments there, in mid-1943 approximately fifty-one percent of operational Luftwaffe aircraft (some 3,415 machines) served with the eastern air fleets.[7] From the opening of Barbarossa until mid-1943, when home defense commitments began to swallow up the Luftwaffe's fighter force, the eastern campaign occasioned the largest concentration of air force combat strength on any one front.[8] For long-range bombardment and ground attack aviation in particular, the USSR remained the primary war theater until the end of the war.

The development of the German air campaign in the east paralleled the fluctuations of German grand strategy to a large extent. Recent West German studies have demonstrated convincingly that the Barbarossa campaign of 1941 is the only endeavor of the entire war to which the German high command consciously employed the Blitzkrieg strategy.[9] Hitler and his generals hoped for a swift victory over the USSR, which would allow the German military to return to the maritime and air war against Great Britain the following year. In line with this decision, Luftwaffe participation in the 1941 campaign sought to bring the air force's power to bear on the strategic objective of defeating the armed forces of the USSR within four months. Likewise, the campaign on the southern front the following spring, code-named Blau, required the fullest possible Luftwaffe support in order to bring about the envisioned rapid decision. In later years, as the Germans were compelled to reduce or abandon their offensive and acquisitive designs on the Soviet Union, the Luftwaffe general staff sought an escape through prewar concepts of air power. They intended to use the Luftwaffe's capability for waging independent air war, even after "a stagnation of the ground front" had occurred,[10] as a means of extricating the German army from the grim battle of attrition that accompanied a defensive posture, and the Luftwaffe from the undesirable position of operating as a mere *Hilfswaffe*, or auxiliary weapon.

The Luftwaffe's limited resources and the nature of the German theory of air power led to the emergence of something of an intellectual dichotomy within the Third Reich's air leadership. Throughout the eastern campaign, a considerable gulf divided the general staff echelons from many of the operational commanders on the scene. This tension manifested itself in the persistent interest at the higher headquarters in independent strategic air operations against the Soviet war industry. At the same time, the more pragmatic commanders of flying units in the east, together with their staffs, grappled with the considerable technical and doctrinal problems of direct army support in tacit acknowledgement (especially after 1941) of the Luftwaffe's limited resources and capabilities.

The debate over tactical and strategic employment of a nation's air assets is a familiar one to historians of Second World War air power, and indeed rages within most air forces to this day. The controversy between Supreme Headquarters Allied Expeditionary Force (SHAEF) and the Allied air chiefs regarding the use of the USAAF and RAF Bomber Command in the months prior to Operation Overlord in preparation for the Normandy landings stands as perhaps the most well-known example.[11] All sorts of vital yet ancillary tasks tended to divert air forces of the Second World War from the execution of a purely strategic air war. These included air transport and resupply, interdiction of enemy road, rail and sea traffic, air defense, direct support of an attacking or retreating ground force, and other missions only peripherally related to the strategic employment of air power. Most successful air forces of the era, willingly or unwillingly, came to grips with the problems these missions posed. Some adhered to strategic bombing principles long after it became impractical or unprofitable to do so. Few have argued that the Luftwaffe fell into this particular trap, yet during the eastern campaign, especially during 1943–1944, the German air force general staff showed a remarkable determination, very reminiscent of its Western Allied counterparts, to carry out strategic air operations even to the detriment of the overall military situation. It should come as no surprise that the Luftwaffe, a typical product of the over-optimistic air power theorizing common in the 1930s, should have in its leadership echelons a large number of true believers in strategic air war. These air power theorists created the intellectual milieu from which sprang the war plans contemplated and executed against the USSR.

The air war in the Soviet Union, however, certainly after the check before Moscow in December 1941, bore little relation to the prewar theories, no matter how much German air planners tried to make it conform to their expectations. That the German air force was able, for several years, to play a significant role in the operational victories of the Wehrmacht in Russia is a tribute to the flexible and realistic elements of its doctrine formulated in the 1930s. Throughout the four years of the eastern campaign, German air force methods for cooperation with the army improved markedly in both the technical and operational spheres. Although equipped with aircraft designs ill-suited for the task, the Luftwaffe gave a good account of itself in support of ground operations from 1941 through 1943. Only when the scope of its operations became impossibly large, owing both to the expanding nature of the war and to its leadership's imprudent assumption of too many tasks, did the Luftwaffe lose the ability to gain a decision "in the third dimension." By late 1943, the once-powerful German air arm resembled a caricature of its own prewar operational air war conception—a force gamely attempting to carry out the entire spectrum of air operations with a force structure barely adequate to meet the demands of any one task. The multifaceted nature of German air power doctrine, formerly an asset, had become a millstone about the necks of its architects.

It is not the primary purpose of this study to recount in detail the course of German air operations against the USSR.[12] Rather, this work intends to delineate the shifts in German air strategy, as well as in the complex interrelationship between operational art, aviation technology, and the strategic ambitions of the German air force general staff during the Russian campaign. As such, this interpretation leans towards an "internal" criticism of the Luftwaffe's performance. The German air force general staff in the later years of the campaign was unwilling or unable to acknowledge that the available air power had little chance of fulfilling the grandiose expectations held for it. Furthermore, the Luftwaffe's status as an independent service may have ultimately been a detriment to the execution of its role in the eastern campaign, as in many cases its participation in the conflict was unresponsive or irrelevant to the requirements of the campaign as a whole. This book is also not intended to be a complete history of the aerial operations of the eastern campaign, giving equal coverage to both the Luftwaffe and the Red Air Force. I have not attempted to discuss the activities of the Axis satellite air forces, such as the Rumanian, Hungarian, Finnish and Italian air arms, that operated alongside the Luftwaffe. The focus of this study remains on the German air leadership and its efforts to apply the available forces towards the goal of victory over the Soviet Union. Accordingly, in many cases I am more concerned with what the Luftwaffe's leaders believed it was accomplishing than what was actually achieved. Rather than a detailed narrative of battles lost and won, this is a study of how a modern air force responded, or failed to respond, to a series of unexpected and eventually overwhelming pressures.

Few historians now doubt that the eastern campaign, in both its military and ideological elements, represented the primary focus for the German army in the Second World War. No such consensus has emerged regarding the employment of the German air force, and it is not the purpose of this study to suggest that the campaign against the Soviet Union had quite the same magnetic attraction for the Luftwaffe as it did for the army. Rather, the German air force, pressed into a four-year bloodletting against an industrially, geographically, and numerically superior opponent, paradoxically had the opportunity to put much of its prewar doctrine and theorizing about air power to the test. If the eastern campaign turned out to be something other than Jeschonnek's "proper war," then at least it proved to be the most revealing campaign the Luftwaffe ever fought. For German air force doctrine, in a manner not duplicated in any of the other theaters, was laid bare, with all of its strengths and weaknesses exposed, in the Soviet Union between 1941 and 1944. Even more importantly, the Luftwaffe's failure in Russia brings to light certain shortcomings common to many military organizations, especially, but not exclusively, those of the Third Reich.

* * *

This project began life as my doctoral dissertation at The Ohio State University, and many people and institutions contributed mightily during the odyssey from initial conception to finished book. I would like to take the opportunity to mention some of them in small remuneration for the assistance they offered.

The lengthy research necessary for this study could not have been accomplished without the help of a Smithsonian/Guggenheim Predoctoral Fellowship in 1988–1989. Moreover, the members of the Aeronautics Department of the National Air and Space Museum provided the best possible environment for aviation history research. I would especially like to thank my Smithsonian advisor, Dr. Von D. Hardesty, as well as Dr. Dominick Pisano, Tom Dietz, Bob van der Linden, Peter Jakab, and Joanne Gernstein for all of the friendship and aid granted me during my stay. My fellow visiting fellows, Tami Davis Biddle, Dr. Jacob Vandermeulen, Dr. Michael E. Neufeld, and Professor John Morrow deserve a special word of thanks. At the U.S. National Archives across the Mall, Mr. Harry Rilley and Dr. Timothy Mulligan were both filled with insights regarding the captured German records.

I must also express my appreciation to the United States Air Force Historical Research Center, Maxwell AFB, for the award of a Dissertation Research Grant in 1988. At Maxwell, Mr. Harry Fletcher and especially Dr. James H. Kitchens III provided wise guidance through the Karlsrühe Collection and the British Air Ministry documents. In addition, Dr. Jürgen Förster of the Militärgeschichtliches Forschungsamt in Freiburg was kind enough to secure for me documents from the Bundesarchiv and initially made me aware of the fascinating story of the Luftwaffe general staff military science department.

The transition from dissertation to book took place with the timely aid of a John M. Olin Postdoctoral Fellowship in Military and Strategic History at Yale University during 1990–1991. My thanks go out to the members of the Yale faculty, especially Sir Michael Howard, Professor Paul M. Kennedy, Dr. Harold Selesky, and Dr. George Andreopoulos for ensuring such a productive year. During the revision process, Mr. Tom Dietz, Dr. Jeff Roberts, Dr. Michael E. Neufeld, Miss Teresa Trautmann, and especially Professor Brian M. Linn of Texas A&M University commented extensively on various versions of the manuscript. Mr. Dietz of the Air and Space Museum in particular provided invaluable assistance in selecting and obtaining the photographs, as did Dr. Tom Crouch and Mr. Larry Wilson. Former Luftwaffe officers Generalmajor a.D. Dietrich Peltz and Oberst a.D. Hajo Herrmann took the time during their visit to Washington in 1990 to answer some of my questions dealing with the war in the east and its impact on the German air force. Mr. Dave Mac-Farland of the USAF Association was kind enough to arrange this interview. My brother Steve Muller drew several of the maps. Thanks are also due my editors at The Nautical and Aviation Publishing Company, Mr. Jan Snouck-Hurgronje and Ms. Linda Brunson, who saw some merit in this project and Sherri Faaborg who saw it through to completion.

At Ohio State, I owe an inestimable debt of thanks to my dissertation adviser and mentor, Professor Wick Murray. His contributions to my understanding of history are profound. The same might be said of Professors Allan R. Millett, Alan Beyerchen, Clayton Roberts, William Childs and John F. Guilmartin. These teacher-scholars deserve much of the credit for any success their students may achieve. Finally, my fellow graduate students at OSU had an impact on my development as an historian that cannot be adequately acknowledged. Their ranks are too numerous to list fully, but Caroline Ziemke, Bill Wolf, Matt Schwonek, Kurt Fryklund, David Young, Tom Arnold, Roger Nimps, Allison Gilmore, Brad Meyer, Rich Hall, Jeff Roberts, George Sinks and the late Paul Manzini had more input into this project than they were ever aware.

Birth of a Concept. Ground crewman handing clusters of "potato masher" grenades up to the observer of a World War I German Air Service Halberstadt CL II ground attack aircraft. This photograph was most probably taken during the spring 1918 German offensive on the western front. (Photo courtesy Peter M. Grosz via NASM)

CHAPTER ONE

PREPARATIONS FOR A PROPER WAR

The Luftwaffe that waged the eastern campaign was the product of years of theorizing and conceptualization about the role air power might play in future conflicts. In addition, the national socialist air arm could draw upon experience gained in nearly two years of operations against the air forces of opponents such as Poland, France, and Great Britain. Its leadership's theories regarding the value of air superiority, close air support, strategic or independent air operations, and other functions of modern air forces all received meaningful evaluation in the crucible of combat. Success in the Balkans and the Mediterranean served to dim the memory of the frustrated air assault on Great Britain that followed the swift fall of France in June 1940. The onslaught against Stalin's Russia, then, put to the test a mature air force, supremely confident in the basic soundness of its equipment, leadership, personnel, and intellectual foundations.

The ideological underpinnings of National Socialist Germany all but ensured that the Luftwaffe's primary battlefield would be the Soviet Union. Few historians now doubt that the cornerstone of Adolf Hitler's foreign and racial policies was a "war of annihilation" and territorial aggrandizement at the expense of, as he expressed in *Mein Kampf*, "Russia and her vassal border states."[1] Although Hitler was notorious

1

for concealing the scope and direction of his ambitions from his military staffs, there is little doubt that the Luftwaffe, like the other armed services the instrument of Hitler's will, prepared during the whole of its existence for a conflict such as the one that greeted it on the morning of June 22, 1941. Its decisive defeat four years later, while certainly the result of the inner failings of the Führer's strategy that mandated the invasion of the USSR, was also an indictment of both the German conception of air power and the prevailing Western belief in the capabilities of modern air forces.

The nature of German air doctrine, both before and during the Second World War, is one of the most complex—and most misunderstood—historical problems to emerge from that conflict. Years of emotional, personality-oriented historiography, fueled by reports supporting the United States Strategic Bombing Survey, skewed interrogations of captured Luftwaffe officers, and narrowly focused studies produced for the USAF have combined to portray the Luftwaffe as an auxiliary weapon or *Hilfswaffe* linked doctrinally and technically to the support of the army.[2] There is, however, little in original Luftwaffe sources to bear out this hypothesis. German air war doctrine, although it evolved under the constraints of geographic and economic realities during the late 1930s, was as ambitious and far-reaching as any developed during this heyday of air power prophesizing; only the aforementioned factors tempered the zeal of the German planners. The Luftwaffe, in fact, developed a concept known as "operational air warfare" (*operativer Luftkrieg*) which seemingly accomplished the difficult task of integrating an independent air force into the conduct of modern "total war." An analysis of the eastern campaign that views the enterprise as merely an aggrandized army support venture by the Luftwaffe fails to provide a rationale for the fluctuations of German air strategy in the east, especially the 1943–1944 attempt to employ the bomber forces in independent operations against the Soviet war economy.

The nature of German air power doctrine also ensured that operations designed to give support to the army played a major role in the war against Russia. The development of an army support capability, a task which many of the air forces of the other powers eschewed during the interwar period, is one of the more notable accomplishments of the Luftwaffe leadership. Few air forces in 1941–1942 could provide ground forces with decisive assistance at a critical juncture of a land battle.[3] The proficiency with which certain Luftwaffe formations carried out this technically difficult task misled both the German army leadership and future historians as to precisely what place direct army support occupied in the German air force's doctrine. In fact, the vaunted close air support capability was a mission for which the bulk of the Luftwaffe was ill-prepared, and one for which the attendant technical problems were not really solved until early 1944.

The experiences that the Luftwaffe acquired during the generally victorious campaigns from 1939 to June 1941 also left their mark on the conduct of the eastern campaign. The leadership drew upon lessons learned in Poland, the low countries, France and the Battle of Britain as it grappled with the even more intractable problems which the Russian campaign posed. Furthermore, Luftwaffe planners during the latter stages of the war in the east made frequent reference to both the successes and failures of the Royal Air Force, the Soviet air force (Voyenno-vozdushnyye sily, or VVS), and the United States Army Air Force when developing operational plans for use against the Bolshevik adversary.

The Russian campaign, then, was in many respects the intellectual as well as the operational watershed of the *Luftwaffe* in the Second World War. The results of the endeavor not only reveal the strengths and weaknesses of German air power, but provide yet another example of the persistent inability of many air forces to reconcile doctrinal preference with operational realities.

THE GERMAN IDEA OF AIR WAR: OPERATIVER LUFTKRIEG

Recent research by both American and German authors has substantially altered the historical perception of German air power doctrine.[4] These authorities have effectively demolished the ideas that the Luftwaffe functioned as an airborne adjunct to the army, and embodied a narrower mentality than the strategic bombardment-oriented air forces of the Western Allies. In fact, the Luftwaffe leadership's theoretical concept of its role and mission was, if anything, more sophisticated, realistic, and comprehensive than that of its later adversaries.

The German military had suffered decisive defeat in the First World War, and this fact had a deleterious influence upon the smooth development of air force theory and technology during the years of the Weimar

Republic (1918–1933). The most obvious strictures concerned the disarmament clauses of the Treaty of Versailles. Certain articles of the treaty placed severe restrictions upon the manufacture even of civilian aircraft in Germany. Other clauses prohibited military aircraft development and the retention of even a vestigial air force organization.[5] The development of air power in Germany therefore took place under constraints not present in the case of the other major powers. One German commentator noted that "until 1933 practically nothing was operational that the Versailles Treaty had expressly forbidden."[6] Perhaps most seriously, the Luftwaffe never recovered from the lag in high performance aircraft engine development resulting from the "lost" Weimar years.[7] The lack of suitable bomber engines was to plague German heavy aircraft development until the end of the Second World War. Nevertheless, interwar Germany proved fertile ground for air power theorizing.

Much of the credit for the preservation of German air power during the Weimar years belongs to Generaloberst Hans von Seeckt, until 1926 the head of the Truppenamt (effectively, a camouflaged general staff) of the Defense Ministry. Seeckt ensured the retention within the 100,000–man Reichswehr of a cadre of former First World War air service officers, despite pragmatic objections from his colleagues that to employ airmen without aircraft was pointless. Although Seeckt does not generally achieve recognition as an air power theorist, his biographer Rabenau credits him with preserving the infrastructure of military aviation in Weimar Germany as well as fostering "air-mindedness" within the German military establishment and population at large.[8] His attitude towards the role of the air force in future conflicts is noteworthy in that it provides a convincing refutation of the idea that the conservative German military establishment downplayed the potential of air power or, at best, viewed it as an adjunct to the ground forces. In a 1929 volume of military reflections entitled *Thoughts of a Soldier*, Seeckt commented,

When we speak of modern military technology, we think first of all of the air weapon. During the World War, and even more since, this branch became a fully-fledged "sister" of the land and sea forces, without changing the fundamental laws of war. We must now admit that an entirely new battlefield with its own peculiar conditions has been created for the soldier and his technical collaborator. The possibility of air attacks on the centers of national resistance, and thus on the extant sources of military strength which have as a result become much more vulnerable, have led to false conclusions as to the necessity of land forces. The difference is only that a military decision can now be obtained in the air, as well as on land or at sea.[9]

Although somewhat unsophisticated in its formulation, Seeckt's prediction foreshadowed some of the basic concepts underlying German air force doctrine in the late 1930s. The air force was to exist as a fully independent service, yet it would carry out its mission and exploit its own unique abilities within the context of the entire conflict and in harmony with the missions of the other services. Later studies produced by the Reichswehr during the interwar period do not differ substantially from Seeckt's formula.[10] For example, in its discussion of the role of air power in modern warfare, the 1931 edition of the standard Reichswehr tactical manual, Die Truppenführung, made no attempt to tie the flying formations to army support tasks. Instead, the manual emphasized that ''the primary task of the bomber units is attack against enemy combat power and the sources of supply that sustain it. Also, they carry out attacks against the economic sources of power (wirtschaftliche Kraftquellen) of the enemy.''[11]

German air force planners would later maintain that ''the idea that the air force alone can decide the outcome of a war has never been expressed.''[12] This statement, narrowly interpreted, is correct: German doctrine always took into account the activities of the other services and sought to formulate a mission for the air force that would permit the most concentrated application of German military power. In spite of this near-consensus, there were proposals in the early years of rearmament following the national socialist Machtergreifung of January 1933 that foresaw a primarily independent mission for the air force. The most celebrated of these was that of Dr. Robert Knauss, business director of Lufthansa, who in May 1933 proposed to Erhard Milch, then State Secretary of the Air Ministry, the creation of a ''risk air force'' (Risiko-Luftwaffe) composed of four hundred long-range four-engined bombers. This force, clearly modeled on an incorrect assessment of the motivations underlying Admiral Alfred von Tirpitz's pre-World War I battle fleet program, would function as a strategic deterrent to protect Germany from a two-front ''preemptive war'' launched by France and

Poland.[13] Tirpitz evidently intended that his battle fleet be actually used to defeat the Royal Navy in a North Sea confrontation, while Knauss intended the air fleet to shield Germany while she passed through a dangerous and vulnerable period of rearmament.[14] Milch, although enamored of Knauss' conception, correctly believed the minuscule German aircraft industry of the time incapable of the rapid construction of such an air fleet. Many of Knauss' ideas, including the use of the bomber force as a diplomatic lever, survived the demise of his proposal and were most evident in Hitler's use of the air force during the last years of peace.[15]

German air doctrine received a more serious and significant codification in 1935 with the publication of its most notable doctrinal statement, L. Dv. 16, *Luftkriegführung* (Conduct of Air War).[16] This manual was the brainchild of one of General Erich Ludendorff's former staff officers and the first chief of the Luftwaffe general staff, General Walther Wever. The final version was the result of a group effort utilizing the talents of staff officers such as General Helmut Wilberg and Major Paul Deichmann.[17] The manual itself contained no list of contributors, in keeping with Moltke the Elder's decree that "general staff officers should be nameless." Wever himself, due no doubt in part to his untimely demise in an air crash on June 3, 1936, remains something of a conundrum among both his peers and historians. Most are in agreement with Milch on his abilities:

> He was the most significant of the officers taken over from the army. If he had remained in the army he would have reached the highest positions there as well. He possessed not only tremendous professional ability, but also great personal qualities. He was the only general staff chief since the end of World War I who came close to Moltke [the Elder].[18]

There is less consensus on what Wever's ideas meant for the future mission of the Luftwaffe. One of the strengths of *Luftkriegführung* was its flexibility and breadth of scope;[19] this same quality also allowed for the appearance of contradictory interpretations. Generalmajor Herbert Rieckhoff was convinced that Wever was a "fanatical Douhet scholar," who believed, as did the Italian air power prophet General Giulio Douhet, that the independent air force should emphasize strategic bombing.[20] Generalmajor Hans-Detlef Herhudt von Rohden, after the war, maintained that Wever's formulation placed too little emphasis on striking at the enemy heartland in favor of such support tasks as interdiction of the enemy's transportation system.[21]

In fact, Wever's manual, although he was not granted the opportunity to expand or elaborate upon it, contained all of the ingredients of the later theory known as "operative" or "operational" air warfare. *Luftkriegführung* combined an awareness of Germany's continental position and need to coordinate the actions of all of the armed forces with a keen appreciation of the potential of air warfare. Accordingly, the manual gave pride of place to the bomber arm, "the bearer of offensive air warfare."[22] Beyond this admittedly Douhetian emphasis on bombardment aviation, the manual dealt at some length with issues such as air superiority, operations in support of the army and navy, the human element in war leadership (beyond the simple assertion of many writers that bombing would cause enemy morale to collapse), and other issues which would decide the coming conflict. "The task of the Luftwaffe," Wever and his collaborators maintained, was:

> Through the conduct of war in the air to attain the following objectives in the context of the overall war (Gesamtkrieg):
>
> To combat the enemy air force; thereby weakening the enemy's armed forces while at the same time protecting our own armed forces, our people, and their living space.
>
> To intervene in the operations on land and sea in direct support of the army and navy.
>
> To battle against the sources of power of the enemy armed forces [strategic bombing of industry], and to interrupt the flow of supplies between the rear areas and the front [interdiction].[23]

While carrying out these general tasks, the Luftwaffe, "an integral part of the entire military force," had to augment "the totality of military action" by all the services.[24]

Central to success in a modern war, the manual maintained, was the principle of concentration of force in time and space against a decisive objective.[25] The Prussian military philosopher Carl von Clausewitz had insisted that "there is no higher and simpler law of strategy than of *keeping one's forces concentrated* [italics in original]."[26] It is likely that Wever in stressing this concept also drew upon Seeckt's vision of how modern armed forces ought to function. Of all the air power principles

espoused in prewar Germany, it is this rule of force concentration that
played the greatest role in the campaign against the Soviet Union. The
German air force's operational successes in 1941–1942, including the
virtual annihilation of the Red Air Force and the conquest of the Crimea,
stemmed from a ruthless adherence to this principle. Likewise, the Luftwaffe's decline as an offensive force resulted in no small measure from a
strategic neglect of this policy, which in turn led to a dilution of German
air power in the eastern theater and elsewhere.

   Also significant for the coming campaign in the east was Wever's
idea, doubtless a reaction to the experiences of the First World War, that
strategic attacks upon enemy "sources of power" offered an escape
from the attrition caused by trench warfare.[27] This recoil from the mud
of Flanders was hardly unique to Wever and his collaborators; it was
arguably the motivating factor behind most air power theories of the era.
Douhet observed that the technical advances of the First World War
greatly favored the defensive; if that war was used as a basis for future
planning, only a ghastly replay of 1914–1918 would ensue.[28] Overflying
an enemy's ground defenses and striking at "vital centers" promised a
solution. In contrast to Douhet's formulation, which emphasized the
use of poison gas against urban centers, the German manual "rejected
on principle" the execution of "reprisal" or "terror" raids against
enemy noncombatants. This was a proscription that did not survive the
opening campaigns of the Second World War, and in the case of the war
against the USSR the contemplation and execution of such attacks were
commonplace.

   As significant as *Luftkriegführung* undeniably was for the Luftwaffe's
conduct of the Second World War, other factors influenced the development of the German idea of air war. One of these concerned the force
structure and aircraft production situation of the German air force during the years leading up to the outbreak of war. The Luftwaffe that
eventually evolved represented an uneasy compromise between the
ideal force, capable of performing the diverse tasks which German planners set for it, and the product of an immature, overheated industry
struggling to match raw material shortages and technical constraints to
the grandiose aims of Nazi foreign policy.[29]

   Nowhere was this conflict reflected more clearly than in the case of
German heavy bomber development. The German aircraft industry
attempted to supply the nascent force with aircraft that would fulfill the

widest possible range of missions. These included a capable medium-range bomber force eventually equipped with the twin-engined Junkers Ju 86, Heinkel He 111, and Dornier Do 17. The development of a heavy long-range four-engined bomber (which Wever portentously christened the Uralbomber after its presumed ability to reach industrial targets beyond the Ural mountains in the eastern USSR), in contrast, suffered a critical miscarriage. Two prototypes which the Junkers and Dornier firms produced in the mid-1930s, the Ju 89 and the Do 19, did not possess acceptable performance. Both types were underpowered, unwieldy machines, and there is little evidence to support their backers' postwar contentions that ''with systematic further development, they would have been equivalent or superior to American and British heavy bombers.''[30] As a result of the poor showing of the Uralbomber proto-types, the Luftwaffe staff in mid-1936 chose to bypass the first genera-tion of heavy bomber aircraft entirely, and proceeded instead to issue specifications for a heavy bomber with greatly advanced performance. This aircraft, initially known as ''Projekt 1041,'' later as the Heinkel He 177, succumbed to technical problems and never had the desired impact on Luftwaffe force structure.[31] As a result, the German air force faced the impending conflict with a strategic bombing capability effectively limited to the area of central Europe.

A second factor coloring the growth of German air power doctrine was the intellectual response within the Luftwaffe both to Wever's man-ual and to the course of Adolf Hitler's diplomatic and military policy. The years between 1936 and 1939 were exceedingly productive ones for the development of air power theory in Germany. The contributions of this often-overlooked second generation of air theorists, half-forgotten majors and lieutenant-colonels such as Erwin Gehrts, Hans-Detlef Her-hudt von Rohden, and Hans Freiherr von Bülow, did much to bridge the gap between Wever's theoretical formulation and Luftwaffe operational practice during World War II.[32]

As several authors have pointed out, the bulk of this theorizing concerned strategic applications of air power, rather than the develop-ment of army support doctrine.[33] In general, the offensive-minded con-ceptions implicit in Luftkriegführung received greater emphasis than did the many other elements of the theory. General Franz Halder, the army chief of staff from 1938–1942, recalled that ''the German air force . . . based itself on the idea of strategic air warfare, i.e. it adapted the ideas laid down in the Italian and French literature on the subject."[34] In fact, the theories of Douhet enjoyed far more thorough scrutiny and acclaim in Germany than in many European nations. German air theorists praised Douhet for recognizing the need for an independent air service, for touting the principle of force concentration, and for recognizing that air supremacy would be decisive in a future conflict.[35] Beyond this rather generous reading of the heavy-handed general's writings, a Luftwaffe analyst cautioned that Douhet's technical prescriptions regarding the destructive effects of area bombing were overly optimistic, and that "it would have been wrong to measure, for example, the British power of resistance by Italian standards."[36]

More significant than any foreign influence were the refinements of Germany's indigenous air power thinkers. Luftwaffe authors writing in the service journals addressed such diverse topics as the lessons of the strategic bombing campaign against Britain during World War I and the concept of the "decisive blow" in air warfare.[37] Most stressed the independent nature of the air arm, and its ability to strike at portions of the enemy war machine hitherto out of range of the other two services. Bombing of enemy industry, accordingly, received much attention from these writers. Such attacks would place such intolerable demands upon an enemy nation already locked in combat with Germany's other armed services that rapid collapse would ensue. Air power was therefore an essential component of the "total war of tomorrow."[38] This concept of air force employment became known as *operativer Luftkrieg*, or "operational air war," and was the central tenet of German air power theory.[39]

During the mid-1930s, the term *operativer Luftkrieg* was applied to a number of air force missions. There was even a danger that the term had a usage so flexible as to render it meaningless. German historian Horst Boog related one graphic illustration of *operativer Luftkrieg*'s amorphous meaning:

> The Bomber Chief of the Operations Department of the Luftwaffe General Staff, Major Deichmann, told me that when in 1936 he called together all General Staff officers and made them write down their definition of the concept . . . he got as many definitions and interpretations as there were officers present.[40]

In the course of the following years, a more precise meaning for the concept evolved, primarily through the exertions of military officers contributing theoretical articles to the military publications. *Operativer Luftkrieg* came to refer to an air force, using its unique attributes of range, speed, and surprise, striking at the sources of enemy military, economic, and moral strength (war industries, population and communication centers, and military installations) in order to achieve a strategic decision in concert with the more traditional branches of the armed service. In operational terms, the German concept embraced many of the elements of Anglo-American strategic bombing doctrine, especially in its identification of "centers of national resistance" vulnerable to attack from the air. Noticeably absent was the assertion that the other services were irrelevant or at best peripheral to the air force's activities. In fact, most German writers believed that the actions of the three services were synergistic. In a typical scenario, the bulk of the bomber units assigned to "operational air war" tasks would smash the enemy's war industries sustaining the armies in the field, the power stations supplying the war industries with electricity, and the communications systems linking the enemy's heartland to the military forces. The concerted pressure of air attack and combat losses at the front would bring about the collapse of the enemy and a strategic victory for Germany.

Perhaps the most eloquent champion of this concept in the late 1930s was a young general staff officer, Major Hans-Detlef Herhudt von Rohden, arguably Germany's most significant prewar air power theorist and certainly the most prolific.[41] Herhudt von Rohden accurately foresaw the future significance of force-to-space ratios, air superiority, productive capacity and other issues which many of the more popular air power apostles of the period ignored. His lengthy 1937 essay entitled "Reflections on Air War" was held in sufficient esteem by the military establishment to warrant four-part treatment in the War Ministry's prestigious red-bound journal *Militärwissenschaftliche Rundschau*. Most official publications and edited collections of the era that touched upon air warfare listed him among their contributors.

The four-part article also appeared in book form in 1938 under the title *On Air War* (*Vom Luftkriege*): *Thoughts on the Command and Employment of Modern Air Forces*. The Clausewitzian allusion in the title was no accident: his intention was to provide his audience with a comprehensive theory of air warfare and its basic principles.[42] Like Clausewitz, Herhudt von Rohden attempted to delineate the role of the various branches of the armed services and to achieve a theoretical balance between them. He was, no less than his nineteenth century role model, particularly concerned with the attainment of strategic and tactical surprise. The conduct of war in the third dimension in his view required an appreciation of complex psychological, technical, and geopolitical factors. Mastery of these attributes amounted to nothing less than "military genius."[43]

Of all the diverse elements comprising this revolutionary form of conflict, Herhudt von Rohden regarded geopolitical considerations as most decisive. He was a disciple of Professor Karl Haushofer and accordingly espoused the pseudoscientific dictates of geopolitics and sought to adapt them to the "revolution in warfare" brought about by the growth of air power. The United States, he maintained, was by virtue of its size and location of its bases uniquely favored by geography to wage future strategic air operations. Germany, surrounded by potentially hostile states, found herself in a much less enviable position.[44] Even taking into account these physical difficulties, he believed that for Germany "the destruction of enemy production centers and their supply of raw materials is an all-important task of operative air warfare." Germany, so it appeared, would need to develop and implement an air strategy by which all her military forces could acquire geographic "triangles" of increased depth in order to shore up her defenses from outside encroachment from land as well as from the air. Then, the "bearer of operational air warfare," the long-range bomber arm, could turn to its most effective employment.

Much of the intellectual ferment of the 1930s naturally concerned scenarios for a war limited to the confines of central Europe; Poland and Czechoslovakia were often mentioned as potential adversaries. While many of the scenarios reflected Germany's continental orientation, air theorists did not ignore the injunction that since aviation promised the spanning of great distances, "the nature of air war is therefore intercontinental."[45] Accordingly, considerations of a future air war against the Soviet Union appeared in the military literature of the 1930s. Herhudt von Rohden regarded the geographic triangle of European Russia, with apexes at Leningrad, Sevastopol, and Gorki, as a suitable basis for *operativer Luftkrieg* against the west. Russia's geopolitical situation therefore served to render that of Germany even more unfavorable by comparison.[46] In 1936, another Luftwaffe officer and air power theorist, Oberst Hans Freiherr von Bülow, anticipated Herhudt von Rohden's senti-

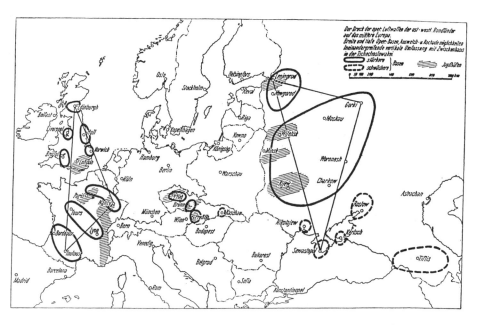

Map 1. Germany is surrounded by potential enemies in this illustration from Herhudt von Rohden's 1937 article, "Reflections on Air Warfare." An Anglo-French alliance to the west and the USSR to the east possess "geographic triangles" from which to wage strategic air war against the Third Reich.

ments in emphasizing the danger Soviet air power posed for Germany, poised as it was on "the gateway of Western European culture."[47] Moreover, Bülow drew attention to both the enormous productive capacity of the Soviet aircraft industry and the progressive designs that emanated from it. The consensus of Luftwaffe officers in the mid- and late 1930s, remarkable in contrast to the attitudes that would prevail in 1941, was that the USSR was a first-rate, rapidly modernizing air power. Its technical sophistication was augmented by formidable industrial, raw material, and geopolitical advantages.

Even so, to some German officers war against the Soviet Union offered certain possibilities. The precise form that such Luftwaffe employment might take was the subject of a two-part article that appeared in the German air force general staff's military science journal, *Die Luftwaffe: Militärwissenschaftliche Aufsatzsammlung*, in 1937–1938. Given the thesis of the article, the study, by a Major Macht, is of great relevance to the present discussion. Entitled "Bottlenecks in the Russian Defense Economy," the article outlined certain aspects of the Soviet "planned economy" of the First Five-Year Plan that were "of special interest to the airman."[48] Macht's thesis was a familiar one for European and American air power planners of his time. He argued that the destruction of a few vital structures from the air would create a crippling effect throughout the economy of a potential adversary. Macht believed that the vast Russian spaces made her transportation system unusually vulnerable to disruption, and he also isolated the Caucasian oil fields as vital targets.[49] The conclusions which Luftwaffe intelligence was to draw regarding its Soviet adversary in 1943–1944 were remarkably similar to those found in Macht's contribution to air power literature. In the late 1930s, however, Luftwaffe evaluations of the Soviet colossus remained academic exercises.

While it would be idle to suggest that every idea which German air power theorists expressed in print found its unaltered expression in air force planning, the geopolitically-based theories of Herhudt von Rohden and others do account for the method by which the Luftwaffe waged its campaigns during the Second World War. Also evident during these times were the beginnings of an intellectual divergence within the command echelons of the Luftwaffe. Implicit in Wever's and Herhudt von Rohden's writings was the need to wage a ground campaign to secure Germany the time and space necessary to wage strategic air warfare. This campaign would require a specialized capability on the part of the German air force. Out of this prerequisite for *operativer Luftkrieg* grew the famed German tactical air arm.

THE STEPCHILD THAT GREW SLOWLY: THE LUFTWAFFE'S ARMY SUPPORT CAPABILITY

Both early Reichswehr planners and "operational air war" theorists foresaw the various branches of service cooperating to reach a strategic decision. This formulation looked fine in theory, until the planners realized that close cooperation with the army called for the difficult task of coordinating ground troops, often rapidly advancing motorized or armored forces, and air units amid the "fog of war" of the industrial battlefield. While a considerable percentage of the Luftwaffe's force structure in 1939 was well suited for what the Germans termed "indirect army support" (*mittelbare Heeresunterstützung*), closer cooperation between the services presented formidable problems. German bomber units could operate effectively in the depth of the battle area and carry out interdiction of supply lines and communications. Even attacks on the war industry of a hostile nation, "strategic bombing" to most American and British planners, sometimes fell under the heading of "indirect army support" since they prevented enemy combat power from being brought to bear at the front.

On other occasions, German air power in a future conflict might have to intervene more directly in the conduct of ground operations. Advancing mechanized troops engaged in a breakthrough operation would require air support to deal with particularly stubborn pockets of enemy resistance; such air support might be even more vital for troops on the defensive. For an air force to be able to provide this type of support, or in German parlance, "direct army support" (*unmittelbare Heeresunterstützung*), a specialized capability was necessary.

As was the case with much of German air power doctrine, the body of experience from which the Luftwaffe's architects drew their operational and strategic lessons regarding support of the army dated back to the latter years of the First World War. Prior to this time, aviation technology was too primitive and the number of available aircraft too small to allow for any meaningful conceptualizing about the role and potential of air power. During the first two years of that conflict, the airplane evolved into an effective artillery spotting platform. The need to protect these observation aircraft led in turn to the quest for air superiority, one of the most enduring principles of air warfare. As late as 1916, however, the Imperial German Air Service viewed its role in the sphere of inter-service cooperation in only the most vaguely-defined terms: "no battle must be fought on the ground without the air force making its honorable contribution."[50]

After the so-called "Race to the Sea" in autumn 1914, the front line evolved into a trench system of increasing complexity, making the prospect of breakthrough battles, with or without air force participation, unlikely. Since it took opposing ground forces three years to solve the two-dimensional problems such a static situation posed, it is not surprising that the evolution of a complementary air support capability was less than rapid. Not until July 1917 did German aircraft provide direct support for attacking army units during a local offensive.[51] In the ensuing months, as the Germans perfected the infantry infiltration or "stormtroop" tactics that were to revolutionize warfare on the western front, related innovations took place within the air service. Germany led the other major powers in the development of specialized army support aircraft. Initially designated "infantry aircraft," by 1918 these planes, including the Halberstadt CL II and IV, the Hannover CL IV, and finally the well-armored, all-metal Junkers J 1, were known as *Schlachtflugzeuge*, or "ground attack aircraft."[52] Alongside the techno-logical advances in aircraft development, the German air service evolved procedures through which these aircraft might provide needed air support to the infantry. These included visual signals and, in some cases, rudimentary wireless contact between ground troops and air-craft.[53] By the time of the Michael offensive (or Kaiserschlacht) in March 1918, the Germans deployed thirty-eight ground attack *Staffeln* (squadrons), which the German command regarded as "an extremely effective and mobile reserve weapon for attack and defense."[54] Aircraft of the *Schlachtstaffeln* attacked enemy trenches with hand grenades and machine gun fire, often with devastating effect.[55] The aircraft employed were also capable of defending themselves against Allied fighters, and must be regarded as one of the more significant aviation developments of the First World War.

As is the case with many military innovations, a number of problems emerged. The March 1918 offensive restored a measure of fluidity to the hitherto stagnant western front. The rapid initial German advance high-lighted a problem that was to haunt Luftwaffe close support operations until the end of the Second World War: the difficulty of providing direct air support to ground troops once positional warfare gave way to a war of movement. General der Kavallerie Ernst von Höppner, commander of the German air service at that time, referred to the "difficulties regarding the use of air power in a war of movement" as arising from the "maintenance of cooperation between headquarters and unit com-manders and between the troops and aerial observers."[56] The ensuing years of peacetime rearmament, first clandestine, then overt, did little to ameliorate this situation. In addition to the limitations of technology, German ground attack units in the final months of the war had to contend with ever more severe losses to Allied fighters. The high cost of ground support operations no doubt helped to diminish their attractive-ness in the eyes of postwar German military planners.[57]

Army support aviation accordingly remained a low priority for the planners who shaped the embryonic Luftwaffe. The initial aircraft pro-duction plan in 1933-1934, designed mainly to prime the pump of the minuscule German aircraft industry, contained no types suitable for the close air support role at all.[58] This apparent regression from World War I practice resulted from the German military planners' belief that the ground attack formations in the 1918 Imperial German Air Service were a reaction to the peculiar conditions of trench warfare.[59] The *Schlacht-staffeln* were a weapon designed to break the stalemate of the Western Front; planners could with some justification point out that their useful-ness in military scenarios of the 1920s and 1930s was questionable. The dominant vision from the First World War was arguably the Gotha bomber raids on London and the deployment of General Hugh Tren-chard's Independent Air Force, coupled with the more prosaic task of aerial reconnaissance. Most of the emphasis during the Luftwaffe's buildup went towards the creation of bomber, reconnaissance, and fighter units, with the quantity and types of aircraft reflecting a desire to wage operational air war in central Europe. The close support mission received a disproportionately small amount of attention. Until 1938, the Luftwaffe did not possess a single unit trained or equipped for this type of mission.[60]

For its part, the army was not particularly insistent that the Luftwaffe alter its approach to war planning in any substantive fashion. As noted earlier, army manuals acknowledged the independence of the air force. Not until 1936 did a series of maneuvers, known as Grosse Herbstübung 1936, take place with the express purpose of coordinating armored troops and aircraft. Many senior Luftwaffe commanders and general staff officers participated, among them Major Paul Deichmann. Deichmann coordinated the exercise entitled "Cooperation of Ground Troops with Air Power."[61] Results were anything but gratifying. Assessments by armored units taking part revealed dissatisfaction even with the methods for transmission of aerial reconnaissance reports.[62] Deichmann continued to maintain after the maneuvers were completed that enemy industry should be the prime target of the Luftwaffe in the next war.[63] Even progressive army generals, such as Heinz Guderian, were not overly sanguine about the prospects for developing battlefield air support. Guderian, in a 1936 work dealing with the cooperation of tank units with other branches of the armed forces, had little to say about the possibilities of using aircraft in a cooperative role.[64] Aircraft were, in his view, best employed in attacking rear areas, staff headquarters, and other targets behind the front lines. He foresaw more of a future for mass drops of parachute troops (then being developed in the USSR) than for direct air support of the *Panzer* force.

The gestation of a true close air support capability for the Luftwaffe began with the German participation in the Spanish Civil War, 1936–1939. Some German sources maintained that the experience gained by the small German air component, known as the Condor Legion, occasioned "a reversal of previous conceptions regarding the employment of the Luftwaffe in direct support of the army with units specially equipped and trained for the task."[65] Even so, the development of direct air support procedures had a distinctly ad hoc character about it, as the initial experiments involved obsolete Heinkel He 51 fighter aircraft which had become unsuited for their intended role. Although the Luftwaffe, on the basis of its Spanish experience, came to embrace the dive bomber concept as an economy measure owing to its greater bombing accuracy,[66] the influence of the Spanish conflict on Luftwaffe operational preferences was ambiguous. Herhudt von Rohden, for example, regarded the conflict as a "special case." He likened the Spanish Civil War to the conflicts in China and Ethiopia in the 1930s, and argued that there were numerous contrasts between these "little wars" and a potential European confrontation between the great powers.[67] The minute size of the forces engaged, the lack of sophistication of the societies involved, and the low moral fiber of the populations caught in the "little wars," in his view, diminished the relevance of these experiences for German air planners.

Perhaps most significantly, the conflict in Spain brought to the fore the Luftwaffe's most outstanding proponent of army support aviation, Oberstleutnant Wolfram Freiherr von Richthofen, the cousin of the World War I fighter ace Manfred von Richthofen, the Red Baron. Richthofen's early career gave little indication of his future role as a tactical innovator. On the subject of direct battlefield air support, Richthofen was heard to remark that the concept of aircraft "diving below 6600 feet is complete nonsense."[68] During his tenure with the Luftwaffe's technical office in the mid-1930s, he even attempted to discontinue development of the Fieseler Fi 156 Storch spotting and liaison plane, a type he would later use extensively during his service in Russia.[69] Yet like many German general staff officers, Richthofen did not allow his preconceptions to override operational reality.[70] In a short time, he developed the tiny Condor Legion into a formidable weapon able to carry out a wide variety of tasks, including close air support. The tactical lessons proved to be extremely valuable, and as one Condor Legion commander, General Karl Drum insisted, "of all the experience gained by the Condor Legion in Spain, it was that pertaining to the methods of tactical air employment which was most significant and most far-reaching in its effects."[71]

There was to be no swift reorientation of a large number of Luftwaffe formations to the ground support role following the end of the Spanish venture. In fact, when the conflict with Poland opened on September 1, 1939, the Luftwaffe possessed only one specialized ground attack *Gruppe* in its entire force structure: II./(Schlacht) LG 2, equipped with obsolescent Henschel 123 biplanes. The bulk of the Ju 87 dive bomber units, later the symbol of German close army support, were at the time of the war's outbreak considered part of the strategic bombing force. The great bombing accuracy of the Stuka made it ideal for pinpoint strikes against industrial targets.

The Luftwaffe general staff's attitude towards the close support mission was ambivalent on the eve of the Second World War. General Dietrich Peltz, later commander of the German bomber force, recalled that emphasis in the Luftwaffe command on high altitude level bombing persisted up to the outbreak of the war.[72] The chief of the general staff,

General der Flieger Hans Jeschonnek, believed that army support tasks were secondary to the attainment of air superiority, particularly in the opening days of a conflict. He also noted:

The direct support of the army is the most difficult task facing the flying forces. Such a mission is analogous to a cavalry attack. It may, if it gains surprise, bring about great success; yet if the enemy is well-prepared, success is nil and losses heavy.[73]

Jeschonnek believed that "the requests of the army for direct support may consequently only be answered if the possibility of bringing about an unconditional, immediate and sensible result exists." In fact, Luftwaffe procedures for direct army support in 1939 seem to indicate that the problem was considered less a technical than a spiritual one: it depended heavily on the personalities and cooperative spirit of the commanders involved.[74]

Preparations for Operation White, the campaign against Poland, accordingly adhered closely to the *operativer Luftkrieg* formulations of the previous few years. The Luftwaffe planned to open the campaign with a decisive strike "with the full weight of [its] power" against the Polish air force, in order to secure air supremacy. Only then were the bomber units to support the advancing German army through a combination of "direct" support and, more frequently, attacks on the Polish army's mobilization centers, supply system, and march routes. Finally, the bomber forces were to stand ready for a strategic attack against the "defense installations and armaments factories in Warsaw."[75] The subsequent victory over the Poles, therefore, was a victory for Wever's multi- level concept of air strategy, not for any reorientation of the Luftwaffe towards close army support. The available forces for the operation were appropriate for the Luftwaffe's intended mission. On August 31, 1939, the German air force had on hand the following combat strength:

Long-range reconnaissance	257
Short-range reconnaissance	356
Stukas	366
Long-range bombers	1,176
Ground attack	40
Transport	552
Zerstörer	408
Fighters	771

Ninety percent of this combat force was serviceable the day war broke out; a state of affairs not often repeated during the coming conflict.[76]

The Luftwaffe in Poland, then, was ideally suited for *operativer Luftkrieg*: the acquisition of air superiority, followed by deep interdiction missions combined with attacks on vital centers of national resistance. That any significant number of direct army support missions took place at all on the first day of the campaign was on account of bad weather over the intended strategic targets. The Luftwaffe command, exploiting the flexibility of its units to the fullest extent, carried out its air strikes on Polish airfields and rendered close support to the German army prior to its armored breakthrough of the overstretched Polish defense lines. The latter task was a distant second in terms of the number of sorties flown. Once the panzer units achieved their breakthrough, the old problem of coordinating air strikes with mobile operations returned. The bulk of the army units did not report any significant cooperation with the air force at all. Some of the advancing field-grey columns were even bombed and strafed by their own aircraft.[77]

The results of the Polish campaign did not lead immediately to any major reforms in cooperation procedures between army and Luftwaffe. If the army presented valid complaints about the promptness, accuracy, and duration of the Luftwaffe's forward air strikes, the air force could point out that the success of missions against the Polish air force, communications lines and the capital city of Warsaw justified the substantial emphasis they had received. Both army and Luftwaffe noted severe problems with the communications systems, especially once the movement phase began.[78] For attacks on fixed fortifications and defensive lines preceding the armored breakthrough, however, the Luftwaffe command was fairly satisfied with results. In fact, the Luftwaffe's procedures for conducting operations of this type did not fundamentally change for the rest of the war.

This is not to say that the Luftwaffe ignored the problems posed by its experiences in the Polish campaign. Richthofen had since June 1939 commanded a special detachment known as the Fliegerkorps zur besonderen Verwendung (special duties air corps), later designated Fliegerkorps VIII, the Luftwaffe's premier close support force.[79] His experiences in Spain had convinced him of the value of close air support in much the same manner as the successes of the panzer arm in Poland had converted initially skeptical infantry officers such as Gerd von Rund-

stedt and Erwin Rommel into advocates of the "armored idea." Richthofen, among other achievements, pioneered the use of radio-
equipped armored car detachments which, while accompanying the
army units, could send back to air corps headquarters the most recent
information regarding progress of the ground battle.[80] Yet, in keeping
with Richthofen's motto, "the Luftwaffe is not a whore who performs
according to the wishes of the army, nor a fire brigade which immediately puts out every fire, large or small, on the ground front,"[81] his air
corps could perform a diverse range of operational tasks.[82]

Interestingly, it was not the specialized Fliegerkorps VIII, the bene-
ficiary of close air support experience in Poland, that was to participate
in a series of exercises just prior to the start of Fall Gelb (the offensive
against France and the low countries) designed to solve the problem of
supporting armored units with Stukas. The Luftwaffe high command
decided that Fliegerkorps VIII's skills might find more worthwhile
employment against French, Belgian, and Dutch airfields in the path of
the largely non-motorized Army Group B to the north. Consequently,
the exercises took place between General Heinz Guderian's XIX Panzerkorps and the Ju 87 dive bombers of Bruno Lörzer's Fliegerkorps II,
the unit that would actually support the armored thrust through the
Ardennes.[83]

The studies, conducted in April 1940, incorporated most of the air
support techniques available for use in the French campaign. They also
left no doubt that it was the Luftwaffe, not the army, that made the final
decision as to how or where the air force would take part in the ground
battle. The army corps' requests went to the *Nahkampfführer* ("close
combat leader") at *Fliegerkorps* level who "reserved to himself the final
attack order." For his part, the *Nakafü* conducted daily briefings with the
wing commanders actually leading the missions and took the army's
needs into account when issuing the following day's orders. Of course,
the system had less value once the movement phase of an operation
commenced. It was most successful during the preliminary phase of an
armored breakthrough, as at Sedan on May 13, 1940. In an attempt to
keep an advancing force supplied with air support, army and air force
staffs together agreed on a series of "security" or "safety" lines
(*Sicherheitslinie*), analogous to artillery fire zones, behind which, at pre-
scribed times, German troops could be reasonably certain of not being
bombed by their own aircraft. The operational orders resulting from

these studies warned pilots of the importance of always knowing the location of the front line. Likewise, the troops were cautioned to mark their own positions clearly, often by simply displaying a red, white, and black swastika banner on the ground or on the turret of an armored vehicle.[84]

Once the movement phase began, planning was less certain. The army's representative laconically concluded, "the production of a safe cooperation between tanks and aircraft at this point encountered difficulties." Use of a Do 17 reconnaissance aircraft as a flying command center proved abortive due to the inadequate radio equipment on hand. The army's recommendations for the campaign about to begin did not extend much beyond using a combination of swastika flags and yellow ID markers to indicate the front line. The difficulties of using this system in the "fog of war" can readily be imagined. The Luftwaffe believed that the experiments suggested ideas that might eventually bear fruit, while both participants agreed that direct radio contact between ground troops and their supporting aircraft was an essential next step in the evolution of air support procedures.[85] With A-day for Fall Gelb only a few days away, no such technical provisions were possible.

As both army and Luftwaffe participants expected, close air support broke down once the movement phase of the operation commenced. In breakthrough battles such as the Meuse crossing on May 13, 1940, however, Luftwaffe intervention, in some cases only yards in front of the waiting German troops, played an important role in the success of the operation. While actual material damage inflicted on the French was minimal,[86] Jeschonnek's belief that close air support was valuable primarily for its "shock" effect seemed to have been borne out. Air superiority and battlefield interdiction had meanwhile played a vital part in the victory over the French. Rather than binding the Luftwaffe closer to the ground forces, the victory in France seemed to bear out the principles of *operativer Luftkrieg*: that successful air operations required coordination with, not subordination to, the activities of the other services. This lesson would have important consequences for the campaign against the USSR the following summer.

Other lessons which the Luftwaffe learned, and mislearned, during the "years of triumph" were less immediately apparent but would, in the fullness of time, play their role as well. The Luftwaffe's foray into independent air operations, the series of raids from July to November

1940 known as the Battle of Britain, did not end happily for the German air force. With the German army and navy virtually idle, the Luftwaffe improvised an air strategy which ignored the principles of force concentration in all but the most general terms. While the ostensible objective of the Luftschlacht um England remained the acquisition of air superiority and the destruction of the Royal Air Force Fighter Command, the constantly shifting and indecisive target selection procedure that Luftwaffe intelligence employed rendered even the occasional German operational successes of little consequence.

In theory, the attack against the British Isles was intended to clear the way for Operation Seelöwe (Sea Lion), the amphibious invasion of the island. Invasion preparations were amateurish at best; the German navy command in particular was obstructionist and unenthusiastic during the entire planning phase. The Luftwaffe's campaign went through a number of phases, including closing the English Channel to British shipping, strikes against RAF Fighter Command's airfields, attacks on British seaborne communications, and finally an attempt to defeat the RAF in the air through attacks on Central London. The various phases had little to do with one another; the so-called Adlerangriff (Attack of the Eagles) had all of the hallmarks of a thoroughly improvised operation. The RAF undeniably defeated the Luftwaffe and frustrated it at every turn. The lessons for the German air planners were evidently unclear. The absence of a strategy incorporating all three fighting services led some Luftwaffe commanders to view the campaign against England as an unpleasant aberration, and their enthusiasm for operativer Luftkrieg ''in the realm of the entire conflict'' did not diminish.

Even while the German bomber and fighter wings took punishing losses over the British Isles, the planning staffs were already turning to the problem of mapping out the next campaign. The invasion of the Soviet Union, as far as the Luftwaffe was concerned, was a task well within its capabilities. While the scale of the operations would present some technical problems, the campaign promised to be little different from the ones so successfully concluded against Poland and France. The principles of Wever and the other German air power theorists were, unbeknownst to their spiritual heirs, about to receive rigorous evaluation.

Hard Use. The crew of a Ju 88 celebrate their 1000th combat mission on the eastern front. Such mission totals in the latter years of the war were commonplace: KG 55 alone by mid-1944 had flown over 50,000 sorties. (National Air and Space Museum, Smithsonian Institution, Photo No. 74-3030)

CHAPTER TWO

THE 1941 CAMPAIGN: THE VERTICAL ENVELOPMENT

On April 1, 1941, representatives of the Hungarian Military Mission attended a conference dealing with the technical and tactical issues of air warfare put on by the Office of Air Armament at the imposing new Reich Air Ministry building in Berlin. One of the members of the Hungarian delegation, a General Littay, posed a somewhat delicate question: in a theoretical war against Russia, what sort of air force would be most effective? Littay was particularly interested in the relative proportion of dive bombers to long-range heavy bombers within this hypothetical force.[1] General Littay's hosts, "on account of the present political circumstances surrounding" his query, did not offer a response.

The German officers escorting the Hungarians, had they been so inclined, might have been more forthcoming. Since the autumn of 1940, the Luftwaffe operational planning staffs were aware of Hitler's intention to turn on his eastern treaty partner. On December 18, 1940, the Führer issued Directive No. 21, which outlined the Luftwaffe's main tasks for the invasion.[2] German reconnaissance planes had begun encroaching on Soviet airspace, and detailed planning conferences between *Luftflotten* and army groups and *Fliegerkorps* and army corps were well in train.

The prospect of a campaign against the Soviet Union offered a unique opportunity for the playing out of the prewar conceptions of air war the Luftwaffe embraced. In contrast to the lengthy and frustrating air campaign against Great Britain, the German army would be an active participant in the offensive, code-named Barbarossa. The Luftwaffe would therefore be in a position to contribute to the strategic decision according to the principle of concentration of all of Germany's military forces. Ideally, the Russian campaign would allow it to attain a "decisive victory" of "Schlieffen-like" scope: "the idea of a 'deep envelopment' of the enemy's flanks in the third dimension."[3] Experience the Luftwaffe gained in Poland and France indicated that the campaign might be too brief for attacks on enemy industry to have any noticeable impact on the outcome. Accordingly, the planning for Barbarossa emphasized the multi-dimensional cooperative aspects of air war outlined in *Luftkriegführung*. Luftwaffe staffs made only the most rudimentary plans for prolongation of the campaign into 1942, as did the army, should Soviet resistance prove stronger than anticipated.

One can find little to criticize regarding the execution of the first phases of the Luftwaffe's war against the USSR. German bomber and fighter units exceeded the most optimistic hopes of their commanders when they virtually annihilated the Soviet air force during the first two days of the campaign; the destruction (even by Soviet estimates) of twelve hundred aircraft by noon on June 22 constitutes an accomplishment never repeated on such a scale during the entire course of the Second World War.[4] It is likely that this campaign against the VVS at the campaign's onset was the Luftwaffe's major contribution to the course of the war. The momentous German advances of summer and early fall 1941 took place under conditions of general air supremacy; it is doubtful that they could have occurred otherwise.

Following the strategic strikes against the Soviet air force, the Luftwaffe was free to carry out its second mission: support of the advancing German army. As in Poland, the support comprised a preponderance of "indirect" (primarily interdiction) missions against the Soviet rear areas and communication zones. In certain cases, and with the deployment of certain formations (particularly Fliegerkorps VIII), the German air force rendered direct support to the Ostheer as it drove deep into European Russia. The combat history of Fliegerkorps VIII is instructive in this regard. The rapid transfer of Richthofen's close support corps from army group to army group indicates not only the high premium which the Ostheer placed upon Luftwaffe close support, but also the very restricted ability of the German air force to carry out this type of mission. The bulk of the combat strength of the eastern air fleets could not, except under exceptional circumstances, readily carry out this task. Although the specialized skills of Fliegerkorps VIII were highly valued by the army, the status of the Luftwaffe as an independent service, with full authority over the method and nature of its employment, remained unquestioned in Richthofen's command.

Dispersal of the Luftwaffe's close support assets mirrored an ominous development within German grand strategy in the Soviet Union. The three-axis advance, necessary to ensure the destruction of the Soviet frontier armies, became, once this task was discharged, a source of discord among members of the German high command. At key points during the brief 1941 campaigning season, the weight of German effort shifted from the center to the north (Leningrad), to the south (the Ukraine), and finally back to Moscow for the commencement of Operation Taifun in the autumn. Such strategic vacillations destroyed the possibility of concentrating the forces against any one objective; as a result one of the underlying principles for *operativer Luftkrieg* was jeopardized. Well might the chief of the army general staff, Generaloberst Franz Halder, note as early as July 1 that "OKL [Oberkommando der Luftwaffe] planning for the massing of air strength is again in an absolute muddle due to misconstrued talks of the Führer with ObdL [Göring]."[5] Once the Luftwaffe turned from its savaging of the Red Air Force to the other levels of its operational tasks, its ability to concentrate its forces, and thereby maximize its strategic effectiveness, fell victim to the vagaries of the overall German strategy in Russia.

The Luftwaffe's conduct of operations, however, gave cause for satisfaction. At those sectors where the German command managed to concentrate the Luftwaffe's air corps, "[their] appearance signified victory."[6] Time and again, air power contributed materially to German success in the great encirclement battles of summer and fall 1941, achievements that convinced even skeptics that total victory over the Bolshevik colossus was imminent. Although the German air commands on occasion indulged in unprofitable and irrelevant diversions from the strategic task at hand, as with the lengthy series of air attacks on Moscow and other industrial centers from July 1941, Luftwaffe operational direction that summer exhibited a single-mindedness and a sound foundation seldom replicated during the four lengthy years of the eastern campaign. Luftwaffe successes seemed a clear vindication of German prewar air power principles that emphasized operations that might decisively "assist in the overall conduct of the war." Only when the army and Luftwaffe staffs discarded these principles did the "proper war" begin to unravel.

THE LUFTWAFFE AND OPERATIONAL PLANNING

German air force participation in Operation Barbarossa had to serve one overriding strategic aim: the destruction of the military power of the Soviet Union "in a rapid campaign" designed to last "six to eight weeks, or three to four months at the most."[7] In the early stages of the Barbarossa planning, the Luftwaffe was to have an additional strategic task following the defeat of the Red Army. In a grandiose version of the "air control" philosophy that the Royal Air Force employed on the fringes of the British Empire, the Luftwaffe was to operate from bases in the conquered European Russian *glacis* and "smash Russia's strategic areas."[8] While echoes of this desire to "police" the unoccupied hinterland of the USSR persisted in Führer directives as the war dragged on, much of the pre-Barbarossa planning involved the air force's role in achieving a decision at the start of the campaign. It is therefore worth examining the relevant portions of Führer Directive No. 21, "Case Barbarossa:"

> The *Air Force* will have to make available for this Eastern campaign supporting forces of such strength that the Army will be able to bring land operations to a speedy conclusion and that Eastern Germany will be as little damaged as possible by enemy air attack . . .
>
> The final objective of the operation is to erect a barrier against Asiatic Russia on the general line Volga-Archangel. The last surviving industrial areas of Russia in the Urals can then, if necessary, be eliminated by the air force.

Directive No. 21 also provided a number of general yet significant constraints on the method of employment of the Luftwaffe in the campaign:

It will be the duty of the Air Force to paralyze and eliminate the effectiveness of the Russian Air Force as far as possible. It will also support the main operations of the army, i.e., those of the central Army Group and of the vital flank of the Southern Army Group. Russian railways and bridges will either be destroyed or captured . . .

In order that we may concentrate all our strength against the enemy air force and for the immediate support of land operations, the Russian armaments industry will not be attacked during the main operations. Such attacks will be made only after the conclusion of mobile warfare, and they will be concentrated first on the Urals area.[9]

Whatever its flaws (and there were many), Führer Directive No. 21 at least reinforced the cardinal principle underlying successful air operations: the need to keep the limited reserves of air power concentrated upon the immediate objective. Postwar critics have drawn attention to the prohibition on strategic air operations as a major error;[10] in fact, as will be demonstrated, when such operations did occur they were generally irrelevant, or even detrimental, to the attainment of the strategic objective.

The directive did, in contrast to those of the second year of the campaign, leave the details of Luftwaffe participation to the discretion of the service staffs. It remained to Jeschonnek, his operations chief General Hoffmann von Waldau, and the personnel of the *Luftflotten* and *Fliegerkorps* to determine the precise character of Luftwaffe activities during the operation. In devising the final operational plan, the Luftwaffe staffs used as their model the Polish campaign of September 1939, with a few modifications in recognition of the peculiar conditions that would confront them in the Soviet Union.

The basic Luftwaffe table of organization was the one that had served so well in previous campaigns. German air power was concentrated in a number of *Luftflotten* (air fleets). Each *Luftflotte* was a self-contained air force command, analogous to an ''Air Force'' within the United States Army Air Forces (there was no direct Royal Air Force equivalent). A *Luftflotte* contained all types of flying units (fighter, bomber, dive bomber, ground attack, reconnaissance) as well as signals and antiaircraft (*Flak*) formations. Each *Luftflotte* in turn contained one or more

Fliegerkorps (air corps), smaller multi-purpose air commands that preserved a broad mixture of flying units. Smaller special purpose command structures, the *Fliegerdivision* (air division) or *Fliegerführer* (air commander) could be dispatched to sectors of a front where a larger
formation was either inappropriate or unavailable. In the coming years,
increasing commitments forced a fragmentation of the Luftwaffe command structure, but for the 1941 campaign, German air power was most
often committed in *Fliegerkorps* strength. The composition of
Fliegerkorps V, assigned in June 1941 to Luftflotte 4 in the southern
sector of the eastern front, was typical. It contained three bomber wings
(KG 51 and 54 with Ju 88s and KG 55 with He 111s), one fighter wing (JG
3, with Messerschmitt Bf 109s), and its complement of communications,
transport and reconnaissance aircraft.[11]

Within the *Fliegerkorps*, the combat power of the German air force
was grouped according to mission and aircraft type. The largest homo-
geneous flying formation was the *Geschwader*, comprising 90–120 aircraft. Each *Geschwader* was in turn subdivided into *Gruppen* (thirty to
forty machines), and finally into *Staffeln* (twelve to fifteen aircraft). The
striking power of the *Luftwaffe* was concentrated in the *Kampfgeschwader*
(long-range bomber wings), equipped with the proven twin-engined
designs Heinkel 111, Junkers 88 and Dornier 17. Of the three types, the
Do 17 had all but disppeared from front-line service by the spring of
1942, while the Ju 88 and He 111 soldiered on until the end of the war.
The twin-engined bombers equipping the Luftwaffe are often erroneously described as ''designed for army support;'' in fact they were
entirely inappropriate for this task. They were, rather, aircraft intended
for long-range bombardment of enemy industrial, communications, and
population centers within the context of a Central European war.

Complementing the long-range bomber force were the *Stukageschwader*, or dive-bomber units. These formations, the symbol of the
Blitzkrieg in Poland and France, operated the Ju 87B single-engined dive
bomber. The greater accuracy imparted by this method of attack made
the Stukas a logical choice for direct army support duties. In fact, this
was only one of the many tasks facing the dive bomber formations in
June 1941. The Ju 87's lack of adequate armored protection and corresponding vulnerability to small-arms fire made it a less than ideal close-
support weapon. The Luftwaffe did possess a few specialized army
support aircraft at the beginning of the campaign. These were a single

Gruppe of Henschel Hs 123 biplanes (II./Lehrgeschwader 2); the fact that this type remained in service until 1944 is more a reflection of the absence of a suitable successor than of the type's usefulness.

The bomber and dive bomber forces were to play a decisive role in the assault against the Red Air Force. The task of protecting the bomber units and maintaining air superiority over the front fell to the Luftwaffe's fighter forces, organized into a number of *Jagdgeschwader*. These units flew the famed Messerschmitt Bf 109F single-engined fighter, certainly the best fighter aircraft in the eastern theater in 1941. The great bulk of the crippling losses which the VVS sustained in aerial combat during the first year of the campaign were the result of encounters with these well-trained German fighter units and their superior aircraft; even allowing for the exaggerations of wartime propaganda and the difficulty of authenticating aerial combat claims, the victory totals of German fighter pilots serving in the eastern theater are unrivalled. The fighter units were augmented by so-called *Zerstörer* (destroyer) formations equipped with the Messerschmitt Bf 110 twin-engined long-range fighter and light bomber. A failure over Great Britain in 1940, the 110's range, varied weapon load, and speed gave it a new lease on life in Russia.

Only in the deployment of certain reconnaissance units did the Luftwaffe command not employ the principle of concentrated and centralized direction of flying units. The *Luftflotten* and *Fliegerkorps* staffs retained full control over long-range reconnaissance formations, but tactical reconnaissance units were at the beck and call of the army commands. The short-range tactical reconnaissance units, sometimes allocated even to individual *Panzer* divisions, flew the Henschel 126, an obsolescent parasol-wing monoplane. The Henschel 126 was later supplanted by the twin fuselage Focke-Wulf FW 189, known as the "Flying Eye" owing to its extensively glazed cockpit. Control of the short-range reconnaissance force was the one concession the Luftwaffe high command allowed the army; as events would demonstrate, the arrangement was not without its flaws.

In conclusion, the Luftwaffe in 1941 was a formidable force. In addition to possessing aircraft types generally superior to those equipping the Red Air Force, the Luftwaffe aircrews were far better trained and possessed more combat experience than their VVS adversaries. Moreover, the command organization of the German air force allowed for

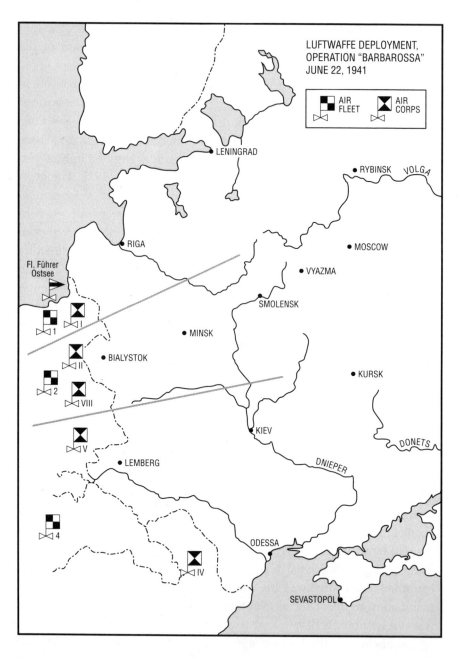

Map 2. Map indicating deployment of air fleets (*Luftflotten*) and air corps (*Fliegerkorps*) for Operation Barbarossa, the attack against the USSR, June 21, 1941.

tremendous flexibility. Units could be transferred rapidly across vast sections of the front. An efficient signals network greatly eased the tasks of command and control of the scattered formations, thereby allowing the concentration of air power at any decisive point. In matters such as supply, particularly of essential items such as fuel, spare parts and ammunition, however, the Luftwaffe possessed severe if as yet concealed weaknesses. Servicing and refuelling conditions, especially on the unimproved airfields from which the Luftwaffe operated as the invasion progressed, were often minimal. In a campaign intended to last not more than four months, none of these weaknesses appeared particularly troublesome.

As was the case in Poland and France, each of the army groups participating in the invasion had one *Luftflotte* allocated to it. Generalfeldmarschall Fedor von Bock's numerically strongest force, Army Group Center, had the support of the most powerful air fleet: Generalfeldmarschall Albert Kesselring's Luftflotte 2. This force contained Fliegerkorps II and VIII, the last still commanded by Richthofen. At the same time, Generaloberst Hans Keller's much weaker Luftflotte 1 (with Fliegerkorps I and Fliegerführer Ostsee) was to support Ritter von Leeb's Army Group North in its drive on Leningrad. Finally, Generaloberst Alexander Löhr's Luftflotte 4, with Fliegerkorps IV and V, supported Army Group South's operations in the Crimea, Dneiper, and Don regions.[12] The placement of the air fleets reflected a desire to concentrate force along the axis of advance. In no way did the deployment subordinate the air fleet to the army group in whose sector it operated. With the aforementioned exception of the tactical reconnaissance force, none of the Luftwaffe's flying formations were under army jurisdiction any more than they had been in earlier campaigns.

This service autonomy became manifest well before the attack began. When planning discussions between the staffs of Luftflotte 4 and Heeresgruppe Süd commenced in April 1941, the army group representatives understood that the air fleet's task was to "prevent as far as practicable the intervention of the Red Air Force and to support the operations of the army group."[13] The army planners delineated a wide range of support tasks for the air fleet, including direct support of the attacking spearheads (Sixth Army and Panzer Group 1) as well as deep interdiction of Soviet reinforcement movements and attacks on communications and logistical centers. If the army staffs anticipated a subservient air support orientation from Luftflotte 4, the course of the planning sessions swiftly disabused them of this notion. On being presented with the army group's requests, the Luftwaffe representative unequivocally replied:

> Luftflotte 4, faced with a numerically superior opponent, will require a considerable period of time in order to achieve absolute air superiority. In view of the manifold tasks of the air fleet, the troops must not count on the same type of support that they have grown accustomed to in previous campaigns. Officers and men must be aware that the Luftwaffe may support the operations of Army Group South only at the immediate Schwerpunkt of the attack. The tendency to call in a Stuka attack at the first sign of enemy resistance must from now on be resisted at all costs.[14]

Emphasis on the air superiority mission was not a new characteristic of Luftwaffe planning. It had, in fact, survived virtually unchanged from the theory of the 1930s to its incorporation into operational practice during the victorious campaigns of 1939–1940. Jeschonnek, before the Polish campaign, noted:

> The most proper and essential task is the battle against the enemy air force, and it must be executed vigorously and at all costs. The second task, the support of the army, in the first days of the war cannot claim the same level of importance as the battle against the enemy air force. What may be achieved in the first two days by using one's own air force against an opposing army does not compare with the damage an enemy air force may inflict if it remains battleworthy.[15]

The one consistent element of the Luftwaffe's pre-Barbarossa planning is the refusal to accede to the army's wishes for immediate and concentrated air support of the attacking divisions at the expense of the counter-air mission. A number of army commanders, both at the time and in postwar accounts, argued that the Luftwaffe would more profitably have been employed in the army support role from the outset.[16] In this instance, Luftwaffe planners were far more cognizant of operational realities than were their army counterparts. As late as June 20, Luftflotte 4 liaison officers were still informing their Army Group South counterparts that virtually none of the army's extravagant demands for air support during the first days could be met, "as the whole of the available air strength will be sent against the enemy air force."[17] At later junctures of the campaign, the Luftwaffe's status as an independent service would have a harmful effect on German strategy; but few in the Wehrmacht would have cause to regret the assertion of that prerogative in this instance.

The Luftwaffe staff's insistence on performing a rigid triage of its accustomed missions reflects a departure from the methods employed in Poland and France. In the context of the Polish campaign, the air force carried out three more or less simultaneous missions (attainment of air superiority, direct and indirect army support, and strategic bombing of industrial, communications, and population centers).[18] In Russia, the Luftwaffe planned to fulfill its role in a series of distinct phases.[19] This amounted to a tacit admission that the magnitude of the task rendered simultaneous execution of the missions impracticable.

With the Red Air Force effectively eliminated, both Directive No. 21 and the Luftwaffe's operational orders envisioned that the air force was "to support German ground operations" until the collapse of Soviet organized resistance. The Luftwaffe, as its operations indicate, took a rather wide view of its "army support" role. In its planning, it defined the two major forms this mission would take:

   a. a direct support of the army on the battlefield (*unmittelbare Heeresunterstützung*)
   b. to destroy the Russian lines of communication near the front which would make it difficult and probably even impossible for enemy units to regroup and make new concentrations far behind the lines.[20]

The Luftwaffe displayed a marked preference for the latter task, generally referred to as *mittelbare Heeresunterstützung*, or "indirect army support." Some clarification of the German terminology is necessary. While the concepts of "direct" and "indirect" army support correspond roughly to the United States Air Force's formulations of "close air support" and "battlefield air interdiction" respectively, the Luftwaffe's interpretation of its tasks was by 1941 somewhat broader. Direct army support, the type which the army requested most frequently throughout the Russian campaign, involved operations immediately above, and designed to assist, ground forces involved in an offensive or defensive battle, with the German ground forces often "locked in combat" with the enemy. It was not a task for which the Luftwaffe found itself particularly well-equipped, and many of the tactical reforms addressed in this study represented efforts on the part of operational commands to correct this shortcoming. The second task, "indirect" army support, defies easy categorization within USAF parlance. While it encompassed most of the tasks commonly referred to as "battlefield interdiction" (bombing of supply lines, enemy columns on the march, staging areas, and similar targets) the Luftwaffe viewed as *mittelbare Heeresunterstützung* any air operation with the potential to influence the outcome of the ground battle. General Wilhelm Speidel noted that "the indirect support of the army is . . . a part of the conduct of *operativer Luftkrieg*. It is not so much dependent upon the tactical conduct of the army's battle, but rather with its operational objectives."[21] Therefore, even bombing of enemy industry could (and often did) fall under the rubric of indirect army support. In such a manner did the Luftwaffe general staff manage to evade the prohibition on attacking war industries prior to the cessation of mobile operations.

Thus did the Luftwaffe staffs translate the vague guidelines of Führer Directive No. 21 into concrete missions which the flying formations would then carry out. One significant factor separated the Luftwaffe's preparations for Barbarossa from previous experience: the specter of the multi-front conflict. In prior campaigns, the Luftwaffe managed to concentrate an overwhelming percentage of its force for the duration of the campaign. This had been the case in both Poland and France. In the case of Barbarossa, the Luftwaffe had not only to divide its strength between three major offensive thrusts, but was compelled to devote scarce resources to a holding campaign against Britain in the west, to the battle for the North Atlantic sealanes, as well as to the prosecution of the unwanted Mediterranean diversion. Despite enlargement of the Luftwaffe as a whole, the force sent against the USSR on June 22, 1941 was scarcely larger than the one that operated against France in May 1940. On the eve of Barbarossa, the eastern air fleets, including Luftflotte 5, engaged in anti-shipping operations in the far north, deployed 3,904 aircraft of all types (of which 3,032 were operational). The force included 952 bombers, 965 single-engined fighters, 102 twin-engined fighters, and 456 Ju 87 dive bombers, the heart of the close army support force.[22] After a scant two weeks of combat, the strength of these main combat

AIRCRAFT STRENGTH OF OPERATIONAL LUFTWAFFE UNITS
ACCORDING TO AIRCRAFT TYPE
July 5, 1941[23]

	Luftflotte			
Aircraft Type	1	2	4	5
Fighter	144	279	286	18
Twin-engined fighter	—	78	—	10
Bomber	211	293	243	12
Stuka	—	164	113	37
Total	355	814	642	77
Grand Total		1,888		

types, which had totalled 2,475 on June 21, 1941, had considerably decreased.

On numerous occasions, the numerical weakness of the Luftwaffe in the east was to prove the determining factor in its success or failure. Shifts in emphasis which the German command elected to undertake invariably forced the wholesale redeployment of large portions of the Luftwaffe, particularly close support forces such as Fliegerkorps VIII, across the vast expanses of European Russia.

Furthermore, in contrast to the Polish and western campaigns, the Luftwaffe did not enjoy a lengthy period of preparation and recovery prior to Barbarossa. Unlike most German army units, the Luftwaffe had been in heavy action up to the eve of the campaign against the Soviet Union. The situation of Richthofen's Fliegerkorps VIII is illustrative if extreme. His air corps operated throughout the period of the campaign against France and the Battle of Britain. Its dive bomber force sustained crippling losses, and was finally withdrawn from the attack on Britain on August 18, 1940.[24] Its other units continued operations throughout the remainder of the daylight raids and the London Blitz. In late March 1941, Fliegerkorps VIII found itself rushed to the Balkans to assist with unexpected campaigns against Greece and Yugoslavia. Scarcely had the Balkan campaign ended on April 27 when the air corps redeployed on hastily constructed Greek airfields for Operation Merkur, the airborne assault on Crete.[25] While Richthofen's dive bombers were still heavily engaged against the Royal Navy around the island, the Fliegerkorps VIII staff prepared to proceed to Krampnitz, near Potsdam, to coordinate the transfer of the flying units and the ground organization to Suwalki, their initial base of operations against the USSR. The hasty transfer was marked by delays, missing supplies, motor transport gone astray, and other complicating factors. Richthofen himself noted on June 21, "[w]e are greatly concerned that our units are as yet unready."[26] While not every Luftwaffe unit had undergone such extensive recent use, the fact remains that the German air force commenced its largest operation of the war with force structure and serviceability at dangerously low levels.

Knowledge of the capabilities and numerical strength of one's opponent can in some measure redress a quantitative imbalance. In the case of the Luftwaffe about to embark on its Drang nach Osten, however, its intelligence service exercised an influence on the campaign that, in spite of tactical and other short-term successes, was generally baneful. The intelligence branch was one of the least prestigious in the Luftwaffe; along with the quartermaster section, it was a posting most qualified officers, intent on attaining an operational command, sought to avoid at any cost.[27] The effect of the intelligence branch on the outcome of the Barbarossa campaign was twofold. First, Luftwaffe intelligence reinforced prevailing racial and national stereotypes about the Soviet enemy. The Red Air Force, according to German estimates, "was not an independent part of the armed services," and therefore possessed little flexibility or resilience.[28] Most of the "4,000–5,000" aircraft in the inventory, particularly the medium bomber force, were described as "inferior," "old," "obsolete," or "fair game for German fighters."

Many of the individual items of information presented in Luftwaffe intelligence briefings regarding the strength and character of the Red Air Force were correct.[29] German analysts duly noted that the Red Air Force was in the process of transitioning to a new generation of aircraft; as a result, many of the flying units in mid-1941 would be equipped either with obsolete aircraft or unfamiliar new ones. The Soviet official historians candidly admitted that "the war caught the air forces of the border military districts during a period when they were undergoing extensive reorganization and retraining of the personnel."[30] The Red Air Force was in fact in much the same condition as the French Armee de l'Air had been in May 1940, when the German attack caught and destroyed it. The aircraft types present in the greatest number in June 1941, including the Polikarpov I-15 and I-16 biplane fighters, and the DB-3 and SB-2 medium bombers, were of outmoded design. Luftwaffe veterans had encountered most of these types in the Spanish Civil War; the VVS was also known to have performed poorly against the Finns during the Winter War of 1939–1940.[31] Soviet training and operational proficiency were well below German standards; lack of adequate radio equipment was a particular shortcoming.[32]

The cumulative effect of Luftwaffe intelligence work, however, was to provide a seriously distorted picture of the latent capabilities of the Red Air Force. The German analysts underestimated the number of Soviet aircraft available;[33] more seriously, they fecklessly disregarded the significance of Soviet technical improvements in aircraft design as well as the productive capacity of Soviet industry. The entire new generation of Soviet combat aircraft that appeared in 1940–1941, including the Yak-1, MiG-3, Pe-2, and Il-2, was generally absent from intelligence estimates and recognition manuals prior to the invasion.[34]

There was little excuse for this state of affairs. As recently as March-April 1941, a German commission of engineers and technicians from the RLM and German industry, accompanied by Oberst Heinrich Aschenbrenner, the German air attache in Moscow, had toured the Soviet air armament industry. The tour covered two airframe plants, three aero-engine works, a light metal and a ball-bearing factory, and an air force experimental installation.[35] In the course of this inspection, Luftwaffe experts were shown mass production facilities for and prototypes of a modern all-metal single-seat fighter, identified as the ''I-(18?, 61?)'' and which was most probably the MiG-3, and a twin-engined light bomber and attack aircraft, the Pe-2.[36] Such tangible evidence of Soviet productivity and technical advances made little impression on Luftwaffe intelligence. Oberst Josef Schmid, Jeschonnek's intelligence chief, regarded information to the effect that ''the aero-engine facilities at Kuibyshev alone were bigger than Germany's six main assembly factories'' as a product of Soviet deception and the gullibility of the German engineers making the reports.[37]

The failure of Luftwaffe intelligence to produce a complete assessment of Soviet capabilities was to have dire consequences on both the strategic level in the coming years and on the tactical conduct of the first campaigning season. On the strategic level, the underestimation of Soviet resilience and industrial capacity led to a failure to appreciate until 1943 that Soviet production was capable of making good combat losses. In addition, the cavalier dismissal of the principles of Soviet air power employment left Luftwaffe and Heer commands alike ill-informed of the danger that a rejuvenated VVS posed. Once operational attrition and geographic dispersion weakened the Luftwaffe's combat strength, the Red Air Force would be in a position to put its operational doctrine into practice.

Soviet air power theory, although not as sophisticated as the German, was at least in principle similar to that of its future adversary. According to the Field Regulations of the Red Army in January 1941:

> The main mission of aviation is to contribute to the success of the ground forces in battles and operations, and to achieve air superiority. It may also be given independent missions: to attack major and important political, industrial and military centers deep in the enemy's rear.[38]

In practice, the main mission of the Red Air Force was direct and indirect support of the Red Army. Its doctrine was predominately oriented towards the offensive. The VVS was intended to support the "deep operations" of the Soviet armored and motorized units. Use of the air force would therefore "facilitate the development of a tactical success into an operational success." Soviet sources admit that the air doctrine in place in June 1941 was ill-equipped to withstand the German surprise attack or to recover quickly. At the same time, German intelligence failed to inform either the Luftwaffe operations staff or the German army leadership of the potential for recovery of the VVS and its likely employment if it was given the opportunity to do so.

Of more immediate concern to the German troops fighting in the USSR in 1941 was the unpleasant tactical surprises that resulted. Typical of such an unwelcome jolt was this report from an army *Flak* unit serving with Army Group North:

> On August 14 and 15 a total of three Russian ground attack fighters were shot down. This new type is equipped with two 2 cm cannon, two machine guns and numerous bombs. This type of fighter has all of its vital areas protected by armor, so that light antiaircraft fire has virtually no effect on it.[39]

The "new fighter type" in question was of course the Il'yushin Il-2 "Shturmovik," justly regarded as "a triumph of Soviet aviation and technical thought"[40] and probably the best close air support aircraft of the Second World War. Luftwaffe intelligence failed completely to inform the fighting units of the existence of this formidable new weapon. Even though Il-2s had been in action since the first weeks of the campaign, Luftwaffe intelligence paid little attention to Soviet technical innovations. The German intelligence branch could provide only minimal information (and a thoroughly inaccurate silhouette) of the Il-2 in an October 1941 recognition manual.[41] Only after captured examples of the aircraft became available for evaluation did the Luftwaffe gain a thorough appreciation of the capabilities of this aircraft. This lack of information was not an aberration; most of the information on other modern Soviet aircraft designs was as spotty. Even as the 1941 campaign progressed, neither army nor Luftwaffe intelligence saw a need to revise their judgments of the VVS. In November 1941 an intelligence assessment concluded, ''the Red Air Force is materially and with regards to its training clearly inferior to the German.''[42] German intelligence analysts appear to have given scant thought to the possibility that this situation might not be permanent.

In certain other respects, Luftwaffe intelligence and its agencies facilitated the swift advance of the German army in the first weeks of the campaign. The activities of a secret long-range reconnaissance formation, known as the Rowehl-Geschwader after its commander, Oberst Theo Rowehl, for some months prior to Barbarossa carried out photo-reconnaissance surveys of most of European Russia.[43] Flying to a penetration depth of three hundred kilometers, Rowehl's specially pressurized high-altitude reconnaissance planes ascertained the location of Red Air Force bases, one reason the target selection on June 22 was so prescient.[44]

Even after the failure of the Barbarossa offensive, Luftwaffe intelligence continued to underestimate the Russian adversary. While the intelligence analysts gradually acknowledged that the caliber of Soviet equipment was improving, they still demonstrated a persistent tendency to view the Soviet state, morale, and economy as more fragile and vulnerable to disruption than their Western counterparts. The attitude of German air intelligence, then, was to play an increasingly prominent role when the Luftwaffe command began to prepare strategic air operations against the USSR in 1943–1944.

The German air force's preparations for Barbarossa represent an extraordinary mixture of thorough planning, realistic formulation, and

almost unbelievable insouciance. There is little to indicate that the Luftwaffe staffs regarded the campaign as anything more than an operation—albeit a wide-ranging and geographically immense one—that was
to last only a few months. Once they had adopted this outlook, there
was little reason not to abdicate strategic direction of the campaign to the
Führer and the OKH. As a result, despite its jealously-guarded status as
an independent branch of the Wehrmacht, the Luftwaffe would be vulnerable to strategic errors to which it was not directly party. If the objectives described in Directive No. 21 were not attained, the German air
force's only recourse would be a series of ever more desperate
improvisations.

THE CONDUCT OF OPERATIONS:
THEORY IN PRACTICE

The Luftwaffe formations flew over the Soviet border at 3:30 A.M. on
June 22, 1941, and touched off the largest land-air campaign in history.
The results of the first phase of operations exceeded the expectations of
even the more optimistic Luftwaffe planners. "We could hardly believe
our eyes," recalled a young Bf 109 pilot. "All of the runways were thick
with [Soviet] reconnaissance planes, bombers and fighters, lined up in
long rows as if on parade."[45] The Luftwaffe struck at thirty-one Soviet
airfields on the first morning, and by noon claimed the destruction of
eight hundred Soviet aircraft for a loss of only ten German planes.[46]
During the first two days, the VVS lost 1,811 aircraft, 1,489 of them on
the ground. By June 26, the Luftwaffe had attacked some 123 airfields,
destroying 4,614 Soviet aircraft by the end of the month for a loss of only
330 German planes.[47]

German propaganda agencies made a great commotion over the success;[48] the reality comprised a virtually unqualified victory for the Luftwaffe in its air superiority mission. The Red Air Force in addition proved
as vulnerable in the air as on the ground. The poorly trained and
equipped Soviet pilots were shot down in appalling numbers, entire
formations at a time. Kesselring, then commanding Luftflotte 2, referred
to the destruction of the VVS bomber force as "sheer infanticide."[49] The
Luftwaffe effectively attained air superiority on the first day of the invasion, a goal that eluded them for all of the months of the Battle of Britain.

On June 25, therefore, the Luftwaffe was able to turn to its second
task: direct and indirect support of the German army which was pro-

ceeding with the successful battles along the frontier. Most army corps after-action reports for this period refer to the "minimal enemy air activity"[50]—testimony to the success of the Luftwaffe's primary mission. Even when the VVS appeared over the battle area, its contribution was often ludicrously ineffective. An officer of the Seventh Panzer Division recalled:

It soon became clear that the Russian air force had only obsolete machines at its disposal, but above all that the pilots did not function nearly as well as our fighter and dive-bomber pilots, or the pilots of our Western opponents. This was naturally a great relief to us, and when Russian aircraft appeared, we hardly bothered to take cover. We often had to smile, in fact, when, for want of bombs, thousands of nails rained down on us from their bomb bays.[51]

The campaign against the shattered Soviet air force continued for weeks after the army support phase began, heralding the first of what were to be many divisions of the Luftwaffe's effort.[52]

Direct German air force intervention in the army's operations had been on occasion decisive in the earlier campaigns in Poland, France, and Flanders. Extending the conflict to the third dimension did not, however, commit the bulk of the Luftwaffe to the close support role. The Luftwaffe's own conception of its mission after June 25 was to perform a "vertical envelopment" (*vertikalen Umfassung*) of the enemy forces while protecting the flanks of the fast-moving *Panzer* groups and attacking Soviet formations and installations far to the rear.[53] This choice of missions grew out of both doctrinal preference and the state of German air armament, as the Luftwaffe command naturally conceived a mission to which its entire force structure could profitably contribute.

Fliegerkorps VIII's own delineation of its tasks serves to emphasize this point. Richthofen's command could still lay claim to being the only "specialized Close Battle Corps" in the entire Luftwaffe during the summer of 1941.[54] Even so, "direct cooperation with the armored forces" ranked well down on its list of mission priorities. "Attacks on airfields in order to neutralize enemy air power during the initial attack, destruction of lines of communication, isolation of higher command staffs, bombing attacks on the principal points of troop concentration and reserves of material" absorbed much of the air corps' combat power during the movement phase.

By this stage of the war, the system of cooperation between the two services represented an evolutionary change from that in use in September 1939. Experience from previous campaigns led to a strengthening of some elements of the chain of command and to a downgrading of others. The system in use during the Barbarossa offensive varied widely from unit to unit and from sector to sector. Local commands improvised cooperative procedures on the spot; frequently, the personalities of the commanders involved determined the quality of the air support. The traditional German military principle of *Auftragstaktik*, or goal-oriented tactics, allowed low and medium level commanders considerable leeway on the battlefield.

In the 1941 campaign, the precise nature of Luftwaffe support for the army's operations was not the direct responsibility of the high command. Führer Directive No. 21 defined the Luftwaffe's primary missions, but it was the commanders on the scene, generally no higher than those at *Armeekorps* and *Fliegerkorps* level, who decided upon the type, time, and location of air force support for a given operation. As with the pre-invasion planning described earlier, the air force could be most insistent on pursuing an independent line. Kesselring's claim that he instructed his commanders "to consider the wishes of the army as my orders"[55] definitely did not reflect the attitude or the performance of most *Fliegerkorps* commanders. Richthofen, himself one of Kesselring's subordinates, although the most effective army support commander in the Luftwaffe, devoted as much of his energy to opposing the senior service as to cooperating with it. He believed that the air force's "consent must first be asked whether it will be profitable in the long run . . . for the Luftwaffe to assist the armies in reaching a decision."[56]

The evolution of the mechanism through which the two services cooperated during the campaign is a fascinating study of the German military mind in action. During the Luftwaffe's early campaigns, the primary (or at least highest-ranking) officer responsible for liaison with the army was the *General der Luftwaffe beim ObdH* (air force general with the army commander in chief). In a similar fashion, the air force command assigned officers to represent its interests at army group and army level. These officers were designated *Kommandeur der Luftwaffe*, invariably abbreviated *Koluft*. Since these officers were within the army chain of command, their major responsibility was not the allocation of major Luftwaffe combat units, much less the coordination of air strikes. Their duties instead concerned overseeing the reconnaissance squadrons that were directly subordinated to army formations.[57] In the campaign against the USSR, the only flying formations obligated to carry out army orders were these invariably overstretched reconnaissance units, and for this reason the command level of *Koluft* existed through the 1941 campaign. In a method of employment little different from that of the First World War, the tactical reconnaissance aircraft cooperated closely with the ground forces.

Naturally, the army favored an extension of the *Koluft*'s duties to include active air support of ground operations, as this would enhance the ground force's control over the available air support. The Luftwaffe successfully resisted this attempt at interservice cooperation, with the result that the *Kolufts* stood rather uneasily outside the mainstream of air force command channels. By the 1941 campaign, close air support was entirely under the control of the *Fliegerkorps* staffs. The Luftwaffe did not win this victory without cost; late in the war a Luftkriegsakademie lecturer noted that the exclusion of the army-controlled reconnaissance units from the Luftwaffe chain of command had been "most disadvantageous," resulting in wasteful duplication of effort.[58]

With the *Kolufts* effectively removed from the command system for battlefield air support, the Luftwaffe still had to solve this technically intractable problem through its own exertions. Richthofen's chief of staff, Generalmajor Karl-Heinrich Schulz, reduced the dilemma of close air support to a simple formulation: the need to balance the ability to concentrate forces, which called for centralized control of air power, with the need to react to a rapidly developing military situation at a crucial point in the ground battle.[59] The essential problem was one of command and control; to keep the air corps staff apprised of the conditions at the front and able, quickly and decisively, to dispatch the massed ground attack formations to the *Schwerpunkt*. Schulz elaborated:

[I]f one went too far down the chain of command, justice would, of course, be done to the demand for a close, undelayed liaison between the ground forces and the Luftwaffe and for as quick a realization of the effects of the air force as possible. On the other hand, one would also run counter to the principle of the

point of main effort . . . One encountered the danger of ineffective splitting-up of forces in the overall situation and of employing the forces in a manner that was not always tactically suitable.
Furthermore, the necessary mobility in shifting points of main
effort was sacrificed.

If one went *up* too far on the chain of command, the principle
of the point of main effort was, of course, taken into account. In
doing so, however, the danger arose that the air force command
would become unfamiliar with the situation and awkward
because the liaison with the ground forces would become bother-
some and time-wasting, the commitment therefore [did not take
place] in a sufficiently quick manner, and could not be adapted to
the particular exigencies of the situation on the ground with the
necessary precision and adaptability.[60]

Responsible for the smooth and balanced implementation of army
support tasks were the *Nahkampfführer* (close combat leader) and the
Fliegerverbindungsoffizier (air liaison officer) or *Flivo*. The post of
Nahkampfführer existed during the western campaign within those air
corps charged with army support tasks.[61] In May 1941, the Luftwaffe
operations staff established the position on the staff of every *Fliegerkorps*
preparing for the Barbarossa campaign. The *Nahkampfführer* was often
the commander of one of the flying units; he was expected to coordinate
all Luftwaffe support with the corps staff of the army units. He disposed
of all of the *Fliegerkorps'* forces available for air support missions, gener-
ically known as *Nahkampfverbände* (close combat units). Since the Luftwaffe had few specialized units for such tasks, the type and number of
aircraft under his jurisdiction fluctuated constantly. Any type of combat
unit—dive bomber, fighter, heavy bomber or *Zerstörer* formation-might
be earmarked for such missions.[62]

Even such a specialized officer as the "close combat leader" had
duties more far-reaching than his title might suggest. "The tasks of the
Nahkampfführer are not limited to the battlefield," ran the operations
staff's manual on the subject distributed to the army commands. "His
combat responsibilities extend to the rear concentrations, reserves and
troop movements of all kinds in the depths of the army's zone of operations."[63] In practice, the concept of the *Nahkampfführer* personally leading his units into battle proved unworkable, and the formal title gradu-

ally disappeared from use. In most cases, the *Fliegerkorps* or *Fliegerdivision* commander, most notably Richthofen, issued the orders for ground support to the flying units through normal *Fliegerkorps* channels.

The most important officer at the tactical level was the *Fliegerverbindungsoffizier*. At the onset of Barbarossa, *Flivos* were assigned down to *Panzer* division level; this soon proved inadequate, and their numbers grew accordingly. By October 1941, during Operation Taifun, there were no fewer that thirty-one *Flivos* in the field reporting back to Fliegerkorps II, with an additional nine "on the staff."[64] By 1942, it was not uncommon for even individual infantry regiments to possess their own air liaison officer.[65] The officers acted as intermediaries between the army and air units, informing ground commanders of the possibilities for air support and relaying reports, observations, and requests back to the air corps command. At the beginning of the campaign, their function was merely to serve as a conduit for communication. Their role would undergo considerable expansion as the campaign progressed.

One technical change from previous practice was the disappearance of safety lines, the predetermined bombing zones that had led to mixed results in Poland and France. Since the movement phase of Barbarossa gave every indication of being sustained, a more flexible system began to come into use, especially in Richthofen's command area. This system involved the use of large white fabric visual panels which troops placed in their own forward positions. Various combinations of panels indicated the location of the front line as well as the direction and location of centers of enemy resistance. The new methods often appeared in conjunction with the swastika flags, flares, and smoke cartridges previously employed.[66] Despite the crudeness of this system (little different from that used in conjunction with the *Schlachtstaffeln* in the First World War), units reported good results as long as the Luftwaffe retained local air superiority. Problems persisted when supporting a rapid advance. Army and Luftwaffe did not as yet possess common radio frequencies, and the firm control over air strikes which the air corps command maintained tended to make the system excessively cumbersome. Even Richthofen's specialized force could not guarantee a response time of under two hours "from request for air support to carrying out of bombing," because of the weather, enemy air activity, the distances to the targets, and other variables. For units other than Fliegerkorps VIII, the ability to carry out the direct army support mission was minimal. Since the Luftwaffe would make its contribution in other ways, however, its commanders did not see this as a serious shortcoming. Common during the days of the rapid German drive across the expanse of European Russia was the phenomenon of the Luftwaffe sealing off the battlefield, blunting Soviet counterattacks and striking communications lines, particularly the vital rail network, far behind the front. The success of these "indirect" army support tasks probably did as much to aid the army's advance as did the air superiority which the Luftwaffe had attained.[67] Halder on July 11 noted, "the Luftwaffe now seems to have succeeded in wrecking Russian railroads far to the rear of the enemy communication zone. The number of lines with immobilized rail transport is growing . . . and the good work is being continued."[68] Fliegerkorps VIII played a decisive role in this manner during the encirclement battles of Bialystok and Minsk in late June.

Contrary to many postwar accounts, the bulk of the Luftwaffe's missions during this time were geared to indirect army support. Given the Luftwaffe's force structure, the lack of Soviet air activity, and the preponderance of suitable targets, this was not a misuse of the Luftwaffe's bomber forces. As General Hermann Plocher pointed out,

On the subject of troop movements it can be said that in the first few days and weeks in particular, such movements were profitable targets for the bomber forces. Moving in two, and very often in three or four columns abreast on a single road (during the summer months the terrain on either side of the road was used as a summer roadway, so that the roads were often up to 100 yards wide) in close order, with motor and horsedrawn vehicles between troops marching on foot, [the Russian forces] were pressing eastwards and fell easy prey to our bomber forces.[69]

This potentially decisive use of the air force continued up to the failure of the autumn 1941 drive on Moscow, and the Luftwaffe staffs only reluctantly abandoned it after the Soviet counteroffensive in December. For this phase of the campaign, the Luftwaffe's effort seemed to be in accord with the army's desires. Requests for air support passed on by the *Flivos* were very simply worded, leaving the details of Luftwaffe participation unspecified. XLI Armeekorps' instructions to the Luftwaffe for the drive on Leningrad, for example, were simply, "Fliegerkorps I will continue to support the attack of XLI Army Corps with bomber and fighter units.''[70] Orders to the close-range reconnaissance formations were much more specific, reflecting the close cooperation between the spotter planes and their parent divisions.

There can be little doubt that Luftwaffe participation during the opening weeks of the eastern campaign was one of the major reasons for the unprecedented success of German arms. Three factors, however, were already at work that would render the Luftwaffe's contribution first inadequate, and finally irrelevant. The first concerned the inability of the German strategic planners to agree on how to translate the operational victories of June–July 1941 into strategic success; the second was the fact that, even in the first few months of the advance, German units reported a resurgence in the activity of the VVS.[71] The final factor was a refusal of the Luftwaffe staffs to restrict the scope of German air force activities.

THE RAIDS ON MOSCOW

At the height of the army support phase of Barbarossa, the Luftwaffe embarked upon an activity that represented a steady and considerable drain on its ability to intervene decisively in the ground battle. From as early as July 1941, in technical disobedience to the spirit and the letter of Führer Directive No. 21, the Luftwaffe attempted to wage a strategic air offensive against the Soviet Union. Such an effort was certainly in line with German air force practice in earlier campaigns, particularly in Poland and the Battle of Britain. Yet with the Luftwaffe stretched thin along an eighteen hundred-mile front, this evident adherence to prewar doctrine was unrealistic.

When the advancing German spearheads reached the Smolensk area in mid-July, the Luftwaffe acquired bomber bases that placed a number of vital Soviet armaments centers within practical striking range. The first mission against Moscow took place on July 21, 1941 with a raid by 195 bombers, primarily from Kesselring's Luftflotte 2 (KGr 100 [pathfinder], KG 2, KG 3, and KG 53, all from Fliegerkorps II).[72] At least one bomber *Gruppe*, III KG 4 (newly arrived in the eastern theater after participating in the Blitz on London), from Luftflotte 1 also participated.[73] This raid inaugurated a series of missions that, until it ended on April 5, 1942, consisted of seventy-six night and eleven day attacks on the Soviet capital.[74] None matched the strength of the first attack; most involved fewer than fifty aircraft. Yet even with the strength of the Luftwaffe at its lowest point of the year, in late November-early December 1941 (after the transfer of most of Luftflotte 2 to the Mediterranean) the attacks continued. For example, on November 30, Fliegerkorps VIII, fully committed to the support of the dying German advance on Moscow, devoted thirty bomber sorties (out of 204 total on that day) to a Moscow raid.[75]

What is significant about these attacks is that they occurred at all. Strategic bombing activity was fairly heavy during the month of October, also the period of the greatest commitment of Luftwaffe units to direct and indirect support of the Taifun offensive. In that month alone, Moscow was raided thirty-five times, and Leningrad received thirty Luftwaffe visitations.[76] The armaments centers of Kharkov, Rostov, Gorki, and Rybinsk also appeared on Luftwaffe target lists.

An examination of the motivation for this air campaign reveals much about German operational doctrine in the east during 1941. The raids were in violation of the principle of *Schwerpunktbildung* to which most Luftwaffe commands adhered during the first campaign year against the Soviet Union. Luftwaffe records dealing with the subject are fragmentary (in sharp contrast to later attempts at "strategic air operations" in the east); still, enough information exists to suggest a number of conclusions.

The raids appear to have been a part of a larger pattern of channeling Luftwaffe effort away from direct army support tasks and into a more broadly-based air strategy. Certainly the city of Moscow in particular, especially after the launching of Taifun, was an objective within the Army's projected zone of operations.[77] Furthermore, prewar German air force doctrinal statements seem to provide a rationale for the launching of long-range bombing attacks even at a critical juncture in the ground battle:

> In close cooperation with the Army and Navy, the air force, and especially its bomber force, frequently cannot find targets against which they can bring their striking power to bear and the destruction of which would bring effective support to the Army or Navy.
>
> It makes more sense to attack distant targets, the destruction or neutralization of which will decisively influence the operations of the Army or Navy.

Therefore, attacks on the "sources of power" might be called for even during cooperation with the Army and Navy.[78]

Thus, the strategic attacks on Moscow and similar targets fell within the gray area between "indirect army support" and independent air operations in much the same fashion as did some of the Luftwaffe General Staff's more ambitious plans of 1943–1944.

In early July, the OKW and, subsequently in Führer Directive No. 33, Adolf Hitler in effect lifted the prohibition on strategic bombing, at least against Moscow and Leningrad.[79] The High Command left the details of the execution of the raids to the *Luftflotte* and *Fliegerkorps* staffs. They carried out the missions with varying degrees of enthusiasm. After the war, Field Marshal Kesselring recalled:

> The raids on Moscow caused me great anxiety. Crews shot down had to be written off, the effectiveness of the Russian AA guns and searchlights impressing even our airmen who had flown over England.[80] Also as time went on Russian defense fighters appeared in increasing numbers, luckily only in the daytime. Results did not quite come up to my expectations, but in relation to the size of the target our forces were not any too strong, the dazzling effect of the searchlights was disturbing and the weight of bombs that could be carried was greatly reduced by the increased fuel load . . .[81]

Kesselring's uncharacteristically pessimistic assessment of the raids' value was in absolute terms correct. The Moscow strikes amounted to little more than harassing attacks.[82] Most German sources dismiss them as "prestige attacks . . . an attempt of inadequate means and scope, a demonstration of strength at a moment of confidence in victory."[83] Göring, when questioned by the Americans in 1945 about the attacks on Moscow, replied off-handedly that they were never pressed home with the requisite strength, as they were only "in response to Hitler's sarcastic question, 'Do you believe that the Luftwaffe has a *Geschwader* with the courage to fly against Moscow?'"[84] If Hitler did in fact make this remark, it was more likely later in the war when the Luftwaffe contemplated renewed operations against Moscow. Certainly in late summer of 1941, Hitler had little reason to criticize the Luftwaffe's performance.[85] It seems clear that there was something more substantial motivating the attacks, however poorly executed, than a desire for mounting prestige operations. The parallel waging of a strategic bombing offensive and a protracted army support campaign was simply the result of the Luftwaffe's attempt to carry out its semi-independent air power concept with entirely inadequate forces.

Even Luftwaffe officers with extensive experience in army support operations were sympathetic to the principle of attacking a nation's armament centers. General Paul Deichmann, a leading close air support proponent who also played a role in the prewar Uralbomber program, later pointed out that the destruction of a Soviet armored division on the battlefield represented a huge effort, as well as a task unsuitable for the heavy bomber force. He further argued that the same number of sorties directed against the tank factory at Gorki, for example, would yield results on a far greater scale. A 1943 Luftwaffe general staff study defended the air force's 1941 position by deeming it unacceptable to have left the Soviet "centers of national resistance . . . intact and unimpeded."[86] The problem with this line of reasoning is that it ignored the impact of the Barbarossa directive's insistence on a rapid military decision. Since the effects of an industry bombing campaign would not become evident for months, such a campaign at the expense of battlefield interdiction in the summer and fall on 1941 represented an unjustifiable dilution of the Luftwaffe's combat power.

"The primary task of the strategic air force," reiterated the aforementioned Luftwaffe general staff study, "is the waging of operational air war against the enemy strong points of every kind, and against transportation targets." That the effort against the "strong point" of Moscow was not of a more sustained and concentrated nature in the summer and fall of 1941 reflects operational realities, not doctrinal unwillingness. Moreover, the information possessed by Luftwaffe intelligence regarding the precise location of Moscow's war industries and its strategic importance was, in 1941, minimal. Only in 1943, on Jeschonnek's insistence, did a sustained intelligence gathering effort commence.[87] The lack of such information in part accounts for the haphazard and ultimately unsuccessful attempt by the Luftwaffe to adhere to one of its operational precepts during Barbarossa.

LENINGRAD AND MOSCOW: THE CASE OF FLIEGERKORPS VIII

The strategic attacks on Moscow took place at a time when German strategy in the east began to fall into disarray. As successful as the massive cauldron battles of encirclement had been, the Red Army remained a viable fighting force, the VVS showed signs of recovery, and Hitler and his military staffs engaged in increasingly acrimonious debates regarding the "decisive objective," the capture of which would end the campaign by autumn. For the Luftwaffe in general, and for its army support forces in particular, this meant the loss of any opportunity to concentrate its force for a strategic engagement. Rather, the Luftwaffe staffs rushed the flying formations as airborne "fire brigades" to reinforce the offensive drives that Hitler and the OKH deemed most important.

For Fliegerkorps VIII, the center of operations following the initial advance, was to be Leningrad in August and September and the Moscow front from October to January. In the course of the Barbarossa campaign, Fliegerkorps VIII headquarters shifted its location no fewer than eighteen times; its component flying units, dispersed on a number of air bases, had to exhibit an even greater degree of mobility.[88] Some of these movements were unavoidable and reflect the rapidity of the German advance and the scale of Russian geography. Others took place as a result of the overall lack of close air support capability in the Luftwaffe, and the need to use the powerful formation as a battering ram, leaving other sectors virtually stripped of air support.[89]

On August 3, 1941 Fliegerkorps VIII, on the personal orders of the Führer, left the command area of Army Group Center and journeyed to the Leningrad sector to support I Army Corps in its drive on Novgorod in the direction of "the cradle of Bolshevism." The sector of Army Group North was in dire need of air support, particularly since Hitler decreed the opening of a major offensive in the region on August 10. Fliegerkorps I, the primary air force command in the northern sector, had proven to be unequal to the task of providing the necessary army support. On August 2, one of its *Flivos* gloomily informed the Sixteenth Army command, "we cannot hold out much hope for air support, as the number of available aircraft is utterly unsuited for the task."[90] The Luftwaffe officer even admitted to a loss of air superiority in the sector.

Richthofen descended upon the scene and began "new-brooming" the air support procedures in the Sixteenth Army sector in preparation for the drive on Leningrad. By August 8, his force, which was not very large even at the start of the campaign, comprised only the eighty-seven heavy bombers of KG 1 "Hindenburg," the fifty Stukas of StG 2

"Immelmann," II./SKG 210's twenty-two twin-engined Bf 110 fighter-bombers, twenty-six obsolescent Hs 123 ground attack machines from II./LG 2, JG 27's sixty-six Bf 109 fighters, and the eleven reconnaissance machines of 2./(F) 11.[91] Richthofen was nevertheless determined to employ this modest force "in the strongest, most concentrated strikes" in conjunction with the attacking army formations to ensure a break-through of the enemy defenses. An indication of how atypical were the methods Richthofen employed may be gleaned from Sixteenth Army records. Prior to the arrival of Fliegerkorps VIII, air support conferences were infrequent, desultory, and general affairs. Once Richthofen appeared on the scene, the frequency of such conferences quadrupled as the liaison staffs of Fliegerkorps VIII made certain that all participating German army units were aware of the specialized cooperation pro-cedures Richthofen had developed. In a remarkably short period, Fliegerkorps VIII established an efficient and comprehensive communi-cations network, ensuring rapid communication between Richthofen's headquarters, the airfields housing his flying units, the main Luftwaffe signals net, and the army group, army, corps and division headquarters requiring air support.[92] The planning of the individual air strikes in support of the attack and its continuation was precise, and constant communications from and occasional Storch flights over the battle area by Richthofen and his staff ensured that the air support given to I. Armeekorps was among the most successful and concentrated of the entire campaign.

A typical army support operation, such as the one involving an attack by units of I. Armeekorps on August 5, 1941, would unfold as follows. At daybreak, German fighters would fly protective patrols over the army's jumping-off positions. Fifteen minutes prior to the attack, bomber units would target enemy artillery positions; these attacks were to continue throughout the day. Five minutes before the German advance, Richthofen's dive-bombers would engage enemy front-line positions, some only one hundred meters from the waiting German infantry. As the attack commenced, the ground attack units struck enemy infantry directly in the path of the advancing German troops with bombs and machine gun fire. Meanwhile, twin-engined fighters attacked any enemy movements behind the front lines, while Stukas, each capable of carrying out four attack sorties in the space of two hours, continued to press the attack as the situation demanded.[93] The system was simple and effective. Most importantly, all parties involved, army and Luftwaffe, were fully apprised of the procedures.

Indeed, it was only that the high command once more changed its mind and downgraded the Leningrad front to "a subsidiary theater of operations" that nullified any strategic benefit that might have accrued from the advance of Heeresgruppe Nord. As it turned out, Fliegerkorps VIII had little to show for the 4,742 sorties flown and 3,351,350 kilograms of bombs dropped in twelve days of intensive operations. Of Richthofen's unit, twenty-seven aircraft were destroyed and 143 damaged. The heavy losses habitually suffered by units under Richthofen's control was a source of some concern at Luftwaffe headquarters. Koller regarded Richthofen as "heartless" and felt that he paid no heed to high casualties since, "owing to his privileged position" with Göring and Jeschonnek, he could always count on an adequate flow of replacements.[94] The ruthless application of the Luftwaffe's most effective strike force in this case secured only the winning of another German tactical victory without strategic benefit with which the eastern campaign is replete.[95]

One other result of the Leningrad diversion was that the level of air support for the final offensive of the 1941 campaign, Operation Taifun, the assault on Moscow, would hardly be commensurate with the importance of the task. The German forces by the autumn of 1941 had advanced so far into European Russia and the Ukraine that both army and air force strength was seriously dispersed. When one takes into account the harsh climatic conditions and primitive airfield facilities, the picture for the German air force becomes even bleaker. One German officer noted:

> The constant movement of flying formations, usually without adequate ground personnel, resulted in such bad servicing that a *Luftflotte* had often on a sector of about 400 km only 10–12 serviceable fighter aircraft. Only the strictest concentration of our resources, the most careful selection of targets, and the provision of better servicing facilities could improve our position.[96]

"Strictest concentration of resources" for the assault on Moscow meant committing the whole of Luftflotte 2, including Fliegerkorps II and VIII, to the operation. Richthofen and his chief of staff, Oberst Rudolf Meister, spent late September conferring with Bock's headquarters about the coordination of the air support for the operation. Richthofen grimly noted that his force was fifty percent weaker than preliminary planning for Taifun had foreseen. In fact, on October 1 the Luftwaffe's finest army support commander refused "for the first time in [his] life" to accept responsibility for the outcome of an operation in which he participated. He cited as reasons the overall weakness of his forces and the unwillingness of the army command to appreciate their condition.[97]

In any case, Taifun went off as scheduled. Richthofen noted in his diary, "Great address by the Führer, that today in the central sector of the front the great and final decisive battle of the year (?) begins." The battles before Moscow in October 1941, especially the double encirclement battle of Bryansk-Vyazma, were the high water mark of the Wehrmacht's operational proficiency. At 5:30 A.M. on October 2, units of the Ninth Army and Panzergruppe 3 jumped off on the northern flank between Smolensk and Byelov, with Fliegerkorps VIII in full support. Aircraft from all units of the air corps averaged four sorties on the first day, with Stukageschwader 2's Ju 87s flying no fewer than six.[98] The attacks centered on the usual mixture of "direct" and "indirect" objectives: "enemy tanks, horses, retreating columns, enemy airfields." The bomber unit KG 76 claimed to have bombed the headquarters of General Timoshenko, erroneously identified as the overall Soviet front commander in the breakthrough sector.

Despite the imposing list of potential targets, Richthofen seems to have made a particular effort to keep his forces concentrated over the *Schwerpunkt* of the attacking *Panzer* formations. Bruno Lörzer's Fliegerkorps II, supporting the attack of the Second Army and Guderian's Panzergruppe 2 on the right flank of Army Group Center, carried out a somewhat wider variety of missions. In the main, these were intended to seal off the "cauldron" area of the Bryansk pocket and prevent the escape of the shattered Soviet formations that were slowly being drawn into one of the greatest battles of encirclement in military history.

Between October 4 and October 10, Fliegerkorps II performed an intensive vertical envelopment, achieving great success despite the depleted forces at its disposal. The reports of the 31 *Flivos* coordinating the air support reveal the scope of the air corps' operations. One such account ran:

> The units of Fliegerkorps II were today in the main responsible for halting the enemy's withdrawal, as well as for providing direct support and protection to our advancing army units . . . Numerous attacks were directed at rearward railway lines and roads, trains, villages, airfields . . . The visibly destructive effect on the enemy was entirely the result of our units' activities. The enemy has again sustained grievous material and personnel losses.[99]

Fliegerkorps II destroyed artillery positions on the right flank of the Second Army, carried out a sustained counter-air campaign against Soviet airbases in the Moscow area, and gave direct support to the 2nd SS Panzer Division "Das Reich" around Vyazma.

Probably due to the more rapid turnaround time possible for the dive bomber units, the number of Stuka sorties in support of the Bryansk/ Vyazma battles approximated that of the more numerous heavy bomber units participating in the "indirect" phase of the operation.[100] Furthermore, a significant portion of Luftflotte 2's heavy bomber force performed tasks peripheral to the decisive effort on the ground. Some of Fliegerkorps II's Heinkel units, and even on occasion the scarce dive bomber formations, feverishly dropped millions of propaganda leaflets (244,000 on October 5 alone) along the Smolensk-Moscow highway.[101] Other bomber *Geschwadern* continued to attack the Soviet armaments industry at such diverse locations as Voronezh, Aleksin, Kashira, Balabanova, and Tula.[102] More in keeping with the operational goals of Taifun, Fliegerkorps II, as the encirclement battle drew to a close, embarked upon ambitious interdiction operations designed to cut off the escape routes of the Soviet forces.[103]

Tactically, the dual battle of Bryansk-Vyazma did not occasion the introduction of any new air-ground cooperation procedures. Both Richthofen's Fliegerkorps VIII and Lörzer's Fliegerkorps II referred in afteraction reports to the familiar system of colored markers, swastika flags, and smoke signals to indicate the front-line positions of German troops. Even so, incidents of air attack on German troops by Luftwaffe aircraft continued to occur.[104] Yet the sheer volume of experience which the two air corps had accumulated in army support operations contributed materially to the success of the encirclement battles. Fliegerkorps II up to October 10 claimed the destruction of 264 Soviet aircraft in the air and on the ground, as well as seventy-eight locomotives, innumerable motor vehicles, and other vital targets.[105] Richthofen, for his part, was full of praise for his own formations when he noted, "For the third time I set out unready, unrested, with some units still in transit or insufficiently prepared for the attack. If one attempted this with an *army* unit . . . !"[106]

The remarkable victory at Bryansk-Vyazma, which Halder described as "downright classical,"[107] did not yield the anticipated strategic dividends. The completion of the encirclement had tied down most of the German mobile formations. The onset of the "mud period" coupled with growing supply difficulties deprived the *Ostheer* of the opportunity to exploit their "classical" victory. In early November, Halder observed:

> The problem of supply dominates the situation . . . viewed as a whole, the situation is determined by railroad capacity and flow of supplies. There is no point in pushing operations outward before we have, step by step, established a solid foundation for them. Failing to do that inevitably would bring fatal reverses down upon us.[108]

The poor weather and parlous supply situation had a predictable effect on Luftwaffe operations, although on the few clear days the sortie level increased dramatically. This was in large measure to the credit of Richthofen's ground organization, which repaired many of the damaged machines while the units were grounded. Yet more and more of Luftflotte 2's bomber force had to resupply the bogged-down German spearheads around Kalinen, one of the last major towns before Moscow to fall to the Germans. Waldau, Jeschonnek's chief of operations, on October 16 noted, "The boldest hopes fade under rain and snow."[109] The Luftwaffe, under conditions of near-total stagnation, could accomplish little.

The effect of the other theaters in which the Reich was engaged, and to which the timely conclusion of Barbarossa would have allowed the Luftwaffe to return, began to impinge on operations in the east. The bulk of Luftflotte 2, including the powerful Fliegerkorps II (minus Nahkampfführer II, a rump close air support force which remained behind on the Moscow front) was transferred in mid-November to the Mediterranean in order to support General Erwin Rommel's African campaign.[110] As one German historian pointed out, the transfer of Kesselring's *Luftflotte* came at precisely the wrong moment. The air fleet left the Moscow front before a decision had been reached there, and completed deployment in the Mediterranean too late to prevent Rommel's retreat following Operation Crusader, British General Sir Claude Auchinleck's counteroffensive in early December 1941.[111] Thus did the assumption that the Russian campaign could be completed before the demands of the other fronts made themselves felt prove to be a drastic miscalculation.

The air support for the last gasp of the German 1941 offensive thus devolved almost entirely onto Fliegerkorps VIII, for all intents and purposes a temporary (and extremely understrength) air fleet. In late November and early December Richthofen's force continued its operations, although bad weather increasingly hampered the battered air corps. On December 3, for example, Fliegerkorps VIII could put only sixteen aircraft into the air; five days later, it could field only three.[112]

On the latter date, Hitler ordered the cessation of offensive operations on the eastern front. Not only was the bulk of the German army immobilized by this time, but the so-called "Stalin Offensive" had begun along the entire front on the sixth. So critical had the military situation become that Richthofen ordered even his ground specialists and flying personnel to participate in the containment of local Soviet breakthroughs. For a brief period, Richthofen himself commanded VI Army Corps after its commander was sacked.[113] Stalin's simple Order of the Day, a copy of which the German forces had captured on December 10, said simply, "The German armies are on the point of collapse—attack everywhere!"[114] On the same day, Richthofen admitted in his own Order of the Day that the 1941 offensive had come to a close:

> Our run of victories has taken us deep into the densely-populated Soviet Union and to the very gates of the Red capital. Bialystok, Minsk, Smolensk, Novgorod, Schlüsselberg, Kiev, Bryansk and Vyazma, Kalinen, Orel and Mozhaisk are the mileposts of our success . . .
>
> In recent weeks, during which the Russians fought especially tenaciously for their capital city, our combat strength was severely reduced by distance and climate . . .
>
> Alongside the establishment of winter quarters, the continued support of the hard-pressed army units is our primary task. Leave, training, re-equipment . . . all preparations for the

resumption in the spring of the final destruction of Bolshevism, will follow the discharging of these tasks.[115]

Richthofen's belief that the "crisis" phase would be temporary was to prove unfounded. In one sense, the Luftwaffe never really escaped from the emergency army support role which the collapse of the Wehrmacht's Drang nach Osten forced upon it. As long as the Luftwaffe possessed anything approaching an adequate force structure, use of the flying units to buttress the ground forces represented a small percentage of the overall air effort. Only with the Soviet counteroffensive of December 1941 did the *Fliegerkorps* commanders place their forces at the disposal of the army. Only when the eastern front was in danger of total collapse did the Luftwaffe reluctantly commit not only the dive bomber and ground attack units, but even the long-range bomber formations, the "bearers of *operativer Luftkrieg*," towards stabilizing the desperate ground situation. Herhudt von Rohden pointed out,

> With the start of the Russian attacks in December 1941, it became clear that all parts of the flying units had to be used for the immediate support of the army; this meant bombers too, which were not fit for that type of mission, involving as it did low level attacks on small targets. The bombers themselves lacked speed in low-level flight, and were poorly armored . . .[116]

Oddly enough, the German high command's orders in light of the grave military situation proposed to increase the spectrum of Luftwaffe operations. Hitler's stop order of December 8 also called for the Luftwaffe to "[disrupt] the recovery of the Russian armed forces through attacks on armaments and training centers, especially Leningrad, Moscow, Rybinsk, Gorki, Voronezh, Rostov, Stalingrad, Krasnodar . . ."[117] Alongside this familiar formula, the Luftwaffe was to continue "to support the army with its defensive battles." This order reversed Führer Directive No. 21's ban on strategic bombing until the cessation of mobile ground operations because the war no longer promised to be a four-month affair. The air force's task became even more complex when the Luftwaffe assumed responsibility for the resupply of surrounded German formations at Kholm and Demyansk.[118]

The order for the resupply of these "fortified places," which were themselves the consequence of holding the front line at all costs, came from Hitler himself. Provisioning of the stalled army groups was one of the tasks he delineated in the December 8 directive, and the high command insisted on the aerial resupply of frontline units and encircled pockets well into March 1942.[119] On December 18, 1941, Fliegerkorps VIII received five transport groups from within the Reich territory, and one additional group detached from Luftflotte 4. These units, operating the trustworthy Ju 52/3m trimotor, assembled near Smolensk under the command of Transportführer Oberst Fritz Morzik.[120]

It is hardly surprising that the Luftwaffe should be asked to assume a large part of the resupply tasks, given the vastness of the theater and the supply difficulties which Halder outlined. What is surprising is how readily the air force leadership accepted the additional tasks, which were bound to place a nearly intolerable burden on the weakened frontline units. Nonetheless, Generaloberst Keller of Luftflotte 1 declared, "Whenever personnel in any position are surrounded, we will provide for them."[121] Predictably, the supply missions to the "fortified places" proved to be very costly. For the Demyansk pocket alone, Fliegerkorps VIII recorded 14,435 operational flights by transport aircraft and their fighter escort and lost 265 aircraft in the process. Since the number of Ju 52s available proved to be insufficient, He 111 long-range bombers were pressed into service as well. This "temporary" reassignment of the Heinkel formations "led to an unsound change in the relationship between transport and bombardment aircraft."[122] Thus began an imbalance within the Luftwaffe's force structure it would spend the next three years attempting to arrest. Such emergency measures no doubt helped to prevent the complete collapse of the Ostheer and enabled it to resume the offensive the following spring; few Luftwaffe planners found them particularly edifying. The air transport mission furthermore began a pattern that was to have disastrous consequences when a much larger German formation was trapped at Stalingrad in November 1942.

The German repulse before Moscow is correctly viewed as one of the turning points of the Second World War. Although many impressive victories lay ahead for German arms in Russia, failure to complete Barbarossa according to the intended timetable was a strategic disaster of the first magnitude. The risks taken by the German planners in embarking on a multi-front war, of failing to make the necessary industrial and technical preparations for a protracted campaign, and in dismissing the recuperative powers of the Red Army and VVS would now come home to roost.

The 1941 campaign presented Luftwaffe commanders with a number of conflicting lessons on which to base the unexpected second year of combat against the USSR. For the operational commanders of Fliegerkorps in the east, the Barbarossa offensive had validated the concept of air power assisting the army in achieving an operational decision. On the other hand, the Luftwaffe general staff was faced with the prospect of the loss of service independence in favor of a decentralized control of air assets if tactical air operations attained too much prominence. The succeeding years of the "proper war" would highlight the relative merits of the competing approaches.

Stukas. In many respects the symbol of Barbarossa, a wedge formation of eight Ju 87B-2 dive bombers of Stukageschwader 77 drones over the southern sector of the eastern front. (National Air and Space Museum, Smithsonian Institution, Photo No. A-5224)

CHAPTER THREE

ANOTHER SHORT CAMPAIGN: THE LUFTWAFFE'S SECOND YEAR IN RUSSIA

'''Tanks up front, artillery to the rear and planes above'—these were the methods of the entire high command which led to the ruin of the Luftwaffe in the east.''[1] So remarked General Karl Koller, last chief of the Luftwaffe general staff. Koller's bitter observation reveals the mounting frustration within the Luftwaffe's leadership, who came increasingly to blame the army and the high command for the emasculation of the Luftwaffe's strategic bombing capability. Koller, a representative of the "external" school of thought regarding the causes for the Luftwaffe's defeat, believed that its degeneration into a "fire brigade" or, in Richthofen's graphic phrase, "the army's whore,"[2] was not the fault of its own officer corps. It was instead the German army leadership, blind to the possibilities air power offered, that shackled the air force to a two-dimensional orientation with ultimately disastrous results. Such a simplistic explanation underestimates the complexity of the strategic situation facing the German armed forces in early 1942. Once again, the success or failure of German ambitions was to hinge on the outcome of a brief, theoretically decisive campaign. Either the Luftwaffe could throw its weight behind this endeavor, or it could violate the precepts of its own *operativer Luftkrieg* doctrine and prosecute an air campaign peripheral to the decisive struggle on the ground. For a variety of reasons, its leadership chose the former course. As long as German strategic planning dealt in terms of months rather than years, the Luftwaffe adhered to the principle of *Schwerpunktbildung*, or concentration of its weakened force on what was presumably the critical point. The German air force staffs on the whole accepted this operational constraint, and Richthofen and other combat commanders embraced it enthusiastically. By pursuing the correct operational employment of the Luftwaffe in the south, the officers of such formations as Luftflotte 4 and especially Fliegerkorps VIII believed that they were making a strategic contribution. Only when the Stalingrad disaster revealed that this policy rested upon false assumptions did Luftwaffe staffs seek an escape from the strategic straitjacket in which operational success in army support ventures had placed them. Yet it was the air arm's success in such ventures that made any such reorientation all the more difficult.

PRELUDE TO BLUE: THE CRIMEAN CAMPAIGN

The 1941 campaign marked the end of the Luftwaffe's ability to function as an independent service in the east, although few air force commanders in December 1941 recognized this fact and would not do so for some time afterwards.[3] The attempt to achieve a decision according to the precepts of *operativer Luftkrieg* had come close to success, as had the German army's bold effort to subdue the Soviet Union within the brief time allocated in Führer Directive No. 21. The unexpected campaign of 1942 displayed elements of both the 1941 Blitzkrieg effort and the later concept of the limited offensive employed at the battle of Kursk in July 1943. For the Luftwaffe, the operational and doctrinal ramifications of this unexpected second campaigning year were immense, and the tendency for "institutional schizophrenia" within its leadership would become ever more pronounced.

The operation known to the OKH planners as "Case Blue" and its supporting components reflected the inability of the Wehrmacht to attempt anything as grandiose as the three-pronged assault of the previous June. Neither army nor air force in early 1942 possessed the manpower or material resources for such an undertaking. The offensive power of the German forces in the East lay concentrated in the southern wing of the front, in the operational area of Luftflotte 4.

The situation in the southern area of the eastern front in the late winter and early spring of 1942 reflected the unfinished nature of the 1941 campaign. German forces had occupied much of the Ukraine and the Crimean peninsula, but late in the year General Erich von Manstein's Eleventh Army had fallen back from the gates of Sevastopol after a costly effort to capture the Black Sea port. In the Crimea, German and Soviet forces faced each other across the ''Parpach line,'' a sophisticated belt of modern fortifications stretching across the narrow Kerch Peninsula. Hitler's War Directive No. 41, issued on April 5, 1942, stressed the necessity for a ''mopping-up operation in the Kerch peninsula and the capture of Sevastopol,'' both as a part of the general stabilizing operations following the winter Soviet counter-offensive and as a precondition for the drive on Stalingrad and the Caucasian oilfields.[4]

Directive No. 41 never made clear the strategic reasoning behind the Crimean campaign. Most Anglo-American writers downplay the strategic significance of the venture.[5] German authorities, both contemporary and postwar, advance a complex geopolitical argument in favor of the conquest of the peninsula. Luftwaffe General Staff analysts referred to Crimean War precedents for the vital importance of occupying the region, and even cited the French Baron Cesar de Bazaucourt's nineteenth century account:

> To dominate the Crimea confers the ability to hold a central position in the Black Sea, the key to all Russian dreams . . . Sevastopol is the arsenal of his sea power . . . it is here that Russian ambitions breed continually . . .[6]

More twentieth century-oriented arguments concerned the vulnerability of the Rumanian oilfields to Soviet bombers based in the Crimea (a rather curious rationale, as the Soviet Union had only a rudimentary long-range bombing capability), as well as the consequences the loss of the peninsula would have for the Luftwaffe's ability to support the main spring offensive.[7] Undoubtedly the capture of a modern fortress like Sevastopol carried with it a powerful prestige element. Finally, German strategic planners placed a high premium on ''the favorable effect the capture of the peninsula was expected to have on the attitude of Turkey.''[8] Whatever the motivation, the Crimean operation enjoyed the support of not only Hitler, but also that of more traditional military minds, such as Manstein and Richthofen.[9]

In May 1942, therefore, the peninsula was the focal point of German operations in the east. As a case study of Luftwaffe operational practice, the campaign is extremely enlightening. For all of the postwar German historiography that refers to the campaign as "the high water mark of German fortunes in the east,"[10] the attack in the Crimea reveals instead the weakened state of German air power in the second spring of the Russian campaign.

On March 31, 1942, Manstein issued the preliminary directive for Operation Trappenjagd (Bustard Hunt) to his Eleventh Army.[11] In the case of previous army operations, the commands on the scene worked out the nature of the air support among themselves. Trappenjagd marked a departure from this practice. Hitler left the army's plan for the assault on the Parpach line intact, while assuming responsibility for Luftwaffe participation himself.[12] Initially, Hitler saw to the dispositions of Luftflotte 4 only. In a lengthy conference on April 17, 1942, the Führer insisted on a strong concentration of force for the upcoming Kerch reconquest.[13] Such concentration was to be achieved even if "the remaining front of Heeresgruppe Süd must during this time do without air force support."[14]

The conference portended another shift in German air planning. Hitler, whose interest in army weaponry is well known, was by 1942 beginning to meddle in questions of air armament as well. A significant portion of the conference was devoted to a discussion of such minutia as the availability of SD 2 fragmentation bombs and specially developed canisters for these weapons. They were to be used against "living targets" in combination with the heavier bombs needed to take out the field fortifications of the Parpach line. The Führer also discussed measures to raise the aircrew strength of the air fleet in light of its increased commitments.[15]

Shortly after this conference, the potential for concentrating German air power in the Crimea increased dramatically. Richthofen, who interceded personally with Hitler, convinced the Führer of the need to employ Fliegerkorps VIII in the operation.[16] The powerful close air support force had recovered its strength somewhat after a month's refit in Vienna. It was in transit from Army Group Center to Army Group South, as OKL had earmarked it for support there of the main Blue offensive. On April 20, 1942 Richthofen's staff, followed by most of the air units under his command, arrived instead at the Crimean front en route to their most well-known operational successes.

The command situation in the south indicates the greater emphasis placed on close air support operations in the wake of the Moscow defensive battles. In the 1941 campaign, Fliegerkorps VIII operated under the overall direction of the air fleet responsible for a particular sector of the front. Its rapid transfer from the central front to the Leningrad sector in late summer also subordinated it, however nominally, to Luftflotte 1 in the north. In both cases, the air corps' operations were part of the overall mission of the Air Fleet. In the Crimea, in contrast, the specialized close support force did not come under the command of Luftflotte 4. Instead, Fliegerkorps VIII was directly responsible to the *Oberbefehlshaber der Luftwaffe*,[17] and of course Richthofen was in effective operational control. Richthofen, in consultation with Manstein, would see to realization of the Führer's desire for *Schwerpunktbildung*.

Not even the air support for the armies advancing on Leningrad in August-September 1941 was as meticulously planned as the Trappenjagd operation. Manstein freely admitted that the timing, and indeed the execution, of the entire attack depended solely upon air force support. "The attack will under no circumstances be carried out without the Luftwaffe,"[18] Manstein declared on April 6. He spoke of creating an aerial "point of maximum effort," and stressed the need for the air force liaison officers to be of the highest possible rank. He need not have worried: Richthofen preferred to carry out all but the most mundane liaison tasks himself. Indeed, by April 22, as preparations for Trappenjagd proceeded apace, orders from XXX. Armeekorps instructed its staff to deal directly with the Fliegerkorps VIII staff rather than proceeding through normal *Luftflotten* channels as in past campaigns.[19]

The liaison procedures for air support of the operations, despite the fairly brief preparation period, displayed a complexity not seen at any time in the 1941 campaign. Air reconnaissance missions, carried out by the army-subordinated unit 3.(H)/13, assembled the necessary aerial photos of the Parpach defense system. The various corps artillery staffs coordinated Luftwaffe support with their own fire plans. Such discussions involved not only Fliegerkorps VIII personnel, but representatives of other participating formations such as Fliegerführer Süd (Air Commander South, normally concerned with Black Sea anti-shipping actions) and Fliegerkorps IV, a general purpose air corps attached to the

Fourth Air Fleet. The close involvement of such formations in the detailed planning of a ground assault shows that the Luftwaffe's status as an independent service was slipping away.

Of course, Richthofen was ever-mindful of his service's prerogatives. Throughout the planning phase, the VIII. Fliegerkorps commander's view carried a disproportionate amount of weight. He was never at a loss for an opinion regarding the wisdom of the army's operations. The army postponed the offensive several times solely on Richthofen's request, and he even requested a major diversionary attack by XLII. Army Corps a few days prior to the main offensive in order that some of his newly-refitted formations might gain needed combat experience. The request went all the way up to Eleventh Army command before being squelched. Manstein reasoned that a diversionary attack would divide the available air assets, a contingency Richthofen was himself usually at pains to avoid, and would forfeit the advantage of surprise, as any activity in the narrow Kerch region would alert the Soviets to German intentions.[20]

Unlike the general orders for the Luftwaffe's participation in earlier operations around Leningrad and Moscow, the requests of the XXX. and XLII. Army Corps were detailed and specific. Operational orders for the German air force's role in Trappenjagd outlined particular tasks for individual types of Luftwaffe units. Beginning at 4:30 A.M., dive bomber units were to attack "targets located on the antitank ditch (bunkers and dug-in tanks) between the sea and Lake Parpach, with the point of main emphasis (*Schwerpunkt*) on the highway Dalnya Kamyski-Arma Eli (3 km. south of Parpach)."[21] In addition to the predetermined air strikes, the army could request additional Stuka attacks "with a period of one and one-half hours between request and execution."[22] The coordination of Stuka strikes in a fast-moving breakthrough situation remained a most difficult technical problem even for Fliegerkorps VIII.

The support which the army requested of the long-range bomber units was almost entirely of the "direct army support" type. The heavy bomber units were to attack individual Russian artillery batteries once they betrayed themselves by their muzzle flashes. In addition to the requests made by the army, Fliegerkorps VIII and the other Luftwaffe formations also planned a series of attacks on Soviet airfields on the Kerch peninsula and the Caucasus region, and these raids in fact commenced a few days prior to the May 8 start date of Trappenjagd.[23]

Attacks on the Soviet Black Sea Fleet, as well as on merchant ships bringing reinforcements to the battle sector, represented the remainder of VIII. Fliegerkorps' "indirect army support" contributions. Yet the bulk of the more than two thousand sorties flown by Richthofen's air corps during Trappenjagd directly assisted the Eleventh Army's frontal assault on the fortified Parpach sector.[24]

The mechanisms of air-ground cooperation were not significantly different from those in use during Taifun the previous autumn. Every command staff in the field down to divisional level had a *Fliegerverbindungsoffizier* attached. The *Flivo* reported the immediate situation back to air corps headquarters and kept the German army command apprised of forthcoming air operations, thus facilitating "a constant exchange of ideas." In case of radio failure, the *Flivos* could rely on reports sent by Storch liaison aircraft. An operational order from Fliegerkorps VIII that summer succinctly outlined the duties of such liaison officers:

Air liaison officers are bound to transmit to Fliegerkorps VIII staff in the first instance the demands of ground units for air support, and also to keep the *Fliegerkorps* informed of the situation on land, of the plans of the ground forces command, and of the disposition of command posts. The air liaison officers must work in close contact with the officers of the ground forces delegated for liaison with the air force. This contact is achieved by joint allocation of command post positions. In places where there are no Army officers delegated for liaison with the Air Force, their duties are carried out by air liaison officers.[25]

These procedures differed only slightly from earlier practices within Richthofen's command. No provision as yet existed for direct contact between ground units and the aircraft operating overhead. Troops were, as usual, requested to mark their own forward positions clearly, as "only then may effective support of the ground battle take place."[26] A series of orders in late April 1942 standardized the types of cloth identification panels, and smoke and light signals throughout the Eleventh Army to minimize the possibilities of confusion.[27] All of these preparations added up, in Manstein's view, to "concentrated air support the like of which has never existed."[28]

The bulk of the close air support burden still rested with the Ju 87 dive bomber units. By 1942, those formations had reequipped with an upgraded version of the 1935 design, the Ju 87D. Furthermore, the few specialized *Schlachtgeschwader* units received an entirely new design for operational trials during Trappenjagd: the Hs 129, a heavily armored close air support machine.[29] Like so much of the Luftwaffe's air armament, the Hs 129 suffered from technical problems and, as events demonstrated, the aircraft never lived up to the promise of its specialized design.[30]

In spite of the Soviet counteroffensive near Kharkov on May 12 (which forced the hasty, if temporary, redeployment of Fliegerkorps IV and portions of Fliegerkorps VIII to that area) and bad weather on the ninth, the Luftwaffe's actions assisted the Eleventh Army in making a swift and decisive breakthrough in the Parpach sector. The entire Kerch peninsula was in German hands by May 16. The Eleventh Army claimed to have destroyed three Soviet armies and taken some 170,000 prisoners.[31]

Soviet accounts indicate that the Red Army's defense of the Parpach position was in disarray and that the VVS, only partially recovered from the mauling it received during the 1941 campaign, could accomplish little in the face of Richthofen's coordinated air strikes. The Soviet official history, in summing up the Kerch disaster, noted:

> The unconcern of the Army and Front staffs, the insufficiently camouflaged command posts, and the failure to periodically move their locations, facilitated the German aviation, which bombed these posts in the first attack, destroying wire communications and the control of troops. The command of the Front . . . absolutely failed to effect coordination of ground and air forces. Our aviation operated outside the general plan of the defensive operations and despite ample opportunities was not able to damage the enemy's air forces.[32]

While the VVS found it difficult to make an operational contribution, the Luftwaffe materially assisted the German army in attaining the preconditions for the spring offensive. As if symbolic of this new era in army-Luftwaffe cooperation, Richthofen and Manstein observed the final stages of the assault on Kerch from a nearby hill.[33] Manstein, in describing Trappenjagd in his postwar memoirs, singled out Richthofen's units for special praise:

VIII Air Corps, which also included strong antiaircraft units, was by its structure the most powerful and hard hitting Luftwaffe formation available for the support of military operations. Its commanding General, Baron von Richthofen, was certainly the most outstanding Luftwaffe leader we had in World War II. He made immense demands on the units under his command, but always went up himself to supervise any important attack they made. Furthermore, one was always meeting him at the front, where he would visit the most forward units to weigh up the possibilities of giving air support for ground operations. We always got on extremely well together, both at Eleventh Army and later on at Southern Army Group. I remember von Richthofen's achievements and those of his Air Corps with the utmost admiration and gratitude.[34]

The final phase of the Crimean campaign involved the taking of Sevastopol. As indicated earlier, most German sources place a disproportionate amount of emphasis upon this achievement. To both the participating army and air force commanders came the highest honors: Manstein received his field marshal's baton, and Richthofen took over command of Luftflotte 4 from Löhr on July 13, 1942.[35] The battle certainly indicated that Richthofen's close air support formula had reached a peak of effectiveness, and there is little doubt that Luftwaffe intervention significantly aided the Eleventh Army's success. The attacks on a single fortress (even the "strongest land and sea fortress in the world") on the tip of an already-occupied peninsula, however, represent a much more restricted objective than the Luftwaffe pursued in support of the Taifun offensive. Nevertheless, the self-congratulatory tone of the German wartime communiques survives in many postwar accounts of the campaign. More muted are the indications that, even under ideal conditions, there were limitations to the efficacy of German air power in the east. Despite the impressive operational success, the campaign against the fortress reveals to an even greater degree than Trappenjagd the overall weakness of the Luftwaffe. Aside from the month-long maximum effort against the fortress in direct support of the Eleventh Army, Luftflotte 4 in the south was capable of accomplishing little else.

The Sevastopol battle represented a notable endeavor, particularly by the Luftwaffe units taking part. Richthofen's self-contained close air

posed of a total of 390 combat-ready aircraft. Another
.r so machines belonged to other formations operating in
. Once again, Richthofen used his access to the Führer to
.ie whole of his combat force against this objective—and once
Fliegerkorps VIII was under direct ObdL control. Richthofen calculated that for the assault on the fortress, he would require six long-
range bomber *Gruppen*, three dive bomber *Gruppen*, two ground attack
Gruppen, five fighter *Gruppen* for the protection of his bombing formations, and three long-range reconnaissance squadrons.[36] Fliegerkorps
VIII on June 1, 1942 actually possessed one more bomber *Gruppe* than
Richthofen had deemed necessary, but was slightly weaker in fighter
protection and reconnaissance strength. Units deployed by the air corps
included reconnaissance Staffeln 3.(H)./11 and 3.(H)./13; dive bomber
Gruppen I., II., and III./StG 77; bomber Gruppen I. and II./ KG 51, I.
and III./KG 76, I./KG 100, and III./LG 1; fighter Gruppen II. and III./JG
77, and III./JG 3. Fliegerführer Süd additionally contributed the long-
range reconnaissance Staffel 4.(F)/122, bomber Gruppe II./KG 26 (also
trained in anti-shipping warfare), and fighter Gruppe I./JG 77. For once,
even Richthofen's extravagant force requirements could be met nearly in
full.[37]

The air corps commander was not alone in his insistence upon overwhelming force. Halder, in his diary, likened the coming assault to a
First World War battle of attrition, and he mandated the lavish use of the
heaviest artillery and its Second World War counterpart, air support.[38]
Hitler had as early as mid-April authorized the dispatch of several giant
mortars, including the "Dora," a super-heavy 800 mm piece, to use
against Sevastopol's fortifications. As one historian observed, the use of
such World War I throwbacks as the "Dora" fit in nicely with the conception of the entire battle, which was itself an anachronism.[39]

The Luftwaffe's own operations research, carried out by the military
science department of the general staff following the Sevastopol battle,
likened the assault to several precedents, including the contemplated air
assault on the Maginot Line and to Fliegerkorps VIII's own efforts
against the fortified Metaxas Line in Greece.[40] Yet the June 1942 operation was unique in the annals of Second World War air operations. As
well as serving as a laboratory situation (and a benchmark) for German
army/air force cooperation in the east, the attack on Sevastopol occurred
under conditions unlikely ever to recur on any front.

For one thing, VIII. Fliegerkorps did not need to wage an air superiority campaign prior to the Eleventh Army's assault. By June 1942 the VVS in the Crimea was so weak, consisting as it did of a motley collection of sixty antiquated land and sea planes,[41] that it could mount only an insignificant fifty sorties each night. Both the Luftwaffe and the German army could therefore carry out their operations under conditions of complete air supremacy. Further easing the Luftwaffe's task was the fact that the fortress and its approaches had been thoroughly covered by air reconnaissance the previous autumn. VIII. Fliegerkorps could therefore commence army support operations as soon as it deployed.[42]

These combat operations were among the most intense of the entire campaign, as the Luftwaffe pitted its army support capability against the concrete and steel of twentieth century fortification technology. Although not yet completed, the defenses of Sevastopol were formidable by any standards. Permanent defenses, eventually to total twenty batteries in rotating armored turrets, included the enormous positions "Maxim Gorkii I and II" with two 30.5 cm. guns each, capable of dealing with a land or sea assault. Such artillery protection enhanced two concentric belts of field fortifications, consisting of "innumerable" bunkers, field positions, and entrenchments, all of which had to be overcome by the air/ground assault.[43] German intelligence reported the defenses to be well-manned by so-called "fortress" or "defensive" divisions which, although not of the quality of "maneuver" formations, could perform adequately in positional warfare. Finally, the ships of the Black Sea fleet (against which the Luftwaffe would expend a disproportionate amount of effort) rounded out the Soviet forces available to defend "Fortress Sevastopol."

By late May 1942, the Eleventh Army had taken up assault positions for a simultaneous advance on Sevastopol from the north and south. The infantry assault to carry the fortress would commence after a fierce, five-day artillery preparation (*Feuerschlag*) combined with an all-out aerial bombardment from VIII. Fliegerkorps.[44] Determination of the Luftwaffe's mission during the assault underscored a divergence between the expectations of the Eleventh Army command staffs and their VIII. Fliegerkorps counterparts. Army documents indicate the extensive hopes which the ground commanders placed in Richthofen's air units. Most broadly, Manstein's staff counted on the Luftwaffe to maintain air superiority, shatter the defenders' morale, neutralize Soviet artillery, and cut the lines of sea communications through attacks on the Black Sea Fleet. With these preparatory conditions fulfilled, VIII. Fliegerkorps would then directly support the Eleventh Army's advance by concentrating its weight at the spearhead and against Soviet artillery to the rear.[45]

In a series of inter-service conferences during the final days of May, the attack plan took shape in concrete form. First of all, the air force was to enhance the artillery's own preparatory bombardment, paying special attention to enemy reserves deployed close to the fortress and outside effective range of the army's artillery. This request is of a type, although on a larger scale, seen on many occasions in the Eastern campaign: "an extension of the range of the corps artillery."[46]

The second task harkened back to the "indirect army support" phase of the 1941 campaign: "Continual destructive attacks, day and night, on the city and harbor, on supply lines, airfields and sea transport." Although on a much smaller scale than in the Taifun operation, the Luftwaffe was expected to "seal off" the Sevastopol battlefield as well. Geographic factors eased this task, with only the sea lines of communication requiring attention.

"Direct" army support tasks were of two distinct types. Not only was the Luftwaffe to augment the artillery during the five day preparatory bombardment, but it was also supposed to participate in the artillery duels during the battle proper. "In coordination with the *Heeresartillerie*," Richthofen's planes would provide counterbattery fire, especially against important targets such as the coastal artillery casemates. Finally, the air force was to provide "full support to the attacking infantry as it makes its way through the enemy defensive positions." Manstein requested the first day's concentration of missions to be over the LIV. Armeekorps, shifting on succeeding days to the XXX. Armeekorps or the VI. (Rumanian) Mountain Corps as the situation required.[47]

The Sevastopol preparations displayed a curious reversal of the roles normally adopted by the air forces and armies of the Second World War. While the army clearly expected (and their happy experiences at Parpach had led them to believe) that the Luftwaffe would be able to succeed at this wide range of tasks, it was the air corps commander, Richthofen, who recognized the limitations of air power. He felt that one objective must take precedence. Richthofen "believed that the best support for the Eleventh Army's attack was in the breaking of the combat morale of the fortress' personnel."[48] On June 2, Richthofen called for "ceaseless attacks . . . to deny the enemy the slightest pause for psychological recovery . . . [M]orale collapse and heavy losses must ensue."[49] To this end, Richthofen concentrated the bulk of the available forces against the fortress, the city, and the harbor, leaving the interdiction tasks to Fliegerführer Süd and other formations.[50]

At six o'clock on the morning of June 2, 1942, one of the most intense artillery and aerial bombardments of the entire campaign, directed against "the huge armored nut which Manstein set out to crack,"[51] began. The Luftwaffe commenced with a half-hour "shock" bombardment by bomber and dive-bomber units against barracks and other military installations in the southeastern portion of the fortress, followed at 7:00 by twelve continuous hours of a "rolling barrage" from the air on the city of Sevastopol. The Germans flew 723 sorties and dropped 525 tons of bombs on the first day. All the while the short-range reconnaissance machines of Richthofen's air corps adjusted the artillery fire of the XXX., LIV. and VI. (Rumanian) Army Corps. Fliegerführer Süd, as intended, dealt with the Soviet Black Sea Fleet, although, despite reporting the destruction of four destroyers, one submarine, three torpedo boats, and ten cargo vessels,[52] it could not prevent naval resupply of the hard-pressed garrison at night.[53]

The bulk of the tonnage dropped on the fortress consisted of high explosive bombs, many of the heaviest types available. The bombers of Fliegerkorps VIII, from June 3 through June 6, placed a further 1,886 tons onto the target. Some aircraft carried out more than eight sorties per day;[54] this is as much a tribute to Richthofen's hard-working ground organization, which kept a sixty-four percent operational ready rate throughout the battle, as to the tenacity of the aircrews. The Luftwaffe's bases, most notably those in the Sarabus area, in some cases were so close to the fortress that the Ju 88 bombers had barely reached attack altitude by the time they reached the target.[55]

As impressive as the initial German effort undoubtedly was, Luftwaffe analysts in 1944 admitted that "the effectiveness of Fliegerkorps VIII did not come up to expectations."[56] When the XXX. Armeekorps attempted to break through towards Severnaya Bay on the seventh, it found that the outer defense works were still intact, as was Soviet morale. The 8. Abteilung gloomily concluded:

On the basis of these experiences the realization must be made that there is little hope of success for the Luftwaffe in attacking permanent fortifications that have been built up over a period of years.[57]

Following the failure to silence Soviet opposition by bombardment, the units of Fliegerkorps VIII moved on to the even more difficult task of assisting the infantry's progress through the fortified zones.

Richthofen had taken extreme care to coordinate liaison between his air units and the ground forces involved in the push through the fortified "rings." He personally briefed every *Geschwader*, *Gruppe*, and *Staffel* commander about the nature of their tasks, and his personal liaison efforts took in not only the Eleventh Army and participating army corps, but also individual divisions.[58] For nearly four weeks, from June 7 until the last pockets of Soviet troops in Sevastopol ceased resistance on July 3, Fliegerkorps VIII functioned as pure "flying artillery," literally blasting the advance forward. The operation seems to have moved German observers to unusual flights of rhetoric. Manstein recalled:

> On the morning of 7 June, as dawn turned the eastern sky to gold and swept the shadows from the valleys, our artillery opened up in its full fury by way of a prelude to the infantry assault. Simultaneously the squadrons of the Luftwaffe hurtled down onto their allotted targets. The scene before us was indescribable . . . at night, within the wide circumference of the fortress, one saw the flashes of enemy gunfire, and by day the clouds of rock and dust cast up by the bursts of our heavy shells and the bombs dropped by German aircraft. It was indeed a fantastic setting for such a gigantic spectacle![59]

Luftwaffe observers provided similar descriptions of the operation. Even Generalmajor Herhudt von Rohden, whose department produced the somewhat critical operations research study mentioned above, gave a wholly impressionistic description of the attack in a 1946 collaborative study:

> The bombers, flying in formation into the shrinking wasp's nest of defense, could hardly see the fort and harbor because of the impenetrable pall of dust streaked by blood-red explosions.

Nature herself seemed to hold her breath during the howling Stuka attacks and the shrill scream of the bombs. The soldiers on the ground, mercilessly beat by the rays of the burning sun, held theirs for moments on end. These same seconds were eternities for the defenders. Only after the last Russian soldier had found eternal rest or had given himself up was assembly finally called on Cape Khersones.[60]

In fact, the fortress of Sevastopol fell only after protracted infantry combat of a severity that in large measure accounts for the reverence in which the battle is held in both German and Soviet historiography.[61] Such tributes—to the tenacity of the German attackers, the stubbornness of the Soviet defenders—have their place. Whether the Sevastopol operation was the Luftwaffe's finest hour in the east is another matter. At the time of the operation, Manstein seems to have been convinced that the Luftwaffe's presence, as in the battle for the Parpach line, was essential for the army's success. He noted, in a conference with Richthofen, "The Luftwaffe struck the first breaches . . . and then by destructive bombing effects made it possible for German units to push through the fortified zones."[62] It seems clear that the Luftwaffe's own assessment of its efficacy was closer to the mark: air power in the case of the Sevastopol operation was not a panacea; it simply enhanced the effectiveness of German counterbattery and supporting fire. It did not appreciably reduce the need for the application of traditional "siege engines" against the fortifications. Fliegerkorps VIII, in its experience reports, referred to individual aerial actions that seemed to have a "decisive" effect, such as the chance bomb hit by an Oberleutnant Maue on the east turret of the "Maxim Gorki" emplacement, which put the formidable defense works out of action.[63] In fact, it seems more likely that Manstein's amphibious outflanking attack across Severnaya Bay in the early morning of June 29 did more than the massed Luftwaffe support to bring the bloody exercise to a conclusion.[64]

On the other hand, the victorious offensives of spring 1942 indicate a willingness on the part of the Luftwaffe's operational leadership to solve the problems of direct support of the ground forces. The most extraordinary representative of this trend is, of course, Richthofen. Whatever the strategic merits of committing Fliegerkorps VIII to close air support missions, Richthofen's approach was reasonable as long as the Ostheer and the German High Command defined their goals in terms of short-term operational successes, such as occurred at Sevastopol. To leave the army unsupported in such situations would have been unacceptable.

The Crimean campaign in the final analysis had a deleterious impact upon the basic soundness of German air strategy in the east. As an operation conducted under ideal conditions and with a beguilingly successful outcome, the conquest of "fortress Sevastopol" did not immediately lead to any substantial rethinking of the wisdom of using air power in this fashion. Moreover, the army units involved in the drive towards Stalingrad were by the autumn of 1942 expecting the same level of air support for their operations as they enjoyed at Sevastopol. The pursuit of wider objectives, unfortunately, was to be well beyond the Luftwaffe's capabilities. The brilliant victory of July 1942 provided no hedge against future disaster and, most ironically, led eventually to a resurgence of interest in strategic air operations within the Luftwaffe general staff.

THE QUIET FRONTS: AIR POWER IN THE BACKWATER

Although the Crimean campaign precluded other major aerial activity during the spring of 1942, a number of less ambitious operations took place on other sectors of the front, particularly in the area of Heeresgruppe Mitte, virtually denuded of air resources after the winter of 1941–1942. The command authority there was not even an air fleet; instead a smaller command, Luftwaffenkommando Ost (Air Force Command East), under General Robert Ritter von Greim and deploying two understrength *Fliegerdivisionen*, provided the air support for the entire army group.[65] This command came into being on April 10, 1942 and represented the fusing of two even smaller air support commands, Nahkampfführer Nord and Nahkampfführer Süd, as well as the command staff of Fliegerkorps V.[66] The type of Luftwaffe participation in these limited operations illustrates the effect of the heavy commitment of the German air force to the southern flank.

Throughout much of the spring, in the absence of major ground operations, Luftwaffenkommando Ost carried out armed reconnaissance and interdiction of rail and road traffic opposite Army Group Center. In several instances, the Luftwaffe aided the army in anti-partisan operations in a surprisingly typical employment of German tactical air power during periods of relative quiet.[67] On rare occasions, the few long-range bomber units of the command even attempted small-scale strategic attacks, including those on Gorki and Saratov in the late spring.

Another attempt to utilize the Luftwaffe against the sources of Soviet military power took place in the far north, in the operational area of Generaloberst Hans-Jürgen Stumpff's Luftflotte 5. In March, 1942, Göring directed Stumpff to use the small bomber force of Luftflotte 5 (which in February comprised the sixty bombers of KG 30 [Ju 88s] and KG 26 [He 111H-6 torpedo planes]) against Allied lend-lease convoys en route to Murmansk.[68] By late June, the German force had been considerably reinforced to a total of 264 aircraft of all types and played a pivotal role in the savaging of Convoy PQ 17 in July. The next Arctic convoy, PQ 18, better protected by carrier-based aircraft than its predecessor, fared somewhat better.[69]

The Luftwaffe command was not able to capitalize on these initial successes. After the Anglo-American Torch landings in North Africa on November 8, the bulk of the anti-shipping bombers and torpedo planes of Luftflotte 5 departed for the Mediterranean, never to return to the far north.[70] Thus ended the only serious attempt by the German air force to cut off the Red Army from its western allies. Once again, the pressure of other fighting fronts forced the premature abandonment of a promising series of operations.

Luftwaffe attempts in 1942 to strike directly at Soviet domestic war production were likewise stillborn. Generalleutnant Hermann Plocher, one of the authors for the postwar United States Air Force Monograph Project, served as chief of staff to Ritter von Greim at Luftwaffenkommando Ost during 1942. He maintained that the few strategic bombing attacks that did take place, although "mere pin-pricks which had no strategic impact upon the course of the war,"[71] were at least indicative of an awareness among the operational commands that interruption of Soviet arms production by air attack was necessary. Indeed, Plocher noted that an early version of the scheme to attack Soviet power plants (the centerpiece of Luftwaffe strategic planning in 1943–1944) originated with the staff of Luftwaffenkommando Ost:

About summer of 1942, Luftwaffe Command East prepared a number of special strategic studies for systematically conducted operations against the Soviet armaments industry in the optimistic hope that suitable flying units would, after all, be available at some future date for missions of this sort. From the point of view of effective aircraft ranges, the area served by Luftwaffe Command East appeared to be especially suitable,[72] and, by submitting complete plans for such operations, the staff of this command hoped to interest the Commander in Chief of the Luftwaffe.

Special efforts were to be made against long-distance transmission lines carrying electric power from the deep interior of the Soviet Union to the industries in the general area of Moscow which were recovering from recent air attacks.[73]

This humble beginning in fact foreshadowed the efforts in spring 1943 by Luftflotte 6 to wage such an air campaign (see Chapter 4). Luftwaffenkommando Ost in 1942 was in a position to do little other than contemplate such operations. Nearly all of its combat power supported the frontline defenses or occasionally assisted the German army in local offensive activity.

Perhaps the largest ground operations carried out in this sector during 1942 were Operations Seydlitz and Seydlitz II in early July 1942. The purpose of these engagements was to "straighten the front" through the elimination of troublesome Russian salients. Specifically, the German Ninth Army in the two Seydlitz operations intended to encircle and destroy the Soviet Thirty-ninth Army and XI. Cavalry Corps in the Vyazma/Belyi region.[74] XLVI. Panzerkorps, responsible for the Seydlitz II phase of the operation, requested specific assistance from supporting Luftwaffe units. The operational order proposed that "missions of the Luftwaffe be restricted to the support of the attacking 328th Infantry Division, at the expense of simultaneous support for the other two attacking divisions." The order went on to indicate that, due to the weakness of the corps artillery, the Luftwaffe was to keep a wooded area that offered concealment to Soviet forces under surveillance.[75] Air to ground recognition procedures for this offensive consisted of the same yellow identification panels and swastika flags in use everywhere in the east. In the absence of radio contact, the corps requested a system of colored flares and smoke cartridges, fired from reconnaissance aircraft, that would indicate the presence of enemy armored units. Similar indicators were to mark the final bomb release, leaving the way clear for the troops to advance.[76] The army seemed quite satisfied with its procedures for cooperation with the air force. Indeed, the Seydlitz operations proved to be a tactical success. After initial slow progress, the German troops put the Soviet forces to flight, and by June 12 most of the Soviet troops were behind German barbed wire.[77]

Towards the end of 1942, Luftwaffenkommando Ost issued a memorandum dealing with "cooperation between army and Fliegerdivision." This two-page document reveals that, in such backwater areas of the eastern front, air support procedures had progressed little since the days of the Polish campaign. There is no mention of air control detachments, nor of direct radio links with any higher Luftwaffe headquarters. The staffs at army, and in some cases divisional level, worked out air support procedures in consultation with Fliegerdivision personnel. The document does provide a summary of the air support capabilities of each of the basic aircraft types, including recommended safe distances for German troops to stand in order to avoid casualties from friendly fire (200 to 600 meters was considered a sufficiently prudent distance from a Ju 87's bomb release).[78] The tried and true system of consultations, flare signals, and ID panels evidently sufficed for the troops of Army Group Center into 1943.

Operations on other quiet fronts do reveal that the process of improving air/ground cooperation was progressing. Not surprisingly, those air force officers at the lower levels of command were sympathetic to the army's desire for more and better air support. Reports from the *Fliegerverbindungsoffiziere*, the members of the air corps staff working most closely with the army, suggest a low-ranking officer corps willing to make the best of the situation. After-action reports concerning the *Flivos* assigned to infantry units taking part in Operation Blücher, the crossing of the Kerch Straits prior to the invasion of the Kuban Peninsula in September 1942, reveal this operational pragmatism. An unnamed *Flivo* accompanied for the first time the Ninety-seventh Infantry Regiment on September 9. Noting the absence of direct radio contact between the ground troops and the supporting aircraft, he pointed out that "the further testing of such a system would increase the possibilities for direct cooperation."[79] He further recommended development of a portable radio set, similar to the 5–watt *Gerät* which liaison officers used to communicate with air corps headquarters, for the use of the battalion staffs. Another *Flivo* participating in the same operation on September 7 suggested more extensive employment of the Luftwaffe's main air superiority fighter, the Messerschmitt Bf 109G, in the ground support role. He cited the powerful effect of its three 2 cm cannons against entrenched infantry.[80] Examples such as these illustrate that the practical flexibility present in most of the Wehrmacht was not absent from the Luftwaffe's officer corps. Just as the entire methodology of close air support grew up at the tactical level, suggestions for the constant improvement of that capability also originated from the lower echelons.[81]

The Luftwaffe's activity on the so-called "static fronts" remains a footnote in the history of the eastern campaign. The upshot of this diminished capacity was that a large proportion of German troops fighting in the east grew accustomed to positional, defensive and even occasionally mobile warfare with little or no air support—a state of affairs almost unknown to the armies of the Western Allies. The remarkably tenacious performance of German forces in the defense of the *bocage* country in Normandy during the summer of 1944 under conditions of absolute Allied air superiority may well have stemmed from experience accumulated on the vast fronts in the east.

LUFTFLOTTE 4 AND THE DRIVE TO STALINGRAD

To the staffs and aircrews of Richthofen's formations, their deployment, with scant rest, must have seemed reminiscent of the hard use they had experienced during their rapid transfer from Leningrad to the Moscow front in late September of the previous year. The task facing them in 1942 was even greater. The operational development of the southern offensive does not require complete elucidation here.[82] Much has been made of the fragmentation of German offensive power, such as the two-pronged drive towards the Caucasian oilfields and Stalingrad. Hitler's War Directive No. 41, "an untidy disarray of disconnected thoughts, containing many asides and irrelevancies, a hotchpotch of strategy and tactics,"[83] led to the dissipation of the available air support as well. The varied tasks demanded of the Luftwaffe included air defense of the Dnieper crossings and Army Group South's staging areas, interdiction attacks on Soviet concentrations "well in the enemy's rear," especially the Don bridges, and air superiority strikes against the

VVS in the attack area.[84] In tacit awareness of the Luftwaffe's weakness, Hitler added, ''The possibility of a *hasty transfer of Air Force units* [italics in original] to the Central and Northern Fronts must be borne in mind, and the necessary ground organization for this maintained as far as possible.''[85]

The bulk of these tasks devolved onto the units of Luftflotte 4, under the command of Richthofen as of July 18, 1942. The air fleet set up its headquarters in a large school at Mariupol (now Zhdanov) on the Sea of Azov.[86] True to form, Richthofen and his new staff paid ''flying visits'' via Storch liaison aircraft to the air and army commands within the air fleet's zone of operations. That area was immense: it covered the entire Caucasus south to Batum, the Russo-Turkish border to the Caspian Sea, the south and east coasts of the Caspian Sea, and the lower tributaries of the Volga River north to Saratov.[87] Luftflotte 4 was operating in this gigantic region with approximately five hundred fighters, bombers and reconnaissance machines—hardly more than it had deployed against Sevastopol. Moreover, the proposed German advance would require great mobility on the part of the air and supporting units in order to keep sufficient force concentrated in the battle area. This applied particularly to the establishment of the many new airfields that units of the air fleet would require.[88] The drive to Stalingrad would demand the same superhuman effort on the part of the Luftwaffe's ground organization as did the previous year's campaign.

At Sevastopol, the whole might of the Luftwaffe had descended upon a single fortress. In July 1942, the available force had to deal with many, often geographically separated tasks. On July 8, for example, events forced the commitment of a splinter command of Luftflotte 4, Gefechtsverband Nord, created the previous month, to support of Second Army and Second Panzer Army in the Voronezh sector.[89] The commitment of Gefechtsverband Nord was intended to be only temporary; in fact Soviet pressure on the extending flanks of the German southern advance proved a lengthy distraction to that part of Luftflotte 4's striking force. Most of the air fleet was by midsummer fully committed to supporting the advance of the German army up to and past the Don River.

The issue on July 23, 1942 of Führer Directive No. 45, ''Continuation of Operation Braunschweig,'' prompted a further dissipation of the German effort. Directive No. 45 called for the controversial dispatch of

Army Group A to the Caucasus and Army Group B, most notably Generaloberst Friedrich Paulus' Sixth Army, to Stalingrad, "the Red citadel on the Volga." As expected, the Luftwaffe was to provide support for both operations. "The early destruction of Stalingrad is especially important," the directive enjoined.[90] Additionally, Luftflotte 4 was to carry out interdiction missions, especially of shipping on the Lower Volga. The directive also contained a prohibition against strategic air attacks on one notable target:

> In view of *the decisive importance of the Caucasian oilfields* [italics in original] for the further prosecution of the war, air attacks against their refineries and storage tanks, and against ports used for oil shipments on the Black Sea, will only be carried out if the operations of the Army make them absolutely essential.[91]

Luftwaffe intelligence, it must be noted, objected violently to this logic; that same month Ic called for the "absolute rejection of the point of view that air attacks on Soviet war industry must be avoided in order to keep it available for work on German behalf."[92] The point was, in any event, moot: direct and indirect support of ground operations during the multi-pronged advance left no substantial Luftwaffe bomber force in reserve for such a task. Not until mid-October did German aircraft, following Hitler's recognition that the early fall of the Caucasus oilfields was unlikely,[93] strike at Soviet petroleum production. On October 10 and 12, the depleted bomber forces of Luftflotte 4, including the Heinkels of III./Kampfgeschwader 55, bombed the crude oil combine at Grosny; a total of only seventeen bombers from that *Gruppe* (normally forty aircraft strong) participated.[94] These evening raids, although considered successful and mounted with minimal loss,[95] were themselves diversions from the daily business of supporting the battle for Stalingrad.

Through summer 1942 Luftflotte 4, in effect, waged three separate air campaigns, and did its best to fulfill all of the complex tasks. Fliegerkorps IV flew constant interdiction missions against Soviet forces facing Army Group A, while the specialized close air support force Fliegerkorps VIII assisted the Sixth and Fourth Panzer Armies in their drive towards Stalingrad. Gefechtsverband Nord, which by late August had metamorphosed into Luftwaffenkommando Don, commanded by General Günther Korten, continued to assist the Second Army in its defensive battles against General N.F. Vatutin's Voronezh Front.[96] This breaking off of separate commands to attend to secondary fronts dissipated the total force, but it also enabled Richthofen to, in the short run, fulfill his July 24 promise to Paulus to devote his personal attention to supporting the Sixth Army's advance.[97] In practice, throughout the campaign, Fliegerkorps VIII, under Generalmajor Martin Fiebig, functioned purely as the Sixth Army's air support command. Once again, Richthofen made sure that the Fourth Air Fleet's *Schwerpunkt* matched that of the German army.

One of the reasons that the Luftwaffe was able to carry out its mission successfully during the summer 1942 advance was that the Soviets were grappling with even greater dispersal of force problems. Since the German command held the operational initiative, the Luftwaffe could use its demonstrated mobility and flexibility to excellent effect. The Soviets, still reeling from the 1941 campaign and the humiliation of the Crimean battles, were not so fortunate. One Soviet source explains,

> In addition, the Stavka of the Supreme High Command was not able to concentrate the full force of its tactical or long-range bombing aviation on the decisive axis. The cover and defense of Moscow, the Central Industrial Region, and Leningrad required strong air groupings. Consequently, although the Red Army concentrated its main efforts during the second period of the war in the south, the Soviet High Command had kept one-half of all its air formations along the northwest and western axes. In the meantime, the German-Fascist High Command had the capability of maneuvering its forces more freely and of employing along the decisive axis 80%–90% of its air forces then operating on the Soviet-German front.[98]

The VVS in mid-1942 faced precisely the same dilemma that the Luftwaffe would encounter from mid-1943 on.

Richthofen's units were therefore able to make considerable headway towards fulfilling their assigned tasks. Directive No. 45 had called for interdiction of the battlefield; indeed, both VIII. and IV. Fliegerkorps carried out attacks on both rail and river traffic in the Stalingrad area.[99] A systematic interdiction of the entire battle area was, however, quite impossible. Accordingly, on August 19 Richthofen declared, "Our air power will continue to be directed primarily at Stalingrad!"[100] Since further dispersal of Luftflotte 4's flying units to a wide variety of tasks would have been absurd, Richthofen in all probability made the correct operational decision in ordering his air fleet to concentrate on supporting the ground battle. An entry from his *Tagebuch* indicates the success achieved:

> 21. 8. 42. On the battlefield at Kalach are incredible numbers of destroyed Russian tanks and casualties . . . KG 76 twice caught two divisions, which had just bridged the Volga. Fantastic bloodbath![101]

On August 23, the entire available force of Luftflotte 4, led by VIII. Fliegerkorps, carried out a massive bombardment of the city of Stalingrad. In one day, the German air force flew 1,600 sorties and dropped 1,000 tons of bombs, an effort which exceeded in scope even the aerial preparations for the attack on Sevastopol.[102] The bomb tonnage included many incendiaries; most of the residential area of Stalingrad was completely gutted during this attack.

Yet as early as August 27, Richthofen detected a slowing of the German offensive. On that date, the air fleet commander dispatched his operations officer, Oberst Karl-Heinrich Schulz, to present Göring and Jeschonnek with his personal commentary on "weaknesses in nerve and leadership of the army."[103] Richthofen throughout the war was something of an intriguer, and frequently addressed uncomplementary reports regarding the army's performance to Hitler or Göring, to Halder's continual dismay.[104] Halder in this case attributed the delay to "counteroffensives and resistance by a numerically superior opponent."[105] Richthofen also noted that the advance had taken its toll on his own units, as the replacement aircraft, fuel, and spare parts situation gave cause for alarm even as German forces closed in on the battered city.

Richthofen's commentary, although highly colored by his service and personal prejudices, is most illuminating. German combat power had in all probability passed its peak before the battle within the city of Stalingrad had even begun. The Luftwaffe commander regarded this decline in German military power as due more to the morale failings and obtuseness of the army leadership than to any inherent flaws in German strategy. He believed the lack of German progress by early October stemmed from a failure to concentrate forces—an article of faith with the close air support commander. It was in this spirit that Richthofen, when Hitler approached him following the mass air raid against Stalingrad, rejected out of hand the Führer's proposal for redeploying Fliegerkorps VIII for a similar operation against Leningrad. As ambitious as Richthofen undeniably was, he fully realized the need to keep his units committed to the present engagement.

As the battle in the streets of Stalingrad raged uncontrollably, Richthofen at last showed awareness that the usefulness of his air fleet in the battle for the city had just about ceased. On November 1, he told Paulus and General Walther von Seydlitz, the commander of LI. Armeekorps, that the Luftwaffe was being incorrectly employed. He noted that the German and Soviet troops were at such close quarters that his dive bombers had to drop their bombs "less than a hand grenade's throw from the German infantry."[106] On the other hand, Richthofen noted with a certain amount of glee that heavy bomber attacks on the Barrikady factory reminded him of the Sevastopol bombardment, as they were characterized by the same ruthless application of air power as in the battle for the Black Sea port. Many of the bomber and dive bomber units, despite their parlous supply situation, continued to fly up to four missions per day.[107] The dive bomber units oriented themselves over the city by using the roof of the railway station, which was adorned with an enormous red sledgehammer, as a landmark.[108] Richthofen was unwilling to concede fully that the air support formula he had perfected would not achieve a strategic decision in the Stalingrad battle. He did, however, agree to devote some of the railway space allocated to his air fleet for the transportation of artillery ammunition.[109]

An obvious failure of the Luftwaffe at Stalingrad was its lack of interdiction efforts against the Soviet buildup for Operation Uranus, the counteroffensive that eventually trapped the entire Sixth Army within the Stalingrad perimeter. An eerie calm preceded the storm; Richthofen on November 4 noted that "absolute quiet" reigned at Stalingrad.[110] Contrary to what is generally believed, the Luftwaffe had ample evidence that the Soviets were massing for such a thrust; it was the strength and swiftness of that thrust that proved surprising. Extremely poor weather on the days preceding the assault somewhat hampered the Luftwaffe's ability to reconnoiter or harass the buildup.

Richthofen did dispatch Gefechtsverband Hitschold, yet another hastily organized close air support command, to the threatened Rumanian
front on the Don two days before the Soviet attack broke against the
satellite army on November 19.[111] Within a remarkably short period of
time, the Sixth Army found itself trapped (*eingekesselt*) within the Stalingrad perimeter.

One of the most vexing questions in Second World War historiography surrounds the issue of the decision to resupply the Sixth Army by
air. Many accounts seek only to place blame or to exonerate their
authors or protagonists from complicity in the ordering of the so-called
Stalingrad Airlift, one of the blackest pages in the history of the German air force.[112] It is not the purpose of this study to enter into the
debate in any substantial way.[113] However, one should note that the
employment of the Luftwaffe in an emergency air transport role was
not an unusual practice on the eastern front by late 1942. During the
first Soviet winter offensive in December 1941, Generaloberst Hans
Keller of Luftflotte 1 had promised to resupply cut-off German troops
wherever they might be. The Luftwaffe had sustained surrounded
pockets of German troops at Demyansk and Kholm during the first
winter campaign. More to the point, Richthofen's own air fleet, including its bomber units, had, during the months of the drive to Stalingrad, airlifted some 9,223 tons of supplies for the rapidly advancing
German army, including 1,787 tons of ammunition, 4,615 tons of fuel,
and 2,830 tons of equipment.[114] Many more tons of airlifted supplies
consisted of bombs, aviation fuel, and ammunition for the use of the
air fleet itself. Thus, the Fourth Air Fleet was accustomed to operating
in an air transport role, and the decision to resupply Stalingrad by air
and Göring's tame acquiescence thus stem from a greater degree of
continuity with past operational practice than many commentators
have allowed.

Whatever the motivation for the airlift, operational factors combined to plague it almost from the start. As Richthofen and the VIII.
Fliegerkorps commander General Martin Fiebig were quick to point
out, the Luftwaffe did not possess sufficient Ju 52 transport aircraft to
supply the Sixth Army with the minimum three hundred tons per
day the Fourth Air Fleet staff calculated would keep it alive. Fiebig, in
fact, on November 22 bluntly informed the army command that ''an
aerial resupply of the entire Sixth Army in a Russian winter is not

possible."[115] There was certainly not a unanimous body of Luftwaffe opinion opposing an airlift operation at the time Hitler made the decision; Jeschonnek's attitude in particular was equivocal at best.[116] By late November, the resupply operation had acquired its own momentum.[117] A number of factors, including the possibility of an early breakout by the Sixth Army, or a lifting of the siege by a counterthrust led by Generaloberst Hermann Hoth's Fourth Panzer Army, conspired to mute the technical objections raised by the air fleet personnel.[118] By the time the hopeless nature of the airlift became evident, the Sixth Army had no real chance of effecting a successful breakout and there was little the participants could do to reverse the course of events.

In fact, the weeks following the encirclement of the Sixth Army provide a good illustration of what Clausewitz called the "chameleon-like character" of warfare. Had the airlift remained in its initial form, a temporary expedient flown from the well-equipped bases at Tazinskaya and Morosovskaya to keep the Sixth Army's fighting power at a high level until the situation became more favorable, the outcome might not have been so disastrous. The airlift gradually acquired its "doomed" valence as the front line receded at a rapid pace, the forward loading airfields (such as Tazinskaya in the last week of December) fell to the Soviets, and the Red Army continued its advance.

This course of events was not immediately evident to most contemporary observers, and Luftflotte 4 made a considerable effort to put the aerial resupply operation into effect. By December 5, the air fleet had assembled eleven transport *Gruppen* (a total of two hundred Ju 52s) along with two *Gruppen* of Ju 86s (obsolete bomber aircraft culled from the training schools) and four *Gruppen* of He 111s (first-line bombers); many more improvised formations would soon follow.[119] Indeed, by mid-January the resupply force comprised no fewer than fourteen Heinkel *Gruppen*, including the entire effective strength of KG 55 and KG 27.[120] The resupply forces were grouped under a number of ad hoc commanders known as *Lufttransportführer* (air transport commanders). Most prominent of these were Oberst Fritz Morzik, at Svervo with the Ju 52 units, and Oberst Ernst Kühl, operating out of Novocherkassk with most of KG 27's and KG 55's Heinkels; other formations flew out of Stalino and Voroshilovgrad. To augment the airlift, unusual aircraft types made their first, and in some cases their only, appearance in the eastern theater. KG z.b.V. 200, for example, was equipped with four-engined Focke-Wulf FW 200 ''Condor'' four-engined maritime patrol planes, while I./FKG 50 operated out of Zaporozhe with brand-new Heinkel He 177 long-range bombers (with disastrous results). The Luftwaffe even risked prototype aircraft in the resupply operation: the giant Junkers Ju 290V1, capable of carrying eight tons of supplies, crashed with heavy loss of life during the airlift. At peak, nearly six hundred aircraft of all types were assigned to the airlift; the number serviceable on any given day was a mere fraction of this total.

The deployment of the bomber forces to supplying the Sixth Army was one of the many ominous features of the Stalingrad airlift. On one hand, the Heinkel units were in most cases more effective formations than were the hastily assembled Junkers transport *Gruppen*. Milch noted pointedly that the bomber units' serviceability rates were less affected by cold than were the Ju 52 units, as their personnel were well acquainted with the crude but effective cold start procedures for aircraft engines. On a number of days during the airlift, Heinkel crews from KG 55 and KG 27 each made two or three sorties per day into the pocket, for which they were singled out for special commendations. Yet the Heinkel 111, with its narrow fuselage and lack of a loading hatch, made an indifferent transport aircraft. Fiebig, on the twelfth of December, rather coldly noted that the proper place for the bomber aircraft was in support of the Fourth Panzer Army's relief drive towards the city: ''This is of far greater worth than a few tons of supplies more or less flown into the fortress.''[121] The use of the Heinkel formations at Stalingrad, moreover, placed the Luftwaffe's strategic bombing capability at risk. For example, two *Gruppen* of Kampfgeschwader 55 (II./ and III./KG 55), which had been pulled out of the Stalingrad battle that autumn to reequip and retrain on the new Lotfe 7D precision bombing sight, in late December joined instead the air transport force.[122] Many of the Ju 52 formations came from the Luftwaffe's multi-engined pilot training schools, and were crewed by skilled flying and navigation instructors. The consequences for the bomber arm are not hard to foresee.

In any event, conditions for a successful resupply of ''Fortress Stalingrad'' were not auspicious. The besieged Sixth Army had a ration strength of 260,000 men, requiring a minimum of three hundred tons of supplies per day for its bare survival (a further two hundred tons per day would keep the army battle-worthy.) As General Hans Hube pointed out, such figures were consistent with previous experience at Demyansk.[123] The Stalingrad fortress possessed only two acceptable landing grounds (Pitomnik and Bassargino; Gumrak, Karpovka and Stalingradskii were marginal at best), weather conditions were appalling, ground organization on the improvised forward bases used by Luftflotte 4 was almost totally lacking, and there were insufficient numbers of escort fighters to protect the vulnerable, heavily laden transport aircraft during their supply runs into the pocket.[124] The energetic Red Air Force mounted a comprehensive "air blockade" of the Stalingrad garrison. General A. A. Novikov commanded the Seventeenth, Sixteenth and Eighth Air Armies, with some 1,100 aircraft; in late November he ordered his subordinate commanders "to consider the destruction of the enemy's transport aircraft to be their primary mission . . . to assign specially designated fighters and ground attack bombers to this mission of destroying the transports and to explain to the flying personnel of these units the great importance of the mission assigned to them."[125] Soviet air power attempted not only to close off the air corridor but also to attack and harrass the loading airfields, using fighters and Il-2s by day and U-2 biplanes by night. The VVS claimed 1,160 German aircraft destroyed during the Stalingrad operation; if the German official loss figures were more moderate, they were alarming all the same.

An insight into the effect of the difficulties that plagued the airlift operation may be gained from an examination of the contingency planning of Luftflotte 4 and Sonderstab Milch for expansion of the airlift. Those running the airlift calculated that, given the aircraft on hand on January 13 (317 Ju 52s, 181 He 111s, twenty FW 200s, one Ju 290 and ten He 177s), augmented by an additional 87 Ju 52s and 219 He 111s en route from other fronts and the Reich, it would be possible, even assuming a twenty-five percent operational ready rate, to fly approximately 456 tons per day into the fortress.[126] If the airlift continued into February, the tonnage was to exceed 530 per day. Aircraft attrition, the loss of landing strips, Soviet air activity, and the deterioration of the ground situation conspired to negate the efforts of Milch, Richthofen, Morzik, and the aircrews. The actual total flown in on January 20 was a mere fifty-two tons. A statistical overview reveals the enormous gulf between German aspirations and the meager results actually achieved:

THE STALINGRAD AIRLIFT[127]
November 24, 1942–February 3, 1943

Date	# of aircraft operational (Ju 52, He 111, FW 200)	# of sorties completed to Stalingrad	tons flown in
Nov. 24	42	42	84
Nov. 25	43	33	66
Nov. 26	43	35	72
Nov. 27	43	14	28
Nov. 28	39	55	101
Nov. 29	109	25	46
Nov. 30	106	98	129
Dec. 1	105	40	85
Dec. 2	134	70	120.1
Dec. 3	149	0	0
Dec. 4	139	74	143.8
Dec. 5	157	29	61.4
Dec. 6	139	44	72.9
Dec. 7	134	135	362.6
Dec. 8	170	107	209.7
Dec. 9	159	0	0
Dec. 10	105	74	156.6
Dec. 11	115	117	266.3
Dec. 12	145	56	114.7
Dec. 13	134	83	133.7
Dec. 14	132	85	135
Dec. 15	126	50	91.5
Dec. 16	78	94	93
Dec. 17	88	47	129.9
Dec. 18	86	31	85
Dec. 19	111	146	273.3
Dec. 20	126	114	215
Dec. 21	120	144	362.3
Dec. 22	124	114	142.8
Dec. 23	105	32	83.8
Dec. 24	97	0	0
Dec. 25	97	9	7

THE STALINGRAD AIRLIFT[127]
November 24, 1942–February 3, 1943 *(continued)*

Date	# of aircraft operational (Ju 52, He 111, FW 200)	# of sorties completed to Stalingrad	tons flown in
Dec. 26	87	37	78
Dec. 27	51	79	127
Dec. 28	69	10	35.4
Dec. 29	49	96	124.2
Dec. 30	86	85	124.2
Dec. 31	85	158	310
Jan. 1	49	78	205.6
Jan. 2	58	0	0
Jan. 3	53	97	168.4
Jan. 4	58	145	270.9
Jan. 5	91	53	161.3
Jan. 6	62	29	49.5
Jan. 7	51	63	125.5
Jan. 8	90	80	117.6
Jan. 9	94	102	349.7
Jan. 10	99	92	162.2
Jan. 11	93	95	189.6
Jan. 12	90	51	61.7
Jan. 13	47	69	224.5
Jan. 14	63	74	65.2
Jan. 15	89	56	105.1
Jan. 16	77	39	68.5
Jan. 17	61	61	52.9
Jan. 18	62	42	24.1
Jan. 19	62	70	60.8
Jan. 20	79	57	52.2
Jan. 21	56	108	99.4
Jan. 22	56	69	93.2
Jan. 23	88	78	80.4
Jan. 24	82	7	12.4
Jan. 25	71	21	13
Jan. 26	74	52	46.3

THE STALINGRAD AIRLIFT[127]
November 24, 1942–February 3, 1943 *(continued)*

Date	# of aircraft operational (Ju 52, He 111, FW 200)	# of sorties completed to Stalingrad	tons flown in
Jan. 27	75	124	103.4
Jan. 28	127	87	83.1
Jan. 29	129	111	108.7
Jan. 30	108	130	128
Jan. 31	135	89	118
Feb. 1	106	89	73.9
Feb. 2	122	82	98
Feb. 3	35	10	7

Many of the accounts of participants in what Herhudt von Rohden called "the drama of the Sixth Army"[128] have tended to dissolve, understandably, into recriminations. Richthofen remarked to Jeschonnek on December 12, "My confidence in our leadership is rapidly sinking to nothingness."[129] Hube, for his part, regarded the Luftwaffe's failure to fly a ranking officer into the pocket to coordinate the airlift and thereby demonstrate its commitment to the besieged army to be a "cardinal omission."[130] Indeed, Paulus rather petulantly ordered an air control officer out of the pocket, "saying that he had been promised a Luftwaffe general."[131] The command staff of the Sixth Army made it clear that the Luftwaffe was responsible for their plight. On January 20, 1943, Major Erich Thiel, *Gruppenkommandeur* of III./KG 27, a bomber unit operating in an improvised transport role, flew into the pocket. He had orders from Generalfeldmarschall Erhard Milch, who since January 15 headed a special staff charged with expediting the airlift, to contact Paulus. Thiel's report of the exchange that followed his landing at the improvised airfield at Gumrak is justifiably famous:

Generaloberst Paulus began with the following:
"When the aircraft do not land, it means the death of the army. Now it is in any case already too late. Every machine that lands saves the lives of 1,000 men . . . Dropping the supplies does no good. Many supply canisters are not found, as we have no fuel with which to retrieve them. Today is the fourth day my people have had

nothing to eat. We could not recover our heavy weapons, because we have no fuel. They are lost. Our last horses have been eaten. Can you picture the soldiers diving on an old horse cadaver, breaking open its head, and devouring its brains raw?"

This last sentence may have been spoken by one of the other gentlemen, as I was being beset from all sides. "What should I, as an army commander, say when a man comes to me and begs, Herr Generaloberst! A crust of bread? Why did the Luftwaffe say that it could carry out the resupply mission? Who is the man responsible for mentioning this possibility? If someone had told me that it was not possible, then I would not have blamed the Luftwaffe, I would have broken out . . ." General Schmidt broke in, "And now you come and try to vindicate the Luftwaffe, which has committed the worst treachery in the history of the German people? It [aerial resupply] must have been suggested to the Führer! Must an entire Army, this splendid Sixth Army, go to the dogs like this?"[132]

The failure of the airlift was readily apparent by the time the above words were spoken. Only twice during the airlift did supply tonnage flown or dropped into the pocket exceed three hundred tons on any given day; this figure (and the 24,910 wounded soldiers successfully evacuated before Soviet troops captured Pitomnik and Gumrak airfields) is in fact impressive given the dismally low serviceability rates for the transport aircraft supplying the Sixth Army. Throughout the latter stages of the airlift, the Sixth Army had little chance of breaking out, particularly after the failure of Hoth's relief attack, Wintergewitter (Winter Storm). This inability to alter in any significant fashion the final outcome bred fatalism among the air fleet staff: Richthofen referred to himself as merely "a highly paid noncommissioned officer" for the duration of the airlift.[133] German accounts find some small mitigation of the disaster in the heroism of individual officers and men who remained at their posts within the Stalingrad *Kessel* until the last moment. Herhudt von Rohden recounts two such incidents. Oberleutnant Wachsland, a member of Luftwaffe Signals Regiment 129 assigned to Sixth Army, radioed as the southern half of the bifurcated pocket fell on January 30, "The remainder of the unit in Stalingrad today signs off. All best wishes to the homeland."[134] Sixth Army command likewise reported on the 31st that the Russians "are standing outside the door," and that the German officers were destroying their equipment.[135] Individual bravery and self-sacrifice (and there was plenty of both in the final weeks of the Stalingrad encirclement) could not disguise the fact that, with the fall of "Fortress Stalingrad" on February 2, 1943, German strategy for 1942 in the south had become completely unhinged.

In criticizing the conduct of German air operations in 1942, one must acknowledge that the application of air power by the German commanders generally complemented the strategic direction emanating from the Führer's headquarters, however haphazard that direction may have been. Concentrations of Luftwaffe units with few exceptions matched the *Schwerpunkt* of the most important ground operations under way at any given time. It is difficult to conceive of a wiser application of the limited forces available in the theater during, in particular, the first half of 1942. The application of all available force to the decisive point is a principle of German military art dating back at least as far as the time of Clausewitz, and the measures conceived and honed to enable the Luftwaffe to participate effectively in the campaigns of 1942 are a triumph of improvisation and adaptation. It is unlikely that any other air force in the world in 1942 could have contributed so effectively to combined-arms operations of the type and scale which the Germans undertook in southern Russia.

Yet for the historian attempting to grasp the nature of Luftwaffe doctrine, mindset, and leadership, the 1942 campaign in the Soviet Union is one of the most misleading. Few German air force planners had expected the Luftwaffe to be heavily committed in the east for a second year; fewer still had given serious thought to the problems which a lengthy air campaign against the Soviet foe posed. Operations such as the conquest of Sevastopol seemed to suggest a suitable employment for the air force within the context of German aims for 1942. The operational successes gained at Kerch and Sevastopol and the drive towards Stalingrad seemed to render any critical examination of these operations superfluous. German commanders tended to ignore evidence that suggested some of these victories represented special cases, which benefitted from favorable conditions regarding balance of forces, climate or geography.

Those Luftwaffe general staff members who, in 1943–1944, argued for a return to the principles of strategic air warfare frequently cited the

1942 campaign as the antithesis of proper employment of air power.[136] They maintained that, after autumn 1941, a significant portion of the Luftwaffe's striking power might have found more profitable employment in long-range deep interdiction and outright strategic bombing of the enemy armaments industry.

There is little evidence to suggest that many Luftwaffe commanders strongly advocated such a position during 1942. Operational rates in the Luftwaffe's flying units in late winter 1942 were, for one thing, at a dangerously low level, particularly after the departure of Kesselring's Luftflotte 2 to the Mediterranean in late November 1941. A strategic bombing campaign at that time made little sense, especially when one considers that the only "strategic" direction provided to the OKL gave assurances of a swift campaign. Strategic bombing thought was not dead in the Luftwaffe during 1942, but it was certainly subsumed by the desire to provide maximum support for Case Blue and its ancillary operations. As the Luftwaffe's own primary doctrinal statement pointed out,

> In many cases, however, [the effects of strategic air attacks] materialize slowly, and a danger inherent in this type of air warfare is that its results might come too late to influence the operations of the Army . . . Usually, this type of warfare will tie down large forces for a considerable duration.[137]

When the anticipated duration of the war began to increase, the Luftwaffe staff's appetite for strategic bombing operations grew in direct proportion. The Stalingrad disaster and its aftermath set the stage for the Luftwaffe to reveal its true colors as an air force whose officer corps had grown to professional maturity in the 1930s, when belief in the potential of long-range bombardment was at its height.

The German air force willingly accepted the task of army support operations and performed this mission with technical skill and genuine commitment. It was, after all, one of the several major tasks for which it had prepared and armed itself. Only when the operations of the army seemed no longer to promise a strategic decision did the Luftwaffe general staff attempt to find that decision primarily in the "third dimension."

General Robert Ritter von Greim. The commander of Fliegerkorps V, Luftwaffenkommando Ost, Luftflotte 6, and (in the last days of the war) Göring's successor as commander in chief of the Luftwaffe, in the nose of an He 111. (National Air and Space Museum, Smithsonian Institution, Photo No. 90-17311)

CHAPTER FOUR

AFTER STALINGRAD: THE SEARCH FOR AN AIR STRATEGY

The year 1943 looked to be an unrewarding one for the German air force in the east. The previous two campaigning seasons ended with the Luftwaffe's failure to carry its operational air war conception through to a successful conclusion. German air power's contribution to the initial advance during the Barbarossa campaign and its dramatic successes in the Crimea and the advance to Stalingrad were completely negated by the course of German grand strategy. The miscarriage of the Stalingrad airlift and the collapse of the southern front were perhaps the nadir of its fortunes.

The 1943 campaigns began, then, with the Luftwaffe's operational and strategic leadership in no position to contemplate executing an independent air strategy. The derailment of the Ostheer's ambitions at Stalingrad had temporarily surrendered the initiative to the Red Army, and the German air fleet commands had little choice but to throw their forces wholesale into the army support role in much the same fashion as during the crisis before Moscow in December 1941. German air force general staff sources estimate variously that sixty to eighty percent of the Luftwaffe's effort went to "direct army support" in 1942–1943.[1]

Yet 1943 proved to be a pivotal year for the Luftwaffe in the east. In matters of doctrine, operational art and improvisation, the Luftwaffe's attempts to thrash out an air strategy for the remainder of the campaign are perhaps the most revealing chapter in the history of the German air force. Most postwar historiography focuses upon the 1943–1944 home defense fighter buildup and the undeniable if transitory victories these forces won against the USAAF's and RAF Bomber Command's Combined Bomber Offensive.[2] In fact, the general staff's plans for the eastern war in 1943–1944 highlight to an even greater extent the tensions caused by the varying demands placed upon the Luftwaffe on the one hand and its own conception of its role on the other. For the Luftwaffe, 1943 represented an uneasy compromise between improvisations designed to deal with operational exigencies and a persistent, almost desperate attempt to fulfill a role as an independent service once again.

These activities took place during the waning months of the life of Generaloberst Hans Jeschonnek, who was to commit suicide in the wake of the August 17, 1943 Eighth Air Force attack on Regensburg and Schweinfurt and RAF Bomber Command's Peenemünde raid on the same date. Jeschonnek, as chief of the general staff, had presided over the Luftwaffe during its years of greatest success; it was he who had so confidently predicted a German victory in the "proper war" that began on June 22, 1941. Jeschonnek obviously bears a fair measure of the blame for the Luftwaffe's decline. His failure to appreciate the importance of production and industrial mobilization (evidenced by his March 1942 remark to Milch that he did "not know what [he] should do with more than 360 fighters [per month]"[3] certainly cost the Luftwaffe dearly in the multi-front battle of attrition to follow.

Yet to paint Jeschonnek as an officer encumbered by an army-oriented mentality, wedded to a tactical air power formula in a war in which the four-engined strategic bomber was the weapon of choice, does violence to the facts. In both the 1941 and 1942 campaigns in Russia, Hitler and the OKH circumscribed the Luftwaffe's role in both the four-month Blitzkrieg that was Barbarossa and in the subsequent campaigns in the Crimea and the south. In neither campaign were there sufficient time or available resources to conduct a sustained bombing offensive against Soviet industry that would have any decisive effect upon the situation at the front. With the destruction of the Sixth Army at Stalingrad, however, dreams of rapid victory vanished. At this point, references to prewar German air strategy, including *operativer Luftkrieg* and its strategic bombing concepts, came once again to the fore. And, as this chapter will demonstrate, it occurred initially under Jeschonnek's direction, not that of the strategic bombing advocate Korten.

This is not to suggest that support of the hard-pressed German army did not occupy an enormous portion of the Luftwaffe's dwindling resources. The course of the war in the east during 1943 was dominated by the Sixth Army's surrender at Stalingrad, Manstein's desperate and ultimately successful attempts to stabilize the front in the south, and the launching of Operation Zitadelle in July 1943 (the last major German offensive of the campaign). Luftwaffe participation in each of these actions was essential, and one of the striking features of the 1943 search for an air strategy was the efforts of the German air force leadership, at many levels, to address the attendant operational problems.

These attempts included improvements in the capabilities of direct army support aviation. Although its reorganization under a separate *Waffengeneral* (inspector general) would have to wait until the autumn of 1943, reforms within the ground attack arm led by mid-year to an enhancement of the Luftwaffe's army support capabilities. Furthermore, anti-tank aviation and night ground attack units, formerly regarded as expedients to be addressed at the tactical level, began to receive long-overdue attention from the higher command circles of the air force.

The changing nature of aviation technology, the process of doctrinal formulation, and the tremendous difficulty of remedying previous errors in planning and production conspire to ensure that air forces rarely end up fighting the type of war for which they prepared. The Luftwaffe in the Soviet Union in 1943 was certainly no exception. The German air force responded in a manner perhaps typical of the air arms of the Second World War: it adapted its technology and tactical and operational art as best it could to the task at hand, all the while attempting, when military circumstances permitted, to recast its war into a more familiar and congenial form. Although, as one German air force officer later pointed out, this approach "might well have given the impression of operations undertaken without a previous plan,"[4] German air strategy in 1943, on the contrary, aimed at freeing the Luftwaffe from the "reactive" posture forced upon it by the disaster of Stalingrad.

THE DEFENSIVE BATTLES OF EARLY 1943

"The Luftwaffe never had a chance to catch its breath," lamented one of its generals after the war.[5] This statement was never more applicable than to the months following the encirclement of the Sixth Army at Stalingrad. Yet the airlift and its aftermath represent only a part of the story. The defensive struggles all along the eastern front in early 1943 required a continuum of maximum effort by the overstretched German air force. That the Luftwaffe was able at all to contemplate ambitious offensive action in the east during 1943–1944 is a tribute to that force's resilience on one level and to the persistent failure of its leadership to tailor strategic planning to available force structure on another.

Available force structure at the end of January 1943 represented a wartime low for the eastern *Luftflotten*, with the possible exception of the period following the collapse of Heeresgruppe Mitte and the onset of the fuel crisis in summer 1944. On January 30, the German air force in the east possessed 2,165 aircraft of all types[6]—a figure significantly below the 3,664 total strength of all units on June 21, 1941.[7] If operational ready rates are taken into account, the gulf becomes far more dramatic. On the opening day of Barbarossa, 2,815 of the Luftwaffe's aircraft in that theater were *einsatzbereit* (operationally ready),[8] while on January 30, 1943, a mere 989 machines were airworthy.[9] That figure seems even more attenuated when one considers that 479 of the available aircraft were Ju 52 transports hastily assembled for the Stalingrad airlift, and that most of these were about to depart for the Mediterranean theater for another ill-advised airlift operation, this time to speed the German buildup in Tunisia.[10] In view of the months of army support operations the remaining units would have to undertake, the eastern Luftwaffe's recovery by the end of May to 3,415 available machines—just over half the total in the entire air force—was most remarkable.

The most obvious cause for the dramatic decline in Luftwaffe strength was the Stalingrad airlift itself. The war diary of Milch's special staff reported the loss not only of 269 Ju 52 transport aircraft, but also 226 other aircraft, including 169 Heinkel 111 bombers, many from KG 27 and KG 55.[11] Of KG 55's remaining aircraft, only twelve out of fifty-two were operational at the end of January. Hermann Göring was only slightly off the mark when he said that at Stalingrad "died the heart of the German bomber force."[12]

Yet Stalingrad was merely the most visible of the many army support tasks that drained the substance out of the Luftwaffe's force structure in early 1943. In some cases, defensive battles along the front had the same impact upon the Luftwaffe forces engaged as the Stalingrad operation had on Luftflotte 4. One example of this type of action was the German attempt, in accord with Hitler's "fortified places" edict, to relieve the 7,000–man garrison at Velikiye-Luki.[13] Air support for this operation was the responsibility of Luftwaffenkommando Ost, which had to concentrate its entire force on the resupply and attempted relief of the garrison.

Luftwaffenkommando Ost had, as demonstrated in the last chapter, grown accustomed to assisting Army Group Center in local, limited offensives such as Operation Seydlitz. The understrength air formation was ill-equipped for sustained defensive and army support operations. The action at Velikiye-Luki had actually begun the previous November, when the Soviet Third Shock Army of the Kalinen Front trapped a portion of the German combat group "von der Chevallerie" inside the town, optimistically designated a "fortress."[14] A Luftwaffe analyst likened the "sacrificial and costly missions" flown by the German units, who tried to resupply the beleaguered garrison with "supply bombs" and DFS 230 and Gotha 242 transport gliders, to those that took place at Stalingrad.[15] A German relief operation, supported directly by the bombers and Stukas of Luftwaffenkommando Ost, pushed to within a few hundred yards of the Velikiye-Luki Kremlin, in which the remaining garrison had taken shelter.[16] The operation was almost completely futile. During the night of January 16, 1943, fifteen officers and eighty-seven men broke through to the west. The rescue operation cost Luftwaffenkommando Ost no fewer that eighty-one aircraft destroyed or damaged, including thirty-nine irreplaceable Heinkel 111 medium bombers.[17]

The operations in support of the Velikiye-Luki garrison were symptomatic of the Luftwaffe's overcommitment along the entire southern half of the eastern front in early 1942. The collapse of the southern front necessitated the creation of no fewer than seven ad hoc air support commands, analogous to army task forces, "which . . . sprung up in response to immediate operational or tactical requirements."[18] The Soviet advance against Army Group Don, which drove the German forces back to the Mius River line, as well as constant pressure in other sectors, including a push against the Seventeenth Army in the Kuban Peninsula, rendered impossible any German plan to concentrate air assets at any single "point of main effort." Most notably, the bomber and transport aircraft of Luftflotte 4, particularly IV. Fliegerkorps, throughout February and March carried out aerial resupply missions to build up the strategically valueless Taman bridgehead, in the process far exceeding the tonnage flown into Stalingrad during the airlift. On March 23, 1943, for example, the Luftwaffe flew some 590 tons of supplies into the bridgehead.[19] Most of the effort during late January and February, however, consisted of "direct army support" to whichever sector was at the moment threatened with being overrun by Soviet forces.

Fortunately for the German command, the Soviets, while possessing the operational initiative on nearly every sector of the front, chose likewise to dissipate their effort. As a result, Manstein seized the opportunity to prepare his well-known counteroffensive, an undertaking that ultimately stabilized the situation in the south.[20] Less well known are Richthofen's efforts to concentrate his forces in support of the operation. In spite of commitments which the holding of the Taman (later Kuban) bridgehead necessitated, Richthofen managed to redeploy his scattered forces "within the framework of a new offensive program."[21] Luftflotte 4, now operating from more permanent bases in what had been the German army's rear areas, demonstrated a marked recovery by mid-February, flying 1,145 and 1,486 sorties respectively on February 22 and 23.[22] This effort coincided with the opening of Manstein's counterblow, and for the last time in the eastern campaign, the Luftwaffe played a decisive role in the success of a major German offensive operation. This accomplishment is all the more remarkable when one considers that Fliegerkorps VIII did not directly participate. After its bloodletting during the Stalingrad airlift, it had been undergoing recuperation, and was in March 1943 assigned to the temporarily quiescent Seventeenth Army front in the Kuban. Richthofen's air fleet deployed only Fliegerkorps IV, the subordinated Fliegerführer Donez, and Fliegerkorps I, newly arrived from the sector of Army Group North.[23] Generalleutnant Hermann Plocher offered the following explanation for the operational success:

Von Richthofen's Fourth Air Fleet was thrown into the battle for Kharkov as one integrated whole, with the participating commands supporting each other, thereby insuring the availability of maximum air power at the crucial point. The main factors behind Richthofen's successes were extreme flexibility, good coordination, and concentration, the latter being secured through the creation of *ad hoc* battle groups to give air support to spearhead units of the ground forces (SS Division "Das Reich") which led the assault on the city. "Massive concentration," "drastic concentration," "Concentration of all forces to the highest degree," were phrases which appeared again and again in Fourth Air Fleet's battle orders.[24]

The recapture of Kharkov on March 15 capped the last major operational success of German arms on the eastern front, and Luftwaffe participation was essential to the victory. In this case, the task was one within the scope of the available German forces on the front, although the effort required an almost superhuman effort on the part of Richthofen and his staff.[25] Such an effort is an ideal example of the command style of Richthofen and others of his ilk, who saw little beyond the immediate operational situation and deployed all available forces to the task at hand. Given the size of the theater and the overall weakness of the German air force in early 1943, such an attitude made good strategic sense as well. Certainly no other employment of the Luftwaffe in the east during the latter half of the campaign brought so many dividends.

Richthofen's handling of the Kharkov battle is even more remarkable when contrasted to the air campaign which was to follow: the operations over the Kuban Peninsula. Seventeenth Army's defensive operations in the region, designated the *Gotenkopf* position, which would ultimately last much of 1943, had no discernible strategic value.[26] German accounts refer to the need to maintain a position near the Straits of Kerch as a jumping-off point for future operations.[27] Hitler also desired to keep the naval base of Novorossiysk out of Soviet hands, but the Germans were unable to hold that city as they retreated into the bridgehead.[28]

On March 30, 1943, the airlift of German troops into the bridgehead was completed, and I. Fliegerkorps, under General der Flieger Günther Korten, assumed air support duties for Seventeenth Army. What ought to have been a simple holding operation then degenerated into a substantial commitment for the German air force.[29] The army insisted on carrying out local attacks, such as Operation Neptune against the Novorossiysk bridgehead (known to the Soviets as "Little Earth") on April 17, which required massed air support. The German army made no significant progress during these attacks; even the Luftwaffe's claims of enormous totals of Soviet aircraft destroyed do not find corroboration in recent Soviet research.[30] In this fashion did a portion of the Luftwaffe in the south squander an opportunity to rest and refit for the inevitable resumption of major operations.[31] In fact, it is likely that it was the Soviet air force, rather than the German, that extracted the greatest benefit from the Kuban operations. The commander of the VVS, General A. A. Novikov, used the protracted air battles over the bridgehead as a proving ground for his operational and tactical reforms, many gleaned from observation of the VVS's German adversaries.[32]

Since his appointment as commanding officer of the Red Air Force in March 1942, Novikov had pursued the goal of bridging the gap between the VVS and the Luftwaffe in the tactics of modern air warfare. Luftwaffe airmen owed much of their success in the first two years of the eastern campaign both to the technical superiority of the Bf 109 over the Soviet fighters and to their tactical skills as fighter pilots. Soviet industry went a long way towards eroding the German technical edge through the introduction of large quantities of thoroughly modern designs; Novikov accordingly concerned himself primarily with inculcating a grasp of modern air war tactics into the VVS. He established, through the Air Force Ministry Council, the "War Experience Analysis and Generalizations Section."[33] Like portions of the Luftwaffe General Staff's intelligence branch and the 8. Abteilung (the military science section), Novikov's new agency sought to interpret the lessons of the air war, many gleaned from observation of the enemy, and translate them into new methods of operational employment.

Accordingly, the air battles over the Kuban peninsula became for the Soviets "a true school of the flying art." According to one Soviet account:

The pilots approached the task of resolving their combat tasks in a creative manner as they improved their tactics and adopted new methods and approaches aimed at the foe's destruction. They acquired much experience in the conduct of air battles in groups; with each new battle they sharpened their mastery. During the

lulls between fights, the air regiments and divisions held numerous conferences at which combat experiences were exchanged.[34]

The VVS successfully adapted the proven German method of grouping
fighters in mutually-supporting pairs. In addition, the Soviets developed air tactics tailored to low-altitude air superiority battles, with
groups of aircraft echeloned at various altitudes to intercept incoming
German formations. This latter tactic, known as the ''Kuban Bookshelf''
or ''Kuban Escalator,'' proved particularly effective.[35] Chief Marshal of
Aviation K. A. Vershinin recalled, ''Each shelf of the bookcase fulfilled
its own distinct role. In the cases where the enemy aircraft were successful in escaping the attack of one shelf of the bookcase, they immediately
came under the others' fire. This combat formation permitted our
fighters to successfully engage the enemy's aircraft and to provide reliable cover to our own forces against their attacks.''[36]

By honing its combat proficiency in this fashion, the VVS went a long
way towards realizing the potential promised by its prewar doctrine:
that the air force might be a vital contributor to the attainment of an
operational decision. The enormous success gained by the VVS in the
great Soviet offensives of 1944 and 1945 proved the soundness of this
policy; it was not a product of Russian numerical superiority alone. At
the same time, the Luftwaffe gained little from its involvement in the
Kuban operations. In fact, the German air arm, in failing to secure local
air superiority over the peninsula, additionally reduced its chances to
achieve air dominance over more crucial sectors of the front during the
following summer.

In the absence of an energetic central coordinating command, the
eastern Luftflotten therefore used the aftermath of the Stalingrad crisis
period in a number of different and occasionally counterproductive
ways. Luftflotte 1 in the north, released from the constant pressure of
providing direct army support against local Soviet offensives, turned in
May and June towards attacks on enemy supply and communications
traffic.[37] Part of its admittedly depleted heavy bomber force attacked
industrial objectives in Leningrad, and in June participated in Luftflotte
6's strategic bombing attack on the Yaroslavl synthetic rubber factory.[38]
Typically, the leadership of an air fleet followed up a pause in enemy
offensive activity with a period of indirect army support (generally railway interdiction) and strategic bombing.

Luftwaffenkommando Ost, operating in the central front, initially used the pause to recover from the mauling it had taken during the winter defensive battles. Throughout April 1943, air activity by the force increased slowly. Luftwaffenkommando Ost flew 893 sorties during the first third of the month, rising to 1,533 for the second third, and 1,725 for the final third.[39] Many of these represent reconnaissance operations over the Kursk salient (1,638 sorties),[40] but a significant portion of the remainder represent heavy bomber and Stuka sorties against rail traffic and communications centers. The staff of Luftwaffenkommando Ost (as of May 1 upgraded to Luftflotte 6) had high hopes for this attack on the Soviet communications network. "Through this intensive attack upon enemy rail transport by day and night, on account of the lack of density and the limited reserve capacity of the Soviet rail network," Greim and his staff believed, "a carefully planned disruption of enemy supply traffic may be attained, thereby inflicting indirect but considerable damage upon his fighting potential."[41] This railway and transportation attack campaign eventually turned towards preparations for the Kursk offensive, but before that operation took place, the staff of Luftflotte 6, with the assistance of the general staff, launched a far more ambitious plan for restoring the initiative to the German air force in the east.

THE RESURGENCE OF OPERATIONAL AIR WARFARE

It is clear that the return of the Luftwaffe to what amounts to its prewar conception of strategic air attacks against enemy industry and other centers of national resistance was an internal decision, portended by the return of the Luftwaffe to the more congenial business of transportation (especially railway) attacks at the expense of battlefield air support. In terms of its actual target selection, however, the German air force general staff, in its first serious strategic bombing effort against Soviet industrial targets, relied upon target data furnished in part by the German army. One historian has argued that the Heer requested that the Luftwaffe conduct strategic attacks against Soviet tank production in order to prepare for Zitadelle.[42] Army requests for air attacks to offset the Soviet Union's growing material superiority do in fact predate the Kursk operation. The army's awareness that Soviet production capacity might outstrip Germany's was evident as early as the fall of 1941. At that time, the Soviet city that came to represent the common ground between army and Luftwaffe planners on the matter of German long-range bombing efforts in 1943–1944 first appeared in intelligence estimates: Gorki. The subject of Soviet tank production at Gorki came up during prisoner of war interrogations conducted by intelligence officers of the Second Panzer Army from September to November 1941. The commander of the Soviet Twentieth Army, Lieutenant-General F. A. Yershakov, captured in the disaster at Vyazma, referred to a planned Soviet 200-division expansion to take place by Spring 1942.[43] Other Soviet prisoners made repeated references to tank production at Leningrad, Moscow, and Gorki. One prisoner even provided a sketch of the factory complex in the last-named city.[44]

The question of launching a bombing campaign against such industrial targets remained largely in abeyance through 1942. Luftwaffe intelligence, as well as the staff of Luftwaffenkommando Ost, produced a number of studies dealing with aspects of the Soviet war economy and their vulnerability to air attack, but in the context of Führer Directives No. 41 and No. 45 there was little opportunity for the Luftwaffe to pursue a campaign against such objectives. Only the cessation of ground actions following Manstein's stabilization of the southern front (the same period utilized by the army to build up its armor reserves for the Kursk offensive) allowed the Luftwaffe General Staff to address the problems of mounting an aerial offensive against the Soviet Union's industrial capacity. Even then, the lack of harmony among the German air force leadership inhibited strategic direction. Göring, both during and after the war, maintained that "Russia presented only a very few strategic targets to an *operative Luftwaffe*, on the basis of its scattered industry and urban areas; and also few communications centers or marshalling yards in the European or American sense."[45] Many of his commanders felt that the dispersed and unsophisticated nature of the Soviet industrial and transportation system, on the contrary, made it an ideal target for air attack.

One of the more interesting questions regarding the resumption of industrial bombing in the eastern campaign is the precise origin of the shift in air strategy. Documentation on this aspect of the Luftwaffe's war is fragmentary; however, it appears that Jeschonnek and his colleague Generalleutnant Rudolf Meister, then head of the *Führungsstab* (operations staff), were the prime movers. Generalmajor Herhudt von

Rohden, head of the German air force's historical research section, credited Jeschonnek with launching "an effort to create an independent and self-supporting offensive air force in the east,"[46] although the constant need to provide air support to the army frustrated his attempt.

This "resurgence of the strategic vision" grew out of the noticeable shift, in all three eastern air fleets, from a direct army support posture during the crisis of the winter of 1942–1943 to a more far-ranging air campaign against the rear areas of the Soviet Union. The Luftwaffe operations staff seized upon this change of emphasis as a means to free the German air force from serving as the army's "fire brigade." As early as March 5, 1943, the eastern air fleets began conserving their bomber forces for these new tasks. While fully cognizant of the need not to betray the army's trust in the defensive battles following the Stalingrad catastrophe, Richthofen insisted that "crews and units, whose abilities and equipment allow them to undertake long-range penetrations, are only to be committed to close air support tasks in emergencies."[47] Even the renowned army support commander acknowledged that attacks on transportation and production were, in the coming weeks, to take prededence over other tasks.[48] By June 1943, some of Richthofen's bomber units, as well as those of Luftflotte 6, would "carry out attacks against purely strategic targets."[49] These targets ultimately consisted of the Molotov tank factory in Gorki, the synthetic rubber factory and asbestos works at Yaroslavl, and the petroleum refinery and ball bearing industry at Saratov. Had not the Kursk operation intervened, the series of strategic attacks would no doubt have been more extensive. Luftwaffe intelligence had, in fact, compiled its own target list for the summer of 1943, and that list bore only a tangential relationship to the targets eventually attacked that June. Its target list was heavily, although not exclusively, weighted towards the air armament industry.

Unlike some of the appreciations later crafted by this agency, Luftwaffe intelligence's first "in-house" target selection process showed a keen awareness of the capabilities, particularly range limitations, of the German bomber force in 1943. The planners at the operations branch intelligence section rejected out of hand targets beyond Heinkel range. Therefore, Soviet tank production plants were well down on its list of desirable targets. Gorki, with its two armored vehicle plants, paled in comparison with the huge factories in the Ural region, such as the Sverdlovsk complex.[50] The report stated, "The army is extremely interested in the destruction of these factories,"[51] yet the German air force planners believed that attacks on targets such as ball bearing factories might bring about the same overall effect.

One target group stood out above all the others: the aircraft engine industry. The Germans calculated that seven aircraft engine plants supplied the VVS with powerplants; five of these, accounting for fully seventy-eight percent of the production totals, were within bomber range. In order of importance, these factories were Factory No. 24, Kuibyshev, with one-fourth of total production and eighty-five percent of all ground attack aircraft (Il-2) engines; Factory No. 26 at Ufa, with thirty-one percent of total production and sixty percent of all fighter aircraft engine production; Factory No. 16 at Kazan, producing twelve percent of the total and sixty percent of all bomber engines; Factory No. 45, Moscow, with five percent of the total but the remaining fifteen percent of Il-2 engines; and finally Factory No. 466 at Gorki, five percent of the total production and one-tenth of all fighter engine production.[52] The report went on to argue:

> Already the shortfall of these factories has had weighty conse-
> quences for the aircraft production of the Soviet Union. Without
> the Kuibyshev, Ufa, Kasan and Moscow output, the Soviet air-
> craft industry would no longer be in a position to cover its losses
> at the front. The striking power of the Red Air Force may in this
> manner be broken in a short time.[53]

The attitude expressed in the above passage would become more prevalent as the war dragged on: in a battle against the Soviet Union's productive capacity, the Luftwaffe might perform a valuable service to the war effort by augmenting losses inflicted on the Soviet forces in combat by attacking the sources of production with its strategic bomber force. Thus, some elements of the Luftwaffe high command were aware that the war in the east was primarily a war of attrition, one that Germany could not win with its present air strategy.

Other key target industries included ball bearing plants (three of the five or six major plants were within range), synthetic rubber production (including the Yaroslavl factory, with twenty-three percent of estimated output), oil refineries, and iron and steel plants. The light metal industry did not have any major plants within striking range; Luftwaffe intelligence therefore discounted it as a potential target.[54]

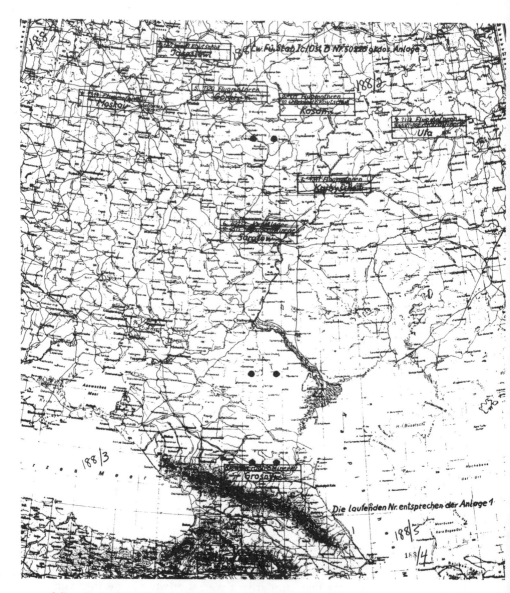

Map 3. Luftwaffe intelligence target map, June 1943. German air intelligence was a prime mover in the target selection process. A central thesis of its estimates was the need to attack the Soviet air armament industry. In this map, Luftwaffe analysts have denoted the aircraft engine plants at Moscow, Gorki, Kasan, Ufa, and Kuibyshev, along with synthetic rubber, crude oil and ball bearing production at Saratov, Grosny, and Yaroslavl. (OKL/2316, NARS T321/247)

The eventual selection of targets by the Luftwaffe high command drew much criticism in succeeding months, most notably from Albert Speer, Minister for Armaments and War Production.[55] Speer, in a postwar interrogation, said that the Luftwaffe staff "lacked appreciation of economic warfare;"[56] this ignorance accounted for the somewhat rudderless target selection process. Nevertheless, the air force general staff was to draw far-reaching conclusions from this incomplete foray into industrial attacks.

Somewhat surprisingly, in view of the great emphasis Ic placed upon the Soviet aircraft industry, it was ultimately the armored vehicle production facilities at Gorki that attracted the most Luftwaffe attention. As mentioned earlier, Gorki was one of the key targets which the army staffs promoted (and would continue to be so after the first series of Luftwaffe raids.)[57] A city of some 644,000 inhabitants, Gorki (formerly Nizhnii-Novgorod) was home to a number of important defense industries, including Armaments Factory No. 112, Krasnoye Sormovo, employing (by German estimates) 12,000 workers and producing 270 T-34 medium tanks monthly (fifteen percent of total production of this tank).[58] As such, it was the most important T-34 factory west of the Urals. In a bit of a targeting miscue, the aiming point designated for the seven raids in June-July 1943 was instead the State Motor Vehicle Plant No. 1 Molotov. The plant, known as the "Soviet Detroit," had been constructed with American assistance between 1927 and 1932; it was the largest automotive plant in the USSR.[59] Luftwaffe intelligence was well aware that this factory, although producing some T-34 components, was in the main turning out T-60 and T-70 light tanks, to the tune of 4,000 per year (an estimated sixty percent of total Soviet light tank output.)[60] One might conclude that the Luftwaffe hit the factory by mistake; the intelligence reports (complete with commentary by a representative of the armaments ministry) leave no doubt that the Molotov factory was the intended target.

Whatever the merits of the factory selected as the aiming point, the bombers of Luftflotten 4 and 6 began by raiding Gorki on four successive nights, June 5 through 8. The Luftwaffe dispatched 420 aircraft with 636 tons of bombs.[61] In the morning hours of June 4, the veteran bomber unit KG 55, with its II. and III. Gruppen, deployed from its main base at Stalino in the Ukraine to its jumping-off bases at Ssetschinskaya and Karatschev. A participant noted that the crews' morale was high after months of air transport and emergency army support operations.[62] The bombers took off on their mission at dusk, flying in the familiar *Kette* (3–aircraft element) formations utilized during the raids on Great Britain nearly three years before. Although the night was quite clear, and terrestrial navigation possible, KG 55 reportedly utilized the Radio Moscow transmitter as a navigation aid.[63]

German intelligence claimed great things for the Gorki operations. The Luftwaffe's effort ultimately totaled seven raids, comprising 682 sorties. The Heinkel 111 units dropped 1,015 tons of bombs, losing in the process only six aircraft (although the Soviets claimed 145).[64] Several aircraft were damaged, including one Heinkel from KG 4 which lost most of its tail section to a ramming attack by a Soviet night fighter.[65] Prisoner of war interrogation reports that filtered back to Luftwaffe intelligence in the following weeks seemed to bear out the initial optimism. On July 31, a POW confirmed that production at the Molotov factory had all but ceased as a result of the Luftwaffe strike.[66] Most fruitful was a series of prisoner interrogations conducted by the intelligence officer of the Grossdeutschland Panzergrenadier division. Four prisoners from the Soviet Fifty-seventh Independent Tank Regiment, who had been stationed in Gorki at the time of the air raids, testified on July 29 that while the Krasnoye Sormovo factory was untouched, the Molotov automobile factory (which, all the prisoners agreed, did in fact manufacture T-34 components) received extremely heavy damage.[67] While the long-term effect of the raids upon Soviet productivity may seem ambiguous, the Gorki complex remained near the top of the Luftwaffe's strategic bombing target list until the end of the war.

The other targets of the June series evidently did not merit the same amount of attention. On the night of June 9 and again on June 20, 102 and 88 bombers, respectively, raided Yaroslavl, dropping a total of 324 tons of bombs. Consultation with experts from the German chemical industry established that vital parts of the synthetic rubber plant SK 1 had sustained crippling damage.[68] Four additional raids between June 12–15 against oil refineries in Saratov added another 181 tons of bombs to the total.[69] The choice of targets here may reflect weaknesses in the Germans' own war economy. Synthetic (buna) rubber was one of the major achievements of the German quest for autarky, and petroleum shortages, as we shall see, eventually crippled the Luftwaffe on all fronts. Luftwaffe intelligence singled out the Saratov plants (target numbers SU 65 75 and SU 65 76) as potential bottlenecks. Despite the Soviet Union's vast oil reserves, only a few plants had the capability to refine crude oil into high octane aviation fuel.[70]

One would be hard pressed to make a case that the significance of these attacks stemmed from the destruction inflicted upon Soviet war potential. It is difficult to see how even the obliteration of the three attack objectives could be expected to "cripple" the Soviet war economy. The attacks on the three targets did portend a major shift in the employment of the Luftwaffe against the Soviet Union. In June of 1943, a number of leading Luftwaffe agencies, as well as army and civilian offices, began to regard strategic bombing as a means to offset Soviet numerical superiority and, in concert with losses inflicted upon the Soviet armed forces at the front, fatally weaken the military power of the Bolshevik enemy.

The mixture of military and civilian agencies reveals the basically social Darwinist aspect of the national socialist state. Competing fiefdoms often battled one other, instead of the enemy at the front, for access to scarce resources or influence. The agencies initially involved in planning and preparation of the strategic bombing program included the Luftwaffe general staff, the operations branch, air intelligence (Fremde Luftwaffen Ost), the Luftwaffe Verwaltungsamt (administrative office, also known as the Steinmann Office after one of its department heads), Milch's Office of Air Armament, Ambassador Walther Hewel of Joachim von Ribbentrop's Foreign Ministry, and most notably a committee set up by the ambitious Albert Speer, since February 1942 head of the Reich Ministry for Armaments and War Production.

In his postwar memoirs, Speer claimed that the impetus to intervene in such an operational matter as air force target selection came about as a result of the famous "Dam Busters" raid on the Möhne, Eder, and Sorpe dams by the RAF on May 17, 1943.[71] The threat which this RAF attack posed alerted Speer, as well as some Luftwaffe planners, to the potential of such precision strikes on vital economic points. In a conference with the Führer on May 30, Speer referred to the futility of "persuading the general staff of the air force to accept the advice of industrialists and engineers on the bombing of industrial targets."[72] This statement was in part untrue; Luftwaffe intelligence estimates of both the Gorki and Yaroslavl attacks refer to consultations with representatives from German industry and from Speer's own office. Speer was correct in his estimation that Luftwaffe targeting decisions in the air war against Britain and the USSR had not in the past reflected sound economic and industrial intelligence. The armaments minister reasoned that centralized direction of the strategic bombing effort was essential.

To that end, and at the height of the initial series of strategic raids, Speer on June 23 formed a committee, known variously as the "Working Committee on Economic Objectives for Air Attack"[73] or the "Carl Committee," after its chairman, Dr. Ing. Rudolf Carl, the Chief of Electric Power Planning. The group consisted of chemist Walter Schieber, also a department head in Speer's ministry; Paul Plieger, Reich Commissioner for Coal; and Walter Rohland, from the steel industry.[74] This group of technocrats was to decide on targeting for air attacks "in close collaboration with the General Staff of the air force."[75] Göring later claimed that he had initiated the collaboration;[76] in this case, Speer's account seems the more plausible. The Carl Committee, as will be seen, ultimately recommended the power plants in the Moscow-Upper Volga area as the most likely "choke point" in the Soviet armaments industry, yet the Luftwaffe had by then reached a similar conclusion through the exertions of its own agencies.

As if to confirm the old adage that "too many cooks spoil the broth," Ambassador Walther Hewel, Ribbentrop's liaison at the Führer's headquarters, on June 12 wrote to Jeschonnek with his own recommendations for air attacks on the Soviet hinterland.[77] Hewel's argument, a fairly simplistic one, maintained that the Soviet industry in the rear areas supplied the fighting fronts and therefore was of vital importance to the war effort. Hewel's support was to be instrumental later that autumn, when Korten and Speer attempted to convince Hitler to sanction the power plant attacks.[78]

As the plans took shape, Jeschonnek and the eastern air fleet commanders set about the task of reorganizing the Luftwaffe to carry out the mission, whatever the target system might turn out to be. Generaloberst Robert Ritter von Greim, commander of Luftflotte 6, the formation deploying much of the bomber strength in the east, acknowledged on June 12 that a military defeat of the Soviet armed forces in 1943 was most unlikely, and that the Luftwaffe needed to continue the strategic bombing policy successfully begun at Gorki.[79] As targets, Greim recommended aircraft engine factories, aviation fuel refineries, tank factories, locomotive works, and "bottlenecks yet to be determined."[80] He went on to argue that Luftflotte 6 benefitted from occupying a central position. Its bomber units, although ill-equipped to hit most of the vital Ural region, at least could reach most targets in central Russia.[81] In conclusion, the Luftflotte 6 staff desired to undertake the offensive against Soviet war production in the central sector of the front, and requested that a special operations staff coordinate the offensive.[82] Greim also requested better intelligence information on Soviet industrial targets.

In his reply to Greim, Jeschonnek "fully and entirely" concurred with the air fleet commander's assessment of the significance of industrial attacks, and desired to see them carried out with the greatest possible strength and speed. He also drew attention to a deficiency that would plague the Luftwaffe throughout its existence: the woeful lack of reliable information on the Soviet economy. Such intelligence would have been redundant had the Barbarossa offensive succeeded; now the German armed forces were paying the price for this lack of information. Jeschonnek even referred to the creation of a separate staff with the sole responsibility for target research, "charged with the study and the appreciation of the Russian war industry in toto, and utilizing all accessible research and press sources."[83] It is this failing in Luftwaffe intelligence that most likely accounts for Jeschonnek's (and later Korten's) willingness both to accept the advice and recommendations of the Carl Committee and, for that matter, to accede to the army's wishes regarding raids on the Gorki tank assembly plants.

That same week, Jeschonnek, in a discussion with Oberst I.G. Fritz Kless, chief of staff of Air Fleet 6, at Robinson, the advance Luftwaffe headquarters, gave his assent to a most specific series of proposals regarding the coming strategic air offensive. He promised the creation of a special staff (*Generalkommando*) to oversee the creation of the long-range bomber force. Strategic bomber units were to be grouped separately from their parent air fleets in the operational area of Luftflotte 6 under a distinct command authority (the suggested title was O. B. Luft Ost, or Supreme Air Commander East.)[84] This proposal anticipates Korten's designation in November 1943 of Fliegerkorps IV as a "pure" strategic bomber force subordinated to ObdL, not to any particular air fleet.

Both officers felt strongly that systematic attacks on the Soviet armaments industry would have a great effect on the overall conduct of the war. Greim further believed that a collapse in Soviet production caused by aerial attack (admittedly a pipe dream for the Luftwaffe in 1943) would have effects on all fronts. He reasoned that the Western Allies, faced with the tasks of building up their forces against Festung Europa, dealing with a renewed U-boat offensive, and other commitments, would then have to contend with the additional burden of propping up a tottering Soviet economy.[85]

The offensive against Soviet armaments centers was off to an uncertain start in June 1943. The Luftwaffe had a long way to go before it acquired the capability to replicate, even on a small scale, what the United States Eighth Army Air Force and RAF Bomber Command began inflicting upon German industry and population centers that year. The opening of the Kursk offensive on July 5, 1943, temporarily brought activity on the strategic bombing program to a halt. When it resumed, the Luftwaffe had a new chief of staff, who would bring many of the reforms initiated under Jeschonnek to a conclusion.

TOWARDS A MORE REFINED ARMY SUPPORT CAPABILITY: THE REFORMS BEFORE ZITADELLE

This chapter has hitherto focused on Jeschonnek's attempt to restore the Luftwaffe's status as an independent service in the months prior to the launching of the Wehrmacht's last major offensive on the eastern front at Kursk in July 1943. Much of Jeschonnek's and the general staff's attention was of necessity riveted upon the coming operation, code-named Zitadelle (Citadel). The Luftwaffe rarely conducted its activities divorced from the overall conduct of the war (*Gesamtkriegführung*). To Jeschonnek, it made little difference if the Luftwaffe defeated the Soviet Union solely through its own efforts or in concert with a decisive thrust by the army. Many of the reforms in the east, therefore, addressed the problem of further enhancing the German air force's ability to support the Ostheer in its offensive and defensive battles.

Prominent in many postwar perceptions of German military aviation have been accounts of the formidable anti-tank capability fielded by the Luftwaffe, particularly in the eastern campaign.[86] One need only mention the widely-read memoirs of Oberst Hans-Ulrich Rudel, who, during his service with Stukageschwader 2 and its successor units, was credited with the singlehanded destruction of 519 Soviet tanks (one-third of one month's production, according to Foreign Armies East's reckoning on

November 1, 1943). Concentration on Rudel's exploits, or on the dramatic sortie by Hauptmann Bruno Meyer's Hs 129 unit against a Soviet armored column during the fighting around Kursk on July 8, 1943 has seriously distorted popular understanding of the true nature of the Luftwaffe's anti-tank capability. Indeed, although this capability underwent some refinement and by mid-1943 was perhaps at the peak of its efficacy, the German air force's ability to execute the difficult task of direct intervention in armored combat from the air remained minimal. Of course, German aircraft from the beginning of the war had attacked armored vehicles when the opportunity presented itself. Most of the Luftwaffe's air armament was nevertheless unsuited to this task. The difficulty of hitting such small targets with bombs can readily be imagined.[87] The Luftwaffe's force structure was much more suited to indirect air support of the type practiced during Barbarossa and Taifun in 1941.

In any case, the deployment in the Crimea and the Kharkov areas during May and June 1942 of small numbers of Hs 129 purpose-built anti-tank aircraft raised the possibility of further exploring the so-called ''tank-busting'' role for tactical aviation. The Hs 129 was in essence a flying gun platform, armed with four 3 cm cannons; the use of forward-firing armament avoided the difficult task of placing a heavy aerial bomb on target.[88] Early use of the Hs 129 seemed promising: the inspector general of fighter aviation, Generalmajor Adolf Galland,[89] reported in March 1943 that newly-equipped Hs 129 units at the battle of Kharkov the previous June had destroyed twenty-three Soviet tanks.[90] In a few instances, the timely appearance of the anti-tank aircraft proved decisive, succeeding where conventionally armed Ju 87 units had failed. Galland reported on one such dramatic engagement:

On January 2, [1943], ground attack aircraft engaged in a ''free hunt'' in the area of Voroshilovgrad-Millerovo observed Soviet infantry escorted by tanks attacking a cut-off German battle group in a small village. After dropping their bombs on the attacking enemy, the cannon aircraft [Hs 129s] attacked the Soviet tanks and destroyed two T 34s, with the result that the remaining tanks as well as the enemy infantry fled.

An aircraft commander, shot down in this engagement, made a lucky emergency landing and was rescued by the German infantry. The German unit (575. Panzergrenadier) reported that it

had escaped destruction at the last minute due to the timely intervention of the ground attack pilots. The men regarded the aircraft
captain as having a "supernatural appearance"—they all wanted
to see, touch and talk with him. Even the wounded extended
their hands. The leader of the battle group, an elderly colonel,
placed himself at his service. There were, however, no cigarettes
left, as they (as well as the weapons and ammunition) had been
destroyed to keep them from falling into enemy hands.

Each grenadier was down to his last ten rounds of rifle ammunition. Only the ground attack aircraft saved the situation . . .[91]

Despite their acknowledgement of sentiments such as these, Galland
and the rest of the German air staff were not overly sanguine about the
extensive employment of these aircraft. In fact, they concluded that the
type had real usefulness only against small numbers of tanks which had
broken through the front lines and were operating in areas where anti-
tank defenses on the ground were weak.[92]

Galland's somewhat lukewarm attitude does not necessarily indicate
an unwillingness within the Luftwaffe to exploit new types of technology. The pessimism which greeted the Hs 129 stemmed instead from a
realistic appraisal of the machine's technical shortcomings. A few
months of operational use demonstrated the extreme vulnerability of the
engines to small-arms fire. Unlike the fuselage, which was heavily
armored, the twin engines of the Hs 129 were virtually unprotected. "At
least 75% of the antitank aircraft downed by enemy action were lost due
to hits in the engines by infantry weapons . . ."[93] Susceptibility to
combat damage was not the only defect in the design; Luftwaffe
mechanics referred to the aircraft's low-powered engines (French
Gnome et Rhône radials) as "veritable dust catchers,"[94] and the unimproved dirt airstrips that were the norm in the east wrought havoc on
the Hs 129's serviceability levels.

Indeed, Galland and his staff regarded the Soviet Il-2 Shturmovik as
a far more suitable aircraft in the ground attack/anti-tank role, despite its
single engine, as that engine was "nearly impervious to shot." In addition, the tiny airframe of the Hs 129 would readily accept neither more
powerful engines nor a heavier weapon.[95] The innovative little Hs 129
had all of the hallmarks of a technological dead end. At the Luftwaffe's
experimental station at Rechlin, work proceeded on a modified Ju 87D

Russian Winter. While a ground crewman lounges on a bomb, a Ju 88A medium bomber of KG 1 waits patiently in the background. (National Air and Space Museum, Smithsonian Institution, Photo No. 90-17316)

Field Marshal Albert Kesselring, commander of Luftflotte 2 during the initial phase of the war against the USSR, arrives at a Luftwaffe airfield in his FW 189. Kesselring, a former artilleryman, learned to fly at a somewhat advanced age after his transfer to the nascent Luftwaffe in the 1930s. (USAFHRC)

Luftwaffe versus Nature II. A Ju 88 of a reconnaissance unit connected to an engine heating truck. More common was the simpler expedient of thinning the engine oil with gasoline and applying the "cold-start" procedure. (USAFHRC)

Generaloberst Hans Jeschonnek, chief of the Luftwaffe General Staff until his suicide in August 1943. He confidently predicted a "proper war" as the Russian campaign opened in June 1941. (USAFHRC)

Aerial Resupply. Long before Stalingrad, the Luftwaffe bore a large proportion of the logistical burden in the eastern campaign. Here a "borrowed" Soviet horse and wagon team is used to unload supplies from a Ju 52 trimotor transport, still in temporary winter camouflage. (National Air and Space Museum, Smithsonian Institution, Photo No. 74-3087)

Mainstay of the Bomber Force. *A Heinkel 111H of KG 53 "Legion Condor," one of the components of General Rudolf Meister's Fliegerkorps IV, taxies out on a bombing mission with an external bomb load. (National Air and Space Museum, Smithsonian Institution, Photo No. 90-17312)*

Russian Mud. *A late-model Heinkel 111H of KG 4 "General Wever" mired in the mud on a grass airfield. (National Air and Space Museum, Smithsonian Institution, Photo No. 90-17317)*

Henschel 123. *Ground crewmen load bombs onto the underwing shackles of this venerable ground attack machine, for many years the sole close air support type in service with the Luftwaffe. (National Air and Space Museum, Smithsonian Institution, Photo No. 90-17307)*

Air Superiority. *Messerschmitt Bf 109Fs of JG 54 "Grünherz" deployed on a grass airfield. (National Air and Space Museum, Smithsonian Institution, Photo No. 73-4124)*

Jeschonnek tries out a motorcycle during a visit to a Luftwaffe base on the Eastern Front in the spring of 1942. (USAFHRC)

Typhoon. Do 17Z medium bomber, probably during the assault on Moscow in autumn 1941. By early 1942, the Do 17 had all but disappeared from front-line service; the Ju 88 and He 111 soldiered on until the end of the war. (National Air and Space Museum, Smithsonian Institution, Photo No. 74-3226)

Stalingrad Airlift. A collection of Ju 52s, assembled from every corner of the Reich (note the variety of camouflage and markings) prepares for the hazardous flight into the Stalingrad pocket during the attempt to resupply the Sixth Army, November 1942–February 1943. During the operation, 269 Ju 52s were lost. (National Air and Space Museum, Smithsonian Institution, Photo No. 90-17313)

Air Reconnaissance. *A Henschel 126 short-range reconnaissance aircraft operating from a frozen lake. Such aircraft generally operated under army control as had their precursors in the First World War. (National Air and Space Museum, Smithsonian Institution, Photo No. 90-17309)*

Close Support. *The FW 190F-8 was intended to replace the Ju 87 as the main close air support aircraft of the Luftwaffe. It never completely did so, but the marriage of the Luftwaffe's finest fighter and a large bomb load was a potent combination. (Photo by the author)*

Ritter von Greim in February 1944 argued for a series of concentrated attacks on Central Moscow in order to disrupt war production and shatter civilian morale. (USAFHRC)

mounting two 3.7 cm weapons, an aircraft type upon which Rudel was to bestow an exaggerated reputation. A special tank-hunting unit, Panzerjagdkommando Weiss, created in February 1943 with the blessing of Hitler, tested new designs under operational conditions.[96]

The military situation kept these German anti-tank aircraft improvisations to the fore even after their unsuitability became manifest. Within a few weeks after the battle of Kursk, General der Flieger Rudolf Meister of the Luftwaffe Operations Staff concluded that the "anti-tank air war," in view of the dramatic increases in Soviet tank production and the likelihood of continued Soviet armored breakthroughs, "[had] assumed greater importance."[97] In recognition of the lack of depth in the Ostheer's defenses, anti-tank aircraft explicitly were to make up for the lack of army anti-tank weapons. The Führungsstab recommended a substantial increase in the number of ground attack units. Moreover, instead of operating as isolated *Staffeln*, they would concentrate deployment in *Geschwader* strength.[98] At this time, the Luftwaffe command also attempted to clarify the minimum performance characteristics for this type of aircraft. These included an ability to carry the heaviest anti-tank armament (including, eventually, 5 cm and 7.5 cm anti-tank guns), high speed, adequate defensive armament, and the capability of returning to base after the loss of an engine to battle damage.

It was clear that none of the aircraft in service were really satisfactory; some in fact met none of these qualifications. The Ju 87 in particular was far too slow, unwieldy, and vulnerable, yet "considering the strained material position, the existing [Stuka] squadrons must remain through the winter as a transition."[99] The operations staff recommended a number of more advanced aircraft as possible successors. As it turned out, none of the aircraft mentioned saw service in the ground support or anti-tank role.[100] Meister concluded that the Luftwaffe's anti-tank forces, inadequate though they were, had to be carefully husbanded. This left them only the rather specialized function of attacking Soviet tanks that had broken through to the rear areas. In effect, like much of the German air force by 1943, the anti-tank units were nothing more than a fire brigade.

The Luftwaffe's efforts to extend its capability in another direction makes the anti-tank aircraft expedient appear carefully planned by comparison. This was the hasty organization in late 1942 of so-called "night harassing squadrons'' (*Störkampfstaffeln*), later termed *Nachtschlacht-flieger-Verbänden* (night ground attack units). Although the personnel of the German air force (especially those in the intelligence branch) tended to regard their Soviet opposite numbers with disdain, they were not above borrowing tactical innovations from the VVS when appropriate. Since the early days of the eastern campaign, small formations of obsolete Soviet aircraft, such as U-2 and Po-2 biplanes, began carrying out harassing attacks with small fragmentation bombs against German troop concentrations and lines of communication behind the front. German troops referred to these antiquated aircraft, often flown by women, as ''sewing machines.'' The constant presence of these nuisance raiders ''caused considerable discomfiture and not a few losses among concentrations of troops who were not yet used to air attack.''[101]

By the fall of 1942, the harassing raids had become a source of inspiration as well as annoyance to the German air force. General Günther Korten, at that time commanding the overstretched Luftwaffenkommando Don (as indicated earlier, most of the German air force's combat power was supporting the Stalingrad offensive, denuding other sectors of the front) cobbled together the first two Störkampfstaffeln out of thoroughly obsolete aircraft (Heinkel 46, Arado 66, Gotha 45, and Focke-Wulf 58, primarily training or observation aircraft never intended for a combat role) which he found in the backwater areas of his command. The aircraft underwent minimal modifications in the field, including the fitting of rudimentary bomb racks, and went into service. Needless to say, the ''harassment units'' did not receive the cream of the Luftwaffe's flying personnel; many such units were in fact derided as ''suicide'' or ''penal'' formations.[102]

Yet such expedients gradually assumed a more prominent role as the fortunes of the German air force in the east declined. Any measure that promised to get useful operational service out of obsolete aircraft seemed to be worth pursuing. By 1943 both army and air force units evolved cooperation procedures for the use of night harassment units. For example, XXX. Armeekorps in October 1943 reported good results from cooperation between its corps artillery and Störkampfstaffel 5 during clashes with Soviet forces opposite the corps' position.[103]. Even Allied intelligence estimates by July 1943 had drawn attention to the successes won by the Germans as a consequence of their developing such a ''second-line air force.''[104]

The increase in effectiveness led to an upgrading of the equipment of the air units. By early 1944, the *Nachtschlachtflieger* units were reequipping with the Ju 87 Stuka, by then too slow and vulnerable for unescorted daytime use.[105] Eventually, even advanced aircraft such as the FW 190 fighter-bomber found their way to the squadrons. An organizational change facilitated the expansion of the concept as well. No longer did the night ground attack units function independently within the frontline commands. The post of *Inspizient für die Nachtschlacht* (inspectorate for night ground attack), held by Oberstleutnant von Mauberge, appeared within the *General der Schlachtflieger*'s office.[106] The ad hoc nature of the units' mission gave way to a coherent doctrine for their employment.

As a response to the eastern enemy's recourse to night movement of troops and supplies, as well as many of the activities of Soviet partisan units, the *Nachtschlacht* units represented a most practical countermeasure. Indeed, the Germans found that the primitive aircraft of the night ground attack units worked best to counter the aerial resupply of partisan bands in the German army's rear areas, itself carried out by obsolescent Soviet aircraft.[107] By May 1944, directives for the utilization of these units indicated little difference in mission between *Nachtschlacht* and first-line German air force units participating in the ground battle by day:

> The main task of night ground attack units is the *direct and indirect support of the army on the battlefield at night* [italics in original] . . . [They] are generally to be employed at the *Schwerpunkt* of the ground battle . . .
>
> The most important targets are: troops on the march, transportation facilities, artillery and antiaircraft positions, quarters and supply depots, airfields . . .[108]

Moreover, command and control procedures, particularly regarding reliance on the *Fliegerverbindungsoffiziere* on the staffs of army commands down to divisional level, precisely corresponded to those employed in daylight support operations in 1941–1942.[109] The solving of problems unique to night operations, such as the provision of navigational beacons, communications apparatus, special weapons canisters, and so forth, required the initiative of the units on the scene. Consequently, the night ground attack squadrons, even when by mid-1944 they possessed nearly four hundred aircraft,[110] seem never to have lost their "improvised" character.

Except for isolated appearances in the Italian campaign and the closing stages of the battle for Germany, night ground attack squadrons remained a phenomenon confined to the eastern theater. Although a small chapter in the history of the air war, the development of the *Nachtschlachtflieger-Verbände* represents in microcosm how the German military faced the problems of the Second World War in general, and of the Russian campaign in particular.

Finally, the capability of the German daylight ground attack arm continued to improve during 1943. The case study of the campaign against Sevastopol presented in the previous chapter serves as an indication of the state of Luftwaffe close support doctrine in mid-1942. Since that time, several organizational, technical, and tactical innovations were underway that would eventually give the German air force a true "close air support" capability. These reforms are analogous to those which occurred in other air forces, notably the VVS in the Kuban and the USAAF and the RAF in the Mediterranean campaign.

The close air support procedures in use during the 1941 and 1942 campaigns possessed obvious limitations. Most difficult was the task of supporting rapidly advancing spearhead units or troops engaged in defensive operations at close quarters to the enemy. The nature of air support operations in the Soviet Union from late summer 1942 on indicated that the Luftwaffe and Heer needed to address jointly the vexing question of close air support procedures. The enhancement of this capability, not to reach fruition until spring 1944, began in the few months of relative quiescence prior to Zitadelle.

In early June of 1943, the operations staff of Army Group Center conducted a study, at the request of the OKH, of the efficiency of cooperation procedures between the close air support units of Luftflotte 6 and army formations during the preceding months. The orders from Heeresgruppe Mitte requested a thorough evaluation of all relevant after-action reports (*Erfahrungsberichte*) from corps and divisions (including *Panzer* and *Panzergrenadier* divisions) that had taken part in either offensive or defensive actions with the support of the Luftwaffe.[111] The army high command was especially interested in the following topics:

Cooperation with the liaison organs of the Luftwaffe (*Flivos*, operations control officers). Methods of liaison.

Request channels and the time necessary for requests [for air support] to be processed.

Indication of target (from maps, through use of signal munitions, or air reconnaissance).

Influence of the season, time of day and terrain on the mission of close air support units.

Possibilities for breaking off an attack by ground attack aircraft which has already begun.

Effects of various aircraft types (Stukas, ground attack, twin-engined fighter) and types of targets especially suitable or unsuitable for attack by these types.

Anti-tank combat from the air.

Conduct of friendly troops before, during and after missions by close-support aircraft.

And particularly [italics in original]:

Indication of own forward line. Prevention of attacks on friendly troops.

Observation of air force activity by the ground troops. Evaluation of that activity.

How may the ground troops take advantage of air activity?

Can the ground troops support the mission of the close support formations by drawing out enemy forces (for example, tanks) so that they become a suitable target for air attack?[112]

The army's response to this request for information was swift, conscientious, and detailed. The variety of responses indicated the lack of unified air support procedures in mid-1943, as well as the inescapable fact that, on the vast eastern front, experiences with Luftwaffe support were bound to exhibit wide variance. The Twenty-fifth Panzergrenadier Division, for example, could only report one instance (in August 1942) in which one of its regiments participated in an action supported by the Luftwaffe's close air support forces.[113] Thus, there existed no "typical" response to OKH's request for information; some general patterns did nevertheless emerge. Taken collectively, these *Erfahrungsberichten* reveal that even the Luftwaffe was a long way from developing a completely effective close air support formula.

The army units reported that they valued the cooperation with the *Flivo* assigned to the ground forces staff immensely. In many cases, a

personal rapport between the divisional commander or operations officer and their Luftwaffe counterparts materially aided the smooth func-
tioning of the liaison process. Fourth Army's report reduced this problem to a simple formula: "Successful cooperation with the *Flivo* is in the
main dependent upon his personality."[114] Thus, wartime experience
seemed to bear out Jeschonnek's 1939 guidelines for successful cooperation between air and ground forces.[115] Army units repeatedly praised
Luftwaffe officers (including, in some cases, the commander of the flying unit itself) who personally acquainted themselves with the terrain
and with the army's operational plans. The commanding general of the
Ninety-fifth Infantry Division further noted that, "in the case of major
operations, personal discussions between the commander of the ground
forces and the air force commander . . . are indispensable. They lead to
100% cooperation."[116] One can detect the influence of Richthofen on the
army's insistence on extensive personal contact in order to guarantee
the effectiveness of Luftwaffe support.

If the army exhibited enthusiasm for the personnel the Luftwaffe provided for air/ground cooperation, it was less happy with the technical
means available. By far the most frequent complaint was the excessive time
required for a request for air support to travel through the necessary army
and Luftwaffe channels and be transformed into an actual air support mission. The many units responding to the survey reported response times
ranging from one and one-half to five hours. In most cases, the army attributed this delay to the lack of direct radio links between the ground troops
and the flying units overhead.[117] During some operations, the *Flivos* had
"air control detachments," or *Einsatz-Leitoffiziere*, serving on their staffs
who accompanied the advancing units and could communicate directly
with the airborne Luftwaffe forces. In many cases, however, these interim
links were not available even for spearhead divisions.[118] Therefore, the
cancellation or redirection of an attack already in progress was a most
difficult task. During periods of close air support, the ground troops had to
fall back on the old procedures of employing flares, smoke cartridges, or the
white and yellow visual panels of the type Fliegerkorps VIII employed in
1941–1942.[119] In sum, most units concurred with Fourth Army's conclusion
that "liaison between ground troops and flying units is not yet close nor
sure enough."[120]

Many of the preferences voiced by the army units were not surprising. All showed a marked predilection for Stuka support, by virtue of

the aircraft's greater bombing accuracy and noticeable effect on enemy morale. Significantly, many units did not believe that tanks could be engaged effectively from the air, due to their small size and the need to score a direct hit in order to cause any appreciable damage. Most of the army units participating in the survey had no firsthand knowledge of such combat, although Fourth Army ventured to guess that "a heavily-armed twin-engined fighter would doubtless prove a dangerous adversary to an enemy tank which has broken through the lines,"[121] a sentiment shared by the Luftwaffe command.

It is unlikely that Luftflotte 6 was able to digest this information in time to put any far-reaching reforms into effect prior to Zitadelle. New manuals and procedures for close air support practice issued in the fall of 1943 or the spring of 1944 under Korten, however, address many of the shortcomings illuminated by Army Group Center's candid examination of existing procedures.

OPERATION ZITADELLE: THE BATTLE OF KURSK, JULY 1943

In the midst of the German air force's reorganization and recovery process came the pivotal event of the summer 1943 campaigning season: the attempt by the reconstituted *Panzerwaffe* to regain the initiative in the USSR through an operational victory against Soviet forces in the Kursk salient. It is not the purpose of this study to enter upon a lengthy debate about the wisdom of such an attempt, or to weigh Hitler's insistence on the offensive against the much-touted "mobile defense," in which Manstein would combine a German withdrawal with an armored riposte. What is significant is how the Luftwaffe approached its task, and what impact the defeat of the German forces at Kursk and their subsequent withdrawal had upon German air strategy.

Luftwaffe participation in preparations for the operation allows one to evaluate for the last time German air force procedures for supporting a large-scale offensive. Many of the techniques familiar in the campaigns of 1941 and 1942 appear for the last time during Zitadelle. Although it was the Germans who took the initiative in launching the offensive, the Wehrmacht, and in particular the Luftwaffe, operated under the constraint of almost continuous action prior to Zitadelle. Therefore, it was undoubtedly the Soviet forces that derived the greatest benefit from the extended period of preparation.

Many historians cite the frequent delays in the launching of the Kursk offensive as one of the principal reasons for its failure.[122] Undoubtedly this is so; the momentary advantages which such an attack might have attained in late spring had all but disappeared by July. From the point of view of the Luftwaffe, however, it is doubtful that its depleted squadrons could have provided adequate support for even a limited offensive in April-May. As discussed earlier, the Luftwaffe, after the Stalingrad airlift, found itself fully committed to emergency defensive battles, followed by the support of Manstein's successful recovery at Kharkov, the resupply of the Kuban, and other tasks. There is no doubt that the Luftwaffe was in dire need of a recuperation period such as the one permitted by the cessation of mobile operations in April 1943.[123] The remarkable numerical recovery of the eastern air fleets would not have occurred had the German air force been in continuous action throughout 1943.

EFFECTIVE STRENGTH OF OPERATIONAL LUFTWAFFE UNITS EASTERN FRONT, May 31, 1943[124]

Aircraft type	Luftflotte			
	1	4	5	6
Short-range recce	45	108	9	138
Long-range recce	37	69	26	62
Fighter	102	171	73	201
Night Fighter	6	17	—	9
Zerstörer/Schlacht	—	166	13	38
Bomber	77	329	50	124
Night Harassment	83	86	—	51
Stuka	35	274	23	102
Transport	—	147	14	62
Miscellaneous	100	361	27	180
Totals	485	1,728	235	967
Grand Total	3,415			

A number of German formations, particularly Fliegerkorps VIII, as of May 1943 under the command of General der Flieger Hans Seidemann, used the pause to conserve and build up their forces for the coming assault, mindful of the key role Luftwaffe support would play in

Zitadelle.[125] Fliegerkorps VIII, charged with supporting the southern pincer of the advance (Fourth Panzer Army and Armeeabteilung Kempf) even to the exclusion of the rest of the breakthrough sector,[126] adhered to this principle of concentration during the opening phases of the battle. Indeed, Fliegerkorps VIII, augmented by elements of the Hungarian Air Corps, in early July boasted 1,185 available combat aircraft.[127] The other formations of Luftflotte 4, Fliegerkorps I and IV, numerically much smaller than Seidemann's force, remained in the Kuban and the southern sectors respectively.[128] In accordance with Göring's directive for the operation, these units had been virtually stripped of flying, anti-aircraft and signals personnel in order to reinforce the *Schwerpunkt*.[129] Only the staffs of I. and IV. Fliegerkorps remained on the Mius front, in part to participate in deception operations.[130] Transfer of their flying units to bases in the Kharkov area proceeded with dispatch. As late as June 26, III./KG 55 was carrying out daily railway interdiction operations under Fliegerkorps IV from its base at Stalino. Less than a week later, the *Gruppe*, now flying out of the field at Rogau east of Kharkov, found itself under Fliegerkorps VIII, and was shortly thereafter heavily committed to support of Zitadelle.[131]

The preparations by Luftflotte 4 for this offensive are entirely consistent with the operational methods of Richthofen. To Manstein's immense agitation, however, Hitler followed up the extraordinary close air support commander's promotion to Field Marshal on February 16, 1943 with his transfer one month prior to Zitadelle to the command of Luftflotte 2 in Italy. Hitler and Göring hoped that the outspoken and forceful Richthofen would successfully organize the air defense of the southern front against the expected Anglo-American invasion.[132] Manstein attempted to have Richthofen kept in command of Luftflotte 4 until the conclusion of Zitadelle, but this effort "led only to a sharp controversy with Göring, who was unwilling to admit how decisively important the influence of such a personality as von Richthofen was for the combat forces."[133] Jeschonnek, who by this time found his position as chief of the Luftwaffe general staff thoroughly untenable, made a concerted effort to take over Richthofen's former eastern front command.[134] Leadership of Luftflotte 4 instead went to an ex-Reichswehr officer, General der Flieger Otto Dessloch, who seems to have left most of the operational planning to the staff he inherited from Richthofen.

Tactical improvements for the operation included a further refinement of the liaison procedures that Richthofen had initiated between
Luftwaffe and Heer. Fliegerkorps VIII made lavish use of *Fliegerverbin-
dungstruppen* among the army staffs: every *Panzer* division, as well as the
staff of the SS-Panzerkorps, III. and XLVIII. Panzerkorps, XI. Armeekorps, Armeeabteilung Kempf, and Fourth Panzer Army, had a fully
equipped, mobile liaison unit attached.[135] Their mission was to provide
both Luftwaffe and Army staffs with a "running commentary" of the
course of operations and to cut down the response time for German air
support strikes. In addition to eight ground attack or dive-bomber *Gruppen*, Fliegerkorps VIII also deployed the antitank unit IV.(Pz)/SG 9, with
approximately sixty Hs 129 tank killers. In some of the ground attack
units the FW 190, a much more modern aircraft, began to replace the
aging Ju 87 dive bombers.

On balance, Fliegerkorps VIII made adequate provisions for logistical support and aircraft replacement.[136] (The same could not be said
for Luftflotte 6, which entered the battle with virtually no reserves
and suffered a corresponding decline in effectiveness as the battle
developed.)[137] Seidemann recalled that each day the air corps'
buildup for Zitadelle required one supply train containing 1,000 tons
of bombs and ammunition as well as 1,020 tons of aviation fuel.[138]
Fliegerkorps VIII relied upon workers from the Reich Labor Service
(RAD) and numbers of Soviet POWs to unload the supply trains.
Attention to such logistical matters in part explains the ninety percent serviceability rate attained by Fliegerkorps VIII on the opening
day of the attack.

In sum, the forces of Luftflotte 4 seem to have adhered closely to the
spirit of the general directives issued by the high command and the OKL
calling for a maximum concentration of Luftwaffe strength for the Kursk
battle.[139] That air fleet, however, was responsible for only the southern
arm of the pincer operation. The northern arm, Generaloberst Walther
Model's Ninth Army, drew its air support from the numerically smaller
Luftflotte 6, under Ritter von Greim. The major striking force of this air
fleet was concentrated in General der Flieger Paul Deichmann's 1.
Fliegerdivision (with approximately 730 aircraft). The command of
Luftflotte 6 possessed a strikingly different attitude towards the coming
offensive than did its southern counterpart. While Luftflotte 4 ruthlessly
concentrated its units for close support duty, Greim's air fleet divided its

combat power among a wide range of strategic, indirect army support, and even psychological warfare tasks.

Although the army initially requested attacks on Soviet armament factories, the series of raids on Gorki and other targets in June 1943 recounted earlier in this chapter grew out of the Luftwaffe General Staff's own efforts to wage independent air operations. There is little doubt that the impressive sortie totals mounted for the June 1943 strategic bombing campaign reduced significantly the amount of preparation, particularly railway interdiction, that the Luftwaffe was able to carry out in the months prior to Zitadelle.

Both air fleets had devoted a large percentage of sorties to the interruption of Soviet transport. Throughout the spring of 1943, Fliegerkorps I, IV, and VIII struck at "vital railway junctions" behind the Soviet front lines with the intention of disrupting Red Army concentrations in the area.[140] The most successful attack of this series was undoubtedly the June 2 mass raid on the Kursk railway station. Luftwaffe intelligence identified the Kursk station as the choke point for the eastward movement of Soviet forces traveling from Voronezh into the Kursk salient.[141] Units of Luftflotte 6 attacked in three waves (at 4:00, 7:20 and 10:30 A.M.) with a total of 164 aircraft. This attack caused heavy damage to the station facilities and destroyed approximately two hundred railway cars.[142] Army sources claim that, as a result of the Luftwaffe's interdiction efforts, "the Russian build-up identified in the Kursk region was disturbed quite substantially."[143] It was nevertheless clear to most observers that the Luftwaffe lacked the strength to carry out the full range of interdiction and support tasks required. Shortly prior to Zitadelle, Jeschonnek remarked to Greim that Luftwaffe strength "was not sufficient to guarantee victory."[144] Jeschonnek's and Greim's policy of carrying out strategic air actions diluted the German effort. In spite of the necessity of stemming the Soviet buildup that summer, railway interdiction suffered as a result of Luftflotte 6's new orientation. Herhudt von Rohden, writing shortly after the war, regarded railway interdiction as a mission more closely in line with the demands of the overall conflict than were the nascent industrial attacks. He maintained, "The correct course of action would have been to concentrate all power against those rail lines whose interruption would lead to the collapse of those Russian concentrations which posed such a great danger at that time."[145] In terms of overall strategic conduct of the campaign, the strategic bombing venture of June 1943 was not only ineffectual, but ultimately harmful to Germany's military position.

Luftwaffe intelligence did, at a late date, attempt to isolate those railway installations the destruction of which might bring long-term or "strategic" benefits beyond mere preparation for the coming offensive. Intelligence planners noted that, of three major routes linking Siberia to European Russia, the southern route (Chelyabinsk-Ryasan-Moscow) offered the greatest possibilities (even to the extent of interrupting lend-lease shipments to the southern and central front.)[146] German intelligence reduced the problem of severing the Soviet communication and supply artery to the destruction of only three railway bridges.[147] The quest for simple solutions through the use of air power may have been compelling; in any event the Luftwaffe, in the weeks preceding Zitadelle, made no attempt to carry out this or any similar mission.

Other employment for the Luftwaffe's bomber force produced a steady drain on Luftflotte 6's capabilities. In a consultation between Jeschonnek and Greim's chief of staff, Kless, the two officers discussed a scheme to dispatch "bomber units in formations of 20 to 30 aircraft" in "systematic terror attacks . . . for the breaking of Russian morale" against Soviet cities behind the front lines.[148] These actions, both in preparation for and reinforcement of Operation Zitadelle, were intended to bring about the collapse of Soviet powers of resistance. The fact that Jeschonnek regarded Luftwaffe strength as inadequate even for the tasks of directly supporting Zitadelle provides yet another example of the inability of the Luftwaffe leadership to make ends conform to means.

Bombs were not the only weapons aimed at Soviet morale prior to the offensive; psychological weapons were also in the arsenal. The *Luftflotten* preparing for Zitadelle referred not only to the collateral effects on morale of bombing attacks, but to the dissemination of propaganda from the air. One of the more interesting aspects of the series of strategic and interdiction attacks launched in June 1943 was the large amount of space allocated in the bomb bays of the Luftwaffe's aircraft for propaganda leaflets. Millions of these small, generally simplistic appeals to Soviet "reason" were scattered across the landscape of the eastern front. Since the 1941 campaign, the high command had believed that such psychological warfare had an important role to play in the conduct of the war against Russia.

In general, the leaflets were merely invitations to desert, little different from the "safe-conduct" passes dropped by Allied forces in Europe
and the Mediterranean. Richthofen himself noted that simple leaflets
brought the greatest results; his own air corps' propaganda in 1941 was
of "classic brevity." The leaflets, accompanied by bombs, read, "'No
one is shot! But, if you do not desert immediately, we will come
again!'"[149] As the war dragged on, German planners did not lose their
fascination for Luftwaffe-delivered propaganda, jointly developed by
the OKH, OKW and German air force intelligence (Ic/IV). In fact, the
Luftwaffe participated in "the most extensive psychological warfare
operation of the campaign"[150] in May 1943, during the period of preparation prior to Zitadelle. This was Operation Silberstreif (Silver Lining),
which consisted of a mass airdrop of propaganda leaflets over the Soviet
rear areas.

German air intelligence, on the basis of prisoner interrogations, concluded that air-dropped propaganda was most effective when scattered
behind the lines, especially in large cities, as opposed to at the front, in
order to ensure maximum exposure to the messages.[151] The Silberstreif
effort adhered to this philosophy, and the impressive total of 84.5 million leaflets cascaded down on the Soviet rear areas between May 7 and
May 15.[152]

Luftwaffe intelligence interpreters seemed quite happy with the
results. The Luftwaffe reported that the number of deserters "doubled"
during that time (although it still amounted in May only to a paltry total
of 2,424),[153] and at least one of the infantry divisions in the area had to
be replaced by a reliable Soviet "Guards" division.[154] POW interrogations revealed that the Soviet command instituted strict anti-desertion
measures, including threats to exile deserters' families to Siberia. Moreover, only "reliable" officers were to collect the scattered leaflets for
burning, and any soldier caught reading said leaflets was to be shot.

The whole German propaganda campaign reveals much about the
attitude of Luftwaffe and army intelligence towards their opponent.
"Principles for active propaganda" against the Soviets included a
reminder to continually repeat a few, easily comprehensible themes, as
this was all that the Soviet soldier might be expected to grasp.[155] Most of
the leaflets referred to the hopeless immediate military situation. One
depicted an iron ring of German armor accompanied by the injunction,
"You are surrounded! But there is a way out . . ." and incorporated a

safe-conduct pass on the reverse. Occasionally, leaflets portrayed political subjects (one depicted the "good ally" Stalin obligingly serving the greedy plutocrat Winston Churchill a dead Soviet infantryman on a platter). Most elaborate, and tragic in view of the treatment actually accorded Soviet prisoners-of-war by their German captors, was a two-page illustrated leaflet extolling the near-ideal conditions of German captivity. Soviet soldiers were shown enjoying cigarettes and accordion music and receiving medical treatment from grinning German army doctors. One unusual departure was a late 1944 leaflet threatening use of the V-1 flying bomb against Soviet cities.[156] One must conclude that the German command, perhaps mindful of the collapse of the Tsarist army in 1917, believed psychological warfare to be an important component of the war against the USSR. In fact, the supposed drain on Soviet manpower through desertion did not seem to have a visible effect on Soviet combat strength. Moreover, in the case of Operation Silberstreif the frequent postponements of the Kursk offensive diluted any impact the psychological campaign may have had.[157]

In conclusion, the Luftwaffe's preparations for Zitadelle ranged from the pragmatic to the irrelevant. Luftflotten 4 and 6 demonstrate effectively the two major currents in Luftwaffe doctrinal thinking at mid-war. On the one hand, the command staffs of Air Fleet 4 toiled ceaselessly and with a fair degree of success to ensure that their force's contribution to Zitadelle would reinforce the efforts of the army, in effect, a somewhat narrow interpretation of *operativer Luftkrieg*, as the *Luftflotte* staff made no attempt to evaluate the operational or strategic soundness of the army's plan. At the same time, Greim's Luftflotte 6, with the blessing of Jeschonnek, undertook far-reaching efforts to expand the capabilities of the German air force in the east, with an almost total lack of appreciation for the serious limitations of the forces at hand. Providing support for the German army in Zitadelle was only one task among many for the air fleet; the result was the failure to concentrate what little force was available.

The actual course of the Kursk operation need not be recounted in detail. The German armored spearheads jumped off in the early morning hours of July 5, 1943, against one of the most elaborately constructed defensive networks ever encountered. Most historians believe that the operation "had not the slightest chance of achieving surprise" due to the lengthy period of concentration, innumerable delays caused in part

by Hitler's desire to concentrate the greatest possible number of Pan-
zerkampfwagen V "Panther" tanks in the armored divisions, and the
limited possibilities for maneuver in the constricted Kursk salient.[158] It is
difficult to understand, then, why the operational directive issued to
Fliegerkorps VIII prohibited air superiority strikes prior to the launching
of the offensive "in the hope of ensuring tactical surprise (time and
place of attack)."[159] To this end, VIII. Fliegerkorps had participated in a
deception attack on the west flank of the southern breakthrough sector
one day prior to Zitadelle; the attack made little progress and its deception value appears to have been nil.

Fliegerkorps VIII's attacking units nearly suffered serious losses on
the first morning of the battle, as a preemptive Soviet air strike aimed at
its forward airfields was only detected and defeated by the narrowest of
margins by the German radar and fighter defenses.[160] The Luftwaffe
was then able to proceed with its mission: the provision of concentrated
air support for the armored spearheads. In the south, Fliegerkorps VIII
placed its main emphasis over the leading units of Armeeabteilung
Kempf and the Fourth Panzer Army, specifically the SS Panzer Corps
and the XLVIII Panzer Corps.[161] Even long-range bomber units participated directly in the ground battle. For example, on the first day of the
offensive, III./KG 55 flew four separate missions against Soviet field
positions and tank concentrations.[162] The vulnerable Heinkel 111s flew
at an attack altitude of 2,600–4,000 meters above the battlefield—hardly
the ideal employment for this type of aircraft.

Both northern and southern German armored wedges made excru-
ciatingly slow progress through the Soviet defensive belts, and it is
unlikely that a greater application of air power by the Luftwaffe could
have materially altered the outcome of the battle. Certain elements of
the Luftwaffe's support forces performed admirably; on a number of
occasions, even the temperamental Hs 129 tank destroyer aircraft
blunted Soviet armored attacks. In Fliegerkorps VIII's sector, air-ground
cooperation procedures worked extremely well, although in some cases
the cumbersome *Sd. Kfz. 305* half tracks carrying the air control detachments could not keep up with the advancing mechanized spearheads.[163]
A more serious flaw was the tendency, on the orders of OKL, to divert
resources from the southern penetration in order to reinforce the less
successful northern drive of the Ninth Army. As early as the afternoon
of July 7, Fliegerkorps VIII surrendered KG 3, JG 3 and SG 3—thirty

percent of its bomber force, forty percent of its fighters, and one-half of its ground attack strength—north to the Orel sector.[164] This redeployment negated much of Fliegerkorps VIII's careful preparations for "massive concentration." German air intelligence claimed that the Luftwaffe achieved air superiority during the operation, and cited fantastic figures of Soviet aircraft destroyed.[165] German intelligence figures for the period July 1 to July 15 alone claim the destruction of 1,961 enemy aircraft, including 705 ground attack planes, 907 fighters, and 207 bombers.[166] Luftwaffe losses for the campaign, however, were in the long run unsupportable, and would ultimately compel the German air force general staff to address the unfavorable aircraft production situation obtaining between the Luftwaffe and the VVS.

Finally, whatever the true ratio of aircraft losses between the Luftwaffe and its VVS adversary, there is no doubt that the Soviet sacrifices, however debilitating they may have been to the Red Air Force's combat strength, contributed to a strategic victory of the first order. The Luftwaffe intelligence analysts, myopically concerned with enumerating the VVS's losses, could make no such claim. The German panzer force on July 12 launched its remaining armored strength on what became known as the "death ride" against the still intact Soviet defensive system and armored reserves. A German noncommissioned officer pronounced the following verdict on the battle's final phase:

> We had been warned to expect resistance from *pak* and some tanks in static positions, also the possibility of a few independent brigades of the slower KV type. In fact we found ourselves taking on a seemingly inexhaustible mass of enemy armor—never have I received such an overwhelming impression of Russian strength and numbers as on that day. The clouds of dust made it difficult to get help from the *Luftwaffe*, and soon many of the T-34s had broken past our screen and were streaming like rats all over the old battle-field . . .[167]

On July 13, 1943, Hitler, citing the Allied landings in Sicily three days earlier, cancelled Operation Zitadelle, but the commitment of both army and Luftwaffe was just beginning. Soviet armies, undisturbed in the regions bordering the Kursk salient, almost immediately turned the German check at Kursk into a full-scale rout. Once again, the Luftwaffe was compelled to fight as an emergency army support arm during the battles of Belgorod, the Orel salient, and other actions in the Soviet 1943 summer offensive. Operation Zitadelle failed on both the operational and strategic levels. Despite the fearful casualties which the German armored force inflicted upon the Soviet mobile formations, the battle's outcome did not redress the Ostheer's unfavorable numerical relationship to its Red Army adversaries. Moreover, the German army did not succeed in recovering the "initiative," one of Hitler's aims for the operation. Assessing the operation's impact upon the German air force is more difficult. In terms of the Luftwaffe's mission, the battles at Kursk and Orel were more reminiscent of the spring 1942 campaign against Sevastopol ("to decide a battle in a limited area")[168] than the 1941 campaign, in which the Luftwaffe was expected to contribute to the strategic decision. Yet the scope of even local offensives had by 1943 increased dramatically. The number of Luftwaffe aircraft committed to the battle against the Kursk salient (some 1,830 operational combat types)[169] was not appreciably less than that deployed against the entire Soviet Union during Barbarossa. The war had attained unparalleled dimensions, and for the Luftwaffe's army support forces, Kursk was something of a watershed. Never again did Fliegerkorps VIII, still the only true close air support force in the Luftwaffe, appear in battle en masse.[170] Even a technically improved close air support formula no longer sufficed to guarantee even operational decisions.

The 1943 campaigning season, then, ended as it had begun: with the Luftwaffe operating in a reactive army support role, rushing without overall strategic or operational guidance from one sector to another. Whereas in previous campaigns the German command generally decided on the location of the *Schwerpunkt*, from summer 1943 on it was the Soviet high command that made the decision. Moreover, the Luftwaffe was fully occupied with buttressing the often inadequate German defense, now that major offensive operations were a thing of the past. The 8. Abteilung in 1944 concluded, "Thus, our air power was dissipated and it was not possible to give any attention to troop concentrations behind the enemy's front."[171]

The path to this state of affairs was a circuitous one. The Luftwaffe command had emerged from the Stalingrad disaster with the realization that army support on the 1942 pattern was not the proper role for the German air force in the east, given its existing doctrine and force structure. The spring of 1943 marked the first sustained attempt by the Luftwaffe general staff and certain air fleet personnel to apply classical strategic bombardment concepts to the war against the Soviet Union. *Operativer Luftkrieg* theory had always stressed the peculiar properties possessed by long-range air power; in mid-1943, these assumed greater importance. At the same time, other elements within the German air force leadership continued to hone battlefield support procedures to a fine edge. The tactical success of the latter was considerable; the strategic effects of the former, negligible. Nevertheless, the Luftwaffe general staff was to draw surprising conclusions from the experiences of the 1943 campaign. The growing numerical superiority of the VVS and the loss of initiative on the main sectors of the eastern front posed an intractable dilemma for the Luftwaffe general staff. The solution they chose was long-range bombardment of the most important enemy war industries; they would adhere to this chimera until the Red Army was poised to cross the Oder and take Berlin.

CHAPTER FIVE

OLD DOCTRINE, NEW DIRECTIONS: THE KORTEN ERA

With the failure of the Kursk offensive, German military planners could no longer argue that the *Schwerpunkt* in the east lay with an attacking German ground force. Instead, the Red Army possessed the initiative, and the Ostheer could only react to the aggressive actions of its numerically superior and operationally proficient adversary. Astute Soviet deception (*maskirovka*) operations confounded German military intelligence as to the time and location of Red Army offensives, reducing still further the Wehrmacht's ability to mount an effective response. Against such a gloomy military backdrop, in which the need for air support of the German army was critical, the resumption of strategic bombing activity by the Luftwaffe seems somewhat curious. In light of German air power doctrine, the shift in emphasis becomes more explicable. Wever's 1936 formulation spoke of a situation that seemed to address the German dilemma in late 1943:

> When a stagnation of the ground battle takes place, the air force is the only means by which a bleeding away of one's own strength may be averted, and a decision be obtained.
>
> This success requires the complete transfer of emphasis to air armament at the expense of other means of war.

149

A shift in the conduct of war requires time and preparation.[1]

Direct support of the Ostheer in a Blitzkrieg style offensive no longer promised to bring about a strategic decision. The experiences of the German air force, particularly the bomber arm, in two winters of emergency defensive operations had convinced a significant portion of the Luftwaffe's leadership that such employment was not cost-effective, or at best should be left to the evolving ground-attack force. For the first time in the eastern campaign, the course of the war allowed the Luftwaffe the opportunity to carry the offensive to the Soviet "centers of national resistance." The objective was still the destruction of the military power of the Soviet Union; that principle remained unchanged from the beginning of Barbarossa. The difference was one of means: in late 1943, the Luftwaffe long-range bomber forces would attempt to strike the decisive blow.

In many histories of the air war, this effort is overshadowed by the simultaneously-occurring air battles over the Third Reich, including the "Big Week" raids in February 1944, that culminated in the destruction of the German fighter arm. Indeed, the air commitment over the home territories seriously and consistently limited the numbers of aircraft and quantity of materiel available to the Luftwaffe in its struggle in the east. The home defense fighter program curtailed the production of multi-engined aircraft, and of those that were manufactured (particularly the latest models of the Ju 88), the lion's share went to the rapidly expanding night fighter force. The fate of the long-range bomber arm is not well understood, since that force failed to have any appreciable impact in the western theater of operations after 1942. Yet air forces are by their nature primarily offensive-minded, and the Luftwaffe was no exception. The attempt to carry out strategic air operations against the Soviet Union and thus employ the special capabilities of air power is in fact much more consistent with Luftwaffe doctrine than is the more frequently studied home defense effort of 1942-1945. Furthermore, the attempt to knock out Soviet armaments production was to the Luftwaffe planners a far more congenial endeavor than the efforts in 1943-1944 to carry out "reprisal" raids against Great Britain. The latter campaign had its roots in the personal vengeance of the Führer and in political necessity, in much the same manner as did the V-weapon attacks on southern England and on the port of Antwerp following the Allied landing on the

Continent. The strategic air campaign against the Soviet Union was, in contrast, a continuation of the Luftwaffe general staff's ongoing attempt to apply air force resources to the decisive point. The undertaking's ultimate failure was less a result of strategic meddling from above as the failure of the air force leadership to design a mission compatible with the Luftwaffe's capabilities.

The impetus for this shift in emphasis lay, as the last chapter has described, with the chief of the Luftwaffe General Staff, Jeschonnek, and a number of the operational commanders of the eastern air fleets. After the failure of German offensive ambitions in Russia in late summer 1943, the inchoate plans for systematic attacks developed by Jeschonnek, Meister, Greim, and Kless assumed a more concrete form. This transformation required the collaboration of a surprisingly wide array of agencies of the Third Reich. The variety of input was necessary on account of the inadequacy of Luftwaffe intelligence for the task of target selection. This somewhat reluctant collaboration eventually resulted in an identification of vulnerable "bottlenecks" in the Soviet war economy. It also rendered the target selection process unnecessarily complex and contributed to the ultimate failure of the undertaking.

This apparent "rediscovery" of strategic bombing as a potential war-winning master stroke is often associated with the appointment of General der Flieger Günther Korten as chief of the Luftwaffe general staff following Jeschonnek's August 1943 suicide. Korten was undoubtedly an enthusiast of strategic bombing, and many ex-Luftwaffe officers have praised him as a man of vision and character, particularly in contrast with the acerbic and brooding Jeschonnek.[2] In fact, the detailed planning for the "new" role of the Luftwaffe in the east originated during Jeschonnek's tenure, although Korten kept the project at center stage until his death as an unintended victim of the July 20, 1944 attentat against Hitler.

Korten was a typical representative of the officers who transferred from the Reichswehr to the nascent Luftwaffe in the early 1930s. He served throughout the First World War on the western front, earning his lieutenant's commission in October 1915. In the course of a career that included service at the Somme, the Chemin-des-Dames, and in the March 1918 offensive, he was wounded and received the Iron Cross, First and Second Class. Transferred to the RLM in October 1934, he was selected the following April for duty with the Luftwaffe General Staff. Significantly, all of his service after June 22, 1941 was on the eastern front. He was Löhr's chief of staff at Luftflotte 4 until August 1942, then commanded Luftwaffenkommando Don in the south and in the Kuban until being given command of Luftflotte 1 at the end of June 1943. Just over two months later, on September 4, 1943, Hitler named him Jeschonnek's successor.[3] The Luftwaffe had, in the 45-year-old Korten, acquired a general staff chief possessing great familiarity with both the Soviet adversary and the peculiar problems of air operations in the eastern theater. Korten would press forward energetically with a new concept of warfare for that front.[4] He also benefited by inheriting plans for a strategic air war against the Soviet enemy that were already well advanced.

Korten's reorientation of the Luftwaffe in late 1943 was a curious admixture of pragmatism and wishful thinking. He oversaw the intensive buildup of the Luftwaffe's single-engined fighter force for Reich defense in order to meet the daylight bombing attacks of the USAAF. The German night fighter arm also attained its highest level of success against RAF Bomber Command during his tenure.[5] Furthermore, Korten concentrated army support aviation under a separate command organization in order to clarify the role of units intended for strategic and tactical employment.[6] He believed that the multi-role capability of most Luftwaffe formations was one of the main causes for their decline in combat effectiveness, since the flexible bomber units could easily be dragged into army support operations. The grouping of flying units into reinrassig (lit. "thoroughbred"), single-purpose formations was his solution.[7] Finally, with mixed success, Korten reorganized the entire command structure of the German air force into its final form, a change designed to eliminate many of the overlapping jurisdictions that had plagued the Luftwaffe in the past.[8]

Korten also advocated a policy which proved to be completely beyond the limited means available to the Luftwaffe by 1943-1944. One of his principal beliefs regarding the nature of air power was that the bomber force's employment should be primarily "strategic." He spent an enormous amount of energy in the creation of an "operational attack corps" in the east "in which the majority of bomber units will carry out strategic attacks against Soviet industry as well as wide-ranging attacks against the rail network in the depth of the Russian hinterland."[9]

One might dismiss Korten's strategic bombing fixation as an expedient measure, an act of desperation intended to recover the Luftwaffe's declining prestige or an attempt to find employment for the German air force's bomber units which had been driven from the skies over Western Europe. Allied intelligence believed this to be the case; in an analysis of the June 1943 industrial attacks, a USAAF officer maintained:

> While it is possible that the Germans have been impressed with the results of Allied heavy bombing operations in the west and believe that by this means they can materially cripple the Russian war effort with limited cost to themselves, it is also true that the long-range bombers represent the one category of aircraft which are not urgently required on other fronts. Thus . . . the new German Air Force policy seeks to make a virtue out of a necessity.[10]

Certainly Göring, his personal position as the number-two-man in the Third Reich considerably eroded by mid-1943, grasped at any straw that promised to revive his flagging fortunes.[11] The *Reichsmarschall* undoubtedly saw in the renewed strategic bombing emphasis a means of recovering the leading position his Luftwaffe once occupied among Germany's armed forces. At his annual address to the Gauleiters on November 8, 1943, Göring announced the inauguration of the new German air force policy with the following remarks:

> At the beginning of the war, Germany was the only nation in the world that possessed a strategic bomber air force (*operative Kampfluftwaffe*) equipped with technologically advanced aircraft. Other nations had divided their air forces into army and naval air arms, and regarded the air force as a necessary and important auxiliary weapon. For this reason they lacked an instrument which could by itself execute concentrated and decisive blows. From its inception, the Luftwaffe was intended to strike deep into enemy territory and exert a strategic effect . . .[12]

Submerged in Göring's characteristically bombastic rhetoric was more than a grain of truth. The Luftwaffe General Staff's plans for the coming air campaign against the Soviet Union had their origins not only in desperation but also in the *operativer Luftkrieg* theories of the 1930s. In order to comprehend more fully how this rediscovery of cherished air power beliefs came about, it is necessary to examine the development of one of Korten's contributions to the intellectual history of air power: the expanded Military History Department of the Luftwaffe General Staff.

THE 8. ABTEILUNG: INTELLECTUAL CHAMPIONS OF STRATEGIC AIR WAR

Albert Speer, in postwar interrogations and in his memoirs, portrayed the Luftwaffe's belated turn towards a strategic concept of air
power as one forced upon it by outside agencies (particularly his own)
and by the unfavorable military situation facing Germany by 1943.[13] It
is, however, clear that the reasons for the Luftwaffe's apparent about-
face were entirely consistent with prewar German air doctrine, as well
as with the German air force's maturation as a fighting service during
the Second World War. The primary guidance for the Luftwaffe's conduct of the eastern campaign came from within its own general staff.
One agency in particular achieved an entirely disproportionate influence over the conduct of German air strategy: the 8. (Kriegswissenschaftliche) Abteilung (Military Science Department) of the general
staff.

The roots of this organization date back to the years immediately following the First World War; its beginnings, like those of the Luftwaffe
itself, were not auspicious. A tiny section of the Defense Ministry concerned itself with the writing of the aviation history of World War I, with a
view towards providing strategic, operational, and tactical lessons applicable to the conduct of future air war.[14] Real progress was, to put it charita-
bly, slow: most of the studies took years to produce and dealt with arcane
topics. Even so, a few of the group's contributors espoused theories of air
power consonant with the much more widely publicized concepts of Giulio Douhet and other interwar air power theorists. Writings such as those
of Major Hans Arndt, who suggested that "[t]he future conduct of land
warfare without air power and without profound appreciation for its
peculiarities is unthinkable,"[15] fit firmly within the mainstream of air
power literature of the 1920s. Once the new Luftwaffe cast off its camouflage in 1935, the historical research agency assumed a more prominent
role. It acquired certain responsibilities for the training, education and
indoctrination of the officers of the new service. In the words of one of its
chiefs, General der Flieger Wilhelm Haehnelt (a former WWI air commander of some reputation), the department was to provide "intellectual
fertilization" for the officer corps and to serve as "the spiritual gas station
[geistige Tankstelle] of the Luftwaffe."[16] Even so, the influence of the often-
redesignated Military Science Department was at best muted until the

summer of 1943, when a series of organizational and intellectual changes brought the department to the peak of its influence. The most visible of these changes was Korten's appointment on August 24, 1943 of then-Oberst Hans-Detlef Herhudt von Rohden as department chief. Herhudt von Rohden possessed wide operational experience, having been chief of staff to two air fleets in the east. He served under Richthofen at Luftflotte 4 until, in one of his more unhappy encounters with the higher Luftwaffe leadership, Milch singled him out for dismissal for mismanagment of the Stalingrad airlift.[17] Most importantly, he was a well-known prewar airpower theorist.[18] His contributions to the German concept of "operational air war" have already been described. Now, in the autumn of 1943, Herhudt von Rohden found himself in a position to influence the conduct of German air operations according to these theories. Under the enthusiastic sponsorship of the like-minded Korten, whom Herhudt von Rohden eulogized as "the founder and supporter of our department,"[19] the Military Science Department strayed rather far from its original brief. Indeed, Korten's organizational changes subordinated Herhudt von Rohden's department directly to the chief of the general staff, bypassing even the operations staff. Herhudt von Rohden's department immediately ceased all "long-range historical work" and turned to projects that could have a swift and decisive impact upon German air strategy and operations.[20]

As indicated earlier, one of Korten's main goals for the coming year was a recasting of German air strategy, particularly on the Eastern Front, where the strategic bomber force was in his view being squandered in improvised army support operations for which it had not been designed. This was an opinion shared by Herhudt von Rohden and the Historical Department's analysts. In December 1943, an 8. Abteilung study pointed out, "The primary task of a strategic air force is the conduct of operational air war against the enemy air force, against the armaments industry, against all types of economically vital points and against transportation targets . . ."[21] As Korten's plans for the reconstitution of the Luftwaffe's strategic bombing capability gained momentum, the 8. Abteilung, in its influential writings and training manuals, proved to be a willing intellectual ally.

Recommendations made by the department reinforced those made by the operations staff under both Jeschonnek and Korten; they called for a regrouping of the bulk of the Luftwaffe's bomber force into an independent attack force against the "centers of national resistance" of the USSR. Even as the German air force as a whole declined in effectiveness, the department's formulations became ever more far-reaching and ambitious. Two new doctrinal/tactical manuals, drafted during the heyday of Korten's tenure, featured increased emphasis on the "operational air war" concepts so congenial to Korten and Herhudt von Rohden.[22] In a time when the front lines in Russia and eventually in Normandy were under heavy pressure, the leadership circles of the Luftwaffe paid increasing attention to strategic applications of air power. Many of the studies and briefings conducted during the planning stages of the attacks on Soviet industry bear the unmistakable hallmarks of the historical department's influence.[23] The 8. Abteilung clarified the usage of the nebulous term *operativer Luftkrieg* to the point where, by early 1944, it referred solely to independent strategic bombing operations.[24] This ambitious intellectual reorientation took place at a time when Luftwaffe capabilities waned as commitments swelled. As a result, during the Luftwaffe's last year of sustained operations in Russia, it functioned as a grotesque caricature of a modern air force.

The transition of the Luftwaffe to the strategic bombing role was not achieved without difficulty. Sustained support of the German army in the Soviet Union had cost the Luftwaffe more than material losses, although those, especially to the bomber force, had been staggering. Many of the highly trained crews with which the Luftwaffe had gone to war in 1939 were dead or prisoners-of-war. Moreover, the command and strategic planning levels had, in the expectation of a short campaign, paid insufficient attention to economic intelligence and target selection that were vital for the conduct of modern strategic air war, and these oversights defied swift rectification. Finally, multi-front commitments and the air armament and aircraft production situation made assembly of the requisite forces by 1943-1944 a daunting prospect. A study of the decision-making and implementation process surrounding such a strategic reorientation illustrates that, for the Luftwaffe at least, the gap between the theory and practice of air war was in large measure unbridgeable.

THE NUMBERS GAME: LUFTWAFFE INTELLIGENCE AND THE WAR OF ATTRITION

Luftwaffe intelligence played a decisive role in facilitating the German air force leadership's shift towards a systematic bombing of Soviet war industries. It not only contributed to the actual target selection process, but its assessment of Soviet war production provided powerful evidence suggesting that combat attrition alone by mid-1943 was insufficient to check the growth of either the Red Army or the VVS, and that air attacks on the industries supplying these forces were not merely desirable, but essential. German air intelligence acted as one of the prime movers of the new strategic bombing campaign, and would do so until the possibilities for realizing such a campaign had all but vanished.

German air intelligence, drawing on meticulously compiled figures provided by the OKW/Wehrwirtschaftsstab Ausland (Foreign War Economies Branch),[25] concluded that Soviet tank production by the summer of 1943 gave cause for alarm. Despite the supposed bloodletting which the *Panzerwaffe* inflicted on the Soviet armored forces at Kursk, the Soviets, drawing upon a tank production of nearly 2,000 vehicles per month, lend-lease deliveries, an energetic battlefield repair service, and vast armored reserves, had managed to make good the losses.[26] Frontline Soviet tank strength still stood at 6,000 vehicles at the beginning of August. In the ensuing months, with no engagements on the scale of Zitadelle to rob the Red Army of its strength, Soviet tank power increased dramatically. By November 1, 1943, the Soviets were credited with 9,500 tanks, a figure that was expected to rise to 11,000 by the following April.[27] Verification of German intelligence estimates is difficult. Figures for armor production given in the Soviet official history correspond very closely to the German calculations. On the other hand, Soviet strength figures (5,400 tanks and assault guns at the beginning of 1944) indicate that German intelligence persistently overestimated the real increase in Red Army combat power conferred by the new production.[28]

Soviet aircraft production seemed no less worrisome. Luftwaffe intelligence calcuiated that Soviet production by the fall of 1943 was outstripping combat losses in every aircraft category, with the single exception of ground attack machines.[29] Only in the first half of July 1943 did the Germans believe that they had inflicted unsupportable losses on the VVS, and the number of Soviet aircraft reported downed following the cancellation of Zitadelle dropped off appreciably.[30] The Germans claimed the destruction of 3,110 Soviet aircraft of all types during July, including 1,961 from July 1 through July 15. The overall lesson contained in these figures was unmistakable: ''The battle against the threatening numerical preponderance of Russian air armament will not be won by relying upon combat victories at the front."[31]

Grand totals available to German intelligence tend to bear out the conclusion that the Luftwaffe needed to augment VVS combat losses by attacking the means of production. In the first year of the campaign, the VVS, by Ic/Fremde Luftwaffen Ost estimates, lost 26,100 military aircraft of all types.[32] During the second campaign year, Soviet losses declined to 20,900. At the same time, Soviet aircraft production "increased uninterruptedly."[33] Replacement of aircraft "invariably exceeded losses" from the end of 1942 on. By early 1944, the Germans would be facing a Red Air Force numerically greater than the one they had destroyed on June 22, 1941 and operating first-rate aircraft.[34] As with the armor production and strength figures, German analysts were unduly pessimistic about Soviet front-line strength. German figures spoke of 23,000 VVS front-line aircraft in November 1943, with an increase to 29,000 by the following April.[35] Comparable Soviet official figures speak of the more modest totals of 8,506 (plus 312 reserve) in January 1944, and 13,428 (with 1,359 in reserve) by June of that year.[36] If the numerical imbalance between VVS and Luftwaffe was perhaps less unfavorable than German intelligence maintained, the corresponding figures for Luftwaffe combat power in the theater (2,312 aircraft in October 1943, 2,726 in January 1944)[37] lent credence to German apprehensions.

German intelligence eventually attributed the decline in Soviet losses to a number of factors:

1.) *Increased experience* [italics in original] of the Soviet aircrews.

2.) *Improvements in the standard of training* of aircrews.

3.) *Increasing numerical superiority* of the Soviet air force.

4.) Noticeable *improvement* in the *types of aircraft* used at the front. Especially in the case of fighter aircraft, the Soviets with their newest types have achieved technical parity.

5.) *Decline in German aircraft strength* on the Eastern Front.[38]

Both Luftwaffe and army planners were in basic agreement regarding the connection between the growth in Soviet combat power and her industrial output. While the two services would ultimately diverge over the target selection process, a remarkable degree of harmony seems to have existed between Heer and Luftwaffe regarding the necessity of industrial attacks. The Luftwaffe operations staff, seeking to buttress its case for strategic bombing, cited a general recommendation from the OKH's intelligence branch:

> One reason for the Russian success is the increased firepower and mobility conferred by the equipment of their forces with a large number of automatic weapons, guns, tanks and vehicles; this has been made possible by efficient war industries. A planned and intensive attack on Russian war industry might achieve a lessening of the pressure brought to bear by the Red Army.[39]

The inescapable conclusion Luftwaffe intelligence drew from this appreciation of Soviet war potential was that the most decisive task German air power might perform was to destroy the war industries feeding this massive Soviet increase in strength. As discussed earlier in this study, the success of Luftwaffe intelligence in the war against the Soviet Union was somewhat spotty. In some ways, Ic's failure stemmed from the same causes as the failure of the entire Luftwaffe: the campaign for which the high command ordered it to prepare was not the campaign it ended up fighting. As a result, detailed information regarding the location, capacity, and characteristics of the Soviet war industry was almost entirely lacking. Such information was essential if the Luftwaffe was to succeed in striking a decisive blow with its relatively weak bomber forces.

Throughout much of the war, Luftwaffe intelligence (Foreign Air Forces East) had been quite adept at discovering Soviet local frontline strengths, unit deployments, and other "operational" information.[40] As long as Luftwaffe intelligence received regular air reconnaissance reports and radio intercepts, Ic was able to present an accurate, though short-range, picture of developments in the combat sector.[41] The efficiency of German tactical intelligence correspondingly dwindled when fewer aircraft were available for reconnaissance missions, or when energetic Soviet fighter activity made it difficult for the reconnaissance units to carry out their tasks. As a result of this blindness, the German command became more vulnerable to Soviet deception operations. Frequently, the apparent presence of a Soviet unit comprised a deceitful piece in a mosaic designed to mask preparations for a major Soviet offensive in another sector of the vast front.

The German intelligence service was often able to augment tactical information through prisoner-of-war interrogations. Captured VVS airmen and any papers found on them were sent to special Luftwaffe intelligence centers, most notably in Smolensk, in order to extract any tactical or technical information.[42] The German attitude towards the subjects of such intelligence gathering reveals much about the racial contempt with which many German officers viewed their adversaries:

> In *one* thing alone, the methods and results of the interrogation of Russian airmen have remained unchanged: the skillful exploitation of the biological factor. Even though the Russian airman, lifted out of the general rut of the eastern masses, represents in a certain sense an individual; yet in mentality he remains two generations behind Western thought. The biological moment of inertia of mind and spirit, and therefore of thought and feeling, have not been able to keep pace with the technical developments of the machine age . . .
>
> The biological immaturity of the blood of the Russian airman necessarily gives him a childlike mentality. This animal fatalism will always break down all the discipline instilled in him to make him keep silence. No regulations, no threats of punishment can at present help the Russian command. The Russian is overcome by his nature as by a primitive force . . . For the interrogation officer it is always a particularly tense, and from the psychological standpoint a dramatic, moment when—and this recurs from case to case with mathematical certainty—the most stubborn silence shown at first is suddenly transformed into an irrepressible urge to talk. Often something like childish vanity and boasting appears . . . *the astonishing thing is that in this state the Russian always tells the truth.*
>
> [T]he specialist in the Russian character, by using methods which are psychologically sound, will crack the hardest Russian nut.[43]

When such evident contempt for individual Soviet airmen was extrapolated to assessments of the sophistication or vulnerability of the entire Soviet state and economy, the constant optimism expressed by German air intelligence about the possibilities for achieving decisive results through strategic bombing becomes more explicable.

Luftwaffe intelligence also relied on these prisoner-of-war deposi-
tions as a means of gauging the effectiveness of the Luftwaffe's activities. Analysts attempted to reconcile the accounts of recently captured
Red Army personnel or intercepted enemy communications with the
combat reports of the *Fliegerkorps*.[44] German air intelligence received
copies of interrogations conducted by army units if they had bearing on
Luftwaffe matters, as with the air attacks on Gorki in June 1943.[45] Yet
such methods, with few exceptions, could only provide information on
the tactical situation on a rather restricted portion of the vast front. The
garnering of what might be termed "strategic" or "economic" intelligence presented a rather more difficult task.

The activities of the "Rowehl squadron" in the months preceding
Barbarossa had likewise provided information within a depth of penetration rarely exceeding a few hundred miles, and the data accumulated,
mostly concerning the location of VVS bases, was again primarily tactical in nature.[46] Some of the information garnered did find its way into
Luftwaffe intelligence's first tentative surveys of the Soviet armaments
industry. For the preparation of the coming campaign, however, far
more sophisticated intelligence was required. This was a shortcoming
which the frenetic efforts of Luftwaffenführungsstab Ic and its subordinate Foreign Air Forces East (Fremde Luftwaffen Ost) only partially
ameliorated. In fact, many key air force and army intelligence estimates
of Soviet industrial capabilities were based in whole or in part upon
open-source propaganda literature published by the Five-Year Plan
office and other Soviet agencies.[47] As late as May 1944, Speer was still
entreating Korten "that air reconnaissance of the Ural district be speed-
ily undertaken."[48] Even target information on objectives well within
Luftwaffe bomber range was uneven. Incomplete photographic coverage existed for many of the proposed targets; in many cases data, such
as the number of workers at a given plant, was seriously outdated.[49]
Estimates concerning the defenses of such familiar targets as Gorki
depended in part on prisoner-of-war interrogations and the reports
(often of dubious validity) of "*V-Männer*," German "confidential
agents" operating behind Soviet lines.[50] In such a manner did Luftwaffe
analysts attempt to assess the productivity of Soviet industrial cities,
their status as "key industries" (*Schlüsselwerke*), and the strength of
fighter and anti-aircraft defenses. Air intelligence noted that, for example, Gorki, which had virtually no *Flak* protection at the time of the

German air attacks in June 1943, had by early 1944 increased its defenses to fourteen heavy and nine light anti-aircraft batteries, fifty searchlights, and two radar sets. Fighter, and especially night fighter defense, although served by "a well-organized air raid warning system," was considered inferior to that possessed by Germany or Great Britain.[51] Luftwaffe intelligence did establish that targets of great military value remained well within German bomber range, even after the Ostheer receded from its high water mark of summer 1942. Ic noted in early July 1943 that the city of Moscow retained its significance as a political, industrial, and communications center.[52] After a few months of intensive information gathering, the intelligence planners were to conclude that the great evacuations of Soviet industry during the summer and fall of 1941 had not in fact moved the bulk of Soviet industry behind the Urals. Indeed, a number of factories which had been moved out of the threatened sector had returned to their former locations once the immediate crisis passed. Luftwaffe intelligence concluded, "today, the Moscow area continues to be an armaments center of the first rank."[53] The German air force's own intelligence agencies therefore established both the desirability and possibility of damaging the Soviet economy through strategic air operations.

The intelligence branch was to play a leading role in the determination of the target systems eventually deemed profitable targets for air attack. Yet, as became painfully clear to Jeschonnek in June 1943, Luftwaffe intelligence's detailed knowledge of Soviet industry was at best incomplete. The need for more informed input into the target selection process opened the door to a number of agencies which had been hitherto on the periphery of operational planning.

One such agency was located within the unlikely confines of the Building and Construction Department of the Luftwaffe's Administrative Office (Verwaltungsamt LD). Its department head, Professor Steinmann, an electric power expert, had prior to the outbreak of the war advocated attacks on a nation's electric power supply as the surest way to cripple a modern industrial state.[54] Steinmann had been one of the technical advisers to Luftwaffe intelligence's well-known appreciation of Britain's war potential, Studie Blau, compiled under Major Josef Schmid in July 1940. Steinmann found that his advice regarding operations against British electric power installations encountered numerous technical objections. Attacks on the electric power industry in Britain never

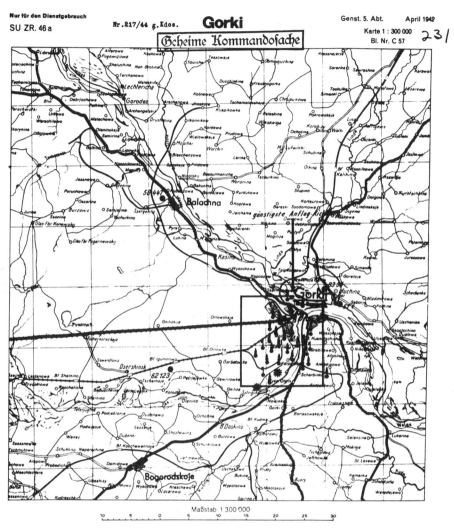

Map 4. Luftwaffe intelligence map of Gorki, the Strategic target most frequently attacked by the Luftwaffe during the eastern campaign. Target data on Soviet industry was sketchy at best; using aerial reconnaissance photographs, German intelligence attempted to determine the location of radar, searchlight, and anti-aircraft gun positions. (OKL/2316, NARS T321/247)

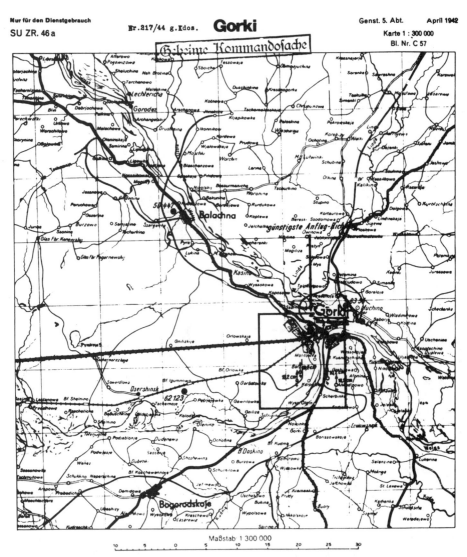

Map 5. German air intelligence also relied on information supplied by agents behind the Soviet lines (*V-Männer*) to augment its knowledge of a target. Here the same map of Gorki indicates agents' reports of anti-aircraft batteries. (OKL/2316, NARS T321/247)

materialized, and the Luftwaffe pursued its own haphazard target selection process during the Battle of Britain.[55] Only the Luftwaffe General Staff's June 1943 appeal for target information on the Soviet Union rescued Steinmann from his mundane duties of providing Luftwaffe installations with power, heat and lighting.

In reality, there was nothing particularly novel about Steinmann's choice of target system. Air power thinkers in Germany and other countries frequently drew attention to the desirability of attacking an enemy nation's electrical industry. Oberst Freiherr von Bülow observed in 1936:

> The life of the large cities, the operations of innumerable factories, and a considerable and ever-growing portion of the transportation system have to rely upon a constant and reliable supply of electric current. The importance of electricity for war industries hardly needs to be highlighted. The technical facilities of large generating and hydroelectric power plants are time consuming and expensive to construct, as well as extremely susceptible to air attack. The simultaneous destruction of most central electrical works will cause the instantaneous crippling of entire industries.[56]

Moreover, in the United States, the air planners at the Air Corps Tactical School at Maxwell Field in the 1930s initially selected the German electric power system as a "primary attack objective" of strategic bombing plan AWPD-1.[57] This aspect of the plan was later rejected on operational grounds, but one of the planners, Major General S. Haywood Hansell, Jr., regarded this as a sin of omission. He wrote after the war, "Nearly all authorities, German as well as Allied, are now agreed that effective disruption of the German electric power system would have contributed as much toward the winning of the war as the campaign against oil."[58] Indeed, electric power generating facilities reemerged as key targets in United States Air Force planning against North Korea in 1950 and North Vietnam during Operation Rolling Thunder.[59]

Although air attacks on the electrical industry of an enemy nation were often contemplated, it is fair to say that concerning the USSR in the 1940s the target had a special significance. To many Soviet leaders, electrification was synonymous with modernity, and was therefore a cure for the "backwardness" afflicting Russian society. V. I. Lenin himself had noted:

Only large-scale industry capable of reorganizing agriculture
. . . can serve as the material base for socialism. But this general
proposition is not enough. It must be made specific. Large-scale
industry corresponding to up-to-date technique and capable of
reorganizing agriculture means electrification of the whole
country.[60]

In December 1920, the Soviets enacted the Goelro Plan, an electrification
scheme designed to implement Lenin's grandiose vision. Under the
authority of the five year plans, enormous power stations and a high-
tension grid spread across European Russia. The result was a modern
and highly centralized power generating system. Soviet literature of the
late 1930s proudly noted, "It should be emphasized that the comparative level of centralization and concentration of the major power systems
of the USSR is higher than in Germany or the USA."[61]

Many German planners believed that very level of concentration
made these huge electrical generating plants the ideal target system for
the Luftwaffe. German studies of the Soviet defense economy in 1942
listed no fewer than thirty-one of the largest electric power generating
stations as "important objectives." These included the huge plants at
Balachna, Krasnaya-Glinka (near Kuibyshev), Rybinsk and Uglich, each
with over 200,000 KW capacity.[62] Steinmann was the first Luftwaffe
planner to utilize data on Soviet electric power to come up with a viable
attack plan. His detailed proposal of July 31, 1943, "Recommendations
for Air Attacks on the Power Supply of the Moscow-Upper Volga
Region," elucidated the major argument for the Luftwaffe's strategic
bombing policy against the Soviet Union which all of the participating
agencies eventually accepted. As a technical expert well-acquainted
with Germany's own strained electrical power situation, Steinmann fer-
vently believed that the USSR must be in an equally precarious position.
Steinmann argued:

In the [Moscow-Upper Volga] area (approximately a triangle
with points at Tula-Ribinsk-Gorki) is located a decisive portion of
the Soviet war industry. This industry is dependent upon electricity. The electric energy is produced primarily by a number of
important power plants and is distributed by an efficient high
tension network.[63]

Steinmann went on to address the relative contribution made by the Moscow-Upper Volga region to the Soviet war economy. In so doing he concurred with Luftwaffe intelligence's assessment that destruction, evacuation, and dislocation of Soviet industry did not substantially reduce the region's importance to Soviet war production. Moreover, wartime exigencies most likely made the region even more dependent upon a few key electrical installations, which his report set out to enumerate.[64]

Steinmann's "electrical taxonomy" of the region, which was to survive in Luftwaffe planning until the end of the conflict, referred to three "sub-regions:" Area I, Moscow and the environs containing its power plants; Area II, the Yaroslavl-Ivanovo region; and Area III, Gorki. Within these three areas, Steinmann drew Luftwaffe planners' attention to twenty-two major power stations. Connecting these power stations to the war industries they served was a network of high-tension cables, itself marked by a number of transformer stations. Twenty of these transformer stations constituted secondary targets.

Steinmann believed that the Soviet electricity supply was more vulnerable than that of other industrialized countries. The 1941 evacuations and disruptions had reduced the Soviets' ability to construct the delicate turbines, generators, and switching apparatus. Replacement of this equipment in destroyed power plants would, therefore, be an extremely lengthy process.[65] Steinmann concluded that "a methodical and precisely conducted attack on the supply of electric current will result in the crippling of the armaments industry of the Moscow-Upper Volga region."[66] He stressed that the attack had to fall more or less simultaneously upon the entire target system, as raids on isolated portions of the network would not deliver the same cumulative effect.

Steinmann's proposal then went before the other agencies contributing to the target selection process. Luftwaffe intelligence initially took a dim view of Steinmann's recommendations. German air intelligence had examined Moscow's power supply as one of the potential target systems within the Soviet capital. They concurred with Steinmann that any attack must take place simultaneously against the entire network; half measures would in this case be "senseless."[67] Ic/IV in this regard believed that the target list which Steinmann proposed was too lengthy. Citing Steinmann's own diagrams, Luftwaffe intelligence demonstrated that an attack on only eleven power generating stations would produce much the same effect.[68] Furthermore, German air force intelligence was as yet unconvinced that power plant attacks were in fact preferable to "concentrated attacks on the largest industrial plants."[69] German air intelligence therefore found itself unable to concentrate on any one target system, and its proposals, which included aero engine, airframe, and ultimately transportation targets promised to dissipate Luftwaffe attack strength.

The Carl Commitee from the Armaments Ministry, however, threw its considerable weight behind the power plant attack concept. Speer's "Working Committee on Economic Objectives for Air Attack" believed that successful pinpoint attacks on eleven major power stations would "preclude the possibility of orderly industrial activity" in the Moscow-Upper Volga region.[70] While agreeing with Luftwaffe intelligence that Steinmann's original target list had been too ambitious, the Carl Committee's findings cited the electrical industry as the sole industrial objective upon which attacks could yield the desired results.

In reaching this conclusion, Carl and the other industrialists used the German electric power system as a model. A report by Carl, later examined by the United States Strategic Bombing Survey in 1945, noted:

> The [German] intra-district power supply could be paralyzed by individual attacks on 56 of the most important generating stations whereby two-thirds of the entire German power production could be eliminated.[71]

The Soviet power system, moreover, possessed far less "depth" and reserve capacity than did its German counterpart. A number of the turbines and other precision components had been manufactured in the United States, or even in Germany (a legacy of the late unmourned Ribbentrop-Molotov pact), and the Carl Committee believed that their replacement under wartime conditions (estimated to take up to one year) would pose nearly insurmountable problems for Soviet industrialists.

There may have been some justification for the optimism of the German planners. Soviet sources suggest that, despite energetic emergency measures on the part of the Stalin regime, the electric power industry was pushed almost to the breaking point by the pressures of war.[72] Even in the absence of German air attacks on the power plants, the People's Commissariat for the Tank Industry reported to the State Committee for

Defense in March 1943 that "in January and February [1943] there were disruptions in the operations of the most important tank plants as a result of the shortages of electric power . . ."[73] The German planners may indeed have pinpointed one of the Soviet economy's most vulnerable components.

Yet other factors mitigated against the German planners reaching a swift and binding decision. The effects of having a number of competing foci of target selection began to make themselves felt. Ultimately, that selection remained the preserve of the Luftwaffe high command, but Speer, whose rationalization of German war production had by late 1943 brought him near the pinnacle of his influence, ensured that the Carl Committee's recommendations (and therefore those of Steinmann) eventually held sway. Moreover, additional proposals by nearly all of the agencies taking part constantly muddied the waters of the target selection process.

Steinmann, while his initial proposal was still under consideration, proposed a complementary strike against the hydro-power plants at Rybinsk and Uglich, which supplied Moscow with more than half of its electric power.[74] He proposed an air attack using special "floating mines" (*Triebminen*) against the power dams and turbines of these power plants as a means of achieving the same effect, in microcosm, of the proposed comprehensive power plant attack. This plan would consume a great deal of time and resources and, since it competed with the main operation under consideration, ended up as an unprofitable deviation from the overall attack concept.

Luftwaffe intelligence, for its part, was dissatisfied with the direction the entire target selection process was taking. In September 1943, Ic instructed its analysts to continue the broadest possible investigation of the Soviet war economy in the hopes of finding the key targets within a variety of manufacturing areas, "for example, the air armament industry," a sure indication that German air force intelligence was pursuing the same line of investigation as it had in the spring of 1943.[75] Indeed, Luftwaffe intelligence, since the beginning of the renewed target investigation process, had refused to tailor the proposals to Luftwaffe capabilities (which renders its initial objections to Steinmann's proposal inexplicable). Ic simultaneously put forth airframe, aircraft engine, synthetic rubber, aviation fuel, ball bearing, and transportation targets as worthwhile objectives, with pride of place given to air armament and medium and heavy tank production.[76] Eventually, Luftwaffe intelligence pared down its target list to aircraft engine assembly plants, most notably those at Gorki, Ufa, Kasan, Kuibyshev, and Moscow.[77] Of these plants, only Moscow and Gorki were by late summer within bomber range; loss of the airfields in the Orel sector following the defeat at Kursk rendered unworkable a plan which in June 1943 had been within the bounds of possibility. Luftwaffe intelligence continued to tout this target group above all others, in the vain hope that the new long-range bomber types, most notably the He 177, might become serviceable in time for the operation.

Meanwhile, various army agencies sought entrance to the target selection process with little success. In a wasteful duplication of the efforts of air intelligence, the OKH pursued its own parallel target research program, utilizing much of the same data. Many of the army's voluminous intelligence appreciations contained quite useless or irrelevant information, such as whether the factory in question had a Jewish plant manager.[78] Beyond acknowledging that Soviet numerical superiority in tanks and planes posed certain intractable problems for German forces in the east, Luftwaffenführungsstab Ic had little interest in the army's input. Thus, when in late September 1943, Army Group Center recommended air attacks on Soviet artillery, motor vehicle, iron, steel, nitrogen, and saltpeter production to the Luftwaffe operations staff, the proposals fell upon deaf ears.[79] Few if any of these proposals were reflected in any of the subsequent target research done by the German air force, although the power plant attack, of course, promised to diminish Soviet production of most of these commodities as part of the general industrial paralysis that would ensue.

In any case, in early November 1943 the Luftwaffe operations staff under Generalleutnant Karl Koller unveiled the definitive plan for the attack on Soviet industrial potential. Koller's study elucidated the main threads of Luftwaffe strategic thinking regarding the war against the USSR: the inappropriateness of using bomber forces for direct army support, the need to bring air power to bear against Soviet productive capacity, and the German concept of strategic air operations. While Koller's cover letter acknowledged that "it is clear that we have let slip our most favorable opportunity and that in the intervening time the difficulties have become very great," Koller believed that the Luftwaffe, even in its weakened state, was still quite capable of delivering a blow to Soviet arms production that would have far-reaching results.

The entire document represented a compromise between the various participating (and competing) agencies. Koller observed that "available target data of Luftwaffe Intelligence has been specially studied and revised by Professor Steinmann of the Administration Office and President Dr. Karl [sic] of the Armaments Ministry," and therefore "the target evaluation may lay claim to a high degree of accuracy."[80] To be sure, Luftwaffe intelligence's aircraft engine target proposal appeared in the final operations staff plan; it was mentioned only insofar as it was deemed unfeasible "with the aircraft types and air bases available at the present time." Perhaps as a sop to Ic, the operations staff observed that an attack on the aero engine plant in Gorki was possible "since the factory is situated next to the power plant."[81] Although the Luftwaffenführungsstab Ia conceded that aircraft engine production comprised an exceptionally concentrated, vulnerable target system, the distance factors, except for converted long-range transport planes such as the Junkers 290, were insuperable.

Soviet power plants made up the primary focus of the definitive attack plan. Employing language borrowed directly from Steinmann's and Carl's proposals, Luftwaffe planners, aware that "only key points and individual especially important factories may be regarded as attack objectives," noted that "the most vulnerable aspect of Russian war industry is the supply of electric power." Using Carl's figures, the operations staff concluded that a loss to the Moscow-Upper Volga region of fifty percent of the normal supply of electricity would cripple eighty percent of all tank engine production, fifty percent of the manufacture of electronics components, and sixty percent of light tank production.[82] The study isolated eleven critical power generating stations, a compromise solution made after consideration of the proposals of the three major contributors to the study. There were five plants in the Moscow area and three each in the Yaroslavl and Gorki regions:

MOSCOW AREA

Rybinsk	(Target Number SU 50 239)
Uglich	(Target Number SU 50 308)
Shatura	(Target Number SU 50 247)
Kashira	(Target Number SU 50 116)
Stalinogorsk	(Target Number SU 50 272)

GORKI AREA

Balachna   (Target Number SU 50 447)
Gorki-Molotov   (Target Number SU 50 762)
Dsershinsk   (Target Number SU 50 64)

YAROSLAVL AREA

Yagres   (Target Number SU 50 95)
Yaroslavl Synthetic Rubber   (Target Number SU 50 710)
  Factory "SK 1"
Komsomolsk   (Target Number SU 50 446)

Destruction of these eleven plants,[83] which produced over a million kilowatts of electricity, was deemed sufficient virtually to halt industrial activity in the region. The operations staff concluded, "The destruction of the sources of [electric] power produces the most permanent effect."[84]

In some respects, the plan had much to commend it. The Luftwaffe's analysts had processed a large amount of information, consulted with outside agencies, and finally designed a mission for the German air force in the east in early 1944 which seemingly promised to bring decisive results entirely consistent with the hopes of prewar air power planners. Even by Soviet admission, electric power generation was one of the most vulnerable sectors of the war economy of the USSR. Moreover, the operation, occasionally referred to in official correspondence as Aktion Russland (Russia Action) or later as Unternehmen Eisenhammer (Operation Iron Hammer), seemed to be faithful to the traditional Luftwaffe principle of concentration of force. Virtually the entirety of bomber strength in the east was earmarked for the operation. Koller was adamant that "the sole prerequisite is that this weapon [the Luftwaffe long-range bomber force] be freed at least temporarily from *direct support of the Eastern Front* or from other tasks."[85]

The plan, in spite of its strengths, contained a number of serious flaws. One of these was related to the available force structure and the aircraft and weapons technology available to the Luftwaffe at that period of the war. The other failing was perhaps more fundamental. With the Luftwaffe leadership supposedly committed to the power plant attack concept, many of its planning staffs tended to divert attention from the

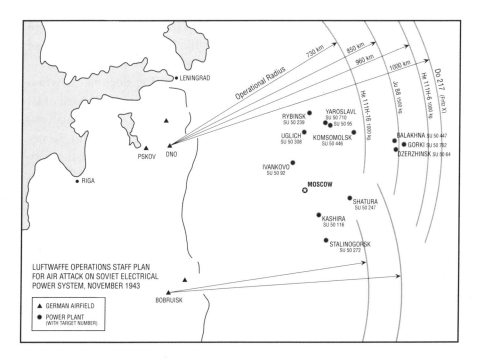

Map 6. Map showing the definitive Luftwaffe operations staff plan for a systematic attack against the Soviet electricity supply in the Moscow-Upper Volga region, November 1944. The major power plants and their target numbers are indicated; concentric circles indicate the operational radius of various German bomber aircraft and the bomb tonnage carried. Notice that the power plants in the Gorki region are barely within bomber range from the bases in the Dno-Pskov area.

task at hand, and advocated schemes that were well beyond the Luftwaffe's limited resources. In an air force struggling to recover its status as an independent service, the temptation to indulge in such grandiose planning is perhaps understandable. For the Luftwaffe, the pursuit of the "strategic vision" was to lead to the bankruptcy of all its options.

The ink was scarcely dry on the major planning documents when Luftwaffenführungsstab Ic commenced work on the second phase of its target selection process: a series of studies entitled "Recommendations for Air Attacks on the Soviet Armaments Industry as a Basis for Strategic Air Warfare" (Vorschläge für Luftangriffe gegen die SU-Rüstungsindustrie als Grundlage für die operative Luftkriegführung).[86] Such an undertaking demonstrates that the power plant attack was not intended as merely an emergency measure, but was to be the first component of a sustained strategic air offensive against the USSR. To inaugurate this ambitious project, Luftwaffe intelligence conducted a discussion at the Robinson headquarters on December 21, 1943. The meeting was chaired by Oberst Rudolf Wodarg, head of the Luftwaffenführungsstab Ic, and his deputy Major i.G. Boie, the chief of Fremde Luftwaffen Ost. Present were Koller, Steinmann, Carl (the latter two in the capacity of "resident experts"), and sundry representatives from the intelligence and operations staffs. The content of the presentations at this meeting was heavily influenced by the air power theories of Herhudt von Rohden's 8. Abteilung, which fostered a close working relationship with the intelligence branch.[87] A briefing presented to Koller stressed that the war against the Soviet Union was only one component of the "total war" being waged on many fronts; yet only in the east did a portion of the enemy's "total armaments potential" fall within the practical range of heavy Luftwaffe attack.[88] The briefing stressed the importance of concepts such as space, time, and the "intercontinental effect" of air power which the 8. Abteilung emphasized. The question facing the Luftwaffe was how to make the strategic bombing force pay the greatest possible dividends in the one theater in which it might operate as originally intended.

Doubtless a portion of this effort was intended as salesmanship. Many authorities, most importantly the Führer, needed to be convinced of the necessity of such a plan if the requisite political impetus and material support were to appear. Certainly spotlighting vulnerable points in Stalin's "planned economy," particularly the concentration of vital war industries into "giant plants" seemingly tailor-made for air attack, was likely to appeal to Hitler's sensibilities and to his intuitive, somewhat eclectic grasp of the principles of air strategy. Detailed wooden models of the Soviet power plants and a graphic presentation of the attack plan assisted the operations staff in convincing the Nazi leadership of the plan's value. Among the operation's devotees were Generaloberst Kurt Zeitzler, the army chief of staff; Oberst Nicolaus von Below, Hitler's Luftwaffe adjutant; Ambassador Walther Hewel of the Foreign Ministry; even the name of noted air power expert Reichsführer Heinrich Himmler occasionally surfaces in connection with the plan.[89] Indeed, by early December 1943, Hitler, with the persuasion of Albert Speer, endorsed the strategic bombing scheme.[90] It was now up to the Luftwaffe planning staffs to bring the Russia Action to fruition.

The public relations aspects aside, Luftwaffe intelligence and the operations staff were earnestly attempting to expand the Luftwaffe's role in the war against the USSR. Throughout December 1943 and January 1944, the target selection process proceeded apace. Some of the recommendations, such as those for repeated attacks upon the eleven power plants to make certain of their destruction, reflected common sense and a sound understanding of the difficulty of inflicting sufficient damage on such small targets.[91] Others promised only a dissipation of the bomber force against a myriad of objectives, many beyond practical attack range.

Luftwaffenführungsstab Ic chief Wodarg, for example, believed that once the destruction of the eleven key power plants had taken place, a number of other "special individual targets" in the Moscow-Upper Volga region, which he referred to as "bon-bons," should be considered as attack objectives.[92] His deputy Boie's recommendations were more concrete. Foreign Air Forces East suggested that the power plant attack be followed up with a comprehensive series of raids on "key industries" in the region, including the production of ball bearings, optical instruments, and aircraft fuselages, as well as the familiar Krasnaye Sormovo tank factory at Gorki.[93] Luftwaffe intelligence no longer restricted its recommendations to those industrial plants within range of the existing bomber force. An additional target selection process took place with a view towards sending small forces of as yet unavailable Heinkel 177 long-range bombers against more distant targets in the Ural region. Hitler had in fact been advocating such a use for the He 177 since 1942.

The possibilities offered by long-range aircraft allowed Ic once again to advance its aero engine plant attack proposal, although even the optimists at German air intelligence had to admit that destruction of the massive factories at Kuibyschev, Kasan, and Ufa would require "stronger forces" than promised to be forthcoming in the near future.[94] Nevertheless, a full-scale target investigation was undertaken for as much of the Ural region as the theoretical attack range of the He 177 would permit, taking in objectives as diverse as aircraft engine plants, ball bearing production, and the petrochemical industry.[95] Despite the unreality that surrounded many of these proposals, both Dr. Carl and (somewhat less enthusiastically) Professor Steinmann concurred on the basic soundness and importance of most of the proposed target lists.[96] Speer, on the other hand, as early as December 7 had complained to Hitler about the Luftwaffe's tendency to "subdivide" the planned operation into too many components.[97]

Many of the assumptions upon which Luftwaffenführungsstab Ic based its calculations were to prove vain hopes, especially the availability of four-engine He 177 aircraft for long-range bombing tasks. Yet the major failing of the target selection process did not rest with such technical shortcomings, however pervasive these may have been. What was to prove fatal to the entire process was the willing acceptance of missions that were far beyond Luftwaffe capabilities. One proposal in particular was to return to haunt the Luftwaffe Operations Staff during the spring of 1944, after the forces for the power plant strike had been painstakingly assembled and trained.

This proposal, so far as may be ascertained, originated with Luftwaffenführungsstab Ic chief Wodarg during January 1944. Wodarg had been most impressed by the American Fifteenth Air Force's systematic interdiction campaign against rail communications between Italy and the Reich during late 1943.[98] American medium and heavy bombers struck at bridges, marshalling yards, and other transportation "choke points" from October 1943 through the year's end, thereby complicating German operational difficulties in the south.[99] Wodarg suggested that the bulk of the Luftwaffe's bomber force, once the power plant attack had taken place, might be sent against the Soviet rail network, producing a collapse of "the entire transportation system" of the Bolshevik adversary.[100] Luftwaffe planners had of course long been aware of the Soviet rail network's vulnerability;[101] Wodarg was merely the first to mention it in the context of proposed missions for the Luftwaffe's rejuvenated strike force. It was a recommendation which would have a profound impact upon operations during the coming spring. When the German bomber force in late winter 1944 found itself in need of a mission, Wodarg's "transportation plan" filled the gap.

REBUILDING A STRIKE FORCE

All of the detailed planning by the various agencies recounted earlier would be for naught if the Luftwaffe command was unable to create the forces necessary for the execution of such ambitious schemes. Owing to the growing air superiority of the Western Allies, the eastern theater was really the only arena by 1943 in which Luftwaffe bombers might operate effectively. As early as May 1943, sixty percent of the Luftwaffe's operational bomber aircraft served with the eastern air fleets.[102] Earlier chapters have demonstrated the hard and continuous use made of the Luftwaffe's bomber forces ever since the eastern campaign began. Diversion of the bomber arm into such tasks as army support and air transport blunted its effectiveness. In spite of the formidable obstacles, the Luftwaffe staffs managed to reconstitute the bomber arm for the projected strategic operations against the Soviet Union in late 1943 and early 1944. Such a recovery is even more remarkable when one considers that the creation of even a small strategic bomber force in Russia faced opposition from advocates of direct army support, Reich defense commitments, and two unproductive attempts to carry out reprisal raids against the British Isles. Opposition from the home defense advocates was particularly insistent. Milch, for example, chided Meister, while the latter was deputy chief of operations under Jeschonnek, that the needs of the Reich defense forces should take priority over those of the fighting fronts. "I keep getting this feeling that we are all sitting out on a limb. At this limb the British keep sawing away! Here at home, I can hear the rasp of the saw. You out there, Meister, are farther away, and are deaf to it . . . ."[103] The commitment to a wide variety of tasks on multiple fronts proved to be an unavoidable and ultimately insurmountable drain on the Luftwaffe's striking power.

The youthful Acting General of Bomber Aviation, Oberst Dietrich Peltz, noted in January 1943, as the Stalingrad airlift continued apace,

ESTABLISHED AND ACTUAL STRENGTH OF LUFTWAFFE BOMBER
UNITS, JANUARY 1943–MARCH 1944[104]

	No. of Bomber Aircraft		
Month	Establishment	Available	Operational
1943			
Jan.	2,106	1,302	653
Feb.	2,025	1,443	811
March	2,025	1,522	844
April	2,034	1,574	864
May	2,109	1,588	894
June	2,111	1,663	1,007
July	2,122	1,419	908
August	2,025	1,134	573
Sept.	2,025	1,080	639
Oct.	2,081	1,357	759
Nov.	2,067	1,380	776
Dec.	2,053	1,604	1,078
1944			
Jan.	2,065	1,642	919
Feb.	2,037	1,441	903
March	1,901	1,331	825

that the bomber aircraft and crew situation had reached critical dimensions. He observed that, on average, the Luftwaffe lost fifty more crews per month than its training organization was able to replace. Peltz somewhat baldly noted that at the present rate, it would take only ten months to exhaust completely the supply of combat-ready crews.[105] He also pointed out that, far from sparing inexperienced bomber crews from combat attrition, such "second-line" tasks commonly used to "break in" junior crews as "antisubmarine operations, fuel transport to North Africa, resupply of surrounded troop formations, etc." instead contributed to his command's spiralling losses.[106] Peltz proposed the most energetic measures to arrest this trend. He called for the withdrawal of the bulk of no fewer than fourteen bomber *Gruppen* from the front lines for refitting. He further recommended the assignment of fully half of the output of training schools to the fourth (replacement) *Gruppe* of active bomber units, while sending the remaining half of the training output to those units reconstituting in the Reich territory. In such a manner did Peltz hope to preserve the core of his flying formations as well as his experienced command personnel. Combat losses among veteran formation leaders during extended army support operations had been exceptionally severe. In many cases, experienced unit commanders had been compelled to fly a large number of missions with the units, in which many were killed, due to a shortage of personnel. Loss of an experienced *Gruppenkommandeur* meant that a younger officer, "without the requisite technical knowledge," had to assume command of the formation. The result was an ongoing drain on irreplaceable leadership personnel that parallelled the wastage of bomber crews skilled in specialized techniques:

> Knowledge and skill acquired in long and costly training in navigation and long-distance bombing is by the very nature of ground attack operations completely wasted. Not only is navigational dexterity and practice lost on missions where only visual navigation is necessary (the crew knows its sector of the front and there is no necessity, and often no opportunity, for complex navigational methods), but the proper mindset for strategic air war is lost as well.[107]

In fact, in the wake of the Stalingrad airlift, early 1943 marked the lowest point in the operational ready rate for properly-trained bomber crews of the entire war.[108]

The demands of the eastern front in particular did not permit Peltz to carry out his reforms to any significant degree. Some units underwent refitting in the spring of 1943, but these were formations worn almost to nothing after months of unremitting operations.[109] The pattern of aerial activity described in the previous chapter did not permit the luxury of a systematic reconstitution of the bomber arm. Only with the greatest difficulty did a few units manage to recover their operational proficiency. I./Kampfgeschwader 4, for example, reduced to a skeleton formation, actually enjoyed a lengthy recuperation period in the Reich from January to October 1943. In April of that year, the entire third *Gruppe* of KG 4 began to train on the Lotfe 7D high-altitude bombsight (a device some Luftwaffe officers regarded as superior to the American Norden bombsight)[110] and to experiment with target-illumination techniques against the day when the Luftwaffe might again make use of such specialized skills.[111]

It is likely that only the Luftwaffe command's return to a policy of offensive warfare in the east saved the bomber arm from premature collapse. In the aftermath of the failure of Zitadelle and the German retreat in the face of the Soviet summer offensive, Luftwaffe formations more than ever became "chained to the support of the ground forces."[112] An additional winter of supporting defensive battles all along the eastern front would in all probability have destroyed the Luftwaffe's bomber force as an instrument of war. The deployment for Aktion Russland against Soviet industry occasioned the last meaningful concentration of Luftwaffe offensive air power (at peak, some 398 operational bombers) in the eastern theater.[113]

Once the OKL and the contributing agencies decided upon the initial shape (although by no means the entire nature) of the "systematic attack against the Russian armaments industry," the eastern air fleets set about assembling the requisite force. Göring, on November 26, 1943, authorized the concentration under Fliegerkorps IV of "the bulk of the heavy bomber units operating in the East, reinforced with special target-finding formations."[114] The former chief of Jeschonnek's operations staff, the bespectacled, schoolmasterish Generalleutnant Rudolf Meister, had on October 13 assumed command of this formation;[115] German sources therefore frequently refer to it simply as "korps Meister." This air corps, it will be recalled, had come to play a role identical with that of most German flying formations in the east, providing primarily direct and indirect army support. Under the new directives, the *Fliegerkorps* would operate in the command area of Luftflotte 6, but came under the direction of the Luftwaffe high command. It was to become a true strategic bomber force, responsible only to the highest command authorities and therefore immune from the daily pressures experienced by the other air corps fighting in the Soviet Union.

Göring initially assigned eight bomber *Gruppen* to the strike force; upon refitting, this would represent a strength of over three hundred aircraft.[116] As preparations for the offensive moved forward, the Luftwaffe staffs would earmark additional forces. Even so, a force of this size was barely adequate for the destruction of such an imposing list of targets; only the fragility and vulnerable concentration of vital segments of the Soviet war economy stood in the German leadership's eyes as a mitigating factor. The inescapable fact was that, by late 1943, the Luftwaffe had the greatest difficulty in assembling a force of even these modest dimensions.

Beginning in December 1943, the units assigned to Fliegerkorps IV concentrated at various rear area airfields under a special interim rehabilitation staff known as Auffrischungsstab Ost (Reconstitution Staff East). The pause allowed the *Kampfgruppen* to replenish their aircraft and aircrew strength, undergo systematic briefings regarding the target system, and in the course of rigorous training, develop the new techniques required for effective nighttime bombardment of the Soviet industrial heartland.[117] Preparations went forward in the greatest secrecy, and specialists from the Steinmann Office and Fremde Luftwaffen Ost arrived in order to brief the command staffs of the bomber units as to the nature of the target.[118]

Some units made a fairly swift recovery, and set about the new task with a will. I./KG 55, for example, in mid-December 1943 left the Crimea, where it had been supporting the Seventeenth Army, for its new base at Ulez near the old Polish-Soviet border. Upon its arrival, the *Gruppe* possessed only twenty-three operational Heinkel 111s. By January 12, 1944 the unit had recovered nearly all of its established strength: thirty-seven aircraft.[119] Upon reaching operational strength, the *Gruppe* began the more difficult task of "training and preparing the crews for strategic night operations."[120] Initially, the training period was intended to last only until February 20; in fact, poor flying weather and other factors conspired to delay its completion until March.

The bomber units of Fliegerkorps IV were attempting to recover a technical advantage which the Luftwaffe had maintained over its adversaries during the early war years. The Luftwaffe in 1939–1940 was superior to all other air forces in the techniques and tactics of night bombing;[121] one need only recall the blind bombing raids used during the Blitz over England, most notably against Coventry on November 14, 1940. Four years of air combat had robbed the Luftwaffe of this specialized capability as the units and crews with the requisite training had been squandered in army support and air transport tasks. The Stalingrad and Tunisian airlift operations in particular stripped the training schools of instrument navigation and night flying instructors.[122] Meanwhile, the air forces of the Western Allies systematically cultivated both precision daylight and effective night area bombing capabilities to the point where a Luftwaffe General Staff analyst could conclude, "The enemy has learned from our conduct of the war, and the pupil is now the master!"[123]

Although the target system and the strategic rationale for the renewed air offensive against the USSR reflected original German planning and the peculiar nature of the Soviet war economy, it is evident from Luftwaffe studies that the tactical measures needed to carry out the attacks were borrowed wholesale from RAF Bomber Command. As the tempo of the Royal Air Force's bomber offensive against the Reich mounted, Luftwaffe intelligence and the operations staff exhibited increasing interest in the methods of, particularly, the specialized "Pathfinder" formations.[124] The Luftwaffe staffs perceived that the success of RAF Bomber Command in its area and occasional precision attacks against German targets stemmed from its use of "special crews with great combat experience, special training, and specialized equipment."[125] The reconstitution of Korps Meister called for improvements and reforms in all of these areas.

The most intractable problem proved to be the creation of special "target finder-illuminator" units. After a thorough evaluation of British practice, Luftwaffe intelligence estimated that fifty "pathfinder" aircraft were required for a large-scale night attack; this would mean retraining two *Kampfgruppen* for this task.[126] It was the original intention of the operations staff to equip the target-marking force with one of the latest bomber types available, the Junkers 188 (a substantially upgraded version of the Ju 88, redesignated so that, in Milch's words, "the enemy gets the impression it's something new.")[127] The limited quantities of this modern type instead went to the bomber units operating with Fliegerkorps IX in the west, raiding Great Britain during Operation Steinbock (Ibex) and intended for use against the coming invasion.[128] The operations staff believed that the Heinkel 111, thoroughly unsuited even for night operations against the Western Allies on account of its obsolescence, would prove to be an adequate pathfinder aircraft for the eastern front. The staff of Luftflotte 6 did not agree; however, the perceived necessity of carrying out reprisal raids against heavily-defended Great Britain meant that Fliegerkorps IV would have to make do with the more venerable bomber type.[129] Ultimately, the operations staff selected KG 4 "General Wever" to operate as the pathfinder force for the air offensive against the Soviet Union. Not until the late spring of

1944 would more modern aircraft such as the Heinkel 177 or Do 217 begin to appear in that theater.[130]

The tactics for illuminating and marking targets adhered fairly closely to RAF practice. Even the terminology employed by the Luftwaffe reflected the debt owed Bomber Command. The British term pathfinder (*Pfadfinder*) was employed interchangeably with *Zielfinder und Beleuchter* (target finder and illuminator), while *Bomberstrom* (bomber stream), another RAF term, described the flight pattern employed during a massed night attack.[131] An advance force of specially equipped aircraft, utilizing in some cases electronic navigation aids, placed marker flares ("Christmas trees") along the route to the target. The target finder unit would deposit prearranged patterns of colored flares at the aiming point; the conventionally armed bomber units would then attack the target with as much concentration as possible with incendiaries and high explosives.[132] KG 4 was to become, by the spring of 1944, quite proficient at the task of target illumination, as its participation in many successful attacks on the Soviet railway system testifies.

Even the non-specialized bomber units needed to relearn some old skills. The *Gruppenkommandeur* of I./KG 55, Major Richard Brunner, noted that his crews required extensive practice in formation flying, conducting massed take-offs at night, and navigation procedures. He observed, however, that his crews were quick to learn, and that the promise of strategic missions against worthwhile targets had infused them with a new zeal and sense of purpose after months of carrying out frustrating army support tasks.[133] Nonetheless, preparing the strike force required a considerable effort from the units taking part. The leadership of Luftflotte 6 called for the most rigorous and intense training possible, and although hampered by bad weather, most of the units seem to have risen to the occasion.[134]

In the later stages of the preparations, the Luftwaffe Operations Staff made a concerted effort to provide Fliegerkorps IV with one of the Luftwaffe's most modern aircraft: the trouble-ridden Heinkel 177 four-engined strategic bomber. As long ago as October 1942, Hitler "had attached great importance" to deployment of the Heinkel 177 against strategic targets in the USSR.[135] Endless technical delays rendered the He 177 unfit for active service for many months after its intended delivery date. Generaloberst Ritter von Greim of Luftflotte 6 had referred to the need for such a long-range bomber at the time of the June 1943 strategic bombing campaign; Dr. Carl of the Armaments Ministry noted that the lack of such an aircraft severely limited the Luftwaffe's target selection options in early 1944.[136] The absence of any coherent policy for the employment of such He 177 units as managed to become operational seriously delayed the aircraft's appearance on the eastern front.

It was not until December 1943 that Kampfgeschwader 1 "Hindenburg" received orders from the Luftwaffenführungsstab to begin reequipment and training with the Heinkel 177 for eventual assignment to Fliegerkorps IV. The intention was to employ the unit as a pathfinder formation. In fact, the lack of suitable ground personnel, trained crews, and specialized equipment delayed deployment of KG 1 to the eastern theater until June 1944, by which time the Geschwader was to carry out daylight precision raids with massed formations.[137] By summer 1944, however, the military situation had rendered the Luftwaffe's strategic bombing program irrelevant. It is not surprising that the official history of KG 1 referred to this period as "the last and saddest chapter in the history of the Geschwader."[138] Fliegerkorps IV was thus compelled to prepare its air attacks in early 1944 with the same basic aircraft types with which it had begun the eastern campaign in 1941. The He 111 H-20 and H-22, the latest incarnations of the aging bomber type, featured incremental improvements in performance, technical equipment and armament, including a power-operated dorsal turret. Even so, the bulk of the Heinkels in the force were the older H-6, H-11, and H-16 models. The Junkers 88 was a somewhat more modern type, but equipped only a few bomber Gruppen of Fliegerkorps IV. The Luftwaffe's Office of Air Armament had failed utterly to put a replacement medium bomber aircraft into production in time to have any effect on operations.

The situation regarding specialized munitions for use against Soviet power stations was equally problematic. Early in the planning stages of the operation, both Luftwaffe and civilian planners recognized that successful attacks on electrical works required a great degree of bombing accuracy. Professor Steinmann noted that a direct hit in the vitals of a power generating station with a standard SC 1000 aerial bomb was an unlikely prospect. Accordingly, the attack planners sought to provide Fliegerkorps IV with a variety of novel weaponry.

The most readily available of these was the Ruhrstahl "Fritz X" radio-controlled glider bomb. Mass production of this effective weapon was already in progress by the autumn of 1943,[139] although many were earmarked for anti-shipping units since the bomb, carrying a 1,400 kilogram warhead, was a proven performer even against enemy capital ships. In September 1943, for example, "Fritz-X"-carrying Do 217s sank the Italian battleship *Roma* as it headed into Allied captivity after Italy's exit from the war.[140] The major factor hindering employment of the bomb was a shortage of aircraft suitable for carrying these heavy and bulky weapons, hence the provision of a single Do 217 unit, III./KG 100, for Fliegerkorps IV. Furthermore, a special Heinkel 111 unit began training with the precision weapons. Dr. Carl and his team estimated that even a small force of "Fritz X" carriers might have spectacular results, although they based their calculations upon some rather optimistic assumptions:

> One may reckon that, given one bomb per aircraft and a 50% on-target rate, a force of 20 aircraft will place approximately 10 bombs within the target area. Of these, perhaps five will hit the vital point; for example, the engine room of a power plant.[141]

In operations against the Royal Navy in the Mediterranean in daylight, the weapons scored hits on the average of one in every fifteen launches.[142]

The "Fritz X" and the "S Bo 53," a "cable bomb" (*Seilbombe*) designed some years earlier for use against high tension wires, required the authorization of Hitler for their deployment.[143] The Führer did in fact grant permission for both of these "secret weapons" to be used over land, where the danger that they might fall intact into Allied hands and allow the enemy "to jam or imitate the device" correspondingly increased.[144]

A less successful effort to develop specialized munitions grew out of a collaboration between Professor Steinmann and the Office of Air Armament's Inspectorate for Aerial Mines. Steinmann noted that the hydroelectric plants mentioned in one of his attack proposals, with their well-protected turbines, presented an especially difficult target for conventional bombing attacks. Accordingly, Steinmann initiated the development of Winterballon (winter balloon) and Sommerballon (summer balloon), specialized devices for attacking these particular targets.[145]

Winterballon and Sommerballon were both floating mines, designed to destroy hydroelectric turbines under any seasonal conditions. Winterballon consisted of an SC 1000 bomb, a guide parachute, a CO_2 cartridge

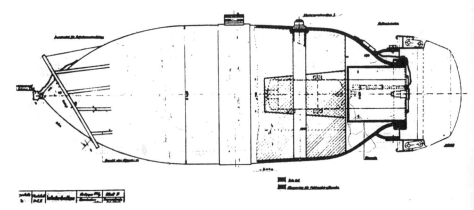

Figure 1. Technical diagram of the Winterballon, a floating mine designed by Professor Steinmann for use against the turbines of Soviet hydroelectric plants. Although the weapon failed miserably during testing, the device was ordered into production and was earmarked for use in Operation Burgund in late 1944.

and balloon apparatus, and a cutting edge fitted to the nose to enable it to pierce protective cable barriers.[146] Sommerballon was intended to "creep" along the bottom while the current drew it into the turbine blades.[147] Neither of these weapons performed well during testing, which in any case began much later than anticipated. On June 27, 1944, tests of Winterballon on a frozen lake in Finse, Lappland, were a complete fiasco, as the mines, released from a Heinkel 111, wound up hopelessly lodged in the bottom mud.[148]

In spite of the fact that neither weapon underwent successful testing, both devices went into mass production. Koller believed that Sommerballon would be ready for action by late summer 1944, with Winterballon following suit that November.[149] By this time, of course, there were no vital Soviet power stations within practical aircraft range. The supply of floating mines then passed to the planners of various "special operations" utilizing unorthodox units and weaponry. Like so much of German "secret weapons" development, these munitions contributed nothing to German fighting power, and their developmental history bore little or no relationship to operational planning or available capabilities.

The short-term success of Auffrischungsstab Ost in restoring the striking power of the Luftwaffe's bomber force in Russia does not obscure the fact that the aircraft production situation in late 1943 and early 1944 permitted virtually no expansion of that force in the foreseeable future; nor was any assembly of reserves possible. Luftwaffe bomber production in 1943–1944 was inadequate even to replace losses. The German aircraft industry's enormous production gains during this period reflected almost entirely a reorientation towards day and night fighter production for home defense; almost none of the expanded capacity was available for the bomber forces. Generalleutnant Karl Koller, Chief of the Luftwaffe Operations Staff, concluded in May 1944 that current production levels would not long sustain even the current force structure of one strong bombardment *Fliegerkorps* in each major war theater.[150] Korten's scheme to create separate home defense, army support and strategic bombing forces may have stood the comparison to realistic Luftwaffe prewar doctrine, but Germany's economic and strategic situation by early 1944 made a mockery of such efforts.

The German air force had by early 1944 thrashed out a strategic mission for its bomber forces and had assembled, however imperfectly,

LUFTWAFFE BOMBER LOSSES AND PRODUCTION, ALL FRONTS
January 1943–March 1944[151]

Month	Destroyed	Damaged	Production
1943			
Jan.	214	122	357
Feb.	185	97	436
March	253	171	354
April	165	119	327
May	261	172	352
June	211	182	350
July	421	266	331
Aug.	356	224	336
Sept.	284	188	326
Oct.	225	191	350
Nov.	219	125	357
Dec.	135	81	341
1944			
Jan.	278	196	300
Feb.	249	200	327
March	319	225	434

a strike force with which to carry it out. Concentration of such a force in the face of the aforementioned obstacles denuded the hard-pressed eastern front of a sizeable proportion of its accustomed air support, and in the process, as Deichmann conceded, "accelerated the retreat of the German front line in the east."[152] There is little doubt that most of the planners involved believed that the power plant operation promised substantial dividends. Deichmann believed that Aktion Russland "would have met with resounding success, and would have paralyzed the Russian armaments industry for a long time."[153] Even the cautious Koller believed that "great success may be achieved even with the small forces available."[154] Most Luftwaffe planners believed that specialized weaponry, well-trained crews and systematic target research, applied against the enemy's most vulnerable point, would tilt the odds in favor of the German air force and make it a truly decisive factor in the campaign once again.

Knowing One's Enemy. A crewman unloading an aerial camera from an FW 189. Luftwaffe tactical intelligence was generally accurate; the same could not be said of strategic or economic intelligence. (National Air and Space Museum, Smithsonian Institution, Photo No. 90-17308)

CHAPTER SIX

THE END OF THE LUFTWAFFE'S OFFENSIVE CAPABILITY

In its years of combat against the Soviet Union, the Luftwaffe's flexibility allowed it to function effectively in diverse roles. Its contributions made possible the rapid advances of summer 1941 and buttressed the reeling German army following the failure before Moscow. The Luftwaffe's successes during Operation Blue temporarily masked the strategic failings of the venture. It had never, however, been able to deal an unassisted decisive blow against the eastern enemy. In early 1944, in contrast to previous campaigning seasons, the Luftwaffe command had the desire, the sanction from above, and even the nominal means to execute a coordinated independent air strategy whose expectations, if not its scope, matched those of the Western Allies. The United States Strategic Bombing Survey concluded that "air power's most vital role would be to reach far into the enemy's country and destroy his sustaining sources of military power."[1] The objectives of the Luftwaffe's belated attempt to shatter Soviet combat power, and even the wording of the documents that supported this effort, were almost identical to the American formulation.

The history of air power during the Second World War is often one of grandiose expectations followed by results ranging from ambiguous stalemates to dismal failures.[2] The reasons for these frequently unedifying conclusions to carefully planned air operations are as complex as was the planning for the operations themselves. In the case of Aktion Russland, an explanation for the eventual diversion and miscarriage of the operation must consider the dynamics of the ground situation on the eastern front, the effects of the campaign in the west, Luftwaffe technical capabilities, and the ambitious general staff planning as well as seemingly arbitrary interference and second-guessing by outside agencies. Therefore, the account given by Speer and others that suggests that Hitler capriciously ordered the irreplaceable strategic bomber corps into a railway interdiction campaign in which it was "annihilated" does not withstand close scrutiny as an adequate explanation.[3] The failure of Aktion Russland stemmed as much from the shortcomings of the Luftwaffe's own planning staffs as from convenient "external" factors. The result was to be the destruction of the last vestiges of the offensive capability of the Luftwaffe on any front. As if to symbolize the complete collapse of that once-formidable force, the bomber strength of Luftflotte 6, the air fleet that had intended to carry the war to the Soviet industrial heartland, consisted in early February 1945 of the single squadron 14./(Eis.) KG 55, operating seven obsolescent He 111 bombers against the expanse of the Soviet rail network.[4]

Luftwaffe intelligence had correctly identified the Soviet war industries as the power source underlying the grave threat to German presence in the east. During 1944 and 1945, the years Soviet combat power was at its height, the Red Army and the VVS, amply supplied with first-rate equipment produced in factories untouched by German bombers, drove the battered Ostheer through eastern Europe and back to Berlin. Only a greatly diminished Luftwaffe opposed the "Bolshevik hordes," yet it was an air force top-heavy with close air support capability. It remains a supreme irony that during the final one and one-half years of the campaign the Luftwaffe, its strategic bombing capability gone, at last perfected the technical and organizational means with which to provide reliable close air support for the ground forces. Although outnumbered by its Soviet adversary by a factor occasionally approaching 10:1, the Luftwaffe ground attack arm remained a considerable factor in defensive combat in the east almost until the final days of the conflict. Like the majority of Second World War air forces, the Luftwaffe mastered this difficult mission, for which it had entered the war poorly prepared, only after years of combat experience and improvisation. The result was an impressive capability, but one that came into being only after the German air force was unable to conduct *operativer Luftkrieg* in any of its permutations.

DEMISE OF AN INTELLECTUAL CONSTRUCT: THE FAILURE OF AKTION RUSSLAND

Had the completion of Fliegerkorps IV's formation, deployment, and training coincided more closely with the Luftwaffenführungsstab's operational recommendations, the Luftwaffe might well have launched the "systematic attack upon the Soviet Union's armaments potential" in late 1943 or during the first months of 1944. Speer informed Korten on February 4, 1944 that:

> [E]ven today the prospects are good . . . for an operative air campaign against the Soviet Union . . . I definitely hope that significant effects on the fighting power of the Soviet Union will result from it . . .[5]

As it happened, completion of the "rehabilitation" period that kept the Luftwaffe's bomber forces out of the furnace of the eastern front, originally intended to end by mid-February, dragged on until late March 1944.[6] Muddy airfield conditions and the need for a full moon period to accompany the attack created additional postponements.[7]

With the training period delayed, events on the ground had a crucial effect on the conditions necessary for the operation. On February 6, 1944, Luftflotte 6 presented its recommendations for final jumping-off bases for the launching of the long-awaited power plant strike. Greim intended to deploy his bomber force (which by that date comprised eight *Gruppen* of Heinkel 111s, two of Junkers 88s, and one of "Fritz-X"-carrying Dornier 217s) at seven airfields in the Minsk-Bobruisk-Orsha area.[8] Noticeably absent from this deployment plan were the northern airfields of Dno and Pskov, at which the operations staff had contemplated basing the three *Gruppen* of bombers with the three power plants at Gorki as their targets. Soviet offensive activity aimed at the final relief of Leningrad and the clearing of the Baltic States threatened to force a German withdrawal into the so-called *Pantherstellung* (Panther position), a "retrograde motion" which would deny Fliegerkorps IV use of these bases.[9] Greim proposed to Korten and Koller the possibility of using alternate bases in the Karelian

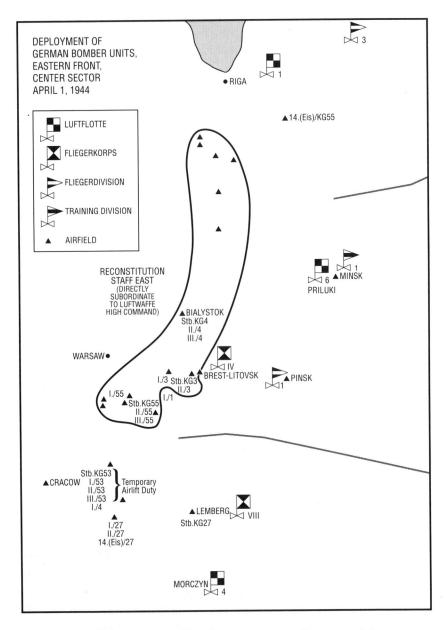

DEPLOYMENT OF
GERMAN BOMBER UNITS,
EASTERN FRONT,
CENTER SECTOR
APRIL 1, 1944

LUFTFLOTTE

FLIEGERKORPS

FLIEGERDIVISION

TRAINING DIVISION

▲   AIRFIELD

RECONSTITUTION
STAFF EAST
(DIRECTLY
SUBORDINATE
TO LUFTWAFFE
HIGH COMMAND)

● RIGA

▲ 14.(Eis)/KG55

6 ▲ MINSK
PRILUKI

▲ BIALYSTOK
Stb.KG4
II./4
III./4

WARSAW ●

▲
I./3 Stb.KG3
II./3
BREST-LITOVSK

PINSK

I./55 ▲
▲ Stb.KG55
II./55 ▲
III./55
I./1

▲
Stb.KG53
▲ CRACOW   I./53   Temporary
II./53   Airlift Duty
III./53   ▲
I./4

▲
I./27
II./27
14.(Eis)/27

▲ LEMBERG
Stb.KG27
VIII

MORCZYN
4

Map 7. Deployments of Luftwaffe units, central sector of the eastern front, April 1, 1944. Note the grouping of all long-range bomber units in the area of Fliegerkorps IV for the attack against the power plants (and eventually Soviet rail transportation).

Isthmus of Finland for the Gorki operation, but this was the first sign that the limited range of Luftwaffe bombers and Soviet offensive activity was about to render Aktion Russland a geographic impossibility.

More was to come; on February 11, Greim sent Korten his detailed "Proposals for the Commencement of Strategic Air Warfare Against the Soviet War Economy."[10] The air fleet commander's recommendations represented the same curious admixture of realism and *hubris* that characterized the entire strategic bombing venture. Greim correctly prophesied that the military situation portended an early loss of the critical airfields east of Lake Peipus, and that the Gorki portion of the operation would then be effectively scuttled.[11] Greim, who was a popular commander as well as a convinced national socialist (and who has the distinction of being referred to as a "maniac" in the Soviet official history),[12] did not concur with the "expert opinion" of Carl and Steinmann that eliminating the three Gorki power stations from the target list would render the operation pointless. Instead, Greim concluded that "range considerations inevitably place attacks upon the Moscow area more and more into the foreground."

Incredibly, in view of the amount of effort the Luftwaffe operations staff expended in order to determine the most rewarding attack targets, the Luftflottenkommando 6 proposals were remarkably primitive. Moscow city, Greim argued, contained a sufficient number of war industries to qualify it as an attack objective. He cited some intelligence figures from the Aussenstelle des W. Stabes Ausland (Mitte) that in fact tended to undermine his thesis. Factories in Greater Moscow, according to these figures, produced forty percent of the Red Army's optical and precision instruments, yet only five percent of aircraft engines, five to ten percent of the artillery pieces, and ten percent of antitank ammunition. In no manner did these figures suggest that Luftflotte 6 could, by attacking Moscow, expect to inflict crippling damage on the Soviet war economy.[13]

Since Moscow was also a major population center as well as the center of Bolshevik power, Greim suggested that it should be the target of "12 to 15 repeat attacks" by the entire 300–plus aircraft strength of Meister's long-range bomber force. In a formulation strongly reminiscent of Douhet (whose theories in 1943–1944 were undergoing something of a revival of interest within certain Luftwaffe circles)[14] Greim proposed:

Concentrated attacks upon the military-industrial installations in Moscow may cause, alongside the destruction of industrial targets, heavy damage to the densely-packed adjoining urban areas. The working population which has been up to the present time lulled into a feeling of security will suffer heavy casualties, as well as still poorer living and working conditions, and will morally be greatly affected. Furthermore, the regime will in all probability be temporarily crippled.[15]

This extraordinary proposal has all of the hallmarks of desperation, an attempt to keep alive a cherished operational concept that events threatened to render superfluous. Luftwaffe intelligence evidently suffered from the same malady, as by selective juggling of the Steinmann Office's figures, Fremde Luftwaffen Ost, on February 28, 1944 came to the conclusion that "a systematic assault upon the power supply in the Moscow-Upper Volga region is still possible, even if the area around Gorki is not attacked."[16] Major Boie pointed out that the 639,000 kilowatts generated by the Gorki plants represented only twenty-five percent of the total power reserve of the area, and the loss could be made up simply by striking additional plants in the Moscow area.

Koller of the Luftwaffe operations staff replied to these proposals on March 6. Though he still had faith in the basic soundness of the power plant concept, Koller admitted that the loss of key air bases had thrown the operation into disarray.[17] He proposed a number of alternate targets, including using S Bo 53 cable bombs against the high-tension network carrying electricity from the Gorki region as a substitute for attacks on the power plants themselves, but offered no definite remedy.

Koller was, however, adamant in rejecting out of hand Greim's proposals for "concentrated attacks" on the city of Moscow. He correctly noted that "the concentration of armaments industries decisive to the war effort within the city limits is relatively small."[18] Furthermore, Koller possessed a far more realistic appraisal of both the Soviet citizenry's will to resist and the efficacy of terror bombing. He pointedly told Greim:

Considering the demonstrated toughness and Spartan nature of the Russian population, we cannot expect permanent and militarily decisive effects from terror attacks against residential quarters. They are, rather, more likely to give the will to resist of the Russian people new sustenance . . .

Almost by default, one of the other "strategic target systems" in the Soviet war economy which Luftwaffe intelligence had identified now came to the fore. In the temporary absence of a cohesive plan for striking at the "sources of Soviet power," Fliegerkorps IV made ready for attacks against the means of distributing that power: the rail network of the USSR. Much the same logic animated the railway interdiction campaign as had driven the power plant attack concept. German intelligence analysts regarded both the railway network and the electrical supply grid of the Soviet Union as exceptionally vulnerable points in a relatively primitive, centrally directed economy. The railway system lacked density, had many stretches of single-track line, and appeared to offer the possibility of disruption even by relatively weak forces. Attacks against the Soviet rail system had been, of course, a familiar mission for the Luftwaffe since the campaign began. Wide-ranging interdiction of Soviet rail communications during Barbarossa went a long way towards making possible the dramatic successes of summer 1941,[19] and most of the eastern *Luftflotten*, from 1942 on, operated specialized railway attack *Staffeln* which attacked targets of opportunity.[20] As early as August 1943, the operations staff professed awareness of the "special significance" Soviet railways held for the conduct of operations.[21] At that time, the Führungsstab was concerned primarily with the operational and tactical ramifications of attacks against the rail lines, rather than any "strategic" effect such attacks might bring about:

> The weight of the attacks against railways is guided largely by the *situation at the time* [italics in original]. In the case of advances or the launching of operations by the enemy the primary task is the *cutting of communications* on the lines leading to that specific section of the front.[22]

During the search for strategic objectives for the bomber force, Luftwaffe intelligence began to regard attacks on Soviet communications as a means of disrupting the entire Russian war economy. While "sealing off" particular areas of the front in order to assist the German army's defensive situation remained an important goal of the Luftwaffe planners, strategic attacks "in depth" promised far more dramatic effects. In April 1944, Major Boie of Fremde Luftwaffen Ost noted:

> The objective of a systematic attack on the Russian rail transport system must be a complete paralysis of the enemy transit capa-

bility . . . a consistently executed assault on the enemy rail system, carried out with strong forces over a long period of time will not only lead to difficulties for supply of the front; rather, it will at the same time also create great difficulties for the entire economic life of the nation.[23]

Many of Ic's recommendations for rail targets in the Soviet hinterland concerned those lines carrying goods from the now-unreachable key industries of the Soviet war economy. These arteries included Moscow-Rostov, Kirov-Yaroslavl-Moscow, Kasan-Moscow, and Kuibyschev-Ulyanovsk-Moscow.[24] Likewise, most Luftwaffe intelligence appraisals of potential rail system attack targets covered the length and breadth of the eastern front, from Leningrad to Kharkov, not simply those sectors in which Soviet offensive activity appeared likely.[25] The thrust of Luftwaffe intelligence's arguments appears to have been that systematic attacks on the rail lines were yet another means of strangling the Soviet war economy.

In the late winter of 1944, few in German air force intelligence or command circles seemed to believe that using Fliegerkorps IV against Soviet communications constituted a relapse into the despised army support role for the bomber fleet. Indeed, Korten in February 1944 referred to ''wide-ranging interdiction of enemy rail traffic'' as a worthy and important mission for Meister's strategic bomber force.[26] Meister, Korten, and Greim also believed that night mass attacks against communications centers would provide the newly trained crews of Fliegerkorps IV, particularly the pathfinder formations, with the requisite operational experience to become a true strategic striking force.[27] The extended training period required for Fliegerkorps IV, the loss of the forward air bases necessary for the launching of Aktion Russland, and the constantly changing ground situation with the threat of Soviet offensives ensured that the deviation into attacks on the communications system would be a permanent one.

Koller, under postwar interrogation, sought to portray the miscarriage of the power plant attacks as a consequence of the Führer's untutored meddling in air force matters. Koller told his interrogators:

At the last moment everything again fell apart, and the units which had been standing by were ordered against the Russian railroads. The Führer promised me that these missions were, so to speak, merely the last training exercises prior to the big attacks against the power plants, and that after ten days the units would be released for this mission. The promise was not kept, the air corps was never released, and it flew again and again against the railroads . . . until the airfields from which [the power plant attack] had to be flown had fallen into enemy hands.[28]

He also maintained that he had persuadèd Hitler to "limit railway interdiction to twelve days," but that the force had by that time been decimated and Hitler cancelled the power plant attack.

Koller, both during interrogations and in his postwar memoirs, sought to place the blame for the Luftwaffe's defeat on Göring, Hitler, "the German High Command, certain 'know-alls' at the head of German industry," and other familiar scapegoats.[29] In the case of the demise of the strategic bombing program against the USSR, Koller's accusations are misplaced. His own intelligence agencies provided ample strategic rationale for the attack against Soviet rail communications, and the first such attack did not take place until the night of March 27, 1944.[30] This was fully three weeks after Koller himself concluded that, "with the withdrawal of the front into the Panther position," and the concurrent loss of the airbases at Dno and Pskov, the three power plants in the Gorki area had already passed out of Heinkel range.[31] Koller's own staff, as well as the "outside experts" Carl and Steinmann, had stressed that all three power generating areas of the Moscow-Upper Volga region had to be attacked in order to produce the desired effect; therefore, by the time the bombers of Fliegerkorps IV turned to railway targets, the essential conditions for the Aktion Russland plan as described in November 1943 no longer existed.[32] Although Koller on March 6 had proposed an alternative power plant attack, substituting targets at Tula, Aleksin, Ivanovo, and Electro-Peredacha (objectives to which Fremde Luftwaffen Ost only one week earlier referred as "small" power plants),[33] he admitted that this reordering of priorities had to await intelligence evaluation and verification.[34] Fliegerkorps IV was therefore, in late March 1944, effectively unemployed, and there seemed in the meantime to be sound operational imperatives for sending its bomber forces against the rail network.

These operational reasons concerned ominous signs that the Red Army was preparing for another mass offensive that spring. Luftwaffe intelligence prided itself on its ability to discover the probable axis of a Soviet offensive through systematic evaluation of rail traffic reports. Employing certain correction factors applicable to the eastern front ("the volume of Russian rail traffic cannot be measured by Western standards [a German division equaled sixty trains; a Russian infantry division equaled fifteen trains])",[35] Luftwaffe intelligence claimed that "all the Russian operations could be detected in time, and in some cases the date of the launching of the offensive determined to the very day."[36] Without passing judgment upon this last statement for the moment, it is clear that both Luftwaffe and army intelligence believed they possessed compelling evidence of a considerable Soviet buildup opposite the demarcation line between Heeresgruppe Mitte and Heeresgruppe Nordukraine from mid-February 1944.

Observation of both road and especially rail traffic after February 15, 1944 indicated all of the hallmarks of a Soviet buildup for a major offensive in the area of Kovel, roughly eighty miles southeast of Brest-Litovsk, the battle headquarters of Fliegerkorps IV. German intelligence noted particularly heavy activity along the rail lines linking Kiev, Korosten, Sarny, and Rovno. The Germans noted "with certainty" the arrival of thirty-one new Soviet formations in the Luzk-Kovel-Dombroviza area, with a further twenty formations appearing in the rear areas.[37] Fortuitously, this was the same general area in which both Luftflotte 6 and Korten had proposed night operational training exercises against transportation centers. With the carefully planned strike against the armaments industry thrown into abeyance by the "retrograde motion" of the front line, many Luftwaffe planners believed that the frustration of a major Soviet offensive buildup offered a temporary substitute. Other commanders subsequently regarded the railway interdiction campaign as "a slap in the face to the 'Doctrine.'"[38] Much of this dissenting opinion appears to have emerged well after the fact; Koller's own operations staff issued the following appreciation in the latter stages of Fliegerkorps IV's protracted assault on the Soviet rail network:

> The *bomber units* operate most effectively against transportation targets. They delay and interfere with the orderly supply of the combat front, particularly when employed against long-distance troop movements and supply columns and in attacks on supply

centers. The repair of railway installations is observed to be time-consuming.[39]

It is most probable that only in hindsight did the four month long campaign against Soviet rail traffic in the Ukraine appear to be the death knell of the Luftwaffe's last serious strategic bombing venture. That venture had collapsed of its own weight before the first bomb fell on Sarny railroad station on the night of March 27, 1944. Luftwaffe intelligence found the target selection process for this offensive to be a far simpler task than the one that had occupied much of its energy from late summer 1943. It was a fairly straightforward process, from its observations of Soviet rail traffic, to convert the raw data into a determination of "bottlenecks" in the Soviet rail network opposite Army Group North-Ukraine. Indeed, on the staff of every air fleet in the east was an operations officer tasked with the evaluation of intelligence information dealing with rail traffic.[40] In such a manner did the closer relationship between Luftwaffe operational commands and the intelligence branch that began during the highly complex power plant project continue into the last phase of Luftwaffe offensive operations.

General Luftwaffe doctrinal statements prior to the Second World War did not place railway interdiction high on target priority lists. *Luftkriegführung* plausibly (if erroneously) noted that, with the rise of modern motorized armies, rail transport would lose some of the vital significance it possessed during the days of the wars of unification. Wever's formulation also pointed out that "major railway stations and junctions are on account of their size alluring targets. They are, however, in general not to be selected as attack objectives."[41] The framers of the Luftwaffe's basic doctrinal statement believed that major railway stations were heavily defended targets, and difficult to cripple effectively. Bridges and other vulnerable points seemed far more suitable targets.[42]

Luftwaffe experience in the war against the USSR caused the operations staff to modify prewar doctrine to conform to the realities of the theater. The Luftwaffenführungsstab Ia allowed that:

The many-sided character of the operations against the enemy's railroads precludes any fixed assessment of the efficacy of different types of operations, or any rigid treatment of experiences. The greatest possible mobility in the choice of targets and attacking procedures is to be aimed at not only by the higher command but also by the commanders of flying units, so that the enemy defenses will be confused and weakened as much as possible.[43]

The Luftwaffe command recommended attacks on complex facilities such as repair shops, concentrations of rolling stock, and the cutting of individual lines. Railway interdiction had until early 1944 been the province of small groups of aircraft, usually no larger than *Staffel* strength, that patrolled open stretches of railway.[44] Large-scale strikes on major rail depots, such as those that preceded the Kursk offensive, were relatively rare. The attempt in early 1944 to identify "key points" in the rail network in order to produce a decisive effect most certainly grew out of Luftwaffe intelligence's reorientation towards strategic air warfare during the previous year. Even more importantly, the Luftwaffen-führungsstab Ic had to restrict its target analysis to objectives which large formations of heavy bombers, operated by crews trained in long-distance night navigation and pathfinder techniques, might profitably attack. Practically the only targets fitting these criteria were the largest rail yards used by the Red Army command in the buildup for the spring offensive. These installations contained "massed rolling stock" as well as the vulnerable service installations necessary to keep the Red Army rolling.[45] In this manner did the available force structure determine the character of the offensive, just as surely as did the "strategic vision" of the German air force general staff.

The last substantial German manned bomber offensive of the Second World War, code-named Operation Zaunkönig (Wren), commenced on the night of March 27, 1944. Fifty bombers of Meister's air corps attacked the railway junction at Sarny, one of the key railway bottlenecks supplying Soviet forces advancing on Kovel.[46] A much heavier raid on the same target followed on the night of March 31, as Fliegerkorps IV, with more of its bomber units at combat readiness following the training period, continued the offensive.[47] The operation demonstrates yet again the blurred distinctions between the German conception of *operativer* or strategic air operations and indirect army support. Luftwaffen-führungsstab Ic had conceived of the railway interdiction plan as a means of striking at the Soviet war economy, yet the choice of targets fulfilled a "battlefield interdiction," or *mittelbare Heeresunterstützung* role. This point was further underscored when, during the first week of

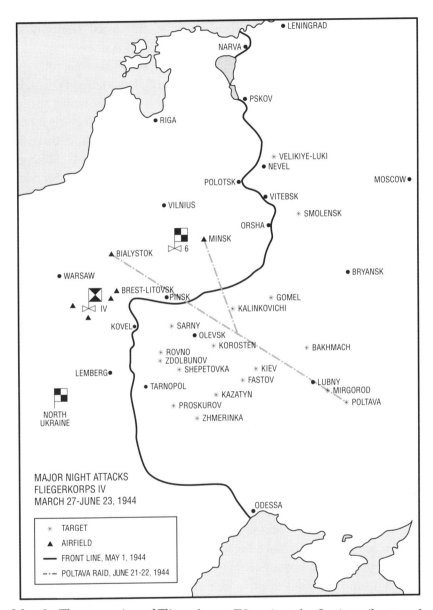

MAJOR NIGHT ATTACKS
FLIEGERKORPS IV
MARCH 27-JUNE 23, 1944

*   TARGET
▲   AIRFIELD
—   FRONT LINE, MAY 1, 1944
-·-··   POLTAVA RAID, JUNE 21-22, 1944

Map 8. The campaign of Fliegerkorps IV against the Soviet rail network, March 27–June 22, 1944. The Luftwaffe was attempting to forestall a predicted Soviet offensive against Army Group North-Ukraine. In addition, the bombers of Meister's air corps struck at the Ukrainian bases of the USAAF shuttle bombing campaign, Poltava and Mirgorod.

April, a number of the irreplaceable bomber *Gruppen* of KG 53 and 55 temporarily functioned as transport units in the aerial resupply of Kovel, which Hitler on March 8 designated a "fortified place."[48]

Even after the immediate Soviet threat to Kovel had passed, the frequency, weight of attack, and effectiveness of Fliegerkorps IV's night raids continued to grow under the assumption that the major spring offensive would also come in this area. The Luftwaffe command's intention was to cut the main rail arteries Kursk-Sheptovka and Briansk-Sarny; the attacks from mid-April through early July 1944 adhered closely to this goal, even when the tactical situation indicated the need for attacks on other points in order to relieve local pressures.[49] Targets attacked most frequently included Sarny, Rovno, Zdolbunov, Sheptovka, Zhmerinka, Korosten, Kiev, Gomel, and Fastov.[50] Drawing upon years of careful observation of Soviet rail traffic, the operations staff devised the following procedures for effective railway interdiction:

> Stretches of line were first blocked by two or three large-scale attacks, after which the unloading stations of the small lines leading up to the front were knocked out by simultaneous attacks by subordinate formations. This was intended to produce a stoppage, which was increased by attacks on intermediate stations. Heavy attacks were then made on the main stations which had been over-occupied as a result of the blockage.[51]

Execution of this bomber offensive required great skill on the part of the command staffs involved.[52] The flying formations had to be far more mobile than was normal for heavy bomber units, which generally operated out of well-equipped, permanent bases. Moreover, many of the targets required penetrations of over five hundred kilometers into enemy territory.[53] The success of the operations, which Herhudt von Rohden subsequently believed was so "convincing and spectacular" as to cause the Luftwaffe staffs to neglect other strategic targets,[54] raises the interesting question of how well Fliegerkorps IV would have performed had it been sent against the power plants, its original *raison d'etre*.

The tactical proficiency of the units taking part indicates both the existence of a cadre of experienced aircrews[55] and that the lengthy training period had at least achieved part of its objective. The crews of the ten bomber *Gruppen* were trained in the use of various navigational aids, most notably the Zyklops, Elektra-Sonne 12, and Egon radio beacons, the latter two located in Warsaw and Pinsk, respectively.[56] Despite these provisions, German crews preferred moonlit conditions for these operations. Actual attack methods put into practice the target marking and illuminating techniques borrowed from RAF Bomber Command's Pathfinder Force. Under ideal conditions, Luftflotte 6 could attack two or three targets simultaneously, each with eighty to one hundred aircraft. Combat losses were remarkably low: during the entire March-July operational career of Fliegerkorps IV, there were fewer than 110 crew fatalities. According to Meister, losses during the training period, attributed to carelessness or overconfidence on the part of veteran combat crews forced to undergo protracted training, had been higher than those caused by enemy action once the campaign began.[57] In stark contrast to the task facing German fliers over Great Britain, night bombing in the eastern theater seems to have remained practical up until the end of the war. The VVS never developed a sophisticated night fighter defense system, and the Luftwaffe's outmoded eastern bomber force could operate almost at will even in 1944. Luftflotte 6's fears that rail centers such as Sarny would in addition possess formidable anti-aircraft concentrations and therefore impose "considerable risk of losses" upon Luftwaffe formations were therefore groundless.[58]

The railway campaign in fact provided one of the few bright spots for the Luftwaffe command on any front. The spring of 1944 occasioned the climactic months of the Eighth Air Force's devastating daylight bombing offensive over the Reich, and the defeat of the German day fighter arm. The reprisal attacks against Britain proved costly and wasteful exercises, and the Anglo-American invasion of the Continent was imminent. Only in the eastern theater, it seemed, was the German air force still earning its keep. The Luftwaffe's own propaganda machinery was quick to promote the campaign. War correspondents' reports, complete with lurid titles such as "Flaming Finale: Rovno and Sarny" and "Target: Sheptovka Railway Station" heralded the "systematic destruction of Soviet supply lines." Some of the observations make interesting reading:

Immediately evident is the moral distinction between these attacks against military objectives of the first rank and the aimless bombing raids of the British and Americans against old people and children . . .[59]

There is little question that the raids did cause the Soviets a certain measure of inconvenience, and doubtless the destruction of rolling stock and war material at the bombed stations was considerable. Even so, the Luftwaffe command managed to squander much of the military value of the revived strategic bomber force through a typically muddled perception of its objectives. Although originally promoted as a campaign calculated to paralyze the entire Soviet transport network, in practice the raids promised only to disrupt a Soviet offensive buildup in one sector: that opposite Army Group North Ukraine.

Certainly the Red Army was reinforcing that sector in the wake of their first unsuccessful attempt to take Kovel in April 1944, but the real weight of the Soviet offensive preparations lay north of the Pripyat Marshes, opposite Army Group Center in Belorussia. Although a number of railway stations in that sector (notably Olevsk and Smolensk) received Fliegerkorps IV attention, there is no doubt that the bulk of Luftwaffe sorties were expended on railway junctions of secondary importance. Both Luftwaffe and army intelligence failed to draw the proper conclusions from observed rail traffic, and sophisticated Soviet camouflage and deception, or *maskirovka*, measures complicated their task.[60] Soviet deception operations preceding the summer offensive in 1944 were on an "unprecedented" scale. Second Ukrainain Front's commander created the impression of massive concentration in his area, while the buildup of the First Belorussian Front was carefully concealed by night movement and zealous attention to camouflage procedures.[61] Fliegerkorps IV's vain effort contains within it a final measure of irony. One of the reasons for the Soviet High Command's selection of the Belorussia sector as the focus of the great summer offensive was that, in the words of the Soviet official history:

> In the triangle of Lepel-Mogilev-Minsk [the area from which most of Fliegerkorps IV's railway interdiction strikes emanated] the enemy maintained aircraft . . . that could pressure the rear areas of the Baltic and Belorussian Fronts on very short notice . . .[62]

In such a manner did the German long-range bomber force, in achieving its last run of operational success, help to bring about the loss of its forward bases to the Soviet counteroffensive it had failed to prevent.

The most noteworthy success of Fliegerkorps IV occurred just as that counteroffensive, known as Operation Bagration after the Tsarist gen-

eral killed fighting Napoleon at Borodino in 1812, was about to commence. Meister's command exerted a strategic effect that none of the
Luftwaffe planners who had brought the long-range bomber force into
being had anticipated. This concerned the derailment of the United
States Army Air Forces' policy of conducting "shuttle" missions from
bases on Soviet soil against industrial and transportation targets in eastern Europe. The policy of shuttle bombing already faced extraordinary
difficulties on account of the touchy political complications surrounding
the basing of AAF bombers on Russian territory. United States Strategic
Air Forces in Europe, Eastern Command employed a "baseball" meta-
phor in explaining the accompanying difficulties:

> The main objective of Baseball . . . is to prove to the other Ball
> Team how well we plan and play the game, so as to convince
> them to let us use their other Ball-fields. Whether they let us use
> their other Ball-fields or not, we are going to be playing some-
> where in that League, and we must profit from both our lessons
> and our failures.[63]

While alliance politics went a long way towards undermining the enterprise, there can be little doubt that prompt and decisive action by the
Luftwaffe operations staff and the Luftflotte 6 command was a prime
factor in the scuttling of the program.

German planners had long dreaded the prospect of strategic air operations launched against them from the eastern theater. As early as October 1943, Foreign Air Forces East drew attention to the consequences for
German war production if the VVS' formidable tactical aviation capability was augmented by strong forces of American B-17 and B-24 four-
engined strategic bombers. The armaments industry of eastern Europe,
including the Skoda works in occupied Czechoslovakia, would be at
risk.[64] With this ominous possibility in mind, Luftwaffe intelligence for-
warded to the OKW reports from German agents in late 1943 and early
1944 indicating signs of interest on the part of the Western Allies in
basing long-range aircraft on Soviet territory. These items included a
"conference between the Anglo-American Military Mission and Air
Marshal Novikov" in December 1943, the appearance of American
bombers in Iraq and Iran, and other bits of information that suggested
the opening of another strategic bombing front against German industry. German intelligence concluded that the most likely rationale for the

buildup was that, since the Soviet aircraft industry was incapable of producing suitable heavy bomber types in sufficient numbers, the American types were required for "an air offensive against Germany from the east."[65] The impetus for Hitler's now-bankrupt Crimean policy had been to keep the Ploesti oilfields secure even from the unsophisticated and ineffectual VVS long-range bomber force.[66] Greim, in his proposal for large-scale raids against Moscow, reckoned that such an offensive would bring reprisal raids against German targets, and recommended concurrent strengthening of home defense forces in the eastern Reich territories.[67] Initially, however, the appearance of USAAF B-17s and their P-51 escorts at the Ukrainian bases of Poltava, Mirgorod, and Piryatin for a June 2 raid on Debrecen marshalling yards "was drowned in the whirl of the [Normandy] invasion."[68] A much larger attack on the hydrogenation plant at Ruhland in Upper Silesia on June 21 galvanized the German air command into action at "lightning speed."[69] Documents retrieved from a crashed AAF Flying Fortress as well as a timely air reconnaissance report provided the cue for Greim to order an immediate strike by Fliegerkorps IV against Poltava and Mirgorod airfields.[70] Koller and the operations staff eagerly endorsed Greim's measure.

The attack required techniques little different from those Meister's units employed in the preceding months against rail targets in the Ukraine. The mobility of Fliegerkorps IV proved essential, as KG 27 and KG 53, based around Brest-Litovsk, quickly deployed to bases in the Bialystok-Minsk area in order that they might reach the American shuttle bases. KG 4, the pathfinder unit, remained at its permanent base at Bialystok. KG 55, with bases at Deblin, Ulez, and Podlovovka, likewise within range of Poltava, also remained in place.[71] In order to save time, ground crews bombed up the aircraft with a mixture of SC 50, fragmentation, and incendiary bombs on their home airfields and topped off the bombers' fuel tanks only upon reaching the jumping-off airfields near Minsk.[72] By mid-afternoon, Meister had in his possession photographs, taken from an He 177, of the long-range reconnaissance unit 2./(F) 100, of the American bases; these "showed a peacetime line-up of the assembled aircraft"—140 B-17s at Poltava and fifty-six P-51s at Mirgorod. Greim, perhaps adhering to the standard procedure for railway station attacks, decreed that at midnight Fliegerkorps IV should simultaneously attack both airfields, even at the cost of dispersing the force. Meister accordingly detailed KG 53 and KG 27 to Poltava, and KG 55 to Mir-

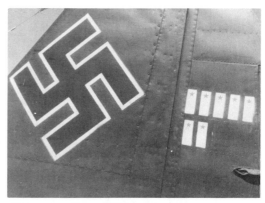

Victory . . . Seven "kill" markings on the rudder of a Junkers 88, all dating from the summer of 1941, attest to the Luftwaffe's stunning successes against the VVS during the opening phases of Barbarossa. (National Air and Space Museum, Smithsonian Institution, Photo No. 87-1807)

Major Ernst Kühl, Geschwaderkommodore of KG 55, inspecting damage to the spinner of his He 111. Kühl commanded the Heinkel-equipped makeshift transport units during the Stalingrad airlift. (USAFHRC)

Special Munitions. The "Fritz-X" guided bomb, intended for use against precise targets such as the turbines of Soviet hydroelectric power plants. Luftwaffe planners envisioned a fifty percent success rate with this weapon. (Photo by the author)

Winter Take-Off. A bomb-laden Ju 87D Stuka takes off from a snow-covered airfield somewhere in the USSR. (National Air and Space Museum, Smithsonian Institution, Photo No. 90-17314)

The "Flying Eye." Focke-Wulf 189 twin-fuselage reconnaissance plane. Note the primitive refuelling procedures common in the eastern theater: the aircraft is being refuelled from fuel drums using a hand pump. (National Air and Space Museum, Smithsonian Institution, Photo No. 90-17310)

A Luftwaffe officer poses on a captured Soviet airfield in Lithuania, littered with wreckage left in the aftermath of the Luftwaffe's June 1941 attack. Most of the damage to the Polikarpov I-15 aircraft pictured was caused by SD-2 fragmentation bombs. (USAFHRC)

The Luftwaffe chief of staff, Generaloberst Hans Jeschonnek, in a moment of apparent bonhomie with Ritter von Greim of Luftflotte 6. The two commanders were in agreement regarding the need to strike Soviet industry with the Luftwaffe's bomber force in June 1943; Jeschonnek's suicide two months later passed the baton to Korten. (USAFHRC)

Soviet warship sunk in Sevastopol harbor by Richthofen's bombers, photographed some weeks after the powerful fortress fell to the Eleventh Army in July 1942. (USAFHRC)

Antitank aviation. *The numerical preponderance of Soviet armor compelled the Luftwaffe to develop an anti-tank capability. The remains of a Soviet tank, victim of ground attack aircraft of Fliegerkorps IV. (USAFHRC)*

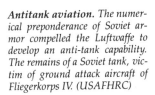

. . . and Defeat. A wrecked Ju 88 lies abandoned on a snow-covered airfield, a microcosm of the fate of the Luftwaffe's bomber arm, worn to nothing after three years of combat in the east. (National Air and Space Museum, Smithsonian Institution, Photo No. 90-17315)

Although the planned attacks on the Moscow-Upper Volga electric power stations were never carried out, Fliegerkorps IV executed a series of successful attacks against Soviet railway centers. A night photograph of Sarny rail station, taken during the attack on April 15, 1944, by a bomber crew of KG 3. (USAFHRC)

Poltava raid. "Reconnaissance photos . . . showed a peacetime lineup of the assembled aircraft." German view of USAAF B-17 Flying Fortresses at the shuttle base at Poltava, attacked with great effect by the bombers of KG 4 (pathfinder), KG 53 and KG 55 on June 21, 1944. The raid was the swan-song of the Luftwaffe's manned bomber force. (USAFHRC)

On October 13, 1943, General Rudolf Meister assumed command of Fliegerkorps IV and began to develop it into an independent long-range bombardment force. Meister (left) greets his predecessor General Kurt Pflugbeil upon his arrival at Kamenka airfield. (USAFHRC)

General Karl Koller, last Chief of the Luftwaffe General Staff and Korten's Chief of Operations. He oversaw much of the detailed planning for the proposed power plant strike. (USAFHRC)

Captured Soviet airmen. Luftwaffe intelligence placed great reliance upon the interrogations of captured Soviet flyers such as these; most subsequently suffered the grim fate of millions of their Red Army counterparts. (USAFHRC)

gorod. Unfortunately, a sudden rain squall drenched KG 27's unpaved airfield, and on account of the soft ground it was deemed impossible to bomb up the Heinkels of that unit in time for the evening's attack. Despite the inauspicious beginning, the operation went off as scheduled, if not as planned. Meister recalled:

> KG 4 took off according to orders received and marked the way for the following formations. The forces attacking both targets were to proceed together on the same route from their bases first to the confluence of the Pripyat and Dnepr Rivers and then as far as Lubny where they were to divide and attack their respective targets. Navigation was carried out by the first pathfinder aircraft using "Egon" procedures. Owing to a mistake on the part of the Mirgorod pathfinders, they mistook their target and flew on to Poltava which had been marked by its own pathfinder force. The Mirgorod pathfinders dropped their markers over Poltava airfield so that it was now impractical to attack Mirgorod at all, but opposition from its fighters was nil, since only day fighters were located there.
>
> This navigational error was regarded . . . as fortunate, as results show how much better it was to have a concentrated attack on the bombers located at Poltava than to dissipate forces by carrying out less satisfactory attacks on two different airfields.[73]

This fortuitous adherence to the principle of force concentration enabled Fliegerkorps IV to place 180 He 111 and Ju 88 bombers (in addition to forty pathfinders from KG 4) over the target. Most of the credit for the timely decision to concentrate on Poltava went to the commander of KG 55, Oberst Wilhelm Antrup, who as "Attack Leader Mirgorod" took responsibility for the change in plans.[74] The German bomber units attacked at leisure with bombs and machine gun fire; I/KG 55 from 11:59 P.M. to 12:32 A.M. dropped 46,000 kilograms of bombs, most of which landed in the target area. Soviet defenses were ineffectual. Returning crews noted only desultory anti-aircraft fire, "two or three" searchlights, and no night fighter opposition.[75] Fliegerkorps IV completed its attack without sustaining any losses. The operation destroyed forty-three B-17s, damaged a further twenty-six, burned 200,000 gallons of aviation fuel, and dealt the already trouble-ridden

shuttle bombing program a blow from which it did not recover.[76] Luftwaffe crews reported that the attack was reminiscent of "the old days,"
including the air superiority strikes on the opening day of Barbarossa.[77]

German bombers followed up the attack with one against Mirgorod
the following evening; since the American aircraft had already departed
it did not match the success of the Poltava strike.[78] Indeed, the Poltava
operation was in many respects the swan-song of the Luftwaffe bomber
force. The days of Fliegerkorps IV were numbered, and its fate was
problematical even prior to its most successful "last bow." One week
prior to the Poltava attack, Koller's operations staff had considered
transferring five of Meister's bomber *Gruppen* (half of the force) to the
western front in order to carry out systematic mining operations
intended to inhibit buildup of the Anglo-American bridgehead in Normandy.[79] The aircraft production program, which Speer, Milch, and the
Jägerstab (Fighter Staff) had of necessity oriented almost exclusively
towards production of single-engine day fighters and twin-engined
night fighters, no longer permitted the maintenance of a strong bomber
force in both east and west.[80] While bomber attrition in the east had
been well within acceptable limits since Fliegerkorps IV went into action
in late March, the same could not be said for the losses that accompanied
Operation Steinbock, Fliegerkorps IX's ill-starred reprisal raids against
Britain, which began on January 21, 1944.[81] Göring insisted that the
raids on London and other British cities "be so conducted . . . that the
operability of the units committed would definitely remain unim-
paired;" this was to prove a vain hope.[82] Losses during these strategically pointless attacks greatly outstripped both aircraft production and
aircrew training output. Moreover, the participating aircraft consisted of
the latest types (Ju 188, He 177, Me 410). The long-awaited third generation of bomber aircraft, with enhanced range, speed, and bombload that
might have made a significant difference to the situation in the Soviet
Union instead found futile employment in the west. Like a candle
burned at both ends, the Luftwaffe's bomber forces by mid-1944 inex-
orably disappeared.

The drastic reduction in multi-engined aircraft production, the
diversion of most Ju 88 production to the night fighter force, the failure
of the Bomber "B" program which had been intended to provide a
modern medium bomber replacement, as well as combat attrition and
other wastage, made the extinction of the Luftwaffe's eastern bomber

force a mathematical certainty. The actual occasion for the disbanding of Fliegerkorps IV was the growing fuel crisis caused by USAAF General Carl Spaatz's decision on May 12, 1944 to target German synthetic oil production.[83] Speer later remarked, "On that day, the technological war was decided."[84] The armaments minister concluded that the American air planners had suffered from the same malady as had the Luftwaffe general staff: the USAAF leadership had since December 1942 been aware of the vital bottlenecks in the German war economy, but only put this knowledge to work in spring 1944. "Before that," Speer noted, "[the enemy] was, at least from his standpoint, committing absurdities."[85]

Meister's long-range bomber force was one of the German air force formations most affected by the fuel crisis of mid-1944. By late June, in all of Luftflotte 6's command area there were only 2,300 cubic meters of B4 aviation fuel (87-octane fuel suitable for bomber aircraft) and 750 cubic meters of higher-octane C3 aviation gasoline (used by fighters and most ground attack aircraft).[86] The location of even individual fuel trains became a vital concern for the eastern air fleets, as they carried out operations according to a hand-to-mouth principle. Koller remarked succinctly, "The biggest problem, now as ever, is the fuel situation." On average, Air Fleet 6 had fuel stocks on hand sufficient for three sorties per aircraft; in effect it had no reserves at all. Within a week of the Poltava mission, Fliegerkorps IV, with ten battle-worthy bomber *Gruppen*, could on account of the fuel shortage send out at most two or three of those bomber *Gruppen* per night. The delayed arrival of a fuel train often rendered operations impossible. The position did not improve; by early August Luftflotte 6's reserves totalled only 265 cubic meters of B4 and 133 cubic meters of C3.[87] The air fleet was, therefore, virtually paralyzed by mid-summer 1944 as the Red Army reached the outskirts of Warsaw.

German air power theorists had both before and during the Second World War referred to the "intercontinental effect" of air power and the close relationship between air warfare and the activities of the other services. The fate of Fliegerkorps IV brought home the truth of these prognostications. Although the German long-range night bomber force performed well and without significant hindrance from the VVS in mid-1944, other developments rendered its contribution virtually worthless. The advance of the Red Army deprived it of its most important operating bases, and the air forces of the Western Allies, with their ''oil program,'' choked off its supply of fuel. These were the kind of wide-ranging developments that the Luftwaffe of 1944 was powerless to prevent.

The fuel crisis also curtailed employment of the Heinkel 177 bomber in the east. After months of delay, Kampfgeschwader 1 ''Hindenburg,'' under the command of Oberstleutnant Horst von Riesen, arrived in early June in East Prussia to begin long-range bombing operations with Luftflotte 6. The big bombers, at last free of the engine problems plaguing the design, carried out a few daylight high-altitude raids against targets such as Kalinkovichi and Velikiye-Luki marshalling yards, but by the end of July the fuel situation rendered further operations impossible.[88] Each He 177 required roughly six tons of fuel per mission; the Luftwaffe had not the capacity to sustain large scale operations of this type.[89] By the end of August, the entire unit disbanded, and the Luftwaffe command redesignated it Jagdgeschwader (Fighter Wing) 7 as the personnel took up duties with the home defense force. Thus, the combat career of the bomber type upon which German long range strategic bombing ambitions in Russia since 1942 had depended came to an end after a few meaningless operations.

The fate of the entire long-range bomber force followed a similar pattern. Fliegerkorps IV's bomber units continued the rail interdiction campaign with reduced strength until early July, then carried out a melange of army support and aerial resupply missions until August.[90] With the front line in the east under heavy pressure and the bulk of Luftwaffe missions consisting of direct support fighter bomber sorties, the rationale for maintenance of a strategic bombing force, with all of the significant targets long out of range, no longer existed. A few of the component units, including III./KG 55, transferred to the western front for the night resupply of the garrisons holding the surrounded English Channel ports, and at least one Gruppe of KG 53 carried out aerial launchings of V-1 flying bombs against Great Britain. The bulk of the bomber formations were simply dissolved. Their aircrews were transferred to the home defense fighter forces of Luftflotte Reich. The force's commander, Meister, became head of the Luftwaffe's Personnel Office; many of the Fliegerkorps IV command personnel joined the staff of the General der Luftwaffe Dänemark.[91] With the demise of Fliegerkorps IV came the effective end of the Luftwaffe's existence as an offensive weapon.

The concept of attacking the USSR's supply of electric power survived even the collapse of the conventional bomber force. One of the more unrealistic proposals originated with Albert Speer. In an effort to employ extraordinary means to keep the power plant attack alive, Speer on May 23, 1944 cited the "poor accuracy of the aim of the Korps Meister" as the reason for proposing suicide attacks, or *totale Einsatz* missions, as the only certain means of destroying the electrical plants.[92] Again on July 28, 1944, Speer referred to the existence of "numerous men brave unto death [who] have rallied around [SS Major Otto] Skorzeny, and also in the air force, who are voluntarily willing to dive with their machines onto the targets."[93] [Speer, in his memoirs, provides a slightly amended version of his proposal: "After the attack the pilots were to abandon their planes over remote areas, parachute to earth, and try to make their way back to the German front."][94] Although Speer indicated that Korten had "promised full support" for the scheme, there is little evidence that the Luftwaffe general staff took serious action on any of the armaments minister's proposals.

The operations staff did make attempts to circumvent the geographic and range limitations and bring at least a portion of the Soviet electric power industry under air attack. Luftflotte 6 in November 1944 prepared an attack, code-named Unternehmen Burgund, using ten He 177s from the special duties Geschwader KG 200 against the familiar power plants at Rybinsk and Uglich, as well as that at Volkhovstroi on Lake Ladoga. KG 200 had been formed in early 1944 as a unit capable of undertaking agent-dropping and similar clandestine missions behind enemy lines. The Heinkels, obtained from the recently deactivated bomber *Gruppe* II./KG 100, were to drop the now ostensibly combat-ready BM 1000 F Sommerballon floating mines in order to destroy the hydro-power plants. Preparation for the operation was to take place "in closest collaboration with the General der Kampfflieger and Professor Dr. Steinmann."[95] In order to secure the requisite fuel for the operation, Dr. Steinmann had literally to resort to barter. Through various machinations, he obtained 100 cubic meters of motor vehicle fuel from Josef Goebbels of the Propaganda Ministry, which he, with Göring's sanction, then exchanged for an equivalent amount of aviation fuel from the Luftwaffe's dwindling stocks. Preparations for the operation went ahead in the greatest secrecy, with aircrews and mine specialists from the Luftwaffe's experimental establishments carefully isolated after being fed suitable cover stories. Unfortunately, KG 200's experts calculated that at least 250 cubic meters of fuel would be required for the operation (and for the reconditioning of the He 177s' engines, which had by that time been placed in long-term storage).[96] Ice build-up around the power plants proved to be the final nail in the coffin of this endeavor. It was postponed until the spring of 1945, and accordingly faded from view.[97]

In early 1945, the same planning agencies attempted to carry out the original systematic power plant attack against the thirteen most important Moscow-Upper Volga installations. This resurrected plan (for which the same wooden models of the targets that had been constructed in 1943 reappeared at the briefings) called for the employment of a combination of Sommerballon-carrying long-range conventional bombers and the Mistel, a composite aircraft consisting of a Junkers 88 night fighter fitted with a hollow-charge warhead controlled by an attached FW 190 fighter. This improbable contraption possessed a combat radius of 1,500 kilometers, just sufficient to reach the targets from bases in East Prussia.[98] The operation, again code-named Eisenhammer, seems to have enjoyed Koller's full support and consumed extensive resources before it was cancelled at the end of March 1945. The Mistel combinations eventually went into action in a futile attempt to halt the Red Army's crossing of the Oder River at Steinau.[99] The entire operation is more illustrative of the inadequacy of the Luftwaffe's equipment than of German innovative weapons design. The Mistel and KG 200 exercise would have been unnecessary had the Luftwaffe's force structure matched its ambitious operational doctrine in late 1943.

Even to the end, the lack of a coherent targeting doctrine continued to divide effort and resources. In an absurd parody of the original debate between aircraft, aero-engine, and electric power target groupings, Luftflotte 6 in November 1944 produced the most detailed target studies to date on the Soviet air armament industry. The study reaffirmed the logic of the mid-1943 efforts by Luftwaffe intelligence to eliminate the huge aircraft factories of the east, but the targets proposed (Kazan, Kuibyshev, Omsk, Sverdlovsk) were by this time completely beyond bomber range.

THE CLOSE AIR SUPPORT FORMULA: FIVE YEARS TOO LATE?

In the midst of the disintegration of the eastern bomber fleets and the military collapse of Army Group Center, the Luftwaffe lost its capable

chief of the general staff. On July 20, 1944, Korten was standing next to
Adolf Hitler in the conference hut at Rastenburg during the afternoon
situation briefing. A piece of flying debris from the explosion of Oberst
Claus Schenk von Stauffenberg's bomb fatally injured him.[100] By the
time of his demise the project that comprised one cornerstone of his
eastern air strategy, the long-range bomber corps and its strategic mission, had just about run its course. One of Korten's other aims had been
the creation of a true close air support capability for the Luftwaffe with
which to assist the army in its defensive battles, and it is to this second
venture, the last chapter of the history of the Luftwaffe in the east, that
we must now turn.

Since the invasion of the USSR in June 1941, the Luftwaffe during
the eastern campaign alternately benefited and suffered from the ability
of many of its units to perform more than one role. Thus, the advancing
Ostheer came to depend upon skillfully applied air support from units,
in particular the bomber wings, whose resources in the view of many
German air force commanders might better be applied elsewhere. The
value which the army placed upon Luftwaffe support perhaps reached
its peak during the Crimean operation, during which Manstein quite
frankly admitted that major operations depended entirely upon air force
support. With the German army in retreat following the failure of
Zitadelle, the ground forces came to view the air force as a three-
dimensional substitute for defense in depth. German army defensive
doctrine was one of the major intellectual achievements of German
arms, but the vast Russian spaces rendered it virtually unworkable
shortly after the campaign opened.[101] Reliance on air force support existed from the highest level of command down to the common soldiers.
Guy Sajer, an Alsatian serving with the Ostheer, remembered one
entirely typical vignette:

Three Messerschmitts passed overhead, and were greeted with a
loud cheer. The confidence which the infantry placed in the Luftwaffe was absolute, and on innumerable occasions the familiar
shape of the planes with the black crosses restored faltering courage and frustrated a Russian attack.[102]

Luftwaffe success in the army support role, particularly that which
Richthofen's command attained, slowly but surely distorted the configuration of German air power in the east, and had been a powerful

inducement for the general staff to pursue the elaborate strategic bombing scheme. With Luftwaffe mission conceptions as flexible as they were, air force commanders found it difficult to refuse requests for direct as well as indirect army support. One of Korten's primary goals was to ensure that a clear separation existed between army support and strategic bomber units. The result came to fruition too late to have any decisive impact, but it did result in the Luftwaffe acquiring by mid-1944 a true close support capability.

Up to the time of Korten's appointment in autumn 1943, responsibility for army support aviation was divided between the Luftwaffe bomber and fighter inspectorates. The Ju 87 units, for example, came under the purview of the General der Kampfflieger, while twin-engined ground attack units (including Bf 110 light bombers and the Hs 129 tank destroyers) were the responsibility of the fighter arm. Korten's reforms provided for a sweeping reorganization of this unwieldy arrangement: as of October 7, 1943, ground attack formations of all types fell under the single direction of the *General der Schlachtflieger* (general of ground attack aviation), with authority equivalent to the bomber, fighter and reconnaissance inspectorates, or *Waffengenerale*. The *General der Schlachtflieger* initially had responsibility for six *Geschwader* staffs, eighteen *Gruppen*, one anti-tank *Gruppe*, and four independent anti-tank *Staffeln*.[103]

This was a decisive step towards the creation of what Herhudt von Rohden and Karl-Heinrich Schulz, both one-time chiefs of staff to Richthofen, believed was the logical solution to the Luftwaffe's strategic dilemma: the creation of separate tactical and strategic air forces.[104] Were it not for the lack of fuel and planes, the concept might well have borne fruit. In addition, there was persistent opposition from the operations staff, who regarded the creation of an "army air force" (*Heeresluftwaffe*) as an unacceptable sacrifice of the German air force's independence.[105] As it happened, the delineation of roles existed only in the most attenuated form, and with the demise of Fliegerkorps IV only the new ground attack arm carried on the fight. In this fashion was the longstanding intellectual dichotomy regarding the proper employment of air forces resolved, in effect, by default.

Korten's redesignation grouped all of the diverse units with a ground attack mission, including Stuka (Ju 87), fighter-bomber (FW 190), night ground attack, and *Panzerjäger* (Hs 129 and Ju 87G) under the single unit designation *Schlachtflieger*.[106] In the broadest terms, units of this type had the task "of keeping the pressure on the enemy at decisive points through prompt concentration of forces and creation of a point of main effort (*Schwerpunktbildung*)."[107] Even Fliegerkorps VIII, during its heyday as the Luftwaffe's only true close army support command, always pursued a wide variety of tasks, including some related only peripherally to army support. Under the new scheme, whole formations of the German air force in the Soviet Union were to operate primarily as "vertical artillery."[108]

Alongside the organizational changes, the creation of the *General der Schlachtflieger* and its unified ground attack command permitted standardization of operational procedures and the technology of army-air force cooperation. These technical reforms "were pursued with the greatest care and energy" by successive Generals of Ground Attack Aviation, Oberst Dr. Ernst Küpfer and, after Küpfer's death in an accident, Oberstleutnant Hubertus Hitschhold.[109] The post had influential responsibilities, including supervision of weapons procurement, training, personnel selection, and development of operational doctrine.[110] Under the direction of the new *Waffengeneral*, shortcomings that had plagued Luftwaffe army support procedures since the war's outbreak finally found a solution.

One such improvement concerned the quality of the aircraft in service with the ground attack units. By early 1944, the Ju 87 dive bomber was of questionable utility even on the eastern front, as it could only operate with fighter escort.[111] Even during Jeschonnek's tenure, a program was under way to replace the aging Stuka with the ground attack version of the FW 190 day fighter. The pressing need for this aircraft for Reich defense duties restricted and delayed its employment in the ground attack role, but by mid-1944 many of the Ju 87 units had reequipped with the modern type.[112] The conversion was never entirely completed for two reasons. Aircraft strength in the eastern theater was so low that the existing Ju 87s had to be retained in service. Furthermore, the Ju 87s utilized the more plentiful 87–octane B4 aviation fuel, while the BMW 801 engine of the FW 190F required the scarcer 100–octane C3 gasoline.[113] The two types of ground attack aircraft therefore served side by side until the end of the war, although the FW 190 was a far more desirable weapon. While a bomb-laden FW 190 was vulnerable in the western theater, the aircraft was a most capable ground attack machine even when operating unescorted against the Soviets.

Probably the most significant reforms in the ground attack arm concerned the actual mechanism for air-ground cooperation at the forward
line, particularly in support of an advancing or (more likely the case by
1944) retreating or surrounded motorized or infantry formation. Past
experience had shown that while certain formations, particularly
Fliegerkorps VIII, enforced the use of standardized liaison and ground
to air recognition procedures throughout their areas of operation, no
such homogeneity prevailed over the entire front. As a result, alarming
discrepancies in the nature and quality of air support emerged even
within a single operation, as with the divergence between Luftflotten 4
and 6 during Operation Zitadelle. The effectiveness of air support too
often depended upon uncertain factors, including the personalities of
Fliegerkorps, Fliegerdivision, and *Luftflotten* commanders, the resourceful-
ness and commitment of the liaison staffs, and the type of flying units
on hand.

One of the first major changes concerned the "methods of liaison"
between the services. In campaigns past, the task of the *Flivos* had been
rather ill-defined; in some cases the liaison officer functioned as a simple
intermediary between *Fliegerkorps* and army unit, while in other cases
the *Flivo* accompanied the ground troops into action, sometimes providing a direct radio link with the flying units overhead. In early 1944 the
Luftwaffe operations staff resolved this ambiguity. The task of the
Fliegerverbindungsoffizier was to function as "the means of liaison of the
air force to the command staffs of the army" at army group and army
level—a formulation rather akin to the original tasks of the *Koluft* in the
early months of the campaign.[114] A newly-designated "air liaison
officer-signals" (*Fliegerverbindungsoffizier-Ln*) fulfilled the liaison tasks at
corps level and with *Schwerpunkt* divisions. Finally, the signals officer
oversaw a mobile *Fliegerleittruppe* (air control team)[115] which provided
the direct communication between ground forces and the *Schlachtflieger*
units operating above.[116] This team was itself under the direction of the
Fliegerleitoffizier (Schlacht) (air control officer-ground attack).[117] This officer served at the focal point (*Brennpunkt*) of the ground battle. His duties
included direct communication with the flying units, informing them of
their precise targets, preventing accidental air attacks on German
troops, and related tactical duties.[118] In this manner evolved a clear
distinction between operational liaison functions and tactical control of
the combat situation, although the system retained the principle of the

"constant exchange of ideas" that had paid such enormous dividends when Richthofen employed it during 1941–1942.

A typical air control team consisted of one officer, one noncommissioned officer/radio operator, and three enlisted men who functioned as reserve operators or vehicle drivers. The team used the *Fu.G 10/12 Volt* radio for communication both with the Luftwaffe command and the Ju 87 units (most of which utilized the older *Fu.G 7a* radio); the *Fu. 5 (Luft)* radio for direct communication with the *Fu. G 16* radio installed in the FW 190 and Hs 129; and the *Fu. 5* for communication with the army units that the team was supporting. In theory, the new arrangement allowed for ground forces to, with minimal difficulty, communicate with every type of Luftwaffe flying formation. The team travelled in either a truck or, if assigned to a *Panzer* or *Panzergrenadier* unit, a *Sd.Kfz. 251/1* half track. In some cases, even a command tank (Panzerbefehlswagen III, IV, Panther or Tiger) was made available to Luftwaffe personnel.[119] These vehicles were recognizable by the large number of radio antennas sprouting from them. This method of providing direct air support, incidentally, is almost identical to the configuration which the Allies adopted for "air support party officers" accompanying armored units in Normandy in summer 1944.[120] Both army and air force liaison officers had bitterly noted the lack of essential and reliable lines of communication between ground and air units; by early 1944 a "simple and generally intelligible" means of such communication came at last to the fore.

In most respects, the new regulations preserved the principle of centralized control of air assets. In the great majority of cases, dispatch of major flying units to a threatened sector was still the responsibility of the Luftwaffe command, and air force personnel retained control of the sortie up to the time of its execution. German air force advocates of strategic air power must nevertheless have blanched at official memoranda that referred to aircraft as "extended-range artillery."[121] Additionally, the Luftwaffe was keenly aware of its inability to provide air control detachments to every army staff along the front. Accordingly, the army and air force jointly developed procedures allowing army personnel, in certain circumstances, to function as air control officers.[122] To facilitate this major concession on the part of the Luftwaffe staff, army and air force at last acquired radio equipment and frequencies in common.

The refinement of air support procedures culminated with publication in March 1944 of the multi-volume manual *Vereint schlagen* (Strike

Together).[123] German air force statements concerning interservice cooperation had hitherto been confined to brief memoranda; the lengthy *Vereint schlagen* contained the accumulated wisdom of years of air support operations and made the refined procedures uniform throughout the German armed forces. The influence of Richthofen's earlier war experience was most evident in the manual; the newly standardized air-ground recognition signals were almost identical to the ones Fliegerkorps VIII employed when supporting Army Group North in 1941.[124] While the bulk of the manual understandably concerned itself with direct support of the army by ground attack aircraft, the general prefatory remarks harkened back to the *operativer Luftkrieg* formulations of earlier times:

> The support of the army by flying units in both attack and defense is one of the tasks of the air force. It may exert a decisive effect on the conduct of the ground battle.
> [The Luftwaffe's] mission may not be limited to the battlefield. It must be decided at the time whether or not attacks in depth, for example against railroads, troop columns or supply lines, will have a greater effect on the operation as a whole.[125]

The overall contents of the manual belied this wide-ranging conception of the Luftwaffe's mission. It was evident to those who carried out the tactical reforms that the greatly enlarged and improved ground attack force was to be a "corset stay" in an overstretched German defense in eastern Europe. The day of the "army's fire brigade" had arrived with a vengeance. Even as the strategic bombing program ran its course, the eastern *Fliegerkorps* and *Fliegerdivisionen* other than Meister's bomber force assumed the character of close air support commands. On June 1, 1944, the Luftwaffe possessed 1,005 operational ground attack aircraft, of which over six hundred were in the east. This made them by far the most numerous German aircraft category in ·the Soviet Union.[126] Fliegerkorps VIII, Richthofen's old command, for once was representative of most German air force formations on the eastern front. In May 1944, the formation, at the time stationed in eastern Poland in the command sector of Luftflotte 4, was top-heavy with ground attack units. Of its 278 aircraft on hand on May 25, 1944, fully 203 of these were the FW 190s, Ju 87s, and Hs 129s of its *Schlachtflieger* units SG 9, SG 10 and SG 77.[127] The remainder of the force consisted of reconnaissance machines,

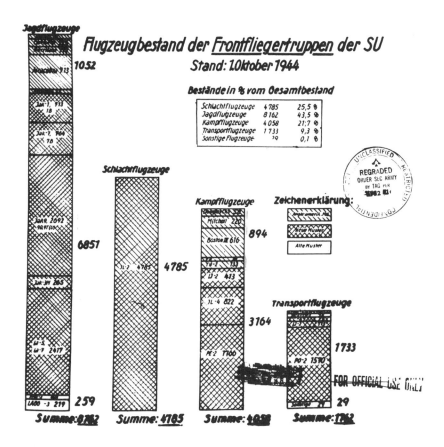

Figure 2. German intelligence's fears of massive Soviet air strength underlay much of the strategic bombing plans in 1943–1944. This diagram, from a Luftflotte 6 survey of the Soviet aircraft industry published in November 1944, is typical: the Soviets are credited with a front-line strength of 4,785 ground attack aircraft (mostly Il-2s), 8,162 fighters, 4,058 bombers and 1,733 transports. Most of these are a result of "new production;" only a small percentage are lend-lease deliveries or obsolete types. The same month, the Luftwaffe had in service in the east only 2,500 aircraft of all types.

thirty-six Bf 109 fighters, twenty-seven night ground attack aircraft and fifteen He 111 bombers of KG 27's railway attack *Staffel*.

Although the concentration of German air strength into a dedicated close support force represented a creditable achievement, the overall balance of force was still most unfavorable. By Luftwaffe intelligence's own reckoning, on the eve of Operation Bagration, the Soviet offensive against Army Group Center on June 22, 1944, the VVS possessed 5,120 Il-2 and Pe-2 ground attack aircraft.[128] Moreover, the Germans discovered from captured documents that the Soviet procedures for command and control of their ground attack force were hardly less sophisticated than their own.[129] Although the Soviets dispensed with the concept that air units were in any way "independent" of the ground forces, by 1944 the same was true of the German close support force.

The result was that the *Schlachtflieger* were capable of no more than a delaying action once Soviet offensive activity commenced. During the early days of Operation Bagration, for example, the VVS even by 8. Abteilung admission swamped the combat area of 4. Fliegerdivision (a force that on June 22 possessed twenty-five operational fighters) with 7,500 sorties.[130] Once the retreat began, provision of air support by the Luftwaffe became an even more difficult prospect. Even so, conditions on the eastern front were far more conducive to German air support operations than were those faced by Luftwaffe units operating in the west. One ground attack unit, the FW 190–equipped III./SG 4, at full strength boasting thirty fighter-bombers, had ten aircraft destroyed, six damaged, four pilots killed and three wounded in just three days of operations over Normandy from June 6. After rehabilitation and transfer to Luftflotte 1 in the Baltic States, the same unit operated from July 4 to October 29 with only thirteen aircraft lost, five damaged, eight pilots killed or missing, and two wounded.[131] While the unit functioned with some effectiveness, its operations could have little effect on the developing strategic situation. By late 1944, in fact, the German air force had lost its ability to concentrate in force and thus achieve local air superiority, even at the expense of denuding vast stretches of the front.

During the Luftwaffe's last months of operation, that force was almost unrecognizable as the bearer of *operativer Luftkrieg* that had invaded the USSR in June 1941. The eastern air fleets, once capable of the full range of missions expected from a modern air arm, had degenerated into mere tactical support corps, even abrogating the air superiority mission to their Soviet adversaries.[132]

Korten's attempt to preserve the Luftwaffe's identity as an independent service in Russia, therefore, was a failure. The German armed forces had not the resources to concentrate on the reconstruction of an air force offensive capability, and the collapse of synthetic oil production in the summer of 1944 drove that point home. Furthermore, the disasters that overtook the German front line and deprived the Luftwaffe of its forward bases only indirectly resulted from the miscalculation of the Luftwaffe staffs. There are, indeed, powerful arguments in favor of "external" reasons why the Luftwaffe's "rebirth" was instead stillborn.

Yet it is clear that the Luftwaffe's own planning in large measure contributed to its precipitous decline. The enormous quantity of material resources, fuel and trained personnel devoted to the reconstitution of Fliegerkorps IV was wasted in the absence of the ability on the part of the Luftwaffe General and Operations Staffs to concentrate on finding appropriate and practical uses for this force. Instead, the long-range bomber force, certainly a potent enough weapon if used selectively, had to function against a daunting and bewildering melange of competing target systems. It is one of the ironies of the Second World War that Luftwaffe intelligence, for long the most despised and neglected branch of the service,[133] was able to achieve such a baneful level of influence at this one juncture. Certainly the dispersal of effort that rendered the strategic bombing program irrelevant originated first and foremost with the analysts of Führungsstab Ic and their backers in the operations branch.

In less dramatic fashion, the remarkable upsurge in tactical air capabilities was also destined to fail. The creation of many new *Schlachtfliegergruppen* and the provision of sophisticated liaison procedures undoubtedly helped to delay the German collapse in Russia and caused the advancing Soviets a considerable measure of trouble. Yet the reforms took place when the aircraft production and personnel imbalance between Germany and her opponents was too wide to be bridged by even the most energetic measures. The growth of the ground attack arm is entirely analogous to the parallel expansion of the home defense fighter force, another of Korten's projects, and its fate was remarkably similar.

Meister awards the Knight's Cross to aircrew of Fliegerkorps IV who distinguished themselves during the four-month long campaign against the Soviet railway network in the spring 1944. By the end of the summer, the air corps was disbanded, its bombers grounded through lack of fuel and its bases overrun by the advancing Red Army. (USAFHRC)

CONCLUSION

FAILURES EXTERNAL AND INTERNAL

The defeat of the Luftwaffe in the campaign against the Soviet Union was only one part of a multi-continental disaster that overtook German arms during the Second World War. Recent accounts of that conflict have stressed that the defeat of Germany, once swift victory against the Soviet Union eluded her in December 1941 and she was caught between the hammer and anvil of capitalist West and communist East, was inevitable.

It would be inappropriate to suggest revisions to this thesis in a work that has examined only one facet of an immensely complex problem. Yet, one leaves an examination of the Luftwaffe's conduct of the war in the east with the sense that errors which the officer corps of that service committed, often in the name of adherence to cherished beliefs in the near-mystical qualities of ''air power,'' did much to hasten the defeat of German ambitions in the east. Although the external factors arrayed against the Luftwaffe and indeed the entire Wehrmacht were formidable, certain measures which the general staff of the Luftwaffe undertook adversely affected their service's ability to redress the balance.

Certainly the external causes for the German defeat are obvious. As early as summer 1940, the British aircraft industry began to outproduce the German factories. By 1943, each of Germany's three major antagonists put forth production totals in most important aircraft categories she could not hope to match. Even the enormous increases in German production in 1943–1944 had to be dispersed over several major air fronts, preventing the Luftwaffe from regaining the initiative anywhere. Muddled aircraft and air armament procurement under Ernst Udet ensured that the Luftwaffe was saddled with obsolescent aircraft while the air forces of her adversaries stole a march on her in the technical race. Well might Luftwaffe intelligence analysts gaze as if hypnotized at graphs of Soviet production of modern aircraft types. Even an air force substantially larger than the Luftwaffe ever became would have been hard-pressed to meet the demands placed upon it by the air activities of the USAAF, the RAF, and the VVS.

The Luftwaffe additionally was subject to the dictates of "Führer strategy," and was compelled to carry out missions that furthered the high command's directives. In addition, after the collapse of the offensive in late 1941, Adolf Hitler increasingly intervened in even the minutia of air force leadership. It is clear that the series of reprisal raids on Great Britain in 1943–1944 were entirely the product of Hitler's desire to pay the British back in their own coin. The Luftwaffe Operations Staff was thus obligated to deploy its most modern aircraft types, the Ju 188s and He 177s that could have been of real use on the eastern front, against the sophisticated British defense system in pursuit of no clear strategic objective. The effect that overall German strategy had on Luftwaffe operations was to make the principle of force concentration unworkable on the strategic level. The Luftwaffe general staff's historical department, in tracing the pattern of the air war in 1944, made a rather significant admission:

The course of the air war since 1941 has been characterized by the fact that the Luftwaffe has not been used again in concentrated attacks against one opponent on one front. It has been forced by simultaneous operations in several theatres of war to direct its blows at the enemy in many directions. The inevitable result has been a decrease in its operational strength on the various sections of the front. Thus the deviation from the previous principles of operational air war [operativer Luftkrieg] in favor of direct support for the army . . . became an established fact. The primary conditions for operations according to the principles of Douhet thus disappeared.[1]

Perhaps the greatest miscalculation that the Luftwaffe general staff made was to not take this strategic constraint into account when determining an operational mission for their service. Clearly front-line commanders such as Richthofen, Fiebig, and Seidemann, although products of the same intellectual background from which Luftwaffe strategic doctrine sprung, sought to develop the means by which the weakened Luftwaffe might still contribute to the conduct of operations in the east. Certainly an appreciation of the Luftwaffe's strategic and economic position vis-à-vis its opponents dictated a need for an air strategy that could extract the most benefit from the attenuated German air force. The development under Korten in 1943–1944 of a viable air defense and close army support capability in the Luftwaffe is testimony to the operational realism that to the end of the conflict was an undeniable characteristic of the German air force leadership. German air force commanders as a rule acknowledged the army's pivotal role in the war plans of a continental power.

Even the dedicated enthusiasts of strategic air power in the Luftwaffe made no attempt to deny that "the Luftwaffe was employed in the Eastern campaign in logically correct fashion until the Dnieper line was attained in the autumn of 1941."[2] At no point in the entire war did the Luftwaffe come closer to achieving its prewar aim of exerting a decisive influence upon the course of operations as during the opening phases of Operation Barbarossa. It is doubtful that any air force in the world in 1941 could have contributed so effectively to success in a major campaign as did the three eastern air fleets in those heady months of summer and early autumn 1941. The German prewar air doctrine that stressed operations in the realm of *Gesamtkriegführung* received its vindication during the strikes against the Soviet air force and in the decisive interdiction and support missions in the course of the Ostheer's encirclement battles.

Even as the war degenerated into a battle of attrition which prewar planners had not foreseen, the Luftwaffe exerted a considerable if diminishing influence on the conduct of the eastern campaign. The nature of German strategy in the east, with its emphasis on operations such as Blau and Zitadelle, intended as decisive thrusts but which instead proved to be costly failures, rendered the task of the Luftwaffe increasingly difficult. Within this unrewarding context, the *Fliegerkorps* and *Fliegerdivision* staffs worked closely with their army colleagues to perfect the system of battlefield air support that had paid such enormous dividends for German ambitions in past operations. The Luftwaffe's learning process is a case study in military adaptation that rivals that of the much more lavishly equipped USAAF and RAF later in the conflict. In the Mediterranean and in Normandy the RAF and USAAF perfected their own solutions to the technical, command and control problems of air support.

One of the peculiarities of Luftwaffe strategic development is that the same leadership that was capable of realistically assessing the operational situation in the east and furthering the development of such useful innovations and improvisations as close support, night ground attack, or specialized anti-tank aircraft also pursued a policy of strategic bombardment of Soviet war potential that was not merely ineffective, but positively detrimental to the smooth and concentrated employment of German air power in the theater. The series of raids on Moscow during the height of the decisive battle against the Red Army in the summer and fall of 1941 seems by comparison merely a foreshadowing of the grandiose schemes that accompanied the loss of German initiative in the Soviet Union after Stalingrad.

The one lesson German air force planners seem to have gleaned from the Stalingrad debacle was that intensive concentration of the Luftwaffe in support of the army's operations failed to produce a strategic decision. The response of the general staff was to reorient the Luftwaffe to a mission for which it did not possess the material or personnel strength: the deployment of a specialized long-range bomber force against Soviet industry sustaining the war effort on the eastern front. Certainly the desire to use the air force as a means of circumventing a debilitating battle of attrition was not unique to German general staff circles. In fact, this desire underlay the entire air strategy of the Western Allies. While Allied air planners hoped that strategic bombing of German targets might render a cross-Channel invasion and the expected battle of attrition unnecessary, the Luftwaffe staffs hoped to use air power as a means of escaping attrition that was already well underway. The real failure of the Luftwaffenführungsstab was its inability to appreciate that the expectations which it attached to the Aktion Russland scheme bore little relation to the capabilities of the weaponry at its disposal. Certainly the operations staff had in four years of air warfare accumulated sufficient data to indicate that the minuscule bomber strength of Fliegerkorps IV, no matter how carefully husbanded, would hardly have the power to do to the Soviet war economy what much more substantial fleets of Allied bombers had thus far failed to do to the German. Indeed, most lessons German planners seem to have drawn from their "laboratory" of the Anglo-American bombing campaign were negative, except for a concentration on spectacular but strategically insignificant feats such as the March 1943 Ruhr dams raid. For example, the Allied failure to strike the overextended German electric power system seemed a substantial sin of omission. The desire to achieve quick and decisive results through air action, although the cornerstone of most of air power theory in the 1930s, should have been tempered with a more realistic appraisal of previous operational experience.

The November 1943 plan for the "battle against the Russian war industry," although the product of a collaboration between military and civilian experts which was rare in the Third Reich, in reality did not merit the great hopes to which it gave rise. Any real or imagined "fragility" in the Soviet war economy could not alter the fact that the operation was far too demanding for the force available. The supposed heirs of Clausewitz did not consider that night attacks against an imposing series of small, distant and well-protected targets such as the Soviet power plants would occasion an extraordinary amount of friction. Instead, Luftwaffe planners seemed content to accept "expert figures" that under these conditions German bombers might score a fifty percent on-target rate with unproven and temperamental weapons. It is a measure of the lack of realism within both Luftwaffe planning and operational circles that hardly a voice seems to have been raised in protest.

Quite the contrary, once the power plant attack found acceptance within the higher corridors of Luftwaffe leadership, even more far-reaching schemes became the order of the day. Although the history of air power in World War II offers examples of lasting benefits being gained from air attacks on "key industries" and transportation networks,[3] in most cases these victories came only after monumental exertions, appalling losses, and much trial and error. Information contained in official Soviet publications suggests that electric power and rail transportation were indeed vulnerable sectors of the Russian planned economy. Only the opening of the Soviet industrial and economic planning archives will enable historians to assess how closely Luftwaffe intelligence's detailed appraisals of Soviet war production reflected reality.

In one sense, such information would be moot, as the energetic intelligence gathering operation went for naught as the Luftwaffe was unable to carry out even the first phase of the operation.

Belief in the power of the air weapon was not the only intellectual construct that ultimately destroyed German air power in the Soviet Union. Luftwaffe staff officers' confidence in their service was accompanied by a racial contempt for their adversary, his technology, and his economic, social and political institutions. Greim's 1944 proposal that air attacks on Moscow would shatter the morale of the "war-weary" population and the German intelligence officer's smug elucidation of the "biological immaturity" of captured Soviet air force officers sprang from the same crucible that made the Eastern campaign one of the most terrible in all of military history. While the Luftwaffe, because of the nature of its operations, maintained a degree of distance from the atrocities of the "war of conquest and annihilation,"[4] the air force leadership's ready acquiescence in plans to "level Moscow and Leningrad and make them uninhabitable, so as to relieve us of the necessity of having to feed the population through the winter,"[5] as well as its advocacy of terror-bombing, suggest no great ideological gulf between Luftwaffe and army. Indeed, on those few occasions that air force general staff documents refer to grand strategy or "war aims," phrases such as "the protection of Europe from the monstrous danger posed by Jewish-Asiatic Bolshevism" appear.[6] The rare dissenting views, as when in October 1944 Generalmajor Herhudt von Rohden suggested that treating all Russians as "*Untermenschen*" had deprived the Germans of the cooperation of anti-Stalinist elements, only serve to underscore the general trend.[7] The Luftwaffe never believed that it could defeat Britain in 1943–1944 with the weak forces at its disposal; it readily succumbed to the delusion that Stalin's Russia was made of lower-grade steel. Underestimation of the Soviet opponent accounts for a great deal of the reverses that the eastern Luftwaffe suffered. It has also inhibited historical understanding of the conflict. "Revisionism" was already underway within weeks of the German collapse. Captured Luftwaffe officers smoothly told their British interrogators that "the available strength of [German] fighters on the eastern front was sufficient," or, more incredibly:

Never in the whole course of the war did the Russians succeed in decisively preventing operations of the German air force nor did they themselves bring about any decision in a battle in spite of a numerical superiority of up to 10 to 1.[8]

The bulk of the memoir literature emanating from the German side has only served to reinforce this perception.

Many historians accept that critical errors within the leadership of the German army and high command were essential contributors to the eventual German defeat in the war against Russia. It should be recognized that the flaws that brought the Ostheer to grief had their counterparts within the Luftwaffe. Additionally, the air force leadership in many of the other belligerent powers brought to the conflict a vision of air power that promised a reevaluation of the "immutable laws of war." In one sense, the Luftwaffe leadership managed to overcome this illusion in the formulation of doctrine and its conduct of operations during 1939–1941. When the tide of war shifted against the Third Reich, however, the Luftwaffe command proved as vulnerable as any to the lure of the strategic bombing fixation. This helped to ensure, in the words of R. J. Overy, that "the German air force was an expensive liability that brought far less benefit for the costs involved than was the case with the Allied air forces."[9] In many cases, the employment of air forces of the Second World War was uneconomical, ill-considered and costly. In the case of the RAF and USAAF, an enormous raw materials and production base cushioned the long-term effects of such mistakes. But when the Luftwaffe command withdrew its long-range bomber force from army support tasks in November 1943 in order to prepare for Aktion Russland, it was gone for good.

BIBLIOGRAPHIC ESSAY AND NOTE ON SOURCES

This study seeks to fill a void in the historiography of Second World War air power. Despite the tremendous popularity of books dealing with the German air force, only a handful of these works may be described as scholarly. If one restricts the discussion to studies dealing with the Eastern campaign, the number is even smaller. In part due to the extraordinary difficulty of working in Soviet archives, and no doubt reflecting national preferences, western military historians have tended to give the Eastern campaign in general, and particularly its aerial aspects, short shrift. Of the really extraordinary studies of the Wehrmacht's Drang nach Osten, such as Earl F. Ziemke's two volumes, John Erickson's equally monumental pair of works on Stalin's war with Germany, and the somewhat dated but still most readable *Barbarossa* by Alan Clark, few deal with the air war in any substantial way.[1] One exception is the Militärgeschichtliches Forschungsamt's semi-official history *Das Deutsche Reich und das Zweite Weltkrieg*. Volume 4, *Der Angriff auf die Sowjetunion*, contains two excellent chapters by Horst Boog on the Luftwaffe. To date, the series covers only the preparations for war, the campaigns through 1941 and the organization of the German war economy.

Recent works on the Luftwaffe at large contain important insights into the eastern campaign. The most voluminous is Horst Boog's outstanding

Die deutsche Luftwaffenführung 1935–1945: Führungsprobleme-Spitzengliederung-Generalstabs-ausbildung (1982). Boog's book delves into such topics as the social background of the members of the Luftwaffe officer corps, the methods of general staff education, the development of doctrine, and the reasons behind the German air force's neglect of the technical, logistical and intelligence branches. Williamson Murray, in *Luftwaffe* (1985), demonstrates, among other things, how the attrition suffered by the German air force in the Soviet Union, combined with the pressures of other theaters, shattered that force as a viable weapon by the spring of 1944. Matthew Cooper's *The German Air Force 1933–1945: An Anatomy of Failure* (1982), although a justly-acclaimed and thoughtful synthesis, relies too heavily and uncritically on previously published works when discussing the eastern campaign.

One older work deserves mention: the British Air Ministry's *Rise and Fall of the German Air Force: History of the Luftwaffe in World War II* (1946). This study grew out of the Air Ministry's attempt to combine the remnants of the Luftwaffe's historical archive with appropriate prisoner of war interrogations into a well-documented account. This volume is free of many of the popular myths about the nature of the German air force, although it is a distinctly uneven product. Many of the semi-popular works that followed it, particularly Karl Bartz's *Swastika in the Air* (1956) and Cajus Bekker's *Angriffshöhe 4000* (1964), are superficial: both create the impression that the Luftwaffe played little role in the east after the Stalingrad airlift. A recent German account, Franz Kurowski's *Balkankreuz und roter Stern: Der Luftkrieg über Russland 1941–1944* (1984) provides an operational narrative (especially of fighter combat) up to 1943, but the treatment is much more cursory thereafter. Virtually nothing has been published regarding the strategic bombing plans in 1943–1944; the sole exception is RAND Corporation analyst Oleg Hoeffding's excellent short study, "German Air Attacks Against Industry and Railroads in Russia, 1941–1945" (1970).

One significant series of publications deals directly with the topic at hand. During the 1950s, the United States Air Force sponsored an ambitious project involving ex-*Luftwaffe* officers as authors of a series of studies dealing with the German Air Force in World War II. Several volumes of the USAF Monograph Project focused on the war in the east, most notably *Generalleutnant* a.D. Hermann Plocher's three-volume *The German Air Force Versus Russia, 1941–1943*. Plocher meticulously organized his coverage by geographic region (i.e. by air fleet), and his account of month-by-month operations is unparalleled. Other volumes in the series dealt with topics such as German perceptions of the Soviets as adversaries (the USAF was, after all, interested in gaining some utilitarian benefit from its investment).[2]

These studies provide a wealth of operational detail. Plocher's volumes, in particular, are undoubtedly the standard narrative works on the subject. Taken individually or collectively, however, they do not constitute a sufficiently analytical appraisal of the German air force's campaign against the USSR. Critics have correctly noted that the perspectives of the authors—mostly middle-level general staff officers, *Fliegerdivision* commanders and the like—inclined the books heavily towards operational matters. As a result, issues such as the role of strategic bombing of the Soviet armaments industry or the intelligence failure prior to Operation Bagration in June 1944 received scarcely any attention. Understandably, the complete and enduring contempt of many Luftwaffe officers, especially those in the intelligence branch, for their Soviet adversaries does not come through in many of the studies. The present work has relied on the USAF Monograph Project volumes for matters of fact and detail, but clearly a new interpretive framework was required.

The available documentation in large measure suggested that framework. The story of the fate of the Luftwaffe archives is a rather dismal one. The Military Science Department of the Luftwaffe General Staff (8. [Kriegswissenschaftliche] Abteilung d. Genst. d. Luftwaffe), under its last department head Generalmajor Hans-Detlef Herhudt von Rohden, energetically assembled the documents of the German air force while the conflict was still going on. The Department took a hand in matters of officer education, indoctrination and the formulation of air doctrine.[3] One of its primary goals was the creation of a multi-volume history of the Luftwaffe, and to this end Herhudt von Rohden ordered the collection of important German Air Force documents at the 8. Abteilung's headquarters in Karlsbad. In 1944 alone, the department took delivery of no fewer than 17,920 *Kriegstagebücher* (war diaries) of various Luftwaffe formations.[4] The department began the massive writing project in 1943, and indeed continued work on it up to the very last days of the war.

Unfortunately for future historians of German air power, the concentration of the records made destruction of said records en masse a fairly simple task, and the bulk of the documents went up in smoke as the Allied

armies approached Karlsbad, Vorderiss and Heldburg, the major depos-
itories. Herhudt von Rohden saved a portion of the documents himself;
he and those documents were captured by the Americans.

It was no accident that many of the surviving documents dealt with the
eastern campaign. Most of Herhudt von Rohden's WWII service had been
in that theatre (he served as chief of staff to Luftflotten 1 and 4). Moreover,
he considered himself something of an authority on the Soviet Union, and
in fact numbered among his acquaintances Lieutenant General Andrei
Vlasov, head of the ill-fated Russian Army of Liberation.[5] He also benefited from a close alliance with General der Flieger Günther Korten, chief
of the Luftwaffe General Staff from September 1943 to July 1944, and
shared many of Korten's ideas about the efficacy of strategic air operations
against the Soviet Union. Many of Korten's efforts to salvage the Luftwaffe's offensive capability in the east found expression in the Historical
Department's publications.

The surviving documents originating with this agency were of two
main types. First, there are a large number of original documents from a
wide variety of German air force agencies, including an extensive collection of Luftwaffe intelligence (Foreign Air Forces East) studies and estimates, especially those pertaining to Soviet war production and the
power plant attack scheme of 1943–1944; doctrinal manuals; operational
records (including a series of war diaries from bomber units I. and III./
Kampfgeschwader 55); general staff materials and studies; records of conferences; aircraft strength returns from the Quartermaster Department;
and other useful material. Secondly, much of the Historical Department's
extensive output has been preserved. Some of it is extremely valuable,
especially studies of operational effectiveness (based upon war diaries
and other documentation which have since been destroyed); new doctrinal formulations, many produced with Korten's blessing, that shed light
on the German conception of air power theory in the later war years; and
finally drafts of the 8. Abteilung's history of the campaign against the
Soviet Union. This material provides insights and factual information not
presented in the USAF Monograph Project, as they were compiled for the
Luftwaffe's internal use, rather than under the watchful eye of the
victors.[6]

These documents may be found on seventy-three reels of microfilm at
the National Archives and Records Service (NARS), Microfilm Series
T971. Some material from this collection not available at NARS may be

found at the Library of Congress, Microfilm Series 1750. Also contained on these reels are typescripts of a multi-volume history of the Luftwaffe commissioned by the USAAF immediately following the Second World War. Herhudt von Rohden himself headed this small team (which was an effort distinct from the USAF Monograph Project) but his poor health (and premature death in 1951) ensured that the project never saw publication. Most useful is Von Rohden Annex Nr 1a, "Die deutsche Luftwaffe im Kriege gegen Russland."[7] A portion of the Von Rohden documents, dealing with technical air armament, was evidently never microfilmed in the United States and is at the Bundesarchiv/Militärarchiv in Freiburg, FRG.[8]

Other documents of Luftwaffe provenance useful for this study may be found at the NARS, on the T321 series, "Records of Headquarters of the German Air Force High Command (Oberkommando der Luftwaffe/ OKL)." A small portion of this collection is described in Guide 24; an unpublished typescript guide available in the Military Reference Branch details the bulk of the collection (274 reels). This record group contains valuable documentation on the war in Russia, most notably OKL/2316, a complete file on the strategic bombing scheme.

A veritable windfall of documentation dealing with the Luftwaffe exists in the records of the German army units fighting in the Soviet Union. Microfilm series on the army groups (T311), armies (T312), *Panzer* armies (T313), corps (T314) and divisions (T315) contain an enormous amount of information dealing with Luftwaffe operations during the eastern campaign. The nature of the documentation, naturally, varies from unit to unit; the war diary of XLVI. Panzerkorps, for example, contains detailed reports from the *Fliegerverbindungsoffiziere* (air liaison officers) reporting back to Fliegerkorps II during the final offensive against Moscow, while other units make only cursory mention of German air force activities. This imbalance is in itself indicative of the inability of the Luftwaffe (especially after 1941) to appear in strength over non-critical sectors of the vast eastern front.

The use of the army records is especially illuminating regarding the methods of direct and indirect air support that the Luftwaffe employed during the four years of the campaign. After-action reports, operational orders, and official manuals provide an excellent indication of the Luftwaffe's ability and willingness to provide support to the German army's offensive and defensive battles in the Soviet Union. The picture of Luftwaffe operational practice that emerges from an examination of these records is one quite different from the "flying artillery" portrayal of much postwar historiography.

An additional major source of documentation is the so-called "Karlsrühe Collection," the documentary library assembled for the USAF German Air Force Monograph Project. This collection consists of typescripts of original German documents, as well as correspondence from leading participants, used by the former German generals writing for the United States Air Force in the 1950s. Some of this material duplicates the Von Rohden holdings, while some was evidently provided by the officers themselves. It is, in essence, the "raw material" for the Air Force's studies. This collection, contained in a large number of Leitz binders, may be consulted at the USAF Historical Research Center at Maxwell Air Force Base, Montgomery, Alabama. Also at the Center are a number of extremely valuable translations and POW interrogations prepared by the British Air Ministry Historical Branch and Allied intelligence, often concerning documents not easily accessible elsewhere.

This study has also benefited from the use of documents, some unavailable in this country, from the Bundesarchiv/Militärarchiv in Freiburg, FRG. While a large portion of the Freiburg collection is available on this side of the Atlantic on microfilm, certain items seem to have "slipped through the cracks" during the microfilming process prior to the return of the documents to West Germany in the 1960s.

Finally, a number of other NARS record groups provided information essential to this account. These include the Records of the Reich Ministry for Armaments and War Production, microfilmed on NARS T73, and the German Air Force Mission to Rumania, on NARS T405. These record groups, along with the ADI(K) intelligence documents available in the Main Reading Room of the National Archives, provided certain documents necessary to "buttress" portions of this study.

Use of the resources described above allows the researcher in large measure to overcome the absence of a vast central repository of records of German air force provenance in producing an account of the main strategic and operational aspects of the Luftwaffe's war against the USSR. While the near-total absence of unit war diaries precludes the writing of a fully-documented tactical account, such is not the purpose of the present study. The available documents, by both their content and their provenance, suggest the major underpinnings of German air strategy in the east.

BIBLIOGRAPHY

Air Ministry. *The Rise and Fall of the German Air Force: History of the Luftwaffe in World War II*. London: HM Stationary Office, 1946.

Bartov, Omer. *The Eastern Front 1941–1945: German Troops and the Barbarisation of Warfare*. Oxford: Macmillan, 1985.

Bartz, Karl. *Swastika in the Air*. London: Kimber, 1956.

Below, Nicolaus von. *Als Hitlers Adjutant*. Mainz: Hase & Koehler Verlag, 1980.

Boog, Horst. *Die deutsche Luftwaffenführung 1935–1945: Führungsprobleme- Spitzengliederung- Geberalstabsausbildung*. Stuttgart: Deutsche Verlags-Anstalt, 1982.

———. "German Air Intelligence in World War II." *Aerospace Historian* 33 (June 1986):121–129.

———. "Higher Command and Leadership in the German Luftwaffe, 1935–1945." In *Air Power and Warfare: The Proceedings of the 8th Military History Symposium, United States Air Force Academy, 18–20 October 1978*, edited by Alfred F. Hurley and Robert C. Ehrhart, Washington, DC: Office of Air Force History, Headquarters USAF, 1979: 128–158.

———. "Luftwaffe and Logistics in the Second World War." *Aerospace Historian* 35 (June 1988): 103–110.

———. "The Luftwaffe and Technology." *Aerospace Historian* 30 (September 1983): 200–206.

———. "Das Problem der Selbständigkeit der Luftstreitkräfte in Deutschland, 1908–1945," *Militärgeschichtliches Mitteilungen* 1 (1988): 31–60.

———. "The Policy, Command and Direction of the Luftwaffe in World War II," *Proceedings of the Royal Air Force Historical Society* 4 (September 1988): 36–63.

Boog, Horst, Jürgen Förster, Joachim Hoffmann, Ernst Klink, Rolf-Dieter Müller, and Gerd R. Ueberschär. *Das deutsche Reich und der Zweite Weltkrieg, Band 4: Der Angriff auf die Sowjetunion.* Stuttgart: Deutsche Verlags-Anstalt, 1983.

Bülow, Hans Freiherr von. "Die Luftwaffe Sowjetrusslands." *Militärwissenschaftliche Rundschau* 1 (1936): 798–821.

———. "Die Grundlagen neuzeitlicher Luftstreitkräfte." *Militärwissenschaftliche Rundschau* 1 (1936), pp. 78–107.

Carroll, Berenice. *Design for Total War.* The Hague: Mouton, 1977.

Clark, Alan. *Barbarossa: The Russo-German Conflict, 1941–1945.* New York: Morrow, 1965.

Clausewitz, Carl von. *On War.* Edited and translated by Michael Howard and Peter Paret. Princeton: Princeton University Press, 1976.

Clodfelter, Mark. *The Limits of Air Power: The American Bombing of North Vietnam.* New York: The Free Press, 1989.

Cochenhausen, Friedrich von. *Die Truppenführung: Ein Handbuch für den Truppenführer und seine Gehilfen.* Berlin: E.S. Mittler & Sohn, 1931.

Cooper, Matthew. *The German Air Force 1933–1945: An Anatomy of Failure.* London: Jane's Publishing Company, 1981.

Copp, Terry and Robert Vogel. "Anglo-Canadian Tactical Air Power in Normandy: A Reassessment." Presented at the Annual Meeting of the American Military Institute. Richmond, Va: April 1987.

Deichmann, Paul. *Der Chef in Hintergrund: Ein Leben als Soldaten von der preußischen Armee bis zur Bundeswehr.* Oldenburg: Stalling Verlag GmbH, 1979.

———. *German Air Force Operations in Support of the Army (USAF Historical Studies No. 163).* New York: Arno Press, 1968.

———. *The System of Target Selection Applied by the German Air Force in World War II (USAF Historical Studies: No. 186).* Manhattan, KS: MA/AH Publishing, 1980 (2 vols.).

Deist, Wilhelm, Manfred Messerschmidt, Hans-Erich Volkmann, and Wolfram Wette. *Das deutsche Reich und der Zweite Weltkrieg, Band 1: Ursachen und Voraussetzungen der deutschen Kriegspolitik.* Stuttgart: Deutsche Verlags-Anstalt, 1979.

Detwiler, Donald S., Charles B. Burdick, and Jürgen Rohwer, *World War II German Military Studies: A Collection of 213 Special Reports on the Second World War prepared by Former Officers of the Wehrmacht for the United States Army. Vol. 16, part 7. The Eastern Theater.* New York: Garland Publishing, Inc., 1979.

Dierich, Wolfgang. *Kampfgeschwader 55 "Greif."* Stuttgart: Motorbuch Verlag, 1975.

Doerr, Hans. *Der Feldzug nach Stalingrad: Versuch eines operativen Überblickes.* Darmstadt: E.S. Mittler & Sohn GmbH, 1955.

Doughty, Robert Allan. *The Breaking-Point: Sedan and the Fall of France, 1940.* Hamden, CT: Archon Books, 1990.

Douhet, Giulio. *The Command of the Air.* Washington, DC: Office of Air Force History, 1983.

Drum, Karl. *Airpower and Russian Partisan Warfare: USAF Historical Studies No. 177.* New York: Arno Press, 1968.

Eichelbaum, Dr. *Das Buch von der Luftwaffe.* Berlin: Verlagshaus Bong & CO, 1938.

Erickson, John. *The Road to Berlin: Stalin's War with Germany.* Boulder, CO: Westview Press, 1983.

———. *The Road to Stalingrad: Stalin's War with Germany.* London: Weidenfield and Nicolson, 1975.

Feuchter, Georg W. *Flieger als Hilfswaffe: Die Zusammenarbeit zwischen Luftstreitkräften und den drei Wehrmachtteilen.* Potsdam: Ludwid Voggenreiter Verlag, 1938.

———. *"Zusammenarbeit zwischen Flieger und Erdtruppen auf dem Schlachtfeld." Flugwehr und Technik* 12 (1950): 106–108.

Fischer, Johannes. "Über den Entschluß zur Luftversorgung Stalingrads: Ein Beitrag zur militärischen Führung im Dritten Reich," *Militärgeschichtliches Mitteilungen* 2 (1969): 7–67.

Foertsch, Hermann. *The Art of Modern Warfare.* New York: Oskar Piest, 1940.

Galland, Adolf. "Defeat of the *Luftwaffe*: Fundamental Causes." *United States Air Force Air University Quarterly Review* VI (Spring 1953): 18–36.

———. *The First and the Last: The German Fighter Force in World War II.* Mesa, AZ: Champlin Museum Press, 1986.

Gellermann, Günther W. *Moskau ruft Heeresgruppe Mitte . . .* Koblenz: Bernard & Graefe Verlag, 1988.

Glantz, David M. *Soviet Military Deception in the Second World War.* London: Frank Cass, 1989.

Groehler, Olaf. "Stärke, Verteilung und Verlüste der deutschen Luftwaffe im zweiten Weltkrieg," *Militärgeschichte* 17 (1978): 316–336.

Guderian, Heinz. *Die Panzertruppen und ihr Zusammenwirken mit den anderen Waffen.* Berlin: E.S. Mittler und Sohn, 1943.

———. *Panzer Leader.* Washington, DC: Zenger Publishing Company, Inc., 1952.

Gundelach, Karl. *Die deutsche Luftwaffe im Mittelmeer 1940–1945, Band 1.* Frankfurt-am-Main: Peter D. Lang, 1981.

———. *Kampfgeschwader "General Wever" 4.* Stuttgart: Motorbuch Verlag, 1978.

Halder, Franz. *Kriegstagebuch: Tägliche Aufzeichnungen des Chefs des Generalstabes des Heeres, 1939–1942. Band*

III: Der Rußlandfeldzug bis zum Marsch auf Stalingrad (22.6.1041–24.9.1942) Edited by Hans-Adolf Jacobsen. Stuttgart: W. Kohlhammer Verlag, 1964.

————. *The Halder War Diary, 1939–1942*. edited by Charles Burdick and Hans-Adolf Jacobsen. Novato, CA: Presidio Press, 1988.

Hallion, Richard P. *Strike from the Sky: The History of Battlefield Air Attack, 1911–1945*. Washington: Smithsonian Institution Press, 1989.

Handel, Michael I. *Strategic and Operational Deception in the Second World War*. London: Frank Cass, 1987.

Hansell, Haywood S. *The Air Plan that Defeated Hitler*. Atlanta: Higgins-McArthur, 1972.

Hardesty, Von D. *Red Phoenix: The Rise of Soviet Air Power, 1941–1945*. Washington, DC: Smithsonian Institution Press, 1982.

Herhudt von Rohden, Hans-Detlef. "Letzter Großeinsatz deutscher Bomber im Osten." *Europäische Sicherheit* 1 (1951):21–27.

————. *Die Luftwaffe ringt um Stalingrad*. Wiesbaden: Limes-Verlag, 1950.

————. *Vom Luftkriege: Gedanken über Führung und Einsatz moderner Luftwaffen*. Berlin: E.S. Mittler und Sohn, 1938.

History of the Great Patriotic War of the Soviet Union, 1941–1945. Translated by U.S. Center for Military History, Scholarly Resources, 1984, 7 reels (microfilm).

Hitschhold, Hubertus. "Die Schlachtfliegerei in der deutschen Luftwaffe." *Flugwehr und Technik* 12 (1950): 81–84.

Hoeffding, Oleg. "German Air Attacks against Industry and Railroads in Russia, 1941–1945." Memorandum RM-6206-PR. Santa Monica, CA: The Rand Corporation, 1970.

Homze, Edward L. *Arming the Luftwaffe: The Reich Air Ministry and the German Aircraft Industry, 1919–1939*. Lincoln: University of Nebraska Press, 1976.

————. *German Military Aviation: A Guide to the Literature*. New York: Garland Publishing, Inc., 1984.

————. "The Luftwaffe's Failure to Develop a Heavy Bomber Before World War II." *Aerospace Historian* (March 1977): 20–26.

Höppner, Ernst von. *Deutschlands Krieg in der Luft*. Leipzig: Koehler und Umeland, 1921.

Infield, Glenn B. *The Poltava Affair: A Russian Warning, an American Tragedy*. New York: MacMillan Publishing Company, 1973.

Irving, David. *Göring: A Biography*. New York: William Morrow and Company, Inc., 1988.

————. *Hitler's War*. New York: Viking Press, 1977.

————. *The Rise and Fall of the Luftwaffe: The Life of Field Marshal Erhard Milch*. Boston: Little, Brown and Company, 1973.

Kahn, David. *Hitler's Spies: German Military Intelligence in World War II*. New York: Macmillan Publishing Company, 1978.

Kehrig, Manfred. *Stalingrad: Analyse und Dokumentation einer Schlacht.* Stuttgart: Deutsche Verlags-Anstalt, 1974.

Kennedy, Paul M. *Strategy and Diplomacy, 1870–1945.* London: Fontana, 1984.

Kennett, Lee. *A History of Strategic Bombing.* New York: Charles Scribner's Sons, 1982.

———. *The First Air War, 1914–1918.* New York: The Free Press, 1991.

Kesselring, Albert. *The Memoirs of Field Marshal Kesselring.* Novato, CA: Presidio Press, 1989.

Kroener, Bernhard R., Rolf-Dieter Müller and Hans Umbreit, *Das deutsche Reich und der Zweite Weltkrieg: Band 5/1: Kriegsverwaltung, Wirtschaft und Personelle Ressourcen, 1939–1941.* Stuttgart: Deutsche Verlags-Anstalt, 1988.

Kurowski, Franz. *Balkankreuz und roter Stern: Der Luftkrieg über Russland 1941–1944.* Friedberg: Podzun-Pallas-Verlag, 1984.

———. *Luftbrücke Stalingrad: Die Tragödie der Luftwaffe und der 6. Armee.* Berg-am-See: Kurt Vowinckel-Verlag, 1983.

Luck, Hans von. *Panzer Commander.* New York: Praeger, 1989.

Lukas, Richard C. *Eagles East: The Army Air Forces and the Soviet Union, 1941–1945.* Talahassee, FL: Florida State University Press, 1970.

Maier, Klaus, Horst Rohde, Bernd Stegemann, and Hans Umbreit.

Das deutsche Reich und der Zweite Weltkrieg, Band 2: Der Errichtung der Hegemonie auf dem Europäischen Kontinent. Stuttgart: Deutsche Verlags-Anstalt, 1979.

Mason, Francis K. *Battle over Britain.* Garden City, NY: Doubleday, 1969.

Mierzejewski, Alfred C. *The Collapse of the German War Economy, 1944–1945: Allied Air Power and the German National Railway.* Chapel Hill: University of North Carolina Press, 1988.

Moisy, F. Gandenberger von. *Luftkrieg-Zukunftskrieg?* Berlin: Zentralverlag GmbH, 1935.

Morzik, Fritz. *Die deutschen Transportflieger im Zweiten Weltkrieg.* Frankfurt-am-Main: Bernard & Graefe Verlag für Wehrwesen, 1966.

Mulligan, Timothy Francis. *The Politics of Illusion and Empire: German Occupation Policy in Russia, 1942–1943.* New York: Praeger, 1988.

Murray, Williamson. "The Air Defense of Germany: Doctrine and Defeat of the *Luftwaffe.*" Unpublished paper, 1988.

———. *Luftwaffe.* Baltimore: Nautical and Aviation Publishing Company, 1985.

———. "The Luftwaffe and Close Air Support, 1939–1941." Unpublished paper, 1984.

———. "The Luftwaffe Before the Second World War: A Mission, A Strategy?" *Journal of Strategic Studies* 4 (Sept. 1981):261–270.

———. "A Tale of Two Doctrines: The Luftwaffe's 'Conduct of the Air War' and the USAF's Manual 1-1," *Journal of Strategic Studies* 8 (December 1985):84–93.

Neumann, Georg Paul. *Die deutschen Luftstreitkräfte im Weltkriege.* Berlin: E.S. Mittler und Sohn, 1920.

Osterkamp, Theo and Franz Bacher. *Tragödie der Luftwaffe? Kritische Begegnung mit dem gleichnamigen Werk von Irving/Milch.* Neckargemünd: Kurt Vowinckel-Verlag, 1971.

Overy, R. J. *The Air War, 1939–1945.* New York: Stein and Day, 1981.

———. "From 'Uralbomber' to 'Amerikabomber': The Luftwaffe and Strategic Bombing." *Journal of Strategic Studies* 1 (1978): 155–178.

———. "The German Prewar Aircraft Production Plans, November 1936–April 1939." *English Historical Review* (Oct. 1975): 778–797.

———. *Göring: The "Iron Man."* London: Routledge and Kegan Paul, 1984.

———. "Hitler and Air Strategy." *Journal of Contemporary History* 15 (1980): 405–421.

Pickert, Wolfgang. "The Stalingrad Airlift: An Eyewitness Commentary." *Aerospace Historian* 18 (December 1971): 183–185.

Plocher, Hermann. *The German Air Force Versus Russia, 1941 (USAF Historical Studies No. 153).* New York: Arno Press, 1968.

———. *The German Air Force Versus Russia, 1942 (USAF Historical Studies No. 154).* New York: Arno Press, 1968.

———. *The German Air Force Versus Russia, 1943 (USAF Historical Studies: No. 155.* New York: Arno Press, 1968.

Price, Alfred. *German Air Force Bombers of World War II, Vol. 2.* Windsor: Hylton Lacy, 1969.

Price, James T., Richard W. Harrison, Harriet F. Scott, William F. Scott, and John R. Brinkerhoff. "Impact of Aircraft Losses on Soviet Air Operations in World War II." Prepared for the Jet Propulsion Laboratory, January 1987.

Proctor, Raymond L. *Hitler's Luftwaffe in the Spanish Civil War.* Westport: Greenwood Press, 1983.

Rabenau, Friedrich von. *Seeckt: Aus seinem Leben.* Leipzig: Hase und Koehler, 1940.

Reshetnikov, V. "From the Combat Experience of Long-Range Aviation in the Operations of the Ground Forces." *Voyenno-Istoricheskiy Zhurnal* 7 (July 1984): 36–43.

Rieckhoff, Herbert Joachim. *Trumpf oder Bluff? 12 Jahre deutsche Luftwaffe.* Geneva: Verlag Interavia, 1945.

Rothbrust, Florian K. *Guderian's XIXth Panzer Corps and the Battle of France: Breakthrough in the Ardennes, May 1940.* New York: Praeger, 1990.

Sadarananda, Dana V. *Beyond Stalingrad: Manstein and the Operations of Army Group Don.* New York: Praeger, 1990.

Sajer, Guy. *The Forgotten Soldier*. New York: Harper and Row, 1971.

Schreiber, Gerhard, Bernd Stegemann, and Detlef Vogel. *Das deutsche Reich und der Zweite Weltkrieg, Band 3: Der Mittelmeerraum und Südosteuropa*. Stuttgart: Deutsche Verlags-Anstalt, 1984.

Schwabedissen, Walter, *The Russian Air Force in the Eyes of German Commanders: USAF Historical Studies No. 175*. New York: Arno Press, 1968.

Seaton, Albert. *The Russo-German War 1941–1945*. New York: Praeger Publishers, 1971.

Seeckt, Hans von. *Gedanken eines Soldaten*. Berlin: Verlag für Kulturpolitik, 1929.

Speer, Albert. *Inside the Third Reich: Memoirs*. New York: The Macmillan Company, 1970.

United States Strategic Bombing Survey. *Over-all Report: European War*. Washington, DC: 1945.

USSR Committee for International Scientific and Technical Conferences, Krzizhanovsky Power Institute of the Academy of Sciences of the USSR. *Electric Power Development in the USSR*. Moscow: INRA Publishing Society, 1936.

Völker, Karl-Heinz. *Die deutsche Luftwaffe, 1933–1939: Aufbauu, Führung und Rüstung der Luftwaffe sowie die Entwicklung der deutschen Luftkriegstheorie*. Stuttgart: Deutsche Verlags-Anstalt, 1967.

———. *Dokumente und Dokumentärfotos zur Geschichte der deutschen Luft-*

waffe: Aus den Geheimakten des Reichswehrministeriums 1919–1933 und des Reichsluftfahrtministeriums 1933–1939. Stuttgart: Deutsche Verlags-Anstalt, 1968.

Watts, Barry D. *The Foundations of US Air Doctrine: The Problem of Friction in War*. Maxwell AFB: Air University Press, 1984.

Weber, Theo. "Zum Thema Flieger und Panzer: Bemerkungen zu einen neuen Geschichtswerk über den zweiten Weltkrieg." *Flugwehr und Technik* 10 (1948): 77–81.

Weber, Theo. "Zum Thema: Panzerbekämpfung durch Flieger: Bemerkungen zum Buch 'Trotzdem' des deutschen Fliegerobersten H. U. Rudel." *Flugwehr und Technik* 12 (1950): 149–155.

Wehler, Hans-Ulrich. "'Absoluter' und 'Totaler' Krieg: Von Clausewitz zu Ludendorff." *Politische Vierteljahrschrift* 10 (1969): 220–248.

Whaley, Barton. *Codeword Barbarossa*. Cambridge, MA: MIT Press, 1973.

Whiting, Kenneth R. "Soviet Air Power in World War II" In *Air Power and Warfare: The Proceedings of the 8th Military History Symposium, United States Air Force Academy, 18–20 October 1978*. Edited by Alfred F. Hurley and Robert C. Ehrhart. Washington, DC: Office of Air Force History, Headquarters USAF, 1979: 98–127.

Wray, Timothy A. *Standing Fast: German Defensive Doctrine on the Russian Front during WWII: Prewar to March 1943. Combat Studies Institute-Research Study No. 5*. Ft. Leavenworth: US Army Command and General Staff College, 1986.

Zantke, Siegfried, "Der Luftangriff gegen Gorkij, ein großer Erfolg der operativen Luftkriegführung 1943," *Wehrwissenschaftliche Rundschau* 5 (May 1954): 230–233.

Ziemke, Earl F. *Stalingrad to Berlin: The German Defeat in the East, 1943–1945*. Washington: Office of the Chief of Military History, 1968.

———. *Moscow to Stalingrad: Decision in the East*. Washington, DC: US Army Center of Military History, 1987.

Notes

PREFACE

1. Luftwaffenführungsstab Ia op Nr. 8655/43 g. Kdos. Chefsache, 9.11.43, National Archives and Records Service (NARS) Microfilm T321/10/4746780. All translations by the author except where noted.

2. David Irving, *The Rise and Fall of the Luftwaffe: The Life of Field Marshal Erhard Milch* (Boston: Little, Brown and Company, 1973), p. 126; Horst Boog, *Die deutsche Luftwaffenführung, 1935–1945 Führungsprobleme-Spitzengliederung-Gene-ralstabsausbildung* (Stuttgart: Deutsche Verlags-Anstalt, 1982), p. 117.

3. Williamson Murray, *Luftwaffe* (Baltimore: Nautical and Aviation Publishing Company of America, 1985), pp. 223–233.

4. Edward L. Homze, *German Military Aviation: A Guide to the Literature* (New York: Garland Publishing Inc., 1984), pp. 149–150.

5. Air Ministry, *Rise and Fall of the German Air Force: History of the Luftwaffe in World War II* (London: HM Stationary Office, 1946), pp. 407–408.

6. The work of the researchers at the Militärgeschichtliches Forschungsamt in Freiburg, particularly that of Horst Boog and Wilhelm Deist, as well as that of Williamson Murray and Edward Homze in the United States and R. J. Overy in Great Britain has revised substantially the perception of Luftwaffe air power doctrine.

7. Anlage 3 zu Genst. Qu. 6. Abt., Nr. 4713/43 gKdos. (I)v. 17.6.43, "Ist-stärken an Flugzeugen der am 31.5.43 im Einsatz gewesenen fliegenden Ver-bände," Milch 53.10, NARS T321/154/062.

8. Olaf Groehler, "Stärke, Verteilung und Verluste der deutschen Luftwaffe im zweiten Weltkrieg," *Militärgeschichte* 17 (1978), pp. 316–336.

256

9. This is the thrust of Horst Boog, Jürgen Förster, Joachim Hoffmann, Ernst Klink, Rolf-Dieter Müller, and Gerd R. Ueberschär, *Das deutsche Reich und der Zweite Weltkrieg, Band 4: Der Angriff auf die Sowjetunion* (Stuttgart: Deutsche Verlags-Anstalt, 1984).

10. L. Dv. 16, *Luftkriegführung* (Berlin: Reichsdruckerei, 1935), paragraph 31.

11. R. J. Overy, *The Air War, 1939-1945* (New York: Stein and Day, 1981), p. 97.

12. This task would be redundant; the three volumes by Plocher in the USAF Monograph Project series contain 1,300 pages on the subject.

CHAPTER ONE

1. Berenice Carroll, *Design for Total War* (The Hague: Mouton, 1977), p. 91.

2. This contention originated with such early works as Asher Lee, *The German Air Force* (London: Duckworth, 1946), and Air Ministry, *Rise and Fall of the German Air Force*. It has been amplified by some of the volumes in the USAF Historical Monograph Series, written by former Luftwaffe officers for the USAF. These volumes emphasize the lack of strategic thinking or capability in the Luftwaffe, especially when contrasted to the air arms of the Western Allies.

3. See Richard P. Hallion, *Strike from the Sky: The History of Battlefield Air Attack, 1911-1945* (Washington: Smithsonian Institution Press, 1989) for a comparative survey of tactical air power.

4. See especially Boog, *Luftwaffenführung*; Wilhelm Deist, "Die Aufrüstung der Wehrmacht," in Deist et al., *Das Deutsche Reich und der Zweite Weltkrieg, Band 1: Ursachen und Voraussetzungen der deutschen Kriegspolitik* (Stuttgart: Deutsche Verlags-Anstalt, 1979), pp. 473-496; and Murray, *Luftwaffe*.

5. Edward L. Homze, *Arming the Luftwaffe: The Reich Air Ministry and the German Aircraft Industry, 1919-1939* (Lincoln: University of Nebraska Press, 1976), p. 3.

6. Ibid., p. 40.

7. Ibid.

8. Friedrich von Rabenau, *Seeckt: Aus seinem Leben, 1918-1936* (Leipzig: Hase u. Koehler, 1940), pp. 527-532.

9. Hans von Seeckt, *Gedanken eines Soldaten* (Berlin: Verlag für Kulturpolitik, 1929), pp. 91-92.

10. See Reichswehrministerium HL, Literatur, Genst d. Heeres, 5. Abt., 43 h Wi/I 317 Ib, "Die zukünftige Kriegführung in der Luft und ihre Auswirkung auf die Bewegung des Heeres," 26 April 1934, NARS T78/128/6057013ff.

11. Friedrich von Cochenhausen, *Die Truppenführung: Ein Handbuch für den Truppenführer und seine Gehilfen. Teil 1: Mittlere und untere Führung* (Berlin: E.S. Mittler & Sohn, 1931), p. 78.

12. Headquarters, United States Strategic Air Forces in Europe (Rear), Office of the Historian, "Questionnaire on GAF Doctrine and Policy: Answers by Gen. Maj. von Rohden (P.W.) and Col. Kriesche (P.W.) to Questions Submitted by Major Engelman," 14 August 1945, United States Air Force Historical Research Center, Maxwell AFB (USAFHRC) 519.619-7, p. 1.

13. Deist et al., *Voraussetzungen der deutschen Kriegspolitik*, p. 475.

14. On Tirpitz, see Paul Kennedy, "Strategic Aspects of the Anglo-German Naval Race," in his *Strategy and Diplomacy, 1870–1945* (Fontana, 1984), pp. 129–160.

15. Hans-Detlef Herhudt von Rohden, *Vom Luftkriege: Gedanken über Führung und Einsatz moderner Luftwaffen* (Berlin: Ernst Mittler & Sohn, 1938), p. 21; R. J. Overy, "Hitler and Air Strategy," *Journal of Contemporary History* 15 (1980), pp. 405–421.

16. See Williamson Murray, "A Tale of Two Doctrines: The Luftwaffe's 'Conduct of the Air War' and the USAF's Manual 1-1," *Journal of Strategic Studies* 6 (December 1983), pp. 84–93.

17. For an interesting first-person account of how the manual came into being, see Paul Deichmann, *Der Chef in Hintergrund: Ein Leben als Soldaten von der preußischen Armee bis zur Bundeswehr* (Oldenburg: Stalling Verlag GmbH, 1979), pp. 58–63.

18. Matthew Cooper, *The German Air Force 1933–1945: An Anatomy of Failure* (London: Jane's, 1981), p. 12.

19. Murray, *Luftwaffe*, p. 9.

20. Herbert Joachim Rieckhoff, *Trumpf oder Bluff? 12 Jahre deutsche Luftwaffe* (Geneva: Inter Avia, 1945), p. 40. A copy of Rieckhoff's book in the Air University library contains marginal notations by a number of captured Luftwaffe officers; comments such as "Braggart!" and "A poor justification" proliferate.

21. Deichmann, *Chef in Hintergrund*, p. 62. Herhudt von Rohden cited as evidence that *Luftkriegführung* devoted 19 paragraphs to interdiction operations, while only two "sub-paragraphs" within Paragraph 161 dealt with attacks on the enemy industry sustaining the transportation system.

22. *Luftkriegführung*, paragraph 2.

23. Ibid., paragraph 10.

24. Ibid., paragraph 8.

25. Ibid., paragraphs 13–15, 30, 45–47.

26. Carl von Clausewitz, *On War*, tr. and ed. Michael Howard and Peter Paret (Princeton: Princeton University Press, 1976), p. 204.

27. *Luftkriegführung*, paragraph 31.

28. Giulio Douhet, *The Command of the Air* (Washington, DC: Office of Air Force History, 1983), pp. 10–11.

29. See Homze, *Arming the Luftwaffe*, pp. 220–227; Murray, *Luftwaffe*, pp. 1–18.

30. Von Rohden Annex, "Die deutsche Luftrüstung 1933–1945," NARS T971/26/1061.

31. See Edward L. Homze, "The Luftwaffe's Failure to Develop a Heavy Bomber Before WWII," *Aerospace Historian* (March 1977), pp. 20–26.

32. This discussion is concerned with the true air theorists, and thus discounts the activities of the air "publicists," such as Dr. Robert Knauss, whose contribution to the interwar genre of "death from the skies" books was *Luftkrieg 1936*, about a hypothetical European-wide air war.

33. See Williamson Murray, "The Luftwaffe Before the Second World War: A Mission, a Strategy?," *Journal of Strategic Studies* 4 (September 1981), pp. 261–270.

34. ADI(K)/CSDIC, 8 Sept 1945, "Report on further information obtained from PW CS/2513 Genobst aD Halder, 'Cooperation Between German Army and GAF,'" NARS RG 165 Box 649.

35. For the final Luftwaffe verdict on Douhet, see OKL, Generalstab 8. Abteilung, 22.11.1944, "The Douhet Theory and its Application to the Present War," Air Historical Branch Translation No. VII/11, USAFHRC 512.621 VII/11.

36. Ibid., p. 9.

37. For example, see Major Genth, "Der operative Luftkrieg im Weltkrieg, insbesondere gegen England," *Die Luftwaffe* 2 (Heft 2), pp. 3–15; Erwin Gehrts, "Gedanken zum operativer Luftkrieg," *Die Luftwaffe* 2 (Heft 2), pp. 16–39, both on NARS T321/10/747477ff.

38. Gehrts, "Gedanken zum operativen Luftkrieg," p. 17.

39. The best and most detailed discussion of the many permutations of this concept is in Boog, *Luftwaffenführung*, pp. 151–164.

40. Horst Boog, "The Policy, Command and Direction of the *Luftwaffe* in World War II," *Proceedings of the Royal Air Force Historical Society* 4 (September 1988), p. 39.

41. Boog, *Luftwaffenführung*, p. 155.

42. Herhudt von Rohden, *Vom Luftkriege*, forward.

43. Ibid., p. 22.

44. Ibid., p. 10.

45. Ibid., p. 4.

46. Hans-Detlef Herhudt von Rohden, "Betrachtungen über den Luftkrieg," I. Teil, *Militärwissenschaftliche Rundschau* 2 (1937) Heft 2, p. 204.

47. Hans Freiherr von Bülow, "Die Luftwaffe Sowjetrusslands," *Militärwissenschaftliche Rundschau* 1 (1936), pp. 798, 820.

48. Major Macht, "Engpässe der russischen Wehrwirtschaft," 1. Teil, *Die Luftwaffe: Militärwissenschaftliche Aufsatzsammlung* 2 (Heft 3, 1937), p. 53, NARS T971/38/149ff.

49. Oberstleutnant Macht, "Engpässe der russischen Wehrwirtschaft," 2. Teil, *Die Luftwaffe: Militärwissenschaftliche Aufsatzsammlung* 3 (Heft 1, 1938), p. 75, NARS T321/75/4826276ff.

50. Paul Deichmann, *German Air Force Operations in Support of the Army: USAF Historical Studies No. 163* (New York: Arno Press, 1968), p. 6.

51. Boog, *Luftwaffenführung*, p. 151.

52. Georg Paul Neumann, *Die deutschen Luftstreitkräfte im Weltkriege* (Berlin: Ernst Siegfried Mittler und Sohn, 1920), pp. 90–93.

53. Army War College, "The Infantry Airplane and the Infantry Balloon" (British translation of a captured German document dated 1st September, 1917). Copy in National Air and Space Museum Library, Washington, DC.

54. OKL, Generalstab 8. Abteilung, "Development of the German Ground Attack Arm and Principles Governing Its Operations up to the End of 1944," 1.12.1944, Air Historical Branch Translation No. VII/14, USAFHRC 512.621 VII/14, p. 2.

55. Edgar Graf von Matuschka, "Organisationsgeschichte der Luftwaffe von den Anfängen bis 1918," in *Handbuch zur deutschen Militärgeschichte, 1648–1939, Band V* (Frankfurt-am-Main: Bernard & Graefe Verlag für Wehrwesen,

1968), p. 307; Lee Kennett, *The First Air War, 1914–1918* (New York: Free Press, 1990), pp. 211–212.

56. Ernst von Höppner, *Deutschlands Krieg in der Luft* (Leipzig: Koehler und Umeland, 1921), p. 149.

57. Kennett, *First Air War*, pp. 212–213.

58. R. J. Overy, ''The German Prewar Aircraft Production Plans, November 1936–April 1939,'' *English Historical Review* (October 1975), p. 779.

59. Deichmann, *German Air Force Operations in Support of the Army*, p. 32.

60. ''German Ground Attack Arm,'' p. 3.

61. Bestimmungen für die Große Herbstübung 1936 des Gruppenkdos. 2 (Kassel: Wehrkreisdruckerei IX, 1936), NARS T78/374/6337544.

62. Generalkommando III. A.K. (Wehrkreiskommando III) Abt. Ia op Nr. 1633/36 g., Betr.: Zusammenarbeit mit der Luftwaffe, 15. Dezember 1936, NARS T405/6/4834188ff.

63. Flak 34, Flakabteilung Lankwitz, I/Flakregt. 12, Vortrag, 29.10.36, Maj. d. Genst. Deichmann, NARS T405/6/4834546ff.

64. Heinz Guderian, *Die Panzertruppen und ihr Zusammenwirken mit den anderen Waffen* (Berlin: Ernst Mittler & Sohn, 1943), p. 47.

65. ''German Ground Attack Arm,'' p. 3.

66. Murray, *Luftwaffe*, pp. 16–17.

67. Hans-Detlef Herhudt von Rohden, ''Luftwaffe und Gesamtkriegführung,'' in Major Dr. Eichelbaum, ed., *Das Buch von der Luftwaffe* (Berlin: Verlagshaus Bong & Co., 1938), p. 20.

68. Deichmann, *German Air Force Operations in Support of the Army*, p. 35.

69. Irving, *Rise and Fall of the Luftwaffe*, p. 58. On the subject of Richthofen's attitude towards technical innovation, it should be noted that he was an early supporter of the Army Ordnance Rocket Program that led to the A-4 (V-2) ballistic missile.

70. Williamson Murray, ''The Luftwaffe and Close Air Support, 1939–1941,'' unpublished paper, 1985, p. 8. In Murray, *German Military Effectiveness* (Baltimore: Nautical and Aviation Publishing Company, 1991).

71. Raymond L. Proctor, *Hitler's Luftwaffe and the Spanish Civil War* (Westport, CT: Greenwood Press, 1983), p. 257.

72. Dietrich Peltz, personal recollection to author, National Air and Space Museum, Washington, DC, November 1990.

73. Luftflottenkommando 3, Führungsabteilung Nr. 2778/39 g.Kdos., Juni 1939, Verlauf der Generalstabsreise der Luftwaffe, 1939, Von Rohden Collection, Library of Congress Microfilm Reading Room, Series 1750, reel 29.

74. Der Reichsminister der Luftfahrt und Oberbefehlshaber der Luftwaffe, Genst. 3. (takt.) Abteilung (II) Nr. 1240/39 geh., ''Richtlinien für den Einsatz der Fliegertruppe zur unmittelbaren Unterstützung des Heeres,'' NARS T321/76/no frame nos.

75. OKL, Planstudie 1939, Heft II: Aufmarsch- und Kampfanweisungen der Luftwaffe—Weisungen für den Einsatz gegen Osten,'' Milch/249, NARS T321/176/6ff.

76. Figures in Karl-Heinz Völker, *Die deutsche Luftwaffe 1933–1939: Aufbau, Führung und Rüstung der Luftwaffe sowie die Entwicklung der deutschen Luftkriegstheorie* (Stuttgart: Deutsche Verlags Anstalt, 1967), p. 189.

77. Murray, "Luftwaffe and Close Air Support," pp. 20–21.

78. Ibid., p. 20.

79. Karl-Heinrich Schulz, "The Collaboration Between the Army and the Luftwaffe: Support of the Army by the Luftwaffe on the Battlefield," US Army MS #B-791a, p. 3. I am grateful to Dr. Brian M. Linn for providing me with this document.

80. Deichmann, *German Air Force Operations in Support of the Army*, p. 131.

81. Von Rohden Annex Nr. 1b, Heft 1: "The German Air Force in the War against Russia," NARS T971/26/241.

82. Air Ministry, *Rise and Fall of the German Air Force*, p. 40; Boog et al., *Angriff auf die Sowjetunion*, p. 600.

83. Murray, "Luftwaffe and Close Air Support," p. 24; Genkdo. XIX. AK, Ia, Anlagenheft z. Ktb., Nr. 2, "Zusammenarbeit mit der Luftwaffe," NARS T314/615/357.

84. XIX. AK, "Zusammenarbeit mit der Luftwaffe," NARS T314/615/372–393.

85. Ibid., fr. 393–394.

86. Robert Allan Doughty, *The Breaking-Point: Sedan and the Fall of France, 1940* (Hamden, CT: Archon Books, 1990), p. 324.

CHAPTER TWO

1. Generalluftzeugmeister, Chef des Stabes, Betr.: Technisch-taktische Fragen der ungarischen Kommission, Bezug: Besprechung am 1.4.41 im RLM, 24 April 1941, NARS T321/247/no frame nos.

2. Barton Whaley, *Codeword Barbarossa* (Cambridge: MIT Press, 1973), pp. 267–269; H. R. Trevor-Roper, *Hitler's War Directives, 1939–1945* (London: Sidgwick and Jackson, 1964), p. 49.

3. Von Rohden annex 13a, "Der Aufbau der deutschen Luftwaffe-Strategie-Rüstung-Ideologie," NARS T971/27/906.

4. U.S. Center for Military History, trans., *History of the Great Patriotic War of the Soviet Union, 1941–1945* (Scholarly Resources, 1984), Vol. 2, p. 16.

5. Franz Halder, *The Halder War Diary, 1939–1942*, ed. Charles Burdick and Hans-Adolf Jacobsen (Novato, CA: Presidio Press, 1988), p. 440.

6. Von Rohden Annex, "War Against Russia," NARS T971/26/248.

7. Trevor-Roper, *Hitler's War Directives*, p. 49; Von Rohden Annex, "War against Russia," NARS T971/26/231.

8. Halder, *War Diary*, entry for July 22, 1940, p. 231.

9. Trevor-Roper, *Hitler's War Directives*, pp. 49–52.

10. Irving, *Rise and Fall of the Luftwaffe*, p. 126.

11. XXXXVIII. Armeekorps, 16893/2, Anl. zur Vorgeschichte des Kriegstagebuch, Abt. Ia, 28.4.–21.6.1941, NARS T314/1138/550.

12. OKL, Genst. 8. Abteilung, 1944, "Der Luftkrieg im Osten gegen Russland 1941," USAFHRC, Karlsrühe Collection K113.309-3 v. 12, p. 2.

13. Heeresgruppe Süd/Ia, Kriegstagebuch I. Teil, 2. Febr. 41–21. Juni 41, NARS T311/260/8.

14. Ibid., "Unterst. durch die Luftwaffe," record of briefing June 12, 1941, NARS T311/260/115.

15. Luftflotte 2, Planspiele 1939, Verlauf des Generalstabesreise der Luftwaffe, 1939, p. 9, Von Rohden Collection, Library of Congress Microfilm Series 1750, reel 29.

16. Hermann Plocher, *The German Air Force Versus Russia, 1941: USAF Historical Studies No. 153* (New York: Arno Press, 1968), p. 43.

17. Heeresgruppe Süd/Ia KTB I. Teil, "Luftwaffe," 20.6.41, NARS T311/260/131.

18. OKL, Planstudie 1939, NARS T321/76/20.

19. "Air Operations on the Russian Front in 1941: A Lecture Delivered by Hptmn. Baltrusch, 25 March 1944," Air Historical Branch translation VII/34, USAFHRC 512.621 VII/34, p. 5.

20. Von Rohden Annex, "War against Russia," NARS T971/26/231.

21. Boog, *Luftwaffenführung*, p. 157.

22. Figures in Boog et al., *Angriff auf die Sowjetunion*, p. 313.

23. Anlage 2 zu Genst. Qu. 6. Abt. Nr. 4713/43 gKdos. v. 17. 6. 43, "Iststärke an Fugzeugen der am 5. 7. 41 im Einsatz gewesenen Jagd-Zerstörer-, Kampf- und Stuka-Verbände," Milch 53.10, NARS T321/154/61.

24. Francis K. Mason, *Battle over Britain* (Garden City, NY: Doubleday, 1969), pp. 275–285.

25. Air Ministry, *Rise and Fall of the German Air Force*, p. 124.

26. "Russland-Feldzug 1941: VIII. Fliegerkorps, zusammengestellt von H. W. Deichmann, Oberst a.D., damaliger Adjutant des VIII. Fl. K. an Hand von Aufzeichnungen, Umfragen und Tagebuch des Herrn Gen. Feldmarschall Dr. Ing. Frhr. v. Richthofen," p. 2, Bundesarchiv/Militärarchiv, Freiburg (BA/MA) RL 8/47.

27. Horst Boog, "German Air Intelligence in World War II," *Aerospace Historian* 33 (June 1986), p. 122.

28. Halder, *War Diary*, p. 321.

29. Boog, *Luftwaffenführung*, p. 111.

30. *History of the Great Patriotic War*, Volume 1, p. 605.

31. Boog et al., *Angriff auf die Sowjetunion*, p. 289.

32. *History of the Great Patriotic War*, Vol. 1, p. 579.

33. Boog et al., *Angriff auf die Sowjetunion*, p. 286.

34. Boog, "German Air Intelligence," p. 125.

35. Der Reichsminister der Luftfahrt und Oberbefehlshaber der Luftwaffe, Generalluftzeugmeister GL 7, Nr. 1065/41 geh., "Bericht über die INDUSTRIE-BESICHTIGUNGS-REISE vom 28.3.–17.4.41 in Russland," OKL/798, NARS T321/232/no frame nos.

36. Ibid., Anlage 7, 13.

37. Irving, *Rise and Fall of the Luftwaffe*, p. 118 n 3.

38. *History of the Great Patriotic War*, Vol. 1, p. 572.

39. I. Armee Korps, KTB der Abt. Ia, Ostfeldzug, June 22–Oct. 31, 1941, 21941/1, Kdr. Heeres-Flak-Abt. 272, NARS T314/39/886.

40. *History of the Great Patriotic War*, Vol. 1, p. 579.

41. Führungsstab Ic, "Die Kriegsflugzeuge der SU," OKL/2589, NARS T321/81/227ff.

42. PzAOK 2, "Taktische Ein-Mappe XVIII, Russland, PzAOK 2, Ic, 30233/22, NARS T313/135/7384066.

43. See David Kahn, *Hitler's Spies: German Military Intelligence in World War II* (New York: Macmillan Publishing Company, 1978), pp. 115–126, for an account of the Rowehl Squadron's development and achievements. Halder testified to the thoroughness of Rowehl's work; Halder, *War Diary*, p. 403.

44. Boog et al., *Angriff auf die Sowjetunion*, p. 289.

45. Franz Kurowski, *Balkankreuz und roter Stern: Der Luftkrieg über Russland, 1941–1944* (Friedberg: Podzun Pallas Verlag, 1984), p. 57.

46. Halder, *War Diary*, p. 412.

47. Boog et al., *Angriff auf die Sowjetunion*, p. 654. Wartime German internal sources claim 2,582 Russian aircraft by the end of the second day. "Air Operations on the Russian Front," p. 6.

48. See Kriegsberichter Walter Schmitt, Gefr., Feldpost Nr.L. 16904, 7.20.41, "Der Befehl ist da, wir starten," von Rohden 4376/810, NARS T971/10/239.

49. Albert Kesselring, *The Memoirs of Field Marshal Kesselring* (Novato, CA: Presidio Press, 1989), p. 90.

50. See, for one of many possible examples, XLI. Panzerkorps, Anlagen z. KTB, Aug.–Sept. 1941, 18741/6, NARS T314/980/440.

51. Hans von Luck, *Panzer Commander* (New York: Praeger, 1989), p. 53.

52. "Air Operations on the Russian Front," p. 6.

53. Von Rohden Annex Nr. 1a, "Die deutsche Luftwaffe im Kriege gegen Russland," NARS T971/26/43.

54. "Russland-Feldzug 1941: VIII. Flieger-Korps," p. 2, BA/MA RL 8/47.

55. Kesselring, *Memoirs*, p. 89.

56. Von Rohden Annex, "War against Russia," NARS T971/26/292.

57. For an example of the responsibilities of Kolufts just prior to Barbarossa, see XXXXVIII. Armeekorps, Anlage zur Vorgeschichte des Kriegstagebuch, Abt. Ia, 28.4.-21.6.41, NARS T314/1138/554. See also Murray, "Luftwaffe and Close Air Support," pp. 18–19.

58. "Air Operations on the Russian Front," p. 9.

59. Schulz, "Collaboration Between Army and Luftwaffe," p. 5.

60. Ibid., p. 7.

61. Genkdo. XXX. Armeekorps, Ia, Anlagenheft z. KTB Nr. 2, "Zusammenarbeit mit der Luftwaffe," NARS T314/615/357–393.

62. Oberbefehlshaber der Luftwaffe, Führungsstab Ia Nr 1440/41 geh. (II), 8.5.41, "Taktische Merkblatt für die Führung von Nahkampfverbänden," p. 1-5, BA/MA RH 27-18/4.

63. Ibid., p. 1.

64. XLVI. Panzerkorps, Ia, Anlagen z. KTB 3, "Tätigskeitbericht, 5. Oktober 1941—Flivo," NARS T314/997/114.

65. XLII. Armeekorps, Ia, Anlagenband z. b. Z. Gefechts- und Erfahrungsbericht "Blücher," "Erfahrungsbericht über den Einsatz des Flieger-Verbindungs-Offiziers," NARS T314/997/114.

66. AOK 16, Ia, 3.8.41, "Merkblatt für die Tätigkeit der Verbindungsoffiziere und das Verhalten der Erdtruppe im Zusammenwirken mit Fliegerverbänden des VIII. Fl. Korps," p. 1, BA/MA RH/unnumbered.

67. Hermann Plocher, "Die Unterstützung des Heeres durch die Luftwaffe, Osten 1941/42," USAFHRC, Karlsrühe Collection, K113.309-3, p. 10.

68. Halder, *War Diary*, p. 466.

69. Deichmann, *German Air Force Operations in Support of the Army*, pp. 108–109.

70. XLI. Armeekorps (Pz), KTB, "Korpsbefehl, 20.8.1941," NARS T314/980/476.

71. XLII. Armeekorps, 14513/12, KTB, Ic Tätigkeitsbericht mit Anlagen, NARS T314/993/802.

72. Hermann Plocher, "Einsatz gegen Moskau im Jahre 1941," April 1955, USAFHRC, Karlsrühe Collection, K.113.309–3 v. 1, p. 2; Boog et al., *Angriff auf die Sowjetunion*, p. 692.

73. "Geschichte der I./KG "General Wever" 4 vom 1.9.1939-15.7.1944," von Rohden 4407/41a, NARS T971/16/588.

74. Plocher, "Einsatz gegen Moskau," p. 1.

75. HGr. Mitte, Ia, Anl. z. KTB Nr. 1 (Band: Dez. 1941) des OberKdo der HGr. Mitte, Verbindungsoffz. d. VIII. Fl. Korps bei HGr. Mitte, 1.12.41, NARS T311/228/445.

76. Von Rohden Annex, "War against Russia," NARS T971/26/249.

77. Boog et al., *Angriff auf die Sowjetunion*, p. 692.

78. *Luftkriegführung*, paragraph 21.

79. Boog et al., *Angriff auf die Sowjetunion*, pp. 689–691; Trevor-Roper, *Hitler's War Directives*, p. 88: "3. . . .The attack on Moscow by the bomber forces of 2nd Air Fleet, temporarily reinforced by bomber forces from the West, will be carried out as soon as possible as 'reprisal for Russian attacks on Bucharest and Helsinki.'" The OKW decrees, however, refer not to reprisals but rather to "strik[ing] at the center of Bolshevik resistance."

80. Kesselring is entirely correct in this statement. "Geschichte der I./KG 'General Wever' 4," NARS T971/16/582, praises the Soviet air defenses.

81. Kesselring, *Memoirs*, pp. 94–95.

82. Soviet sources for prestige reasons tend to exaggerate the level of Luftwaffe activity against the capital. N. Svjetlisin, "Die Abwehr des ersten massierten Angriffes der deutsch-faschisten Luftwaffe auf Moscow," *Wehrwissenschaftliche Rundschau* 20 Heft 2 (1970), p. 113. In the same vein, the Soviets on November 5 claim to have destroyed 180 out of 187 bombers raiding the capital. E. Lederry, *Germany's Defeat in the East: The Soviet Armies at War, 1941–1945* (London: War Office, 1955), p. 42 n. 1.

83. Boog et al., *Angriff auf die Sowjetunion*, p. 693.

84. "Vernehmung von Hermann Göring," von Rohden 4376/436a, June 1, 1945, NARS T971/14/78.

85. In January 1944, Hitler made similarly disparaging remarks about the Luftwaffe's inability to bomb London in retaliation for RAF Bomber Command's area attacks. Irving, *Rise and Fall of the Luftwaffe*, p. 264.

86. Generalstab 8. Abteilung, "Auswirkungen und Folgerungen aus dem Einsatz von Teilen der strategischen Luftwaffe zur unmittelbaren Unterstützung des Heeres," 24.12.43, NARS T971/37/689.

87. Luftwaffenführungsstab Ic, Nr. 20 362/43 geh. (IVD), 2.7.43, Betr." Die Bedeutung Moskaus als politisches und militarisch. Zentrum," von Rohden 4406/15, NARS T971/22/101.

88. "Gefechtsquartiere des VIII. Fliegerkorps im Russland-Feldzug 1941," Aufgestellt von Hans-Wilhelm Deichmann, USAFHRC, Karlsrühe Collection K113.309-3 v. 2.

89. See also Air Ministry, *Rise and Fall of the German Air Force*, pp. 169–170, for a discussion on the rapid transfer of fighter and dive-bomber units within the theater.

90. I AK, KTB der Abt. Ia, Ostfeldzug, 22. Juni– 31. Okt. 1941, 21941/1, NARS T314/39/842.

91. I AK, Anlage z. Gen. Kdo. I AK, Ia 545/41 gK., 16.9.41, "Tätigkeit des VIII. Fliegerkorps bei der Unterstützung des Durchbruchs des I. A.K. bis zur Eisenbahnlinie Leningrad-Moskau vom 10.8.41-21.8.41," p. 3, BA/MA RL 8/48.

92. Anlage 2 z. Gen Kdo. VIII. Flieger-Korps-Ia Nr. 2155/41 gKdos., in I. AK, Ia Nr. 538/41 gK., NARS T314/93/22ff.

93. I. AK, Ia, Anl. z. KTB, Korpsbefehle, NARS T314/41/1039.

94. "Interrogation of General der Flieger Koller," 17.11.45, von Rohden 4406/275, NARS T971/22/545.

95. I AK, "Tätigkeit des VIII. Fliegerkorps," p. 15.

96. "Air Operations on the Russian Front," p. 8.

97. VIII. Fliegerkorps, Russland-Feldzug: Mittelabschnitt 2. Teil-1941 ab 28.9.1941, Zusammengestellt von H. W. Deichmann, Oberst a.D. damaliger Adjutant des VIII. Fl. K an Hand von Aufzeichnung, Umfragen und Tagebuch-Aufzeichnungen des Gen. Feldmarschalls Dr. Ing. Freiherr v. Richthofen," p. 2, BA/MA RL 8/49.

98. Ibid., p. 2; Boog et al., *Angriff auf die Sowjetunion*, pp. 677–679.

99. Gen. Kdo.d.II. Fliegerkorps, Abteilung Ic, 99. Lagebericht vom 4.10.41, in XXXXVI. AK, Ia, Anlagen z. KTB, 27. Aug.-31. Okt. 1941, NARS T314/1075/68ff.

100. Gen.Kdo. d. II. Fliegerkorps, Abteilung Ic (R), 100. Lagebericht vom 5.10.41, NARS T314/1075/92. On October 5, for example, StG 1 and StG 77 together flew 210 sorties, while KG 3, KG 28 and KG 3 flew a total of 165.

101. Gen. Kdo. d. II. Fliegerkorps, Abteilung Ic (Dr), 102. Lagebericht vom 7.10.41, NARS T314/1075/107.

102. Boog et al., *Angriff auf die Sowjetunion*, p. 691.

103. Gen.Kdo II. Fliegerkorps, Ia, "Tätigkeitbericht des II. Fl. Korps v. 9.10.41," NARS T314/1075/119.

104. Gen. Kdo. II. Fliegerkorps, Ia, Tätigkeit des II. Fl. Korps v. 10.10.41, NARS T314/1075/125.

105. Figures obtained from XXXXVI. Pz. K, Anlagen zum Kriegstagebuch, Korpstruppen v. 27.8.-31.10.41, NARS T314.1075/68ff. The Fliegerkorps II intelligence and after-action reports contained in this war diary provide one of the most complete accounts of a Luftwaffe army support operation extant.

106. "VIII. Fliegerkorps, Russlandfeldzug," p. 2.

107. Earl F. Ziemke, *Moscow to Stalingrad: Decision in the East* (Washington, DC; Office of the Chief of Military History, 1987), p. 37.

108. Halder, *War Diary*, pp. 552–553.

109. Boog et al., *Angriff auf die Sowjetunion*, p. 680.

110. Ibid., p. 681.

111. Karl Gundelach, *Die deutsche Luftwaffe im Mittelmeer 1940–1945: Band 1* (Frankfurt-am-Main: Peter D. Lang, 1981), p. 339.

112. Verbindungsoffz. d. VIII. Fl. Korps bei HGr Mitte, in: Heeresgruppe Mitte, Ia Anl. z. KTB Nr. 1 (Band: Dez. 1941) des Oberkdo der HGr Mitte, NARS T311/228/445ff.

113. Halder, *War Diary*, p. 595.

114. "VIII. Fliegerkorps: Russlandfeldzug," p. 30.

115. Komm. General VIII. Fliegerkorps, Tagesbefehl, 10.12.1941, BA/MA RL 8/49.

116. Von Rohden Annex, "War against Russia," NARS T971/26/252.

117. Boog et al., *Angriff auf die Sowjetunion*, p. 681.

118. Von Rohden Annex, "War against Russia," NARS T971/26/256.

119. Oberkommando der Wehrmacht, *Kriegstagebuch des Oberkommandos der Wehrmacht, Band I: 1 August 1940–31 December 1941* (Frankfurt-am-Main: Bernard & Graefe Verlag für Wehrwesen, 1963), p. 1084.

120. Boog et al., *Angriff auf die Sowjetunion*, p. 693.

121. Von Rohden Annex, "War against Russia," NARS T971/26/256.

122. Ibid., fr. 257.

CHAPTER THREE

1. Von Rohden Annex, "War against Russia," NARS T971/26/253.

2. "Questionnaire on GAF Doctrine: Answers from Rohden and Kriesche," p. 5.

3. German documents by 1944 acknowledged that the 1941 check before Moscow represented something of a watershed. See, for example, Generalstab 8. Abteilung, "Einsatz vom Teilen der strategischen Luftwaffe zur unmittelbaren Unterstützung des Heeres," NARS T971/37/687.

4. Trevor-Roper, *Hitler's War Directives*, p. 118.

5. Alan Clark, *Barbarossa: The Russo-German Conflict, 1941–1945* (New York: Morrow, 1965), voices the majority opinion in pointing out that "Manstein was decorated Field Marshal [in 1942] after both 'leading a campaign in person' (the Crimea) and 'taking a fortress' (Sevastopol). Neither task was of outstanding difficulty or importance" (p. 147n). Also see Ziemke, *Moscow to Stalingrad*, p. 309.

6. OKL, Chef. Genst. 8. Abteilung./Teilkdo. Wien, "Erfahrung und Auswirkung beim Einsätze der Luftwaffe in Kämpfe um Festungen (Erläutert an dem Beispiel des Kampfes um Sewastopol im Juni 1942), von Rohden 4407-114, NARS T971/18/868. A short article, "The Crimean War and its Lessons" also appeared in the same department's periodical *Kriegswissenschaftliche Skizzen für die Luftwaffe* in 1944.

7. Ibid. This argument was put forth by Generaloberst Alexander Löhr of Luftflotte 4 in January 1942. It would recur during the battle of the Kuban bridgehead in spring 1943, and yet again at the evacuation of the peninsula in 1944.

8. Erich von Manstein, *Lost Victories* (Novato, CA: Presidio, 1982), p. 209.

9. Ibid., p. 239.

10. Von Rohden Annex, "War against Russia," NARS T971/26/264.

11. Ziemke, *Moscow to Stalingrad*, p. 262.

12. Ibid., p. 264.

13. OKL, Chef Genstb. 7644/42 Chefsache, "Notiz über die Besprechung beim Führer am 17.4.42 bezüglich: Einsatz der Luftflotte 4," von Rohden 4407/122, NARS T971/18/976ff.

14. Ibid.

15. Ibid., fr. 977.

16. Von Rohden Annex, "War against Russia," fr. 263.

17. "Kämpfe um Festungen," NARS T971/18/872.

18. XXX. Armeekorps, 21574/4, KTB der Abt. Ia vom 1.4. bis 30.4.1942-Parpatsch-Stellung, NARS T314/826/167.

19. Ibid.

20. XXX. Armeekorps, KTB der Abt. Ia, "Besprechung mit dem kommendierenden General des VIII. Fliegerkorps, Generaloberst von Richthofen," 28.4.42, NARS T314/826/235–237.

21. XXX. Armeekorps, "Anlage 6 zu Korpsbefehl Nr. 133-Luftwaffe," NARS T314/826/433.

22. Ibid.

23. Chef Generalstab der Luftwaffe, 8. Abteilung, "Der Luftkrieg in Russland 1942 (Übersicht) 1943/1944, USAFHRC, Karlsrühe Collection, K.113.309-3 v. 5, G/VI/4a, p. 11.

24. Hermann Plocher, *The German Air Force Versus Russia, 1942: USAF Historical Study No. 154* (New York: Arno Press, 1968), p. 184.

25. Fliegerkorps VIII, Ia (Aufkl), Nr. 7790/42 geheim, 29.7.42, "The Duties of Reconnaissance Units," USAFHRC 512.625-3. This document was captured by the Soviets, translated into Russian, and finally into English by Allied intelligence.

26. XXX. Armeekorps, "Anlage 6 zu Korpsbefehl Nr. 133-Luftwaffe," NARS T314/826/434.

27. For a copy of one such order, see Generalkommando VIII. Fliegerkorps, Ia, B.Nr. 7439/42 geh, "Merkblatt für das Zusammenwirken der Erdtruppe mit Verbänden des VIII. Fl.Korps," in HGr. Mitte/Ia, Anl. z. KTB, Erfahrungsberichte, Heft 3, 65002/31, NARS T311/220/717.

28. Ziemke, *Moscow to Stalingrad*, p. 264.

29. XXX. Armeekorps, KTB, "Korpsbefehl Nr. 133-Luftwaffe," NARS T314/826/434. Instructions to the German troops participating in Trappenjagd also alerted them to the presence of the Hs 123, an antiquated biplane first used in Spain.

30. See Chapter 4.

31. Chef Genst. der Luftwaffe, 8. Abt., "Der Luftkrieg in Russland 1942," p. 11.

32. *History of the Great Patriotic War*, Vol. 2, p. 405.

33. Manstein, *Lost Victories*, p. 236.

34. Ibid., p. 235.

35. "Luftflotte 4 vor Stalingrad unter Gen. Oberst Frhr. v. Richthofen ab 20.7.42," USAFHRC, Karlsrühe Collection, K.113.309-3 v. 9, p. 1. This document consists of typed extracts from the private Richthofen diary.

36. "Kämpfe um Festungen," NARS T971/18/871.

37. Ibid., fr. 874.

38. Halder, *War Diary*, p. 612.

39. Ziemke, *Moscow to Stalingrad*, p. 309. Manstein, for his part, observed, "Undoubtedly the effectiveness of the cannon bore no real relation to all the effort and expense that had gone into making it." Manstein, *Lost Victories*, p. 245.

40. "Kämpfe um Festungen," NARS T971/18/860.

41. Ibid., fr. 875.

42. Ibid., fr. 863.

43. Fliegerführer Süd, "Abschlußmeldung über Einsatz der Luftwaffe im Kampf um Sewastopol vom 2.6. bis einschl. 3.7.42," von Rohden 4407-110, NARS T971/51/505.

44. "Kämpfe um Festungen," NARS T971/18/871.

45. Ibid., fr. 876.

46. The phrase "extension of the artillery" appears in both Army and Luftwaffe documents; the latter usage is generally pejorative. See OKL, Genst. 8. Abteilung, "Kriegschronik des Kampfgeschwaders "Hindenburg" Nr. 1– Vom Beginn des Polenfeldzuges (September 1939) bis zur Auflösung des Geschwaders (Ende August 1944) von Hptm. Spohr, Stab/KG 1," von Rohden 4407-78, NARS T971/50/1024.

47. Army operational orders drawn from AOK 11, Ia Nr. 2276/42 gKdos vom 27.5.42 and Abt. Ia Nr. 2304 vom 30.5.42, appended to "Kämpfe um Festungen," NARS T971/18/876.

48. Ibid., fr. 876.

49. Ibid., fr. 877.

50. Fliegerführer Süd, Nr. 3555/42 geh., 3.7.42, "Abschlußmeldung über Einsatz der Luftwaffe im Kampf um Sevastopol vom 2.6. bis 3.7.1942," USAFHRC, Karlsrühe Collection K113.309-3 v. 6, p. 1.

51. John Erickson, *The Road to Stalingrad: Stalin's War with Germany* (London: Weidenfield and Nicholson, 1975), p. 350.

52. Fliegerführer Süd, "Einsatz der Luftwaffe," p. 4.

53. Erickson, *Road to Stalingrad*, p. 351.

54. Some of StG 77's aircraft, once attacks began on the outer ring of fortifications, occasionally flew 12–18 sorties per day.

55. Von Rohden Annex, "War against Russia," NARS T971/26/265.

56. "Kämpfe um Festungen," fr. 863.

57. Ibid., fr. 864.

58. Ibid., fr. 877.

59. Manstein, *Lost Victories*, p. 248.

60. Von Rohden Annex, "War against Russia," NARS T971/26/264.

61. Erickson, *Road to Stalingrad*, p. 351.

62. Plocher, *German Air Force Versus Russia 1942*, p. 206.

63. VIII. Fliegerkorps, Ia, Fernschrieben Nr. 7641 g., 23.6.42, USAFHRC, Karlsrühe Collection K.113.309-3 v. 6. Maue's accomplishment was also reported in ObdL Füstb Ic, "Frontnachrichtenblatt der Luftwaffe" Nr. 42 (1942), NARS T321/83/226. In typical fashion, the army claimed that its own artillery fire had done the deed. Manstein, *Lost Victories*, p. 251.

64. Albert Seaton, *The Russo-German War, 1941–1945* (New York: Praeger Publishers, 1971), p. 264.

65. Plocher, *German Air Force versus Russia 1942*, p. 144; Von Rohden Annex, "War against Russia," NARS T971/26/261. This formation was later designated Luftflotte 6 during the preparations for the Kursk offensive.

66. Chef Genstb. der Luftwaffe, 8. Abt., "Der Luftkrieg in Russland, 1942," p. 23.

67. Ibid., p. 24.

68. Air Ministry, *Rise and Fall of the German Air Force*, p. 114.

69. Ziemke, *Moscow to Stalingrad*, p. 430.

70. Air Ministry, *Rise and Fall of the German Air Force*, p. 115.

71. Plocher, *German Air Force Versus Russia, 1942*, p. 148.

72. This was precisely the argument which von Greim was to advance in June 1943: that Luftflotte 6 should be the standard bearer of strategic warfare against the USSR because of its occupying the "central position." See Chef der Luftflotte 6, Betr.: Bekämpfung der sow. russ. Kriegswirtschaft, BA/MA RL 7/521, p. 2.

73. Plocher, *German Air Force Versus Russia 1942*, p. 149.

74. Erickson, *Road to Stalingrad*, p. 382, Ziemke, *Moscow to Stalingrad*, p. 242.

75. XLVI. Panzer Korps, Ia, Anlagen z. KTB 5, Korpsbefehle, "Einsatz der Luftwaffe für Angriff XXXXVI. Pz. Korps," 29.6.42, NARS T314/65/697.

76. Ibid.

77. Ziemke, *Moscow to Stalingrad*, p. 252.

78. PzAOK 2, 43407/34, Erkennungs u. Verstandigungsdienst Heer-Luftwaffe, Sonderanlagenband 1 zum KTB Nr. 3, PzAOK 2, Ia, Luftwaffenkommando Ost, Führungsabteilung Ia op, "Merkblatt für die Zusammenarbeit zwischen Verbänden einer Armee und Verbänden einer Fliegerdivision," NARS T313/194/7454710.

79. XLII. Armeekorps, Ia, Anl. 2 b.z. Gefechts- und Erfahrungsbericht "Blücher II," 3.8.-19.9.1942, NARS T314/997/114.

80. Ibid.,"Erfahrungsbericht über den Einsatz des Me. 109 im Erdkampf," fr. 115.

81. Schulz, "Collaboration between Army and Luftwaffe," p. 7.

82. Ziemke, *Moscow to Stalingrad*, makes excellent use of the German documents in recounting the unfolding of Operation Blau and its components.

83. Seaton, *Russo-German War*, p. 266.

84. Trevor-Roper, *Hitler's War Directives*, p. 120.

85. Ibid.

86. "Luftflotte 4 vor Stalingrad," p. 1.

87. Von Rohden Annex, "War against Russia," NARS T971/26/268.

88. Generalkommando VIII. Fliegerkorps, Ia, Nr. 7718/42 geh., Betr.: Belegung neuer Flugplätze, 12.7.42, USAFHRC, Karlsrühe Collection K.113.309-3 v. 7.

89. Chef Genst. der Luftwaffe, 8. Abt., "Der Luftkrieg in Russland 1942," p. 14.

90. Trevor-Roper, *Hitler's War Directives*, p. 130.

91. Ibid., p. 131.

92. Oleg Hoeffding, "German Air Attacks against Industry and Railroads in Russia, 1941-1945: Memorandum RM-6206-PR" (Santa Monica, CA: The RAND Corporatioon, 1970), p. 22.

93. David Irving, *Hitler's War* (New York: Viking Press, 1977), p. 437.

94. III./Kampfgeschwader 55, Kriegstagebuch Nr. 8, 28. Sept. 1942-27. Feb. 1943, von Rohden 4406/694, NARS T971/16/140ff.

95. "Luftflotte 4 vor Stalingrad," p. 13.

96. Chef Genst. der Luftwaffe, 8. Abt., "Luftkrieg in Russland 1942," p. 15.

97. "Luftflotte 4 vor Stalingrad," pp. 2-3.

98. *History of the Great Patriotic War*, Vol. 3, p. 384.

99. Chef Genst. der Luftwaffe, 8. Abt. "Luftkrieg in Russland 1942," p. 15; III./Kampfgeschwader 55, Kriegstagebuch Nr. 8, NARS T971/16/119ff.

100. "Luftflotte 4 vor Stalingrad," p. 5.

101. Ibid., p. 6.

102. Ibid., p. 6.

103. Ibid., p. 7.

104. Halder, *War Diary*, p. 371.

105. Ibid., p. 662.

106. "Luftflotte 4 vor Stalingrad," p. 17.

107. For example, see Stukageschwader "Immelmann" Nr. 2, Kriegstagebuch 9, 6.10.42-3.7.43, NARS T971/4/12ff.

108. Von Rohden Annex, "War against Russia," NARS T971/26/278.

109. Ziemke, *Moscow to Stalingrad*, p. 463.

110. "Luftflotte 4 vor Stalingrad," p. 19.

111. Ibid., p. 22.

112. The literature of the Stalingrad Airlift is considerable. One of the most meticulous accounts remains Hans-Detlef Herhudt von Rohden, *Die Luftwaffe ringt um Stalingrad* (Wiesbaden: Limes Verlag, 1950), primarily a compilation of the official war diaries and wireless logbooks accompanied by a somewhat emotive commentary. Franz Kurowski has produced a recent treatment of the subject in *Luftbrücke Stalingrad: Die Tragödie der Luftwaffe und der 6. Armee* (Berg-am-See: Kurt Vowinckel-Verlag, 1983). Irving's *Rise and Fall of the Luftwaffe* is well done but overemphasizes Milch's contributions; Milch arrived at the Stalingrad front only in mid-January, a fact pointed out by Osterkamp and Bacher in their criticism of Irving's *"Milchfreundlich"* account. A number of the USAF Monograph Project volumes offer accounts of the operation, particularly Fritz Morzik's *German Air Force Airlift Operations* (New York: Arno Press, 1968).

The Stalingrad airlift episode generated a large amount of documentation, much of which survives. The diaries of Sonderstab Milch, including the message log, are at NARS as part of the von Rohden Collection. Also in this collection are numerous war diaries of units taking part, as well as the *Erfahrungsbericht* of Oberst und Transportführer Fritz Morzik. The diaries of Fiebig, commander of Fliegerkorps VIII, von Richthofen, Hube, Pickert and other participants are at the USAFHRC.

113. Johannes Fischer, "Über den Entschluß zur Luftversorgung Stalingrads: Ein Beitrag zur militärischen Führung im Dritten Reich," *Militärgeschichtliches Mitteilungen* 2 (1969):7-67.

114. Plocher, *German Air Force Versus Russia, 1942*, p. 233.

115. "Luftflotte 4 vor Stalingrad," p. 24.
116. Nicolaus von Below, *Als Hitlers Adjutant* (Mainz: Hase & Koehler Verlag, 1980), p. 323.
117. Irving, *Hitler's War*, pp. 453–459, provides a controversial yet well-documented account of the decision-making process.
118. Below, *Als Hitlers Adjutant*, p. 324.
119. "Luftflotte 4 vor Stalingrad," p. 31.
120. OKL, Kriegstagebuch Sonderstab Milch, 24.11.42–3.2.43, NARS T321/207/no frame nos.
121. Tagebuch-Forsetzung Teil IV, Genllt. Fiebig, Kdr. VIII. FK, 12 December 1942, copy on file at USAFHRC.
122. III./KG 55, Kriegstagebuch Nr. 8, NARS T971/16/119ff.
123. General der Panzertruppe Hube, "Erfahrungsberichte über die Luftversorgung der Festung Stalingrad," 15.3.43 geheim, USAFHRC K113.309-3 v. 10, p. 3.
124. For an important insight into the problems faced by the transport force, see Kampfgeschwader z.b.V 5, Kriegstagebuch-Luftversorgung Stalingrad, NARS T971/12/05ff. Also Fritz Morzik, *Die deutschen Transportflieger im Zweiten Weltkrieg* (Frankfurt-am-Main: Bernard Graefe Verlag für Wehrwesen, 1966), pp. 152–157.
125. *History of the Great Patriotic War*, Vol. 3, p. 386. Also Von D. Hardesty, *Red Phoenix: The Rise of Soviet Air Power, 1941–1945* (Washington, DC: Smithsonian Institution Press, 1982), pp. 105–119.
126. KTB, Sonderstab Milch, T321/207/no frame nos.
127. Figures compiled from KTB, Sonderstab Milch, NARS T321/207/no frame nos.
128. Herhudt von Rohden, *Luftwaffe ringt um Stalingrad*, p. 85.
129. "Luftflotte 4 vor Stalingrad," p. 33.
130. Hube, "Erfahrungsbericht Festung Stalingrad," p. 7.
131. Irving, *Rise and Fall of the Luftwaffe*, p. 194.
132. Thiel, Major, Kommandeur III./K.G. "Boelcke" Nr. 27, Betr: Meldung über Beschaffenheit des Platzes Gumrak (Kessel von Stalingrad) und Rücksprache mit Herrn Generaloberst Paulus, USAFHRC Karlsrühe Collection K113.309-3 v. 9, pp. 5–6.
133. "Luftflotte 4 vor Stalingrad," p. 28.
134. Herhudt von Rohden, *Luftwaffe ringt um Stalingrad*, p. 117.
135. Ibid., p. 119.
136. Luftwaffenführungsstab Ia op Nr. 8865/43, NARS T321/10/4746778.
137. *Luftkriegführung*, paragraph 22.

CHAPTER FOUR

1. Two publications of the 8. Abteilung from 1944 refer to two different figures, probably a result of semantic differences within the broad German definition of "army support." 8. Abteilung, "A Survey of German Air Operations, 1939–1944," 21.9.44, Air Ministry Translation No. VII/28, USAFHRC 512.621 VII/28, p. 8, refers to "80% of the operations were devoted to tactical co-

operation with the Army, and 1944 showed no appreciable difference.'' Another document by the same agency, Genst. der Luftwaffe, 8. Abteilung, ''Strategischer Überblick über die deutsche Luftkriegsführung, 1939–1944,'' translation appended to A.I. 12, USAFE/M.31, Intelligence Report 31: ''The Part Played by the GAF on the Eastern Front,'' USAFHRC 512.62512M-31, p. 14, gives a sixty percent figure for ''close support.'' 8. Abteilung publications benefited from access to the war diaries of Luftwaffe units at all levels, a source now largely unavailable owing to the destruction of the German air force archives in April 1945.

2. An emphasis first seen in Air Ministry, *Rise and Fall of the German Air Force*, and continued by a spate of later works. Thus, discussions of Korten's tenure as chief of the Luftwaffe general staff tend to center on his association with the ''defensive clique'' (Galland et al.) in 1943–1944.

3. Irving, *Rise and Fall of the Luftwaffe*, p. 150.

4. ''Part Played by the GAF,'' p. 4. This portion of the report consists of the responses of Generalmajor Karl-Heinrich Schulz and Oberst i.G. von Greiff.

5. ''Questionnaire on GAF Doctrine: Answers from Rohden and Kriesche,'' p. 4.

6. Figures calculated from ''Einsatz fliegender Verbände der deutschen Luftwaffe an der Ostfront 1943, 31. Januar 1943,'' USAFHRC, Karlsrühe Collection K 113.309-3 v. 13, p. 3.

7. Boog et al., *Angriff auf die Sowjetunion*, p. 313.

8. Ibid.

9. ''Einsatz fliegender Verbände,'' p. 3.

10. On May 31, 1943, the Luftwaffe quartermaster general reported only 166 Ju 52s serving with *Transport-Gruppen* in the east. ''Iststärke an Flugzeugen, 31.5.43,'' NARS T321/154/062.

11. KTB, Sonderstab Milch, NARS T321/207/no frame nos; Herhudt von Rohden, *Luftwaffe Ringt um Stalingrad*, p. 140.

12. ''Vernehmung Hermann Göring,'' NARS T971/14/77.

13. Murray, *Luftwaffe*, p. 151.

14. Earl F. Ziemke, *Stalingrad to Berlin: The German Defeat in the East, 1943–1945* (Washington: Office of the Chief of Military History, 1968), p. 108; John Erickson, *The Road to Berlin: Stalin's War with Germany* (Boulder, CO: Westview Press, 1983), p. 61.

15. 8. Abteilung, ''Der Einsatz der Luftwaffe im Bereich der Heeresgruppe Mitte im Jahre 1943,'' Bearbeitet 8. Abteilung der Gen Stabs von Oberst Mittmann, USAFHRC, Karlsrühe Collection K 113.309-3 v. 13, p. 1.

16. Ziemke, *Stalingrad to Berlin*, p. 109, ''Bereich der Heeresgruppe Mitte,'' p. 2.

17. Luftwaffenkommando Ost, Führungsabteilung Ia Op, ''Gefechtsbericht über die Schlacht um We. Luki vom 24.11.1942 bis 19.1.1943,'' BA/MA RL 7/549, p. 18.

18. Air Ministry, *Rise and Fall of the German Air Force*, p. 225.

19. 8. Abteilung, ''Luftwaffe im Osten 1943, Auszüge aus KTB Lfl. 4, Marz-Aug. 1943 als Arbeiterunterlage,'' 16.10.44, USAFHRC, Karlsrühe Collection K113.309-3 v. 12, pp. 4–7, 13.

20. Ziemke, *Stalingrad to Berlin*, pp. 91–97.

21. Air Ministry, *Rise and Fall of the German Air Force*, p. 227.

22. 8. Abteilung, "Entwurf der kriegsgeschichtlichen Darstellung Luftflotte 4 vom 1. 1. 43-31. 5. 43," USAFHRC, Karlsrühe Collection K113.309-3 v. 13, p. 7.

23. Air Ministry, *Rise and Fall of the German Air Force*, p. 228.

24. Hermann Plocher, *The German Air Force Versus Russia, 1943: USAF Historical Studies No 155* (New York: Arno Press, 1968), p. 22.

25. Richthofen on February 23 noted the "self-denying and meticulous work" of his support staffs.

26. Murray, *Luftwaffe*, p. 151.

27. Kriegswissenschaftliche Abteilung der Luftwaffe, "Luftkrieg Ost," Jan-Dec. 1943, NARS T971/18/581ff.

28. Plocher, *German Air Force Versus Russia 1943*, p. 10.

29. For a day-by-day account of German air operations over the Kuban see Kriegswissenschaftliche Abteilung der Luftwaffe, "Luftkrieg Ost," NARS T971/18/600ff.

30. The Germans claim the destruction of 2280 Soviet aircraft during the campaign (Plocher, *German Air Force versus Russia 1943*, p. 50), including "more than 300" between April 20 and 30 (8. Abteilung, "Einsatz der Luftflotte 4," p. 11). The Soviets admit to the loss of 296 fighters from April-June. See James T. Price, Richard W. Harrison, Harriet F. Scott, William F. Scott, and John R. Brinkerhoff, "Impact of Aircraft Losses on Soviet Air Operations in World War II." Jet Propulsion Laboratory, January 1987, p. 27.

31. Murray, *Luftwaffe*, p. 152.

32. Hardesty, *Red Phoenix*, p. 141.

33. Ibid., p. 84.

34. *History of the Great Patriotic War*, Vol. 3, p. 399.

35. Ibid., p. 399; Hardesty, *Red Phoenix*, p. 142.

36. *History of the Great Patriotic War*, Vol. 3, p. 399.

37. 8. Abteilung, "Der Einsatz der Luftflotte 1 im Jahre 1943 zusammengestellt durch 8. Abt. d. Gen. Stabs von Oberst Mittmann," USAFHRC, Karlsrühe Collection K113.309-3 v. 13, p. 4.

38. Ibid., p. 5.

39. Figures calculated from A.O.K. 4, Ia, Tagesabschlußmeldungen des Luftwaffen-Kommando-Ost, 1.4.43-20.5.43, Beilage 2 zum KTB Nr. 16, AOK 4 34558/19, NARS T312/203/7752353ff.

40. On April 14, 1943, the short-range reconnaissance unit N.A.G. 3, flew its 4000th operational sortie since its arrival in the Soviet Union on June 7, 1942. Ibid.

41. 8. Abteilung, "Bereich der Heeresgruppe Mitte," pp. 4–5.

42. Hoeffding, "Industry and Railroads," p. 25.

43. PzAOK 2, 30233/22, Taktische Ein-Mappe XVIII, Rußland, PzAOK 2, Ic, IcAO, 11.11.41, "Vernehmungsberichte des Gen.Ltn. Jerschakoff, O.B. der 20. Armee," NARS T313/135/7383902.

44. Ibid. fr. 7383904.

45. "Vernehmung Hermann Göring," NARS T971/14/78.

46. Von Rohden Annex, "War against Russia," NARS T971/26/295.

47. "Abschrift eines Zusatzbefehls des Chef der Luftflotte 4 zur Weisung des Reichsmarschalls," Ob.d.L. FüSt. Ia Nr. 10671/43 g.Kdos. (op. 1) vom 5.3.43, BA/MA RL 7/487, p. 3.

48. Ibid., p. 5.

49. 8. Abteilung, "Bereich der Heeresgruppe Mitte," p. 5.

50. GL/A-Rü, GL/A Nr. 11258/43 geh (Rü), 4.6.43, Meldung an den Herrn Staatsekretär über GL/A Chef. Betr.: Überblick über die entschiedenden Angriffsziele der Wehrwirtschaft der SU (Nach Unterlagen des Luftwaffenfüstabes IcIV), Milch 53.113, NARS T321/154/789.

51. Ibid., fr. 790.

52. Ibid., fr. 788.

53. Ibid.

54. Ibid., fr. 790.

55. Hoeffding, "Industry and Railroads," p. 28.

56. Ibid.

57. HGr Mitte, 65002/46, Anlagen z. KTB d. Hgr. Mitte/Führungsabteilung, Allgemeines Heft 9, 29.1.44, "Betr.: Angriff auf Rüstungswerke im Raum Moskau-Gorkij," NARS T311/222/507-510.

58. Luftwaffenführungsstab Ic, Fremde Luftwaffen Ost Nr. 20 225/44 g.Kdos., 20.1.44, "Zielauswahl für den Raum Moskau-Obere Wolga," OKL/2316, "Operativer Luftkrieg-Gesamtdarstellungen," NARS T321/247/no frame nos.

59. Kurt S. Schultz, "Building the 'Soviet Detroit': The Construction of the Nizhnii-Novgorod Automobile Factory, 1927–1932," Slavic Review 49, No. 2 (Summer 1990), pp. 200–212.

60. Luftwaffenführungsstab Ic Nr. 18 833/43 geh. (IV D), 27.6.43, "Vortragsnotiz Nr. 39-Betr.: Angriffe auf das Kraftwagenwerk Nr. 1 "Molotow" SU 80 47 Gorki-Awtosawod in den Nächten vom 4./5., 5./6., 6./7. und 7./8.6.1943," USAFHRC, Karlsrühe Collection K.113-309-3 v. 12.

61. Ibid.

62. Siegfried Zantke, "Der Luftangriff gegen Gorkij, ein großer Erfolg der operativen Luftkriegsführung 1943," Wehrwissenschaftliche Rundschau 5 (May 1954), p. 231.

63. Ibid., p. 232.

64. Luftwaffenführungsstab Ic, "Vortragsnotiz Nr. 39- "Molotow,"; Hoeffding, "Industry and Railroads," p. 27. According to Zantke, "Luftangriff gegen Gorkij," p. 232, KG 55 suffered only two losses out of 300 sorties, an entirely acceptable rate of loss. History of the Great Patriotic War, Vol. 3, p. 399.

65. Karl Gundelach, Kampfgeschwader "General Wever" 4 (Stuttgart: Motorbuch Verlag, 1978), p. 236.

66. Abt. Fremde Heere Ost IID vom 31. Juli 1943, Nr. 5671/43 geh., von Rohden 4406-228, NARS T971/45/547.

67. PzAOK 2, Ic, Panzer-Grenadier-Division Grossdeutschland, 29. Juli 1943, Gefangenaussagen, NARS T313/185/7443776-7.

68. Luftwaffenführungsstab Ic, Nr. 23 174/43 geh. (IV), 17.7.1943, Vortragsnotiz-Betr.: Angriffe vom 9./10. und vom 20./21. Juni 1943 auf das Werk für synthetischen Kautschuk "SK 1" SU 66 7 und Cordfabrik Nr. 1 SU 66 7A in Jaroslavl," USAFHRC K.113-309-3 v. 12, G/VI/5aa, p.1.

69. ''Deutsche Luftangriffe auf russische Rüstungs-usw. Anlagen im Jahre 1943,'' USAFHRC, Karlsrühe Collection K113.309-3 v. 13, G/VI/5b, p. 1.

70. Luftwaffenführungsstab Ic, Nr. 19477/43 geh. (IV D), Vortragsnotiz-Betr.: Die Angriffe vom 12./13. und 13./14.6.43 auf die Erdölraffinerie Saratow SU 65 75 und 65 76, USAFHRC, Karlsrühe Collection K113.309-3 v. 11, G/VI/5a, p. 2.

71. Albert Speer, *Inside the Third Reich: Memoirs* (New York: The Macmillan Company, 1970), pp. 280–281.

72. Records of the Reich Ministry for Armaments and War Production, ''Conference with the Führer on 30.5.43,'' NARS T73/192/3405658.

73. Arbeitsausschuß ''Wirtschaftsobjekte für Fliegerangriffe Dr. Carl.'' See Hoeffding, ''Industry and Railroads,'' pp. 30ff.

74. Records of the Reich Ministry for Armaments and War Production, ''Punkte aus der Führerbesprechung vom 28. Juni 1943,'' Item 6, NARS T73/192/3405666.

75. Ibid.

76. Der Reichsmarschall des Großdeutschen Reiches Nr. 08978/43 g. Kdos., 8.12.43, von Rohden 4406-379, NARS T971/23/358.

77. Letter, Hewel to Jeschonnek, 12.6.43, von Rohden 4406/73, NARS T971/22/251. The cover letter is all but illegible, but the appendices (intelligence reports and Soviet proclamations) render the thrust of Hewel's argument clear.

78. Von Rohden Annex, ''War against Russia,'' NARS T971/26/308.

79. Der Chef der Luftflotte 6, Br.B. Nr. 241/43 g.Kdos. Chefs., 12.6.1943, Betr.: Bekämpfung der sow. russ. Kriegswirtschaft, BA/MA RL 7/521, p. 1.

80. Ibid.

81. Luftflotte 6's bomber forces at the time consisted of III./KG 1, Stab.,II./,8. and 9. KG 51 with Junkers 88s, and Stab., II./ and III./KG 4 with Heinkel 111s—about 150 operational bombers. Einsatz fliegender Verbände der deutschen Luftwaffe an der Ostfront 1943, 30.6.43, USAFHRC K113.309-3 v. 13, pp. 3–4.

82. Chef der Luftflotte 6, ''Bekämpfung der sow. Kriegswirtschaft,'' p. 3.

83. Der Oberbefehlshaber der Luftwaffe, Führungsstab Ia, Nr. 8437/43 g. Kdos. Chefsache, 18.6.43, Bezug: Der Chef der Luftflotte 6, USAFHRC, Karlsrühe Collection K113.309-3 v. 12, G/VI/5aa, p. 2.

84. ''Besprechungspunkte Oberst i.G. Kless am 17.6.43 in Robinson 4 mit Generaloberst Jeschonnek,'' 20.6.43, BA/MA RL 7/521, p. 1.

85. Chef der Luftflotte 6, ''Bekämpfung der sow. Kriegswirtschaft,'' p. 2.

86. The debate in the late 1970s within the USAF regarding the role of the A-10 anti-tank aircraft occasioned a resurgence of interest in this topic. See, for example, Captain Lonnie O. Ratley III, ''Air Power at Kursk: A Lesson for Today?'' *Military Review* 62 (April 1978), pp. 54–62.

87. Indeed, Colonel Robert Doughty has estimated that in the German breakthrough at Sedan in May 1940, an imposing concentration of close air support by the Luftwaffe accounted for the destruction of only two French tanks. Doughty, *The Breaking-Point*, p. 324.

88. Hallion, *Strike from the Sky*, p. 238–239.

89. Until October 1943, ground attack aviation did not have its own *Waffengeneral*, or service branch inspector general.

90. "Erfahrungen mit Panzerjägerstaffeln: Auszug aus dem Bericht des Generals der Jagdflieger Nr. 673/43 v. 5.3.43," Milch 53.51, NARS T321/154/392.
91. Ibid., fr. 394.
92. Ibid., fr. 392.
93. Ibid., fr. 395.
94. Von Rohden Annex, "War against Russia," NARS T971/26/270.
95. The 3 cm MK 101 installation weighed 231 kilograms, while the proposed 3.7 cm Flak modification weighed in at 450 kilograms. In any event, later models of the Hs 129 did carry enhanced firepower, but at a great cost in maneuverability. Air Ministry, *Rise and Fall of the German Air Force*, p. 212.
96. Generalstab 8. Abteilung, "Einsatz der Luftflotte 4," p. 7.
97. Luftw. FüStb. Ia, Nr. 03300/43 gKdos, 1.8.43, "Plänung für die Panzerbekämpfung an der Ostfront im Winter 1943/44," Milch 53.40, NARS T321/54/295.
98. The Operations Staff reported on August 1, 1943, that five *Staffeln* of Hs 129s (4.(Pz.)/SG 1, 8.(Pz.)/SG 1, 4.(Pz.)/SG 2, 8.(Pz.)/SG 2, and Pz. Jäger Staffel 51) were operational, as well as two Ju 87-equipped units (Pz. Jäger Staffel StG 1 and Pz. Jäger Staffel 2 [Rudel's unit]). In addition, an experimental unit of Ju 88 medium bombers with 7.5 cm cannon was also undergoing operational trials. The planned reorganization called for the grouping of these units, as well as the newly-constituted ones, into a 3-*Gruppen* "*Panzer-Jäger Geschwader*" by the winter of 1943/44. Ibid.
99. Ibid., fr. 296.
100. Types mentioned were the Messerschmitt 410, Heinkel 219, Focke Wulf Ta 154, and the unorthodox Dornier Do 335. Ibid., fr. 298.
101. C.S.D.I.C (AIR), C.M.F., "Initiation and Development of Night Attack (Nachtschlacht) by the G.A.F. on the Russian Front," Report No. 583, 27th July, 1945, NARS RG 165 Box 650, CSDIC Folder 1: CSDIC (AIR) CMF (560-), p. 1.
102. Ibid., p. 2.
103. Generalkommando XXX. A.K., Ia, Kriegstagebuch, Abt. Ia, Flivo, 16.10.43, NARS T314/833/112.
104. Memorandum for Lt. Colonel Melvin Hall, Joint Intelligence Committee, from Major DeForest Van Slyck, Chief, Geographic Section, Informational Division, AC/AS, Intelligence, "Study on Recent German Air Force Trends on the Eastern Front," 10 July 1943, USAFHRC 142.0422-18, p. 2.
105. Oberkommando der Luftwaffe, Führungsstab Ia/Ausb. Nr. 1300/44 geheim, "Merkblatt: Die Nachtschlachtflieger-Verbände," BA/MA RH 11-III/76, p. 5. The operations staff regarded the Ju 87 as "capable on the whole of performing all the tasks which can at present be demanded of night ground attack aircraft."
106. USAFE/Air Ministry Intelligence Party (OKL), Intelligence Report No. 86, "The Role of Night Ground Attack Units in the GAF," USAFHRC 512.62512M-86, p. 2.
107. Karl Drum, *Airpower and Soviet Partisan Warfare: USAF Historical Studies No. 177* (New York: Arno Press, 1962), p. 36.
108. Oberkommando der Luftwaffe, Führungsstab Ia/Ausb., "Die Nachtschlachtflieger-Verbände," p. 3.
109. Ibid., p. 12.

110. Groehler, "Stärke, Verteilung und Verluste der deutschen Luftwaffe," Table 9, p. 325.

111. Oberkommando der Heeresgruppe Mitte, Ia Nr. 5924/43 geh., HGr Mitte Ia, Anl. z. KTB, Erfahrungsberichte Heft 3, 65002/31, NARS T311/220/679.

112. Ibid., fr. 680.

113. 25. Panzer-Grenadier Division, Ia Nr. 779/43 geheim, Betr.: "Zusammenwirken von Erdtruppen mit Nahkampfverbänden der Luftwaffe," HGr. Mitte Ia, Anl. z. KTB Erfahrungsberichte, Heft 3, 65002/31, NARS T311/220/692, "The experience of the Division in cooperation with close air support formations is limited to the offensive and defensive battles in August 1942 in the area Ukolizi-Ulyanavo-Gosskova-Leonovo, in which, of the units of the Division, only the 119th Panzergrenadier Regiment took part."

114. A.O.K. 4, Ia Nr. 6976/43 geh., 1.7.43, HGr Mitte Ia, Anl. z. KTB, Erfahrungsberichte, Heft 3, 65002/31, fr. 701. Many of the other reports echo this sentiment.

115. Reichsminister der Luftfahrt und Oberbefehlshaber der Luftwaffe, "Einsatz der Fliegertruppen zur unmittelbaren Unterstützung des Heeres," NARS T321/76/ no frame nos.

116. 95. Infanterie-Division, Ia Nr. 01333/43 geh., 16.6.43, HGr Mitte Ia, Anl. z. KTB, Erfahrungsberichte, Heft 3, 65002/31, fr. 709.

117. Ibid., fr. 708.

118. Generalkommando IX. A.K., Ia Nr. 1870/43 geh., Betr.: "Erfahrungen im Zusammenwirken der Nahkampfverbände der Lw. mit der Erdtruppe," HGr Mitte, Ia, Anl. z. KTB, Erfahrungsberichte, Heft 3, 65002/31, fr. 706.

119. 299. Infanterie-Division, Abt. Ia Nr. 525/43 geheim, 19.6.43, Betr.: Zusammenwirken von Erdtruppen mit Nahkampfverbänden der Luftwaffe, HGr Mitte, Ia, Anl. z. KTB, Erfahrungsberichte, Heft 3, 65002/31, fr. 685.

120. A.O.K. 4, Ia, 6976/43 geh., NARS T311/220/702.

121. Ibid.

122. Ziemke, Stalingrad to Berlin, p. 132.

123. Plocher, German Air Force Versus Russia, 1943, p. 57.

124. "Iststärke an Flugzeugen, 31.5.43," NARS T321/154/062.

125. Hans Seidemann, "Das VIII. Flieger-Korps im Osteinsatz 1943: Op. Zitadelle," USAFHRC, Karlsrühe Collection K113.309-3 v 12.

126. "Die Weisung für den Einsatz des VIII. Fliegerkorps für das Unternehmen 'Zitadelle,'" USAFHRC, Karlsrühe Collection, K113.309-3 v. 12, p. 20.

127. Seidemann, "VIII. Flieger-Korps im Osteinsatz 1943."

128. Donald S. Detwiler, Charles B. Burdick and Jürgen Rohwehr, eds., The Eastern Theater Continued, Vol. 16, Part 7 of World War II German Military Studies: A Collection of 213 Special Reports on the Second World War Prepared by Former Officers of the Wehrmacht for the United States Army (New York: Garland Publishing, Inc., 1979), p. 193.

129. Plocher, German Air Force Versus Russia, 1943, p. 75.

130. Seidemann, "VIII. Flieger-Korps im Osteinsatz," p. 6.

131. III./Kampfgeschwader 55, Kriegstagebuch Nr. 11 von 25.6.1943 bis 18.8.1943 durch Oblt. Ludewig, von Rohden 4376/676, NARS T971/63/no frame nos. This war diary gives a good indication of the mobility of even heavy bomber units in the Luftwaffe.

132. David Irving, *Göring: A Biography* (New York: William Morrow and Co., Inc., 1988), p. 390.

133. Plocher, *German Air Force Versus Russia, 1943*, p. 75n.

134. Irving, *Göring*, p. 391.

135. Seidemann, "VIII. Flieger-Korps im Osteinsatz," p. 18.

136. Richthofen was one of the few senior Luftwaffe commanders who recognized the importance of logistics in a theatre as vast as the eastern zone of operations. Horst Boog, "Luftwaffe and Logistics in the Second World War," *Aerospace Historian* 33 (June 1986), p. 107.

137. Von Rohden Annex, "War against Russia," NARS T971/26/302.

138. Seidemann, "VIII. Flieger-Korps in Osteinsatz," p. 12.

139. Air Ministry, *Rise and Fall of the German Air Force*, p. 419.

140. 8. Abteilung, "Luftwaffe im Osten 1943," p. 43.

141. Luftwaffenführungsstab Ic Nr. 18 672/43 geh. (IV D), 16.6.43, "Vortragsnotiz Betr.: Angriff auf Bahnhof Kursk am 2.6.43," USAFHRC, Karlsrühe Collection K113.309-3 v. 11, p. 1.

142. Ibid.

143. Detwiler et al., *German Military Studies*, p. 158.

144. Ibid. Jeschonnek noted on June 26 that fighter replacements for the eastern front in particular barely covered losses. "Überlegungen des Oberkommandos der Luftwaffe über den Kräftebedarf für das Unternehmen Zitadelle 1943 an der Ostfront," 26.6.1943, USAFHRC, Karlsrühe Collection K113.309-3 v. 10, p. 1.

145. Von Rohden Annex, "War against Russia," NARS T971/26/301.

146. Luftwaffenführungsstab Ic Nr. 2048/43 gKdos (IVD), 16.6.43, Vortragsnotiz 27, Verkehrssystem SU 40-46, "Unterbrechung der Bahnstrecke Tscheljabinsk-Moskau durch Brückenzerstörung," von Rohden 4406/122, NARS T971/25/45-47.

147. Ibid., fr. 47.

148. "Besprechungspunkte Kless mit Jeschonnek," p. 1.

149. Plocher, *German Air Force Versus Russia, 1941*, p. 99.

150. Ziemke, *Stalingrad to Berlin*, p. 131.

151. Luftwaffenführungsstab Ic(IV), Vortragsnotiz Nr. 53, Betr.: Flugblattpropaganda, von Rohden 4406/137, NARS T971/43/355.

152. Luftwaffenführungsstab Ic/IV, Vortragsnotiz Betr.: Unternehmen "Silberstreif," von Rohden 4406/110, NARS T971/25/13. One has to think of the remark by Air Chief Marshal Sir Arthur Harris regarding the RAF's own leaflet dropping campaign: "I always said that the only thing leaflet raids would achieve would be to supply Germany with toilet paper for the rest of the war!" Dudley Saward, *Bomber Harris: The Story of Sir Arthur Harris* (Garden City, NY: Doubleday and Company, 1985), p. 76.

153. Timothy Francis Mulligan, *The Politics of Illusion and Empire: German Occupation Policy in the Soviet Union, 1942-1943* (New York: Praeger, 1988), p. 170.

154. Luftwaffenführungsstab Ic/IV, "Silberstreif," fr. 13.

155. Oberkommando der Wehrmacht, WPr (AP), "Die Entwicklung der deutschen Flugblattpropaganda in der Sowjetarmee," 3/43, OKW/1560, NARS T77/1425/1ff.

156. Oberkommando des Heeres, Abt. Fremde Heere Ost, "Flugblatt-propaganda," August 1944, NARS T78/540/325.

157. Mulligan, *Politics of Illusion and Empire*, p. 171.

158. Ziemke, *Stalingrad to Berlin*, p. 133. Clark, *Barbarossa*, p. 327, likened the operation to the French Nivelle offensive of April 1917, against a thoroughly alerted German defense.

159. "Weisung für VIII. Flieger-Korps für das Unternehmen "Zitadelle," p. 19.

160. Seidemann, "VIII. Fliegerkorps im Osteinsatz," pp. 25–26.

161. Detwiler et al., *German Military Studies*, p. 201.

162. Kriegstagebuch Nr. 11 der III/Kampfgeschwader 55, entry for 5.7.43, NARS T971/63/no frame nos.

163. Detwiler er al., *German Military Studies*, p. 206.

164. Seidemann, "VIII. Flieger-Korps im Osteinsatz," p. 33.

165. Luftwaffenführungsstab Ic, Nr. 25 038/43 geh (IV), 31.7.43, Betr.: SU-Feindverluste in der Zeit vom 1-28 Juli 1943, NARS T971/45/367.

166. Luftwaffenführungsstab Ic, Nr. 23 473/43 geh. (IV), 20.7.43, von Rohden 4406-136, NARS T971/45/351.

167. Clark, *Barbarossa*, p. 337.

168. Von Rohden Annex, "War against Russia," T971/26/262.

169. Plocher, *German Air Force Versus Russia 1943*, p. 83.

170. Seidemann, "VIII. Flieger-Korps im Osteinsatz," p. 45.

171. 8. Abteilung, "Survey of German Air Operations," p. 8.

CHAPTER FIVE

1. *Luftkriegführung*, paragraph 31.

2. Rieckhoff, *Trumpf oder Bluff?*, p. 275. For an interesting perspective on Korten's leadership, see the interrogation of Koller, NARS T971/22/542ff.

3. Personal details available in Personal-Nachweis, Gen. d. Fl. Günther Korten, von Rohden 4376/424, NARS T971/6/730.

4. Boog, *Luftwaffenführung*, p. 201.

5. Air Ministry, *Rise and Fall of the German Air Force*, p. 289.

6. See Chapter 6 for a discussion of what Korten's reforms meant for the support of the German army in Russia.

7. Hans-Detlef Herhudt von Rohden "Letzter Großeinsatz deutscher Bomber im Osten," *Europäische Sicherheit* 1 (1951), p. 21.

8. Boog, *Luftwaffenführung*, p. 282ff.

9. Generalstab 8. Abteiling, OKL, Kriegstagebuch Nr. 1, 14.12.43-29.6.44, von Rohden 4407-61, NARS T971/49/379. This entry refers to a briefing by Korten on February 15, 1944, in which the general staff chief discussed forthcoming operations.

10. "Study on Recent German Air Force Trends on the Russian Front," p. 4.

11. R. J. Overy, *Göring: The Iron Man* (London: Routledge and Kegan Paul, 1984), p. 196.

12. Von Rohden Annex, "Die deutsche Luftrüstung," NARS T971/26/1121.

13. Speer, *Inside the Third Reich*, p. 283; Hoeffding, "Industry and Railroads," p. 28.

14. For the early history of the historical branch, see Chef Genst. 8. Abt., Nr. 3237/44 g-Chef,31.12.44, "Sonderstudie Heft 7: Überblick über die Entwicklung und Zielsetzen der Kriegswissenschaftlichen Arbeit in der Luftwaffe von 1935 bis 31.12.44," NARS T971/33/83ff.

15. Ibid., fr. 84.

16. Ibid., fr. 88.

17. Irving, *Rise and Fall of the Luftwaffe*, p. 191.

18. Boog, *Luftwaffenführung*, p. 155.

19. Air Ministry/USAFE, Intelligence Report No. 109, A.I. 12/USAFE/M.109, "The GAF Historical Branch in the Service of the General Staff," 3 June 1945, USAFHRC 512.62512M-109, p. 7.

20. A.D.I.(K), June 7, 1945, "Record of Information Supplied by German POWs to D. G. Richards, Senior Narrator, Air Historical Branch, I. Generalmajor von Rohden and Oberst Kriesche," USAFHRC 512.619I, p. 2.

21. Generalstab 8. Abteilung, "Einsatz vom Teilen der strategischen Luftwaffe zur unmittelbaren Unterstützung des Heeres," NARS T971/37/687.

22. The two manuals were: Luftkriegsakademie, "Letifaden-Lufttaktik," 1.4.44, partial copy on NARS, T971/67; and the 8. Abteilung's own "Studien zum Luftkriege Heft 4: Hinweise für den Truppenführer der Luftwaffe," 20/44 g., NARS T971/39/139ff. Also Boog, *Luftwaffenführung*, pp. 161–163.

23. See especially Luftwaffenführungsstab Ic Nr. 52 089/43 g.Kdos. (IV), Vortrag vor Generalleutnant Koller, Chef Luftwaffenführungsstab in Robinson, 21.12.43, OKL/2316, "Operativer Luftkrieg-Gesamtdarstellung," NARS T321/247/no frame nos.

24. Boog, *Luftwaffenführung*, p. 160.

25. Kahn, *Hitler's Spies*, p. 378.

26. Luftwaffenführungsstab Ic, Nr. 29 167/43 geh. (IV), Vortragsnotiz: Betr.: Panzerkampfwagenbestand der SU-Besprechung vom 1.9.43 bei Wehrwirtschaftsstab Ausland Obstl. i.G. Kirsch, Obstl. Seidl, Oberreg. Dr. Klocke, Reg. Baurat Steuber, 6.9.43, von Rohden 4406/167, NARS T971/25/78.

27. Luftwaffenführungsstab Ia, "Kurze Studie: Kampf gegen die russische Rüstungsindustrie," Anlage I, Leistung der russischen Rüstungsindustrie, BA/MA RL 2 II/52, p. 1. These figures were remarkably prescient. A recent Western account provides figures for Soviet armored production within 10% of German estimates. Steven J. Zaloga and James Grandsen, *Soviet Tanks of World War II* (London: Arms and Armour Press, 1984), p. 224.

28. *History of the Great Patriotic War*, Vol. 4, p. 28.

29. Luftwaffenführungsstab Ic Nr. 30 984/43 geh. (IV), Vortragsnotiz- Betr.: Entwicklung der Ausbringung, der Verluste und des Bestandes des SU-Schlachtflugzeuges IL-2, 22.9.43. The Germans estimated Shturmovik losses at 570 per month for the first half of 1943, leaving a current (September 1943) strength of 477.

30. Luftwaffenführungsstab Ic Nr. 23 473/43 geh. (IV), Vortragsnotiz Betr.: Feindverluste SU für die Zeit vom 1.-15.7.43, 20.7.43, von Rohden 4406-136, NARS T971/45/351; and LFüStb Ic Nr. 25 038/43 geh (IV), Betr.: Feindverluste in der Zeit vom 1.-28. Juli 43, NARS T971/45/367.

31. Luftwaffenführungsstab Ic, "Vortrag vor Generalleutnant Koller," NARS T321/247/no frame nos.

32. Oberkommando der Luftwaffe, Führungsstab Ic, Fremde Luftwaffen Ost Nr/ 1403/45 g.Kdos., Bemerkungen zur feindlichen Luftrüstung Nr. 1/45, Sowjetunion-Flugzeugverluste, von Rohden 4407-115, NARS T971/5/587. These included 800 ground attack planes, 15,900 fighters, 7,500 bombers, and 1,900 "other types" lost from all causes between the opening of the campaign and June 22, 1942.

Verification of German estimates of Soviet losses presents many difficulties; however, a recent statistical evaluation of Soviet losses provides some basis for comparison. Analysis based upon recent Soviet sources indicates that the VVS lost 9,500 aircraft in combat in 1941 and a further 10,400 in 1942. Allowing for noncombatant losses, destruction on the ground, etc., the total figure for the entire war "may have been as high as 133,000." In is likely, therefore, that Luftwaffe intelligence was not excessively wide of the mark in its computation of Soviet losses. Price et al., "Impact of Aircraft Losses on Soviet Air Operations," p. 13.

33. OKL, "Sowjetunion-Flugzeugverluste," NARS T971/5/589.

34. Luftwaffenführungsstab Ic, "Vortrag vor Generalleutnant Koller," NARS T321/247/no frame nos.

35. Luftwaffenführungsstab Ia, "Kurze Studie," p. 1.

36. History of the Great Patriotic War, Vol, 4, pp. 28, 238.

37. Groehler, "Stärke, Verteilung und Verluste der deutschen Luftwaffe," Table 12, p. 328.

38. OKL, "Sowjetunion-Flugzeugverluste," NARS T971/5/586-587.

39. Luftwaffenführungsstab Ia op Nr. 8655/43, NARS T321/10/4746780–81.

40. Kahn, Hitler's Spies, p. 384.

41. Boog et al., Angriff auf die Sowjetunion, p. 689.

42. XL. Armeekorps, 19068/13, Anlagen z. KTB 4, Qu. Abt, 2 Jan.–28 Apr. 1942, Gen. Kdo. VIII. Flieger-Korps, Ia/Ic, Br.B. Nr. 695/42 geh., NARS T314/961.

43. A.I. (T), 20. August 1945, "Report on the Means of Intelligence on the Russian Front," Translation, USAFHRC 512.625N, 1945, p. 5.

44. Luftwaffenführungsstab Ic Nr. 52 703/43 geh. (IV), Vortragsnotiz Betr.: Feindmeldungen nach VH und Gefangenen-Aussagen über die Wirkung deutscher Luftangriff im Vergleich mit den eigenen Erfolgsmeldungen in den Kampfraumen des IV. und VIII. Fliegerkorps, OKL/2376b, NARS T321/89/51ff.

45. PzAOK 2, Ic, Gefangenaussagen, NARS T313/185/7443776.

46. Kahn, Hitler's Spies, p. 119.

47. OKW/Wehrwirtschafts-und Rüstungsamt Wi(VI) Nr. 2758/41 g, "Die Wehrwirtschaft der Union der Sozialistischen-Sowjet Republiker (UdSSR)," NARS T78/479/6462223.

48. Reich Ministry for Armaments and War Production, Conference minutes, Item 26, 22–23 May 1944, FD 3353/45, NARS T73/192/3405743.

49. Luftwaffenführungsstab Ic, Fremde Luftwaffen Ost Nr. 20 225/44 g.Kdos., Zielauswahl für den Raum Moskau-Obere Wolga, 20.1.1944, Anlage 4, OKL/2316, NARS T321/247/no frame nos.

50. Luftwaffenführungsstab Ic, Fremde Luftwaffen Ost Nr. 217/44 g.Kdos., Vortragsnotiz Betr.: Abwehrlage im Großraum Moskau- Obere Wolga, 16.1.1944, OKL/2316, NARS T321/247/no frame nos. The value of such agents'

reports was frequently suspect; witness the Gruppe Scherhorn incident of late 1944.

51. Ibid., Anlage 1.

52. Luftwaffenführungsstab Ic "Die Bedeutung Moskaus," NARS T971/22/101.

53. Luftwaffen-Füstb. Ic/IV Nr. 31 786/43 geh., "SU Ziele der Wehrwirtschaft-Ruckverlegung der Rüstungsindustrie," 1.9.43, OKL/2143, NARS T321/67/4817195. Analysis of Soviet sources indicates that German intelligence was correct in this assumption. Hoeffding, "Industry and Railroads," p. 5.

54. Paul Deichmann, *The System of Target Selection Applied by the German Air Force in World War II: USAF Historical Studies No. 163* (Manhattan, KS: MA/AH Publishing, 1980), p. 247.

55. Murray, *Luftwaffe*, pp. 49–59.

56. Hans Freiherr v. Bülow, "Die Grundlagen neuzeitlicher Luftstreitkräfte," *Militärwissenschaftliche Rundschau* 1 (1936) 1. Heft, p. 83.

57. Haywood S. Hansell, *The Air Plan that Defeated Hitler* (Atlanta: Higgins-McArthur, 1972), pp. 80–81.

58. Ibid., p. 261.

59. Mark Clodfelter, *The Limits of Air Power: The American Bombing of North Vietnam* (New York: Free Press, 1989), pp. 17, 102–107.

60. USSR Committee for International Scientific and Technical Conferences, Krzizhanovsky Power Institute of the Academy of Sciences of the USSR, *Electric Power Development in the USSR* (Moscow: INRA Publishing Society, 1936), p. 4.

61. Ibid., p. 65.

62. Der Oberbefehlshaber der Luftwaffe, Führungsstab Ic Nr. 6080/42 geh., "Sowjetunion: Übersicht der Archivunterlagen—Band I: Ergänzuge Rüstungsindustrie (einschließlich. Stromversorgung), Sept. 1942, NARS T321/81/354.

63. Der Reichsminister der Luftfahrt und Oberbefehlshaber der Luftwaffe, Az. 8 n 10 02 Nr. 2161/43 g. Kdos. (LD Ag III 10), "Vorschläge für Luftangriffe auf die Stromversorgung des Bereiches Moskau-Obere Wolga," 31.7.1943, OKL/485, NARS T321/104/109.

64. Ibid.

65. Ibid., p. 4.

66. Ibid., p. 6.

67. Luftwaffenführungsstab Ic, "Die Bedeutung Moskaus," NARS T971/22/104.

68. Ic/IV D, "Stellungnahme zu LD Ag III 10, 'Vorschläge für Luftangriffe auf die Stromversorgung des Bereiches Moskau-Obere Wolga,'" von Rohden 4406-17, NARS T971/22/123; Hoeffding, "Industry and Railroads," p. 33.

69. Ibid., fr. 124.

70. Hoeffding, "Industry and Railroads," p. 34.

71. Hansell, *Air Plan that Defeated Hitler*, p. 289.

72. *History of the Great Patriotic War*, Vol. 2, p. 509.

73. Ibid., Vol. 3, p. 151.

74. Die Reichsminister der Luftfahrt und Oberbefehlshaber der Luftwaffe, LD Ag III 10, Vorschlag für Luftangriff auf die Wasserkraftwerke Rybinsk und Uglitsch, 10 August 1943, von Rohden 4406/18, NARS T971/22/345.

75. Ic/IV D, Vortragsnotiz, Betr.: Zielbearbeitung, 23.9.1943, OKL/2376a, NARS T321/89/43.

76. Ic Wi Nr. 2375/43 gKdos., Bemerkungen zur vorgesehenen Zielauslese im Luftkrieg gegen die Wehrwirtschaft SU, 9.7.43, USAFHRC, Karlsrühe Collection, K113.309-3 v. 11, p. 4.

77. Ic/Wi Nr. 3754/43 gKdos., "Besprechung bei Dr. Carl am 30.9.43 betr.: Luftangriff auf russische Flugmotorenwerke," von Rohden 4406-238, NARS T971/22/505.

78. For example, "die jude Louri" was reported to be in charge of one such armaments plant. Oberkommando des Heeres, Abt. Fremde Heere Ost (IIc), H 3/1456, NARS T78/585/813.

79. Heeresgruppe Mitte, 65002/46, Anlagen z. KTB d. HGr. Mitte/ Führungsabteilung, Allgemeines Heft 9, 29.1.44, NARS T311/222/597-510. Army Group Center argued that attacks on armaments factories "may effect a speedy and effective relief of the fighting troops from the material weight of the Red Army."

80. Luftwaffenführungsstab Ia op Nr. 8865/43, NARS T321/10/4746781.

81. Luftwaffenführungsstab Ia, "Kurze Studie," p. 7.

82. Ibid., p. 2.

83. Ibid., pp. 3–4; Anlage 4.

84. Ibid., p. 6.

85. Luftwaffenführungsstab Ia op Nr. 8865/43, NARS T321/10/4746780-81.

86. Luftwaffenführungsstab Ic Nr. 52 089/43 g. Kdos. (IV), "Notiz über Besprechung am 21.12.1943," OKL/2316, "Operativer Luftkrieg-Gesamtdarstellung," p. 287, NARS T321/247/no frame nos.

87. Genstb. 8. Abteilung, KTB Nr. 1, NARS T971/49/380ff.

88. Luftwaffenführungsstab Ic, "Vortrag vor Generalleutnant Koller," NARS T321/247/no frame nos.

89. Luftwaffenführungsstab Ia op Nr. 8865/43, NARS T321/10/4746781; von Rohden Annex, "War against Russia," NARS T971/26/308; Speer, Inside the Third Reich, p. 282.

90. Records of the Reich Ministry for Armaments and War Production, Item 22, 7.12.43, NARS T73/192/3405711–712.

91. Ic/Ost (D) Nr 63/44 g. Kdos., Zielauswahl für den Raum Moskau-Obere Wolga, 8.1.1944, OKL/2316, "Operativer Luftkrieg-Gesamtdarstellung," p. 257, NARS T321/247/no frame nos.

92. Chef Ic Nr. 162/44 g.Kdos., 12.1 1944, OKL/2316, "Operativer Luftkrieg-Gesamtdarstellung," p. 253, NARS T321/247/no frame nos.

93. Ic/Ost (D) Nr. 63/44 g. Kdos., Zielauswahl für den Raum Moskau-Obere Wolga, NARS T321/247/no frame nos.

94. Ic/Ost (D) Nr. 115/44 g.Kdos., Die Bekämpfung des SU-Rüstungspotentials bis zur Unteren und Mittleren Wolga und zum Uralgebiet, OKL/2316, "Operativer Luftkrieg-Gesamtdarstellung," p. 254, NARS T321/247/no frame nos.

95. Der Oberbefehlshaber der Luftwaffe, Führungsstab Ic Nr. 138/44 gKdos. (Wi), 12.1.44, OKL/2316, "Operativer Luftkrieg-Gesamtdarstellung," p. 251, NARS T321/247/no frame nos.

96. Der Reichsminister für Rüstung und Kriegsproduktion Wag Aussch. 8/44, Geheime Reichssache, Stellungnahme I. zur Zielauswahl für den Raum Moskau-Obere Wolga Nr. 63/44, OKL/2316, "Operativer Luftkrieg-Gesamtdarstellung," p. 237, NARS T321/247/no frame nos.

97. Records of the Reich Ministry for Armaments and War Production, Item 22, 7.12.43, NARS T73/192/3405711-712.

98. Chef Ic Nr. 162/44, p. 253, NARS T321/247/no frame nos.

99. Wesley Frank Craven and James Lea Cate, *The Army Air Forces in World War II* (Chicago: University of Chicago Press, 1949), Vol. 2, pp. 555-559.

100. Chef Ic Nr. 162/44, p. 253, NARS T321/247/no frame nos.

101. Macht, "Engpässe der russischen Wehrwirtschaft," II. Teil, NARS T321/75/4826276ff.

102. "Isstärken an Flugzeugen, 31.5.43," NARS T321/154/062. 580 bombers on that date were in the east; 391 served in the west or in the Mediterranean theater. An additional 617 bombers were assigned to units undergoing rearmament, training or recuperation.

103. Irving, *Rise and Fall of the Luftwaffe*, p. 232.

104. Luftwaffenführungsstab Ia/Flieg. Nr. 9592/44 g. Kdos. Chefs., "Studie über die Flugzeuglage der Kampfverbände," NARS T321/10/4746765.

105. Der Oberbefehlshaber der Luftwaffe, General der Kampfflieger Nr. 4/43 g. Kdos Chefs., 7.1.43, Betr.: Lage der Kampfverbände, USAFHRC, Karlsrühe Collection K113.3019-1, p. 2.

106. Ibid., p. 3.

107. Generalstab der Luftwaffe, 8. Abteilung, "Einsatz von Teilen der strategischen Luftwaffe zur unmittelbaren Unterstützung des Heeres," NARS T971/37/688.

108. Murray, *Luftwaffe*, Table LXIX, p. 292.

109. On January 31, 1943, Stab, I./ and III./KG 27, for example, could together muster only 18 operational machines. KG 55 on the same date had only 12 aircraft operational. "Einsatz fliegender Verbände," USAFHRC K113.309-3 v. 13, p. 3.

110. Interview with Generalmajor a.D. Dietrich Peltz, Washington, DC, November 1990.

111. Geschichte der I./KG General Wever 4, NARS T971/16/623.

112. Von Rohden Annex, "War against Russia," NARS T971/26/305.

113. Groehler, "Stärke, Verteilung und Verluste der deutsche Luftwaffe," Table 9, p. 325.

114. Reichsminister des Großdeutschen Reiches u. Oberbefehlshaber der Luftwaffe, Nr. 8912/43 g. Kdos. Chefsache (Füst. Ia), 11.26.43, NARS T321/10/746460.

115. Plocher, *German Air Force Versus Russia, 1943*, p. 146.

116. The table of organization for the force was as follows: Command level: IV. Fliegerkorps
KG 3 with I. (from Luftflotte 4) and II. (from Luftflotte 6) Gruppe
KG 4 with II. and III. Gruppe
KG 55 with I., II. and III. Gruppe (except for 9. (railway attack)
Staffel (from Luftflotte 4)
III./KG 100 (from Luftflotte 3 in France)

KG 4 and KG 55 were equipped with the Heinkel 111; KG 3 with the Junkers 88, and KG 100 with the Dornier 217, modified to carry the "Fritz X" glide bomb.

117. Luftflottenkommando 6, Der Chef des Generalstabes Nr. 498/44 gKdos/ Chefs., 17.1.1944, Betr.: Übungseinheiten des Auffrischungsstabes Ost, USAFHRC, Karlsrühe Collection K113.309-3 v. 16, p. 1.

118. Teletype, Lfl. Kdo. 6, Chef d. Genst. Nr. 23/44 GKDOS., An LW FUEST IA-ROBINSON, Betr.: Einsatz Auffrischungsstab Ost, OKL 2316, "Operativer Luftkrieg-Gesamtdarstellung," NARS T321/247/no frame nos.

119. Kriegstagebuch Nr. 1, I/Kampfgeschwader 55, 17.5.43-24.5.44, OKL/2878, NARS T321/75/4825717.

120. Ibid.

121. Murray, "Luftwaffe Before the Second World War," pp. 267–268.

122. Murray, Luftwaffe, p. 158: "As one ranking officer told another after capture: 'you cannot imagine how catastrophic the air personnel situation is. We have no crews; all the instructor crews were shot down in the Junkers.'"

123. Generalstab der Luftwaffe, 8. Abteilung, "Gegenüberstellung der Kampfführung der eigenen und der anglo-amerk. Luftwaffe," 22.8.1944, von Rohden 4407-97, NARS T971/51/334.

124. Luftwaffenführungsstab Ic/III, Nr. 34 482/43 geh. Ic/III, "GB Fliegertruppe, Die Schweren britische Kampfverbände (Bomber Command)," Oct. 1943, p. 12, NARS T971/68/no frame nos.

125. Reichsminister der Luftfahrt und Oberbefehlshaber der Luftwaffe, GL-Planungsamt Nr. 800-43 GL/Rü, Berlin, 10. Juni 1943, "Ergebnisse der Beuteauswertung Nr. 14-15, Neuerungen in der Ausrüstung der Britische-amerikanischen Fliegertruppe," pp. 33–36, NARS T971/69/no frame nos.

126. Ibid., p. 33.

127. Irving, Rise and Fall of the Luftwaffe, p. 167.

128. Luftwaffenführungsstab Ia, Flieg., H.Qu. 16.12.43, Aktennotiz Betr.: Zielfindergruppe für Korps Meister, USAFHRC K113.3019-1, p. 1. I/KG 66, I./KG 6 and II./KG 2 were equipped with the Ju 188, and operated against Great Britain and were intended to combat the eventual opening of the Second Front.

129. Ibid., p. 2.

130. Chef des Luftwaffenführungsstabes Nr. 2822/44 geheim, Vortragsnotiz Betr.: Einsatz KG 1 (He 177) im Osten, 18.5.1944, USAFHRC K113.835, p. 1.

131. Wolfgang Dierich, Kampfgeschwader 55 "Greif," (Stuttgart: Motorbuch Verlag, 1975), p. 348; I./Kampfgeschwader 55, Abt. Ia, Br.B. Nr. 167/44 geh., Betr.: Erfahrungsbericht an Waffengeneral, 22.3.44, OKL/2312, NARS T321/247/ no frame nos.

132. For a summary of Luftwaffe target-marking procedures, see Oberkommando der Luftwaffe, General der Kampfflieger Nr. 10050/45 geheim (I/A), Merkblatt über den Einsatz von Zielfinder-Verbänden, 1.1.1945, NARS T971/68/ no frame nos.

133. I./KG 55, "Erfahrungsbericht an Waffengeneral," NARS T971/247/no frame nos.

134. Luftwaffenkommando 6, "Übungseinheiten des Auffrischungsstabes Ost," p. 1.

135. Massnahmen Hitlers zur Behebung des Mangels an Flugzeugen an der Ostfront am 25.10.42, 25.10.42, Chefsachen-Fernschrieben an Major i.G. von Brauchitsch, USAFHRC K113.309-3 v. 6, p. 2.

136. Reichsminister für Rüstung und Kriegsproduktion, Wag Aussch. 8/44, NARS T321/247/no frame nos.

137. "Kriegschronik des Kampfgeschwaders "Hindenburg" Nr. 1, NARS T971/50/1049ff. For the utter lack of readiness among the He 177 units at the time, see Luftwaffenführungsstab Ia/Flieg Nr. 4518/44 g.Kdos., Aktennotiz über Besuch bei KG 1 (Rücksprache mit Kommodore KG 1 und Kommandeur II./KG 1), USAFHRC K113.309-3 v. 15, p. 3.

138. Kriegschronik KG 1, fr. 1052.

139. GL/C Nr. 17759/43 (IIH) gKdos. 8.10.43, Betr.: Meldung über Auslieferungsstand der Empfänger für Hs 293 und Fritz X zum 30.9.43, Milch 53.55, NARS T321/154/414. A shortage of receivers had somewhat reduced production; still, up to September 30, 1943, 1518 "Fritz X"s had been manufactured.

140. Alfred Price, German Air Force Bombers of World War II, Vol. 2 (Windsor: Hylton Lacy, 1969), pp. 28–29.

141. Ic Wi Nr. 5609/43 gKdos., "Besprechung bei Dr. Carl am 25.9.43 über Munitionseinsatz beim Angriff auf Wehrwirtschaftliche Anlagen, von Rohden 4406-28, NARS T971/45/110." The operations staff appears to have concurred in these estimates.

142. Air Ministry, Rise and Fall of the German Air Force, p. 262.

143. Luftwaffenführungsstab Ia, "Kurze Studie," p. 11.

144. Ibid.

145. Hoeffding, "Industry and Railroads," p. 38, is probably correct in assuming that this concept "was clearly inspired by the Möhne Dam attack." The Luftwaffe recovered Barnes-Wallis' "bouncing bomb" apparatus from a crashed Lancaster after the Dam Busters raid in May 1943; in fact, German intelligence's diagrams of the apparatus were far more accurate than any generally available in the Allied countries for years after the war, due to enforcement of the British Official Secrets Act. See RdL u. ObdL, GL-Planungsamt, "Ergebnisse der Beuteauswertung Nr. 14-15," p. 30, NARS T971/69/no frame nos.

146. Erprobungsstelle der Luftwaffe, Travemünde/Gruppe E 6/7 "Winterballon"- Vorläufige Gerätebeschreibung, OKL/2504, Dec. 4, 1944, NARS T321/110/888.

147. Hoeffding, "Industry and Railroads," p. 39.

148. GL/6-7 IVC, Niederschrift über Erprobungsabwürfe "Winterballon" in Finse von 27.6. bis 1.7.44, von Rohden 4406-67, NARS T971/45/226; Hoeffding, "Industry and Railroads," p. 39.

149. Luftwaffenführungsstab, Betr.: Vorschlag Ministerialrat Steinmann, Winterballon und Sommerballon, 15.5.44, von Rohden 4406-61, NARS T971/45/202.

150. Luftwaffenführungsstab Ia/Flieg. Nr. 9592/44 g.Kdos. Chefs. (T), "Studie über die Flugzeuglage der Kampfverbände," NARS T321/10/4746754ff.

151. Luftwaffenführungsstab Ia, "Flugzeuglage der Kampfverbände," NARS T321/10/4746765.

152. Paul Deichmann, "Gedenken zum Thema: 'Heeresunterstützung an der Ostfront 1943,'" USAFHRC, Karlsruhe Collection K113.309-3 v. 13, p. 6.

153. Deichmann, *System of Target Selection*, p. 251.
154. Luftwaffenführungsstab Ia op Nr. 8865/43, NARS T321/10/4746780.

CHAPTER SIX

1. United States Strategic Bombing Survey, *Over-all Report: European War* (Washington, DC: September 30, 1945), p. 3.
2. See Barry D. Watts, *The Foundations of U.S. Air Doctrine: The Problem of Friction in War* (Maxwell AFB: Air University Press, 1984).
3. Speer, *Inside the Third Reich*, p. 283.
4. Luftflottenkommando 6, Führungsabteilung Ia, Kriegstagebuch, 1.2.1945, OKL/385, NARS T321/50/4796024.
5. Speer, *Inside the Third Reich*, p. 282.
6. Oberkommando der Wehrmacht/WFst, KTB Ausarbeitung Ostfront: Zuführung vom Verbänden für den Osten 1.1.44-31.3.44, "Tätigkeit der Luftwaffe im Osten," OKW/1929, NARS T77/1430/701.
7. Luftflottenkommando 6 Nr. 537/44 g.Kdos. Chefs., Überlegungen für der operativer Luftkriegführung gegen die sowjetische Wehrwirtschaft, 11.2.44, BA/MA RL 7/521, p. 1.
8. Luftflottenkommando 6 Nr. 526/44 g.Kdos. Chefs., KR-Fernschrieben an Ob.d.L Füst. Ia (Rob.), Auffrischungsstab Ost (nachrichtl.), 6.2.44, USAFHRC, Karlsrühe Collection K113.309-3 v. 16, p. 12.
9. Ziemke, *Stalingrad to Berlin*, p. 264.
10. Luftflottenkommando 6, Überlegungen für der operativen Luftkriegführung, p. 1.
11. Ibid., p. 1. Greim maintained that Gorki lay at the extreme limit of bomber range from Orsha, although he evidently did not regard a mass attack from this base to be practicable.
12. *History of the Great Patriotic War*, Vol. 5, p. 536.
13. Anlage zu Lfl. Kdo. 6 537/44 g.Kdos. Chefs., "Anteil Moskaus an der Gesamtausbringung der Rüstungsindustrie der SU," USAFHRC, Karlsrühe Collection K113.309-3 v. 16, p. 7.
14. OKL, Generalstab 8. Abteilung, "Douhet Theory," p. 10.
15. Luftflottenkommando 6, Überlegungen für den operativen Luftkriegführung, p. 2.
16. Luftwaffenführungsstab Ic, Fremde Luftwaffen Ost Nr. 885/44 g.Kdos. (D), Vortragsnotiz Betr.: Angriffe auf die Stromversorgung Moskau-Obere Wolga von den Flugplatzen Baranowitschi, Dünaburg und Minsk aus, OKL/2316, "Operativer Luftkrieg-Gesamtdarstellung," p. 170, NARS T321/247/ no frame nos.
17. Der Oberbefehlshaber der Luftwaffe, Führungsstab Ia Nr. 9314/44 g.Kdos. Chefsache, Bezug: Lfl. Kdo. 6, Nr. 537/44 g.Kdos. Chefs. vom 11.2.44, Betr.: Kampf gegen die russische Rüstungsindustrie, An: Luftflottenkommando 6, BA/MA RL 7/521, p. 1.
18. Ibid., p. 2.
19. Halder, *War Diary*, p. 466.
20. A.I. 12/USAFE/M.74, USAFE/Air Ministry Intelligence Party (OKL), Intelligence Report No. 74, "Strategic Bombing in the GAF" (Interrogation of

General der Flieger Rudolf Meister), 3 Dec. 1945, USAFHRC 512.62512M-74, p. 5. These were among the last bomber units to be deactivated during the fuel crisis of summer 1944.

21. ObdL, Füstb Ia Nr. 03510/43 geheim, 25.8.43, "Pamphlet Concerning Operations Against Railways," Translation appended to "Strategic Bombing in the GAF," p. 13.

22. Ibid.

23. Luftwaffenführungsstab Ic, Fremde Luftwaffen Ost Nr. 51 278/44 gKdos., Vortragsnotiz Betr.: Angriffsziele im Eisenbahnverkehrssystem der SU, 13.4.44, in OKH/FHO H 3/1471, Transportverhältnisse u. Brennstofflage in der SU, NARS T78/586/454.

24. Ibid., fr. 453.

25. Luftwaffenführungsstab Ic, Fremde Luftwaffen Ost Nr. 1477/44 g. Kdos. (D), 5.4.44, Vortragsnotiz Betr.: Angriffsziele im Eisenbahnverkehrssystem der SU, von Rohden 4406–82, NARS T971/45/259ff.

26. Genstb. 8. Abteilung, OKL, KTB Nr. 1, NARS T971/49/349.

27. In mid-January 1944, the staff of Air Fleet 6 requested "as part of the training the release of individual bomber *Gruppen* for night attacks on noted enemy supply and rail centers, which may provide relief for the ground situation at the present time; for example Smolensk, Rosslavl, Nevel, Velikiye-Luki, Gomel, Kiev, Zhitomir, etc." Luftflottenkommando 6, Übungseinheiten des Auffrischungsstabes Ost, p. 1. Also see Oberkommando der Wehrmacht/Wfst, "Tätigkeit der Luftwaffe im Osten," NARS T77/1430/700-701: "General Korten reported to the Führer the establishment of a long-range bomber group for the east . . . with a likely readiness date of February 15, 1944 . . . For training of these units they should be sent out against railway targets in the area of Kiev and eastward . . ."

28. Koller interrogation, NARS T971/22/551. Also USSBS interrogation, 30. 5. 1945, Von Rohden Collection, Library of Congress, Microfilm Reading Room, Series 1750, Reel 37.

29. Air Ministry, *Rise and Fall of the German Air Force*, p. 408.

30. Lw. Füst. Ic/Ost (D), "Grossangriff des IV. Fliegerkorps auf das SU-Eisenbahnssystem in der Zeit v. 27. 3.-5. 5.1944," USAFHRC, Karlsrühe Collection K113.309-3 v. 16, p. 1.

31. ObdL, Führungsstab Ia Nr. 9314/44, p. 1.

32. Hoeffding, "Industry and Railroads," p. 46.

33. Luftwaffenführungsstab Ic, Flugplätzen Baranowitschi, Dünaburg und Minsk, NARS T321/247/no frame nos.

34. ObdL, Führungsstab Ia Nr. 9314/44, p. 1.

35. "Report on the Means of Intelligence on the Russian Front," p. 3.

36. Ibid., p. 1.

37. Oberkommando des Heeres, Fremde Heere Ost (I), Nr. 1512/44 gKdos., Entwicklung und Beurteilung der Feindlage im Raum Luzk-Kowel-Sarny für die Zeit vom 15.2-10.5.44, H 3/1158, NARS T78/582/550ff.

38. Von Rohden Annex, "War against Russia," NARS T971/26/313.

39. Oberkommando der Luftwaffe, Lw.-Führungsstab Nr 1920/44 geh. (Ia/ Ausb.), "Taktische Bemerkungen des Oberkommandos der Luftwaffe Nr. 5/44," BA/MA RH 11 III/76, p. 14.

40. "Operations against Railways," pp. 13ff.

41. *Luftkriegführung*, paragraph 173; Hoeffding, "Industry and Railroads," p. 49.

42. *Luftkriegführung*, paragraph 172.

43. "Operations against Railways," p. 14.

44. Gefechtsberichte in Anlagen z. Kriegstagebuch, III./KG 55, Sept. 1, 1943–Nov. 14, 1944, OKL/2391, NARS T321/255/no frame nos.

45. Luftwaffenführungsstab Ic, "Angriffsziele im Eisenbahnverkehrssystem," NARS T78/586/296.

46. LwFüst Ic-/Ost (D), "Grossangriffe des IV. Fliegerkorps," p. 1.

47. I./Kampfgeschwader 55, Abt. Ia, Br. B. Nr. 149/44 geh., "Ausbildungsbericht über der Zeit vom 1.2. bis 31.3.44," Anlage 18 zum KTB, OKL/2312, NARS T321/247/ no frame nos.

48. I./Kampfgeschwader 55, Abt. Ic Br.B. Nr. 18/44 geh., "Erfahrungsbericht über Versorgung der Festung Kowel in der Zeit vom 2.-7.4.44," Anlage 30 zum KTB, OKL/2312, NARS T321/247/no frame nos. In five days of operations, I/KG 55 had eighteen Heinkel 111s damaged. Also Ziemke, *Stalingrad to Berlin*, p. 277, on the "fortified places" directive.

49. "Part Played by the GAF," p. 10.

50. Summary of operations in LwFüst Ic-/Ost (D), "Grossangriffe des IV. Fliegerkorps," pp. 1–13.

51. "Part Played by the GAF," p. 10.

52. Hoeffding, in his remarkable "German Air Attacks on Industry and Railroads," tends to denigrate the scope and effectiveness of the rail interdiction campaign. However, he cites only Von Rohden document 4406-83, compiled on May 9, 1944, and therefore implies that the attacks ended with the May 5, 1944 raid on Kiev-Darnitsa. Examination of the KG 55, KG 4, Fliegerkorps IV and Koller materials indicates that the German bombing effort was far more protracted.

53. Von Rohden Annex, "War against Russia," NARS T971/26/315.

54. "Questionnaire on GAF Doctrine answered by Rohden and Kriesche," p. 5.

55. On May 11, 1944, for example, KG 55 under its *Geschwaderkommodore* Major Wilhelm Antrup flew its 50,000th operational sortie. While few Luftwaffe bomber pilots survived the entire duration of the conflict, the existence of pilots such as Antrup clearly raised unit efficiency and morale. General der Kampfflieger, 12.5.44, I./KG 55, OKL/2312, NARS T321/247/no frame nos.

56. "Part Played by the GAF," p. 11; "Merkblatt über den Einsatz von Zielfinder-Verbänden," p. 4, NARS T971/68/no frame nos.

57. Von Rohden Annex, "War against Russia," NARS T971/26/315.

58. Luftflottenkommando 6, Führungsabteilung Ia op Nr. 1459/44 geheim, 7.2.44, Heeresgruppe Mitte, Anl. z. KTB d. HGr. Mitte/Ia, Akte XIII-Luftwaffe, Heft 8, 1.1.-27.3.44, NARS T311/225/275. This order also tasked Army Group Center for failing to destroy Sarny rail station prior to the German retreat.

59. Luftwaffen-Kriegsberichter-Abteilung beim Luftflotten-Kommando 6, Lt. Hans-Joachim Volland (9. Zug), Bericht Nr. 321/Vol/25, "In die Offensivvorbereitungen der Sowjets: Zwei Monate operativer Luftkrieg im Osten," NARS T971/63/ no frame nos.

60. "Auszüge aus dem Original-Tagebuch von Gen.d.Fl. Koller," 17.6.44, USAFHRC K113.309-3 v. 15, p. 1. On the Soviet deception operations preceding Operation Bagration see David Glantz, "The Red Mask: The Nature and Legacy of Soviet Military Deception in the Second World War," in *Strategic and Operational Deception in the Second World War*, ed. Michael I. Handel (London: Frank Cass, 1987), pp. 213–231.

61. David M. Glantz, *Soviet Military Deception in the Second World War* (London: Frank Cass, 1989), pp. 348–358; *History of the Great Patriotic War*, Vol. 4, pp. 243–249.

62. *History of the Great Patriotic War*, Vol. 4, p. 242.

63. Richard Lukas, *Eagles East: The Army Air Force and the Soviet Union, 1941–1945* (Tallahassee, FL: Florida State University Press, 1970), p. 196.

64. Ic/IV D, Nr. 4195/43 g.Kdos, 30.10, 1943, OKL/809, NARS T321/86/186–190.

65. Dienstelle Walli I Trb. Nr. 2520/44 geh., Betr.: Errichtung einer Luftfront im Osten gegen Deutschland, OKL/762, NARS T321/86/177.

66. See Chapter 3.

67. Luftflottenkommando 6, Überlegungen für der operativen Luftkriegführung, pp. 2–3.

68. Adolf Galland, *The First and the Last: The German Fighter Force in World War II* (Mesa, AZ: Champlin Museum Press, 1986), p. 295; Lukas, *Eagles East*, p. 198.

69. Most published accounts of the German aspects of the Poltava operation are inadequate. Lukas' *Eagles East*, although the standard work on the USAAF/Soviet collaboration, does not describe the raid in any detail. Glenn Infield, *The Poltava Affair: A Russian Warning, an American Tragedy* (New York: Macmillan Publishing Co., Inc., 1973), in addition to being polemical, is most unreliable in its lengthy (and sometimes fanciful) descriptions of German planning and operations.

70. This account of the Poltava raid is based upon an interrogation of General Rudolf Meister in "Strategic Bombing in the GAF," pp. 4–5; Von Rohden Annex, "War against Russia," NARS T971/26/316ff; "Original-Tagebuch Koller;" III/KG 55, KTB, NARS T321/255/no frame nos.

71. Dierich, *Kampfgeschwader 55 "Greif,"* p. 365.

72. Von Rohden Annex, "War against Russia," NARS T971/26/317.

73. "Strategic Bombing in the GAF," p. 4.

74. Dierich, *Kampfgeschwader 55 "Greif,"* p. 367.

75. III/Kampfgeschwader 55, Abt. Ia/Ib, "Gefechtsmeldung 5: Erfolgsmeldung zum Angriff auf Flugpl. Mirgorod vom 21.22.6.44," OKL/2381, NARS T321/255/no frame nos.

76. Lukas, *Eagles East*, pp. 200–201.

77. Kurowski, *Balkankreuz und roter Stern*, p. 413.

78. III./Kampfgeschwader 55, "Erfolgsmeldung zum Angriff auf Flugplatz Mirgorod," NARS T321/255/no frame nos.

79. "Original-Tagebuch Koller," entry for 15.6.1944, item k, p. 2.

80. Luftwaffenführungsstab Ia/Flieg. Nr. 9592/44 g.Kdos. Chefs. (T), "Studie über die Flugzeuglage der Kampfverbände," 5.5.44, NARS T321/10/4746358.

81. Air Ministry, *Rise and Fall of the German Air Force*, p. 322.

82. Deichmann, *System of Target Selection*, p. 268.

83. Murray, *Luftwaffe*, p. 258.

84. Speer, *Inside the Third Reich*, p. 346.

85. Ibid., p. 352.

86. "Original-Tagebuch Koller," entry for 28.6.1944, p. 3.

87. Luftflottenkommando 6, Chef d. Genst, Nr. (illeg.)/44 g.Kdos. Chefs., 7.8.44, BA/MA RL 7/522.

88. "Kriegschronik des Kampfgeschwaders 'Hindenburg,'" NARS T971/50/1052ff.

89. Price, *German Bombers of World War II*, Vol. 2, p. 47.

90. III./KG 55, Gefechtsberichte in: Anlage z. KTB, Sept. 1, 1943–November 14, 1944, OKL/2381, NARS T321/255/no frame nos.

91. "Strategic Bombing in the GAF," p. 4.

92. Records of the Reich Ministry for Armaments and War Production, Vol. 61, pp. 104/109, FD 3353/45 item 26, NARS T73/92/3405743. Hoeffding, "Industry and Railroads," provides an excellent and suitably irreverent discussion of a number of these later attempts.

93. Records of the Reich Ministry for Armaments and War Production, Memo, Speer to Hitler, Nr. 2460/44 geheime Reichssache, Vol. 92, pp. 3128–3143, NARS T73/192/3405944.

94. Speer, *Inside the Third Reich*, p. 546 n. 10.

95. OKL-Füst. (Robinson) Nr. 10360/44 g.Kdos. Chefs., USAFHRC 512.625J.

96. A.D.I.(K) Report No. 398/1945, "A Short History of KG 200," USAFHRC 512.625J AIR MIN, February 1945, p. 6.

97. OKL, Fü.St. (Robinson) Nr. 18436/44 g. Kdos. (op), Betr.: Unternehmen "Burgund," USAFHRC 512.625J.

98. Chef des Generalstabes der Luftwaffe, Nr. 10496/45 g.Kdos. Chefs. FüSt. Ia/Flieg (op), USAFHRC 512.625J. For a recent account of KG 200's operations, see Günther W. Gellermann, *Moskau ruft Heeresgruppe Mitte . . .* (Koblenz: Bernard & Graefe Verlag, 1988).

99. Luftflottenkommando 6, Kriegstagebuch, 1945, NARS T321/51/4798039.

100. Irving, *Hitler's War*, p. 664.

101. Timothy A. Wray, *Standing Fast: German Defensive Doctrine on the Russian Front During WWII: Prewar to March 1943: Combat Studies Institute Research Study No. 5* (Ft. Leavenworth: US Army Command and General Staff College, 1986), offers a fascinating discussion of how the exigencies of the Russian campaign forced amendments to German "elastic defense" doctrine.

102. Guy Sajer, *The Forgotten Soldier* (New York: Harper and Row, 1971), p. 72.

103. "German Ground Attack Arm," p. 5; Boog, *Luftwaffenführung*, p. 193.

104. "Questionnaire on GAF Doctrine and Policy answered by Rohden and Kriesche," p. 9; Schulz, "Collaboration Between Army and Luftwaffe," p. 9.

105. Horst Boog, "Das Problem der Selbständigkeit der Luftstreitkräfte in Deutschland, 1908–1945," *Militärgeschichtliches Mitteilungen* 1 (1988) p. 52.

106. OKL, Ausbildungshinweis Nr. 19--Zusammenarbeit Heer-Luftwaffe, May 1944, tr. in Air Ministry Weekly Intelligence Summary No. 278, Issued by

Air Ministry A.O.A.S. (I) (A.I. 1), 30th December, 1944, USAFHRC 512.625-3a, p. 1.

107. Oberkommando der Luftwaffe-Lw. Führungsstab, "Taktische Bemerkungen Nr. 5/44," 15.7.44, p. 14.

108. Panzergruppe West Abt. Ia/Fliegerverbindungsoffizier Nr. 1600/44 geheim, Merkblatt zur Luftwaffen-Unterstützung, 22.3.44, OKL/2571, NARS T321/51/4798881.

109. "German Ground Attack Arm," p. 5; Hubertus Hitschhold, "Die Schlachtfliegerei in der deutschen Luftwaffe," *Flugwehr und Technik* 12 (No. 4, 1950), pp. 81–82.

110. Hitschhold, "Schlachtfliegerei," p. 84.

111. Der Oberbefehlshaber der Luftwaffe, Führungsstab Ia.Ausb. Nr. 570/44 geheim, "Taktische Bemerkungen des ObdL Nr. 2/44," 1.3.44, BA/MA RH 11 III/76, pp. 15–16.

112. "German Ground Attack Arm," p. 10.

113. Ibid., p. 16.

114. Oberbefehlshaber der Luftwaffe, Führungsstab Ia, "Taktische Bemerkungen Nr. 2/44," p. 18.

115. Analogous to the USAF's "Forward Air Controller" (FAC).

116. "Ausbildungshinweis Nr. 19—Zusammenarbeit Heer-Luftwaffe," p. 2.

117. Oberkommando der Luftwaffe, Lw. Führungsstab, Ausb. Abt. Nr. 2880/44 geheim, "Merkblatt: Der Fliegerleitoffizier (Schlacht)," 26.11.1944, NARS T971/41/124ff.

118. Ibid., fr. 127.

119. Ibid., fr. 128–129.

120. PRO AIR 23/1861, "Report by an Observer with an American Corps in France: Air Support of Armored Columns," appended to: Terry Copp and Robert Vogel, "Anglo-Canadian Tactical Air Power in Normandy: A Reassessment," (presented at the meeting of the American Military Institute, Richmond, VA, 1987).

121. Panzergruppe West, "Merkblatt zur Luftwaffen-Unterstützung," NARS T321/51/4798881.

122. Luftwaffenkommando 6, Führungsabteilung Ia op Nr. 1616/44 geheim, Anl. z. KTB d. HGr. Mitte/Ia, Akte XIII-Luftwaffe, Heft 8, NARS T311/225/265.

123. Der Oberbefehlshaber der Luftwaffe, Führungsstab Ia/Ausb. Nr. 1000/44 geheim, *Vereint schlagen: Zusammenarbeit Luftwaffe-Heer auf dem Gefechtsfeld*, OKL/2085, NARS T321/243/no frame nos (first item).

124. Ibid., Heft 2, pp. 10ff.

125. Ibid., Heft 1, p. 3.

126. "German Ground Attack Arm," p. 17; Groehler, "Stärke, Verteilung und Verluste der deutschen Luftwaffe," Table 9, p. 325. By way of comparison, there were only 475 conventional fighters in the theater; Murray, *Luftwaffe*, p. 269.

127. "Truppengliederung des VIII. Fliegerkorps," Aus Lagekarte Ob.d.L. vom 25.5.1944, USAFHRC, Karlsrühe Collection K113.309-3 v. 16.

128. "German Ground Attack Arm," p. 17.

129. See Ic/Ost, Br. B. Nr. 53210/44 geh., "Übersetzung der Dienstvorschrift über das Zusammenwirken der Fliegertruppe mit den Erdtruppen," He-

rausgegeben vom Generalstab der roten Armee, Militär Verlag des Volkskommissariats für die Verteidigung, Moskau 1944, OKL/2054, NARS T321/67/4817424ff.

130. "Part Played by the GAF," p. 16.

131. Figures calculated from Erfolgsberichte der Gruppe (III./SG 4) vom 4.7.44–29.10.44, von Rohden 4376-477, NARS T971/39/430.

132. For the force structure of Luftflotte 6, which in early February 1945 possessed 1376 aircraft, see Luftflottenkommando 6, KTB, NARS T321/50/4796024ff.

133. Boog, "German Air Intelligence," p. 122.

CONCLUSION

1. OKL, Generalstab 8. Abteilung, "Douhet Theory," p. 10.

2. Luftwaffenführungsstab Ia op Nr. 8655/43, NARS T321/10/4746779.

3. See, for example the excellent new work by Alfred C. Mierzejewski, *The Collapse of the German War Economy, 1944–1945: Allied Air Power and the German National Railway* (Chapel Hill: University of North Carolina Press, 1988).

4. Boog et al., *Angriff auf die Sowjetunion*, pp. 413ff.

5. Halder, *War Diary*, p. 458.

6. Generalstab der Luftwaffe, 8. Abteilung, "Luftflotte 1, 2, 4, 5- Der Luftkrieg im Osten 1941," von Rohden 4407–113, NARS T971/18/801.

7. Herhudt von Rohden's novel recommendations appear in Generalstab 8. Abteilung, Nr. 61/44 geheim-Chef, "Sonderstudie Heft 5: Ein Beitrag zur Frage des russischen Problems," 5.10.44, NARS T971/18/898-911.

8. "Part Played by the GAF," p. 6. The officers under interrogation were Schulz, Richthofen's former chief of staff at Luftflotte 4 and last chief of the Luftwaffe operations staff, and Oberst i.G. von Greiff, also of the operations staff. Both officers were in a position to know better.

9. Overy, *Göring: The "Iron Man,"* p. 204.

BIBLIOGRAPHIC ESSAY

1. For a discussion of the historiography of the air war against the USSR, see Homze, *German Military Aviation*, pp. 127–129.

2. Particularly noteworthy are Klaus Uebe, *Russian Reactions to German Airpower in WWII:USAF Historical Studies No. 153* (New York: Arno Press, 1964), and Walter Schwabedissen, *The Russian Air Force in the Eyes of German Commanders: USAF Historical Studies: No. 175* (New York: Arno Press, 1968). Much fascinating material on the genesis and development of the project is available in the Karlsrühe Collection at the USAF Historical Research Center, Maxwell AFB, Alabama.

3. Richard R. Muller, "A Vision of Air Power: The Luftwaffe General Staff's Military History Department," paper presented at the Ohio Valley History Conference, October 1989.

4. OKL, Genst. 8. Abteilung, KTB 2, 2. 1. 45-4. 4 .45, von Rohden 4407-64, NARS T971/50/0005.

5. Chef. Genst. 8. Abteilung, ''Beitrag zur Frage des russichen Problems,'' NARS T971/18/900.

6. As one might expect, the studies frequently tend towards wild bursts of optimism and hyperbole; when Army Group Center collapsed under heavy pressure in summer 1944, we are told that ''the Luftwaffe, as always, was the backbone of the defense . . .'' As such, these studies are a useful barometer for Luftwaffe General Staff expectations.

7. See ''The Von Rohden Collection,'' *Library of Congress Quarterly Journal of Acquisitions* VI (August 1949), pp. 45–49. The typescript study on the Russian campaign, Von Rohden Annex, ''Kriege gegen Russland,'' NARS T971/26/1ff (also available in English translation in Annex 1b), written by Herhudt von Rohden himself, is extremely useful, although there is evidence of considerable back-pedaling by the Historical Department chief on a number of major issues.

8. Homze, *German Military Aviation*, p. 5.

INDEX